CHILTON BOOK COMPANY

REPAIR MANUAL

OMNI HORIZON RAMPAGE 1978-89

All U.S. and Canadian models of DODGE Omni, Miser, 024, Charger 2.2 ● PLYMOUTH Horizon, Miser, TC3, TC3 Tourismo, Rampage

D0963840

Vice President and General Manager JOHN P. KUSHNERICK
Editor-in-Chief KERRY A. FREEMAN, S.A.E.
Managing Editor DEAN F. MORGANTINI, S.A.E.
Senior Editor RICHARD J. RIVELE, S.A.E.
Senior Editor W. CALVIN SETTLE, JR., S.A.E.
Editor Martin Gunther

CHILTON BOOK COMPANY
Radnor, Pennsylvania
19089

CONTENTS

GENERAL INFORMATION and MAINTENANCE

ENGINE PERFORMANCE and TUNE-UP

ENGINE and ENGINE OVERHAUL

EMISSION CONTROLS

FUEL SYSTEM

CHASSIS ELECTRICAL

629.287
DODGE
1978-89

SAFETY NOTICE

Proper service and repair procedures are vital to the safe, reliable operation of all motor vehicles, as well as the personal safety of those performing repairs. This book outlines procedures for servicing and repairing vehicles using safe, effective methods. The procedures contain many NOTES, CAUTIONS and WARNINGS which should be followed along with standard safety procedures to eliminate the possibility of personal injury or improper service which could damage the vehicle or compromise its safety.

It is important to note that repair procedures and techniques, tools and parts for servicing motor vehicles, as well as the skill and experience of the individual performing the work vary widely. It is not possible to anticipate all of the conceivable ways or conditions under which vehicles may be serviced, or to provide cautions as to all of the possible hazards that may result. Standard and accepted safety precautions and equipment should be used during cutting, grinding, chiseling, prying, or any other process that can cause material removal or projectiles.

Some procedures require the use of tools specially designed for a specific purpose. Before substituting another tool or procedure, you must be completely satisfied that neither your personal safety, nor the performance of the vehicle will be endangered.

Although the information in this guide is based on industry sources and is as complete as possible at the time of publication, the possibility exists that the manufacturer made later changes which could not be included here. While striving for total accuracy, Chilton Book Company cannot assume responsibility for any errors, changes, or omissions that may occur in the compilation of this data.

PART NUMBERS

Part numbers listed in this reference are not recommendations by Chilton for any product by brand name. They are references that can be used with interchange manuals and aftermarket supplier catalogs to locate each brand supplier's discrete part number.

SPECIAL TOOLS

Special tools are recommended by many vehicle manufacturers to perform specific jobs. Use has been kept to a minimum in this guide, but, where absolutely necessary, special tools are referred to in the text by the part number of the tool manufacturer. These tools can be purchased, under the appropriate part number from Miller Special Tools, Division of Utica Tool Company, Inc., 32615 Park Lane, Garden City, Michigan 48135 or an equivalent tool can be purchased locally from a tool supplier or parts outlet. Before substituting any tool for the one recommended, read the SAFETY NOTICE at the top of this page.

ACKNOWLEDGMENTS

The Chilton Book Company expresses its appreciation to the Chrysler Corporation, Dodge and Plymouth Divisions, Detroit, Michigan for their generous assistance.

Chilton's Repair Manual: Omni/Horizon/Rampage 1978–89
ISBN 0-8019-7934-X pbk.
Library of Congress Catalog Card No. 88-43176

General Information and Maintenance

HOW TO USE THIS BOOK

Chilton's Repair & Tune-Up Guide for the Dodge Omni/Plymouth Horizon is intended to help you learn more about the inner workings of your vehicle and save you money on its upkeep and operation.

The first two chapters will be the most used, since they contain maintenance and tune-up information and procedures. Studies have shown that a properly tuned and maintained car can get at least 10% better gas mileage than an out-of-tune car. The other chapters deal with the more complex systems of your car. Operating systems from engine through brakes are covered to the extent that the average do-it-yourselfer becomes mechanically involved. This book will not explain such things as rebuilding the differential for the simple reason that the expertise required and the investment in special tools make this task uneconomical. It will give you detailed instructions to help you change your own brake pads and shoes, replace points and plugs, and do many more jobs that will save you money, give you personal satisfaction, and help you avoid expensive problems.

A secondary purpose of this book is a reference for owners who want to understand their car and/or their mechanics better. In this case, no tools at all are required.

Before removing any bolts, read through the entire procedure. This will give you the overall view of what tools and supplies will be required. There is nothing more frustrating than having to walk to the bus stop on Monday morning because you were short one bolt on Sunday afternoon. So read ahead and plan ahead. Each operation should be approached logically and all procedures thoroughly understood before attempting any work.

All chapters contain adjustments, maintenance, removal and installation procedures, and repair or overhaul procedures. When repair is not considered practical, we tell you how to remove the part and then how to install the new or rebuilt replacement. In this way, you at least save the labor costs.

Backyard repair of such components as the alternator is just not practical.

Two basic mechanic's rules should be mentioned here. One, whenever the left side of the car or engine is referred to, it is meant to specify the driver's side of the car. Conversely, the right side of the car means the passenger's side. Secondly, most screws and bolts are removed by turning counterclockwise, and tightened by turning clockwise.

Safety is always the most important rule. Constantly be aware of the dangers involved in working on an automobile and taking the proper precautions. (See the section in this chapter "Servicing Your Vehicle Safely" and the SAFETY NOTICE on the acknowledgement page.)

Pay attention to the instructions provided. There are 3 common mistakes in mechanical work:

1. Incorrect order of assembly, disassembly or adjustment. When taking something apart or putting it together, doing things in the wrong order usually just costs you extra time; however, it CAN break something. Read the entire procedure before beginning disassembly. Do everything in the order in which the instructions say you should do it, even if you can't immediately see a reason for it. When you're taking apart something that is very intricate (for example, a carburetor), you might want to draw a picture of how it looks when assembled at one point in order to make sure you get everything back in its proper position. (We will supply exploded views whenever possible.) When making adjustments, especially tune-up adjustments, do them in order; often, one adjustment affects another, and you cannot expect even satisfac-

tory results unless each adjustment is made only when it cannot be changed by any other.

2. Overtorquing (or undertorquing). While it is more common for overtorquing to cause damage, undertorquing can cause a fastener to vibrate loose causing serious damage. Especially when dealing with aluminum parts, pay attention to torque specifications and utilize a torque wrench in assembly. If a torque figure is not available, remember that if you are using the right tool to do the job, you will probably not have to strain yourself to get a fasten tight enough. The pitch of most threads is so slight that the tension you put on the wrench will be multiplied many, many times in actual force on what you are tightening. A good example of how critical torque is can be seen in the case of spark plug installation, especially where you are putting the plug into an aluminum cylinder head. Too little torque can fail to crush the gasket, causing leakage of combustion gases and consequent overheating of the plug and engine parts. Too much torque can damage the threads, or distort the plug, which changes the spark gap.

There are many commercial products available for ensuring that fasteners won't come loose, even if they are not torqued just right (a very common brand is Loctite®). If you're worried about getting something together tight enough to hold, but loose enough to avoid mechanical damage during assembly, one of these products might offer substantial insurance. Read the label on the package and make sure the product is compatible with the materials, fluids, etc. involved before choosing one.

3. Crossthreading. This occurs when a part such as a bolt is screwed into a nut or casting at the wrong angle and forced. Crossthreading is more likely to occur if access is difficult. It helps to clean and lubricate fasteners, and to start threading with the part to be installed going straight in. Then, start the bolt, spark plug, etc. with your fingers. If you encounter resistance, unscrew the part and start over again at a different angle until it can be inserted and turned several turns without much effort. Keep in mind that many parts, especially spark plugs, use tapered threads so that gentle turning will automatically bring the part you're threading to the proper angle if you don't force it or resist a change in angle. Don't put a wrench on the part until it's been turned a couple of turns by hand. If you suddenly encounter resistance, and the part has not seated fully, don't force it. Pull it back out and make sure it's clean and threading properly.

Always take your time and be patient; once you have some experience, working on your car will become an enjoyable hobby.

TOOLS AND EQUIPMENT

Naturally, without the proper tools and equipment it is impossible to properly service your vehicle. It would be impossible to catalog each tool that you would need to perform each or any operation in this book. It would also be unwise for the amateur to rush out and buy an expensive set of tools on the theory that he may need one or more of them at sometime.

The best approach is to proceed slowly, gathering together a good quality set of those tools that are used most frequently. Don't be misled by the low cost of bargain tools. It is far better to spend a little more for better quality. Forged wrenches, 6 or 12 point sockets and fine tooth ratchets are by far preferable to their less expensive counterparts. As any good mechanic can tell you, there are few worse experiences than trying to work on a car or truck with bad tools. Your monetary savings will be far outweighed by frustration and mangled knuckles.

Begin accumulating those tools that are used most frequently; those associated with routine maintenance and tune-up.

In addition to the normal assortment of screwdrivers and pliers you should have the following tools for routine maintenance jobs (your Omni or Horizon uses both SAE and metric fasteners):

1. SAE/Metric wrenches: sockets and combination open end/box end wrenches in sizes from ⅛″ (3mm) to ¾″ (19mm); and a ¹³⁄₁₆″ spark plug socket.

If possible, buy various length socket drive extensions. One break in this department is that the metric sockets available in the U.S. will all fit the ratchet handles and extensions you may already have (¼″, ⅜″, and ½″ drive).

2. Jackstands for support;

3. Oil filter wrench;

4. Oil filler spout for pouring oil;

5. Grease gun for chassis lubrication;

6. Hydrometer for checking the battery;

7. A container for draining oil;

8. Many rags for wiping up the inevitable mess.

In addition to the above items there are several others that are not absolutely necessary, but handy to have around. These include oil dry, a transmission funnel and the usual supply of lubricants, antifreeze and fluids, although these can be purchased as needed. This is a basic list for routine maintenance, but only your personal needs and desire can accurately determine your list of tools.

The second list of tools is for tune-ups. While the tools involved here are slightly more sophis-

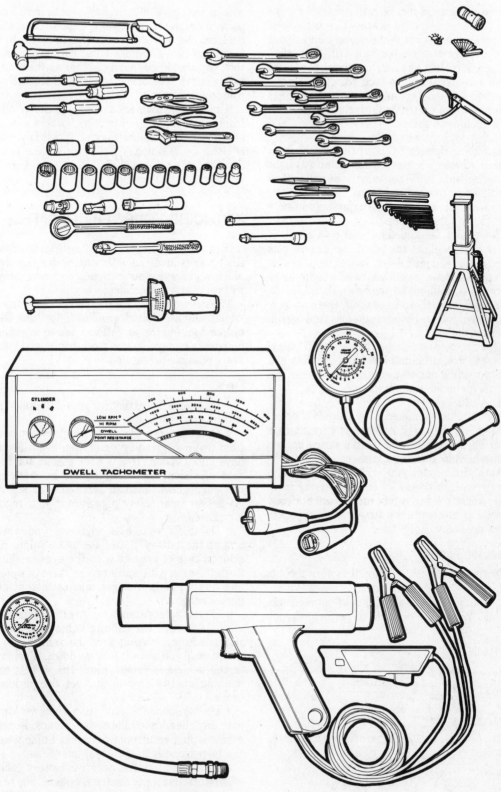

The majority of automotive service can be handled with these tools

ticated, they need not be outrageously expensive. There are several inexpensive tach/dwell meters on the market that are every bit as good for the average mechanic as a $100.00 professional model. Just be sure that it goes to at least 1,200-1,500 rpm on the tach scale and that it works on 4, 6 and 8 cylinder engines. A basic list of tune-up equipment could include:

1. Tach/dwell meter;
2. Spark plug wrench;
3. Timing light (a DC light that works from the car's battery is best, although an AC light that plugs into 110V house current will suffice at some sacrifice in brightness);
4. Wire spark plug gauge/adjusting tools;
5. Set of feeler blades.

Here again, be guided by your own needs. A feeler blade will set the point gap as easily as dwell meter will read dwell, but slightly less accurately. And since you will need a tachometer anyway . . . well, make your own decision.

In addition to these basic tools, there are several other tools and gauges you may find useful. These include:

1. A compression gauge. The screw-in type is slower to use, but eliminates the possibility of a faulty reading due to escaping pressure;
2. A manifold vacuum gauge;
3. A test light;
4. An induction meter. This is used for determining whether or not there is current in a wire. These are handy for use if a wire is broken somewhere in a wiring harness.

As a final note, you will probably find a torque wrench necessary for all but the most basic work. The beam type models are perfectly adequate, although the newer click type are more precise.

Special Tools

Normally, the use of special factory tools is avoided for repair procedures, since these are not readily available for the do-it-yourself mechanic. When it is possible to perform the job with more commonly available tools, it will be pointed out, but occasionally, a special tool was designed to perform a specific function and should be used. Before substituting another tool, you should be convinced that neither your safety nor the performance of the vehicle will be compromised.

Some special tools are available commercially from major tool manufacturers. Others can be purchased from Miller Special Tools; Division of Utica Tool Company, 32615 Park Lane, Garden City, Michigan 48135.

SERVICING YOUR VEHICLE SAFELY

It is virtually impossible to anticipate all of the hazards involved with automotive maintenance and service but care and common sense will prevent most accidents.

The rules of safety for mechanics range from "don't smoke around gasoline," to "use the proper tool for the job." The trick to avoiding injuries is to develop safe work habits and take every possible precaution.

Do's

● Do keep a fire extinguisher and first aid kit within easy reach.

● Do wear safety glasses or goggles when cutting, drilling, grinding or prying, even if you have 20/20 vision. If you wear glasses for the sake of vision, then they should be made of hardened glass that can serve also as safety glasses, or wear safety goggles over your regular glasses.

● Do shield your eyes whenever you work around the battery. Batteries contain sulphuric acid; in case of contact with the eyes or skin, flush the area with water or a mixture of water and baking soda and get medical attention immediately.

● Do use safety stands for any undercar service. Jacks are for raising vehicles; safety stands are for making sure the vehicle stays raised until you want it to come down. Whenever the vehicle is raised, block the wheels remaining on the ground and set the parking brake.

● Do use adequate ventilation when working with any chemicals. Like carbon monoxide, the asbestos dust resulting from brake lining wear can be poisonous in sufficient quantities.

● Do disconnect the negative battery cable when working on the electrical system. The primary ignition system can contain up to 40,000 volts.

● Do follow manufacturer's directions whenever working with potentially hazardous mate-

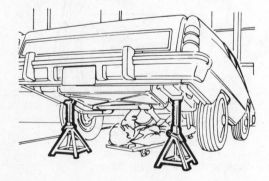

Always use jackstands when working under the car

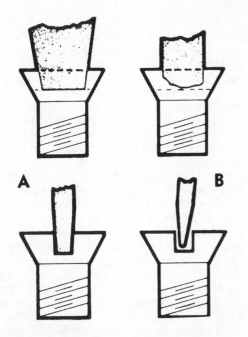

Screwdrivers should be kept in good condition to prevent injury

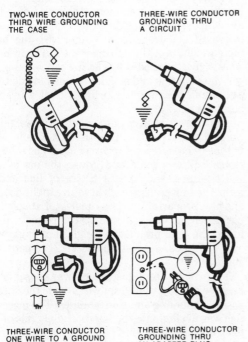

TWO-WIRE CONDUCTOR
THIRD WIRE GROUNDING
THE CASE

THREE-WIRE CONDUCTOR
GROUNDING THRU
A CIRCUIT

THREE-WIRE CONDUCTOR
ONE WIRE TO A GROUND

THREE-WIRE CONDUCTOR
GROUNDING THRU
AN ADAPTER PLUG

Power tools should always be properly grounded

rials. Both brake fluid and antifreeze are poisonous if taken internally.

• Do properly maintain your tools. Loose hammerheads, mushroomed punches and chisels, frayed or poorly grounded electrical cords, excessively worn screwdrivers, spread wrenches (open end), cracked sockets, slipping ratchets, or faulty droplight sockets can cause accidents.

• Do use the proper size and type of tool for the job being done.

• Do when possible, pull on a wrench handle rather than push on it, and adjust your stance to prevent a fall.

• Do be sure that adjustable wrenches are tightly adjusted on the nut or bolt and pulled so that the face is on the side of the fixed jaw.

• Do select a wrench or socket that fits the nut or bolt. The wrench or socket should sit straight, not cocked.

• Do strike squarely with a hammer; avoid glancing blows.

• Do set the parking brake and block the drive wheels if the work requires that the engine be running.

Don'ts

• Don't run an engine in a garage or anywhere else without proper ventilation — EVER! Carbon monoxide is poisonous; it takes a long time to leave the human body and you can build up a deadly supply of it in your system by simply breathing in a little every day. You may not realize you are slowly poisoning yourself. Always use power vents, windows, fans or open the garage doors.

• Don't work around moving parts while wearing a necktie or other loose clothing. Short sleeves are much safer than long, loose sleeves and hard-toed shoes with neoprene soles protect your toes and give a better grip on slippery surfaces. Jewelry such as watches, fancy belt buckles, beads or body adornment of any kind is not safe working around a car. Long hair should be hidden under a hat or cap.

• Don't use pockets for toolboxes. A fall or bump can drive a screwdriver deep into your body. Even a wiping cloth hanging from the

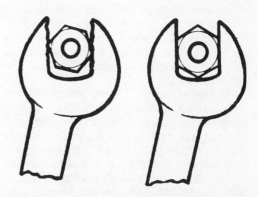

Use the correct size wrench and position it properly on the flats of the nut or bolt

back pocket can wrap around a spinning shaft or fan.

• Don't smoke when working around gasoline, cleaning solvent or other flammable material.

• Don't smoke when working around the battery. When the battery is being charged, it gives off explosive hydrogen gas.

• Don't use gasoline to wash your hands; there are excellent soaps available. Gasoline may contain lead, and lead can enter the body through a cut, accumulating in the body until you are very ill. Gasoline also removes all the natural oils from the skin so that bone dry hands will suck up oil and grease.

• Don't service the air conditioning system unless you are equipped with the necessary tools and training. The refrigerant, R-12, is extremely cold and when exposed to the air, will instantly freeze any surface it comes in contact with, including your eyes. Although the refrigerant is normally non-toxic, R-12 becomes a deadly poisonous gas in the presence of an open flame. One good whiff of the vapors from burning refrigerant can be fatal.

HISTORY

In designing the Omni and Horizon models, Chrysler didn't replace a car as much as design a brand new, efficiency sized car for the U.S. market. The goal was to design a car with outstanding roominess, good handling characteristics, good fuel economy and flexibility of use.

According to chassis and body development studies the new car would be based on these criteria:

• a fuel efficient 4-cylinder engine
• base weight less than 2,100 pounds
• overall length less than 165 inches
• overall width less than 66 inches
• front wheel drive.

The starting point was a fuel efficient, 4-cylinder engine, the first 4-cylinder engine to power a domestic Chrysler Corporation passenger car in 45 years. The last 4-cylinder powered Chrysler Corporation passenger car was the 1932 Plymouth.

The base engine is a 1.7 liter powerplant purchased from Volkswagenwerk AG in the form of an assembled cylinder block and cylinder head. The unit is shipped in special containers to the Trenton engine plant, where samples of each shipment are tested on a dynomometer and completely torn down during a complete quality control inspection. The other components — intake and exhaust manifolds, fuel pump, carburetor and controls, emission controls, alterna-

tor, power steering pump, clutch, air cleaner, ignition system — are all obtained from U.S. suppliers and installed at the engine plant. Since the Omni and Horizon models are Chrysler's first metrically designed models built in the U.S., the cylinder block, head and crankshaft are built to metric measurements. Other components, mostly those obtained from domestic suppliers, such as the power steering pump or alternator retain inch-size dimensions.

In 1981, a new 2.2L (135 cu. in.) 4-cylinder engine was introduced as an option on all models except the fuel efficient Miser.

Early in the design stages, Chrysler engineers realized that even with their design parameters, the luggage carrying needs of people hadn't changed that much. Front wheel drive offered the dimensional advantages to obtain the desired front and rear legroom with a superior luggage carrying capacity, and still stay within the design criteria. The lower floor, made possible by front wheel drive eliminating the driveshaft tunnel, resulted in extra inches that could be devoted to a luggage area.

Front wheel drive also gave advantages in handling. The car was more stable and didn't drift during cornering; directional stability was increased and traction was improved due to more weight over the driving wheels. The front wheel drive transaxle allowed the car to be bigger on the inside and smaller on the outside to achieve the overall length and width parameters.

Emphasis was also put on minimal weight coupled with a solid, substantial look, to appeal to those who were used to larger cars. The solid, stable look was achieved through the use of a wider stance, and careful choice of line and form, the proper degree of curvature to the door and the proportion of body panels. Extensive use of strong, but lightweight, components allowed the final product to weigh in at slightly over 2000 pounds, just under the 2100 pound goal.

A strut type front suspension was chosen to keep weight to a minimum yet provide the best possible handling and ride qualities. The objective was to eliminate the harsh, choppy ride often associated with small cars, through the use of anti-sway bar, soft oval rubber pivot bushings, non-concentric coil springs and well balanced front and rear systems.

The actual design of the cars began in April of 1975, after preliminary planning had settled the issues of length, width, wheel base and configuration. More than 16 different exterior concepts were wind tunnel tested to determine their aerodynamic behavior. The results refined the 4-door hatchback configuration to obtain the minimum aerodynamic drag. Design improvements were translated in half scale, plastic models before producing a total of 84 prototypes that would log over 6,000,000 test miles. The final result, "Job Number One," rolled off the Belvidere assembly line on November 21, 1977.

Popularity of Dodge Omni and Plymouth Horizon in their first full year in the marketplace, achieved a new production record for Chrysler Corporation's Belvidere assembly plant. In calender year 1978, 288,236 cars were built and sold. Demand was so great that the plant capacity was increased from the initial 960 cars per day to the present rate of almost 1,200 per day.

In 1979 the Plymouth Horizon TC3 and Dodge Omni 024 were introduced. The sporty, 2-door hatchback design had all the basic ingredients that made the 4-door version a success, in addition to a low profile, 2 + 2 sport look. The aerodynamically styled 024 and TC3 are about 8 inches longer and almost 2½ inches lower than their sedan counterparts.

In 1982 the 024 Charger and the TC3 Turismo performance version were introduced. The Charger and Turismo body styles were refined versions of the original 024 and TC3 models, with added features such as mellow tuned exhaust, simulated hood scoop and fender exhaust vents. Also included on these models are bold nameplate graphics, rear spoiler and raised white letter tires.

Also an E-Type sedan was added to both the Dodge and Plymouth line. In addition to all the standard features on the other sedans, the E-Type is equipped with European style black-out moldings and mirrors. Also a console and a rallye style instrument cluster is included.

Probably the most radical model introduced in this body style in 1982 was the Dodge Rampage pickup truck which was the first front wheel drive pickup to be built by a member of Detroit's "Big Three". Introduced in both the Sport and High-Line trim packages they share many of the same components with the other Omni/Horizon models. The major difference is in the rear suspension, where the other Omni/Horizon models have rear coil over strut type shocks and independent trailing arms the pickup model has conventional rear shocks, leaf springs and a tubular rear axle in order to support the additional rear weight capacity required in a pickup.

For the 1983 model year Plymouth added a pickup to their model line called the Scamp. This model shared comparable features to the Dodge Rampage pickup introduced the previous year.

Introduced in mid-1983 was the aggressive styled Dodge Shelby Charger. Built to be a high performance "image car" with its high output 2.2 liter engine and 5-speed transmission. Its designer, Carol Shelby, that's right, the same man who brought us the 0-100 and back to zero in ten seconds AC Cobra, and the famous Shelby Mustang once again proved that he could come up with a high performance car that would be popular in the 80's.

Introduced in 1984 is the new high output 2.2 liter engine putting out an impressive 110 horsepower, standard in the Dodge Shelby Charger and optional in the other models.

SERIAL NUMBER IDENTIFICATION

Vehicle (VIN)

The vehicle identification number (VIN) is located on a plate attached to the upper lefthand corner of the instrument panel visible through the windshield. The complete VIN is also on the Safety Certification label located on the rear facing of the driver's door. An abbreviated form of the VIN is also stamped on a pad on the engine and on the transaxle housing.

All 1978-80 VIN's contain 13 digits coded to reveal the following information:

- 1st digit: Car line
- 2nd digit: Series
- 3rd and 4th digit: Body type
- 5th digit: Engine displacement
- 6th digit: Model year
- 7th digit: Assembly plant
- Last 6 digits: Sequential vehicle serial number

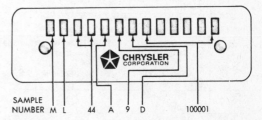

Sample 1978–80 VIN plate (Visible through windshield)

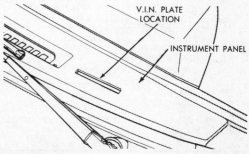

VIN plate location

1978–80 Vehicle Identification Plate Interpretation

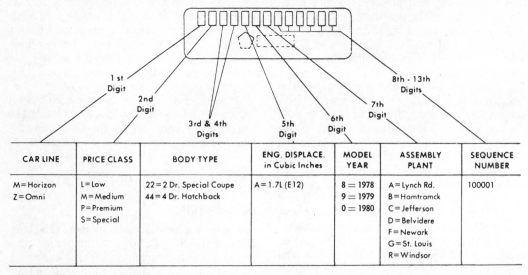

CAR LINE	PRICE CLASS	BODY TYPE	ENG. DISPLACE. in Cubic Inches	MODEL YEAR	ASSEMBLY PLANT	SEQUENCE NUMBER
M = Horizon Z = Omni	L = Low M = Medium P = Premium S = Special	22 = 2 Dr. Special Coupe 44 = 4 Dr. Hatchback	A = 1.7L (E12)	8 = 1978 9 = 1979 0 = 1980	A = Lynch Rd. B = Hamtramck C = Jefferson D = Belvidere F = Newark G = St. Louis R = Windsor	100001

NOTE: A derivative of the Vehicle Identification Number is also stamped on all Production Installed Engines and Transmissions; e.g.:

8	A	100001
Model Year	Assembly Plant	Vehicle Sequence Number

1981 and Later Vehicle Identification Plate Interpretation

POSITION	CODE OPTIONS			INTERPRETATION
1	1 = U.S. 2 = Canada	3 = Mexico J = Japan		Country of Origin
2	B = Dodge C = Chrysler	P = Plymouth		Make
3	3 = Passenger Car 7 = Truck			Type of Vehicle
4	B = Manual Seat Belts D = 1-3000 Lbs. GVW			Passenger Safety System
5	C = LeBaron D = Aries E = 600 T = New Yorker D = Lancer	L = Caravelle (Canada) M = Horizon P = Reliant J = Caravelle (U.S.)	V = 600 Z = Omni A = V Daytona A = C Laser C = LeBaron GTS	Line
6	1 = Economy 2 = Low	4 = High 5 = Premium	6 = Special	Series
7	1 = 2 Dr. Sedan 2 = 2 Dr. Specialty Hardtop 3 = 2 Dr. Hardtop 4 = 2 Dr. Hatchback	5 = 2 Dr. Convertible 6 = 4 Dr. Sedan 8 = 4 Dr. Hatchback 9 = 4 Dr. Wagon		Body Style
8	A = 1.6L C = 2.2L	D = 2.2L EFI E = 2.2L Turbo	G = 2.6L	Engine
9*	(1 thru 9, 0 or X)			Check Digit
10	F = 1985			Model Year
11	C = Jefferson D = Belvidere F = Newark G = St. Louis 1	K = Pillette Rd. N = Sterling R = Windsor	T = Toluca W = Clairpointe X = St. Louis 2	Assembly Plant
2 thru 17	(6 Digits)			Sequence Number

*Digit in position 9 is used for VIN verification

All 1981 and later VIN's contain 17 digits coded to reveal the following information:
- 1st digit: Country of Origin
- 2nd digit: Make
- 3rd digit: Type of Vehicle
- 4th digit: Pass Safety System
- 5th digit: Model Type
- 6th digit: Series
- 7th digit: Body Style
- 8th digit: Engine
- 9th digit: Check Digit
- 10th digit: Model Year
- 11th digit: Assembly Plant
- 12th thru 17th digit: Sequence Number

Engine

The engine identification numbers on the 1.6 and 1.7 liter engines are stamped on a pad on the engine block just above the fuel pump. The 2.2 liter engine has its number stamped on a pad just above the bellhousing.

Transaxle

The manual transaxle serial number is stamped on a metal pad or tag on top of the transaxle, just above the timing window. Four

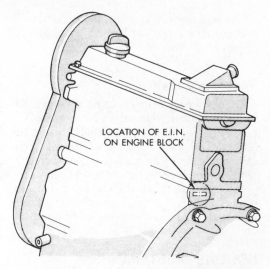

Engine identification number—2.2 liter engine

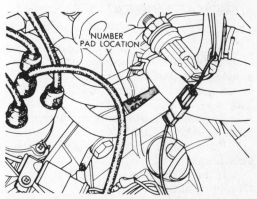

The manual transaxle number is stamped on a pad

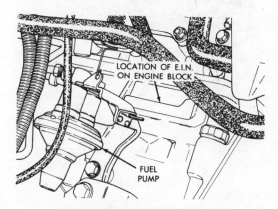

Engine identification number—1.6 liter engine

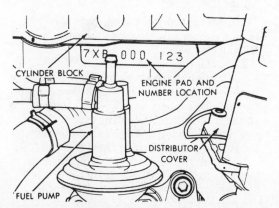

Engine identification number—1.7 liter engine

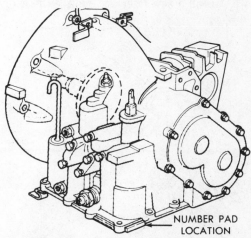

Location of the automatic transaxle number pad

types of manual transaxle are used, the A412 VW design 4-spd., the A460 4-spd., the A465 5-spd., and the A525 close ratio 5-spd., used in the high performance models.

The automatic transaxle serial number is stamped on a metal pad located just above the oil pan at the rear of the transaxle.

Body Code Plate

The body code plate contains important information about your particular car which is usually needed for any correspondence with the factory. The plate is located on the left front fender side shield, on the left side of the upper radiator support or on the wheel housing.

The information on the plate is coded in 6 rows of digits and is read from left to right. The information can be interpreted using the chart.

ROUTINE MAINTENANCE

Air Cleaner

ELEMENT REPLACEMENT

1.7L

The carburetor air cleaner should be replaced every 30,000 miles under normal use. If the car is driven continuously in extremely dirty, dusty or sandy areas, the interval should be cut in half.

1. Remove the 2 wing nuts and unsnap the retaining clips.
2. Remove the air cleaner cover with the filter attached.
3. If the hoses come off, note their location for reinstallation.
4. Unscrew the wing nut on the bottom of the filter element and remove the filter.
5. Install a new filter and replace the wing nut.

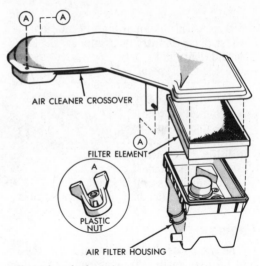

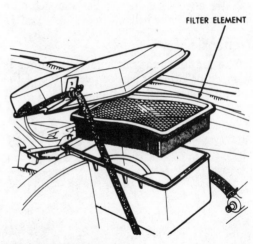

1.6L engine air cleaner

2.2L engine air cleaner

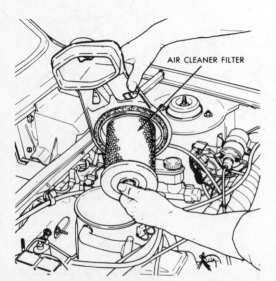

Replacing the 1.7L air cleaner

6. Reinstall the cover and hand-tighten the wing nuts.
7. Snap the retaining clips into place.

1.6 and 2.2L

1. Remove the three wing nuts that retain the air cleaner cover, remove the cover and lift out the element.
2. Install the new element.
3. Position the cover while aligning the three hold-down clips while allowing the two carburetor and one support bracket studs to protrude through each stud hole in the cover.
4. Install a wing nut on each of the carburetor studs first, and torque them to 14 in. lbs.
5. Install the third wing nut on the support bracket stud and torque it to 14 in. lbs.

NOTE: *It is important to follow this sequence to avoid air leaks due to air cleaner body distortion.*

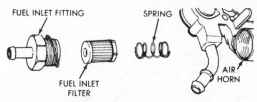

Fuel filter, spring and fitting—1978–79

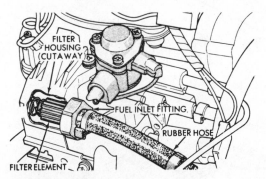

Fuel filter location—1978–79

Fuel Filter

CAUTION: *Never smoke when working around gasoline! Avoid all sources of sparks or ignition. Gasoline vapors are EXTREMELY volatile!*

REMOVAL AND INSTALLATION

Carbureted Engines

1978-79

The fuel filter on the 1978-79 models is located behind the fuel inlet of the carburetor. Under normal operating conditions the filter should be replaced every 15,000 miles.

1. Remove the clamp from the rubber hose.
2. Spread some dry rags under the fuel filter to absorb the ievitible gasoline spillage.
3. Unscrew the fitting and remove the filter.
4. Install a new filter.
5. Install and tighten the fitting.
6. Connect the fuel line. You may want to use a new screw type clamp that will make future filter replacement easier.
7. Run the engine and check for leaks.

1980 AND LATER

There are two fuel filters in the present system. One is part of the gauge unit assembly located inside the fuel tank on the suction end of the tube. This filter normally does not need servicing, but may be replaced or cleaned if a very large amount of extremely coarse material gets into the tank and clogs it.

The 2.2 liter engine usually uses a disposable filter-vapor separator that is located on the front side of the engine block between the fuel pump and carburetor. On some applications, this filter has not only inlet and outlet connections, but a third connection designed to permit fuel to return to the tank so that vapor that accumulates in hot weather will not interfere with carburetion.

A plugged fuel filter can limit the speed at which a vehicle can be driven and may cause hard starting. The most critical symptom will usually be suddenly reduced engine performance at maximum engine power levels, as when passing.

Remove the filter as follows:

1. Have a metal container ready to catch spilled fuel. Make sure the engine is cool.
2. Remove the hose clamps from each end of the filter. Then, disconnect the hoses, collecting the fuel in the metal container.
3. Remove the old filter and hoses. On the reservoir type filter, remove the two mounting nuts inside the air cleaner.
4. Put the new filter into position. If it has mounting studs, pass them through the mounting bracket and then install the attaching nuts snugly. Connect the hoses, and install and tighten the hose clamps (if the hoses are hard to force onto the nipples, you can wet them inside just very slightly). Make sure the clamps are located a short distance away from the ends of the hoses and on the inside of the nipples located on the ends of the filter connections.
5. Start the engine and check for leaks.

Fuel Injected Engines

CAUTION: *Fuel injected engines use high pressure in their operation. This pressure is maintained through the action of check valves even when the engine is off. Therefore, you must be sure to work on the fuel carrying parts of injected cars only when the engine has cooled off and only after you have properly bled the pressurized fuel from the system. Failure to do this could readily cause a fire!*

1. Relieve fuel system pressure as follows:
   a. Loosen the fuel tank cap to release any accumulated air pressure that may be there.

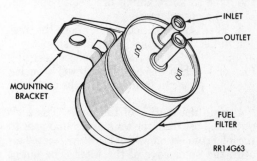

Fuel filter-fuel injected models

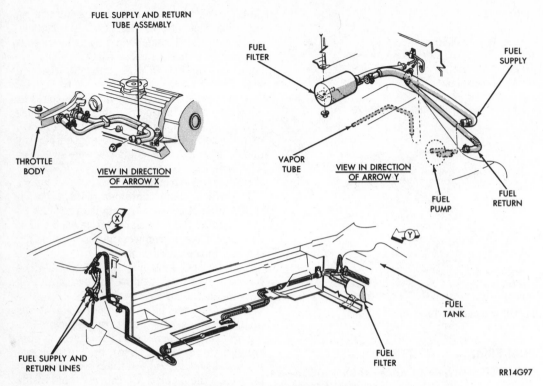

Fuel filter location-fuel injected models

Then, disconnect the electrical connector at the single fuel injector on the throttle body on cars with throttle body injection. On cars with multi-point injection, disconnect the electrical connector on the injector closest to the battery.

b. Use a jumper wire to ground one of the injector terminals for whichever injector you've disconnected.

c. Connect one end of a jumper wire to the other injector terminal. Then, just touch the other end of the second jumper to the battery positive post for nearly 10 seconds. *Make sure you do not maintain this connection for more than the maximum of 10 seconds or the injector could be damaged.*

2. Remove the retaining screw that mounts the filter to its retaining bracket so you can reach the hose clamps.

3. Then, loosen the clamps for both the inlet and outlet lines. Quickly wrap a shop towel around these connections to collect escaping fuel safely. Then, dispose of this towel in such a way as to protect it from heat the the chance of fire.

4. Note the routing of the hoses. The high pressure hose from the tank and pump goes to the inlet connection, which is always located toward the outer edge of the filter. The outlet hose to the engine is labeled on some filters and is always at the center. Pull the hoses off the connections on the filter. Replace the filter, draining fuel into a metal container and disposing of it safely. Inspect the hoses and clamps and replace defective parts as necessary.

WARNING: *Chrysler uses and recommends hoses that meet their specifications and are labeled EFM/EFI18519. Make sure you use either this type of hose or an equivalent, high pressure (up to 55 psi) type of fuel hose available in the automotive aftermarket. Be sure not to use ordinary rubber fuel hose, as this is not tough enough for high pressure use and may not be able to resist the destruction caused by certain types of contamination. Also, if hose clamps require replacement, note that the original equipment clamps have rolled edges to keep the edge of the band from cutting into this hose, due to the necessary use of high clamping forces with a high pressure fuel system. Make sure that you use either an original equipment clamp or a similar type of clamp available in the aftermarket.*

5. Reconnect the hoses, using the proper routing noted as you disconnected them. You may want to very slightly wet the inside diameter of the hoses to make it easier to install them onto the filter connections. Install them as far as possible, until they are well over the bulges at the ends of the connectors. Install the clamps

so they are a short distance away from the ends of the hoses but well over the bulged areas at the ends of the filter connections. Tighten both clamps securely. If you have an inch lb. torque wrench torque them to 10 in. lbs.

6. Remount the filter on the bracket snugly with the screw. Start the engine and check for leaks, tightening the hose clamps, replacing parts, or forcing the hoses farther onto the connectors, if necessary.

PCV Valve

Omnis and Horizons are equipped with a closed crankcase ventilation system. The PCV valve is located in a line running between the cylinder head cover and the air cleaner.

This valve must be kept clean for optimum engine performance and fuel economy. The PCV valve should be inspected every 15,000 miles and replaced every 30,000 miles. In extremely dusty conditions or if the car is subjected to extensive idling or short trip operation, the interval should be halved.

PCV VALVE INSPECTION

There are 2 ways to check the PCV valve. If a valve fails either test, replace it with a new one.

Engine Idling

1. Remove the PCV valve from the rubber grommet in the cylinder head cover.
2. If the valve is not plugged, a hissing noise will be heard and a strong vacuum will be felt when you cover the valve with your finger.

Engine Stopped

1. Remove the PCV valve from the rubber grommet in the cylinder head cover.
2. Shake the valve; a clicking noise should be plainly audible if the valve is free.

PCV VALVE CONNECTING LINE INSPECTION

After a new PCV valve is installed, perform the test under "Engine Idling." If a strong vac-

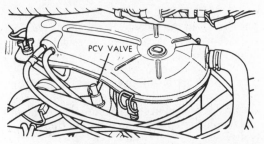

Location of PCV valve—1.7L engine

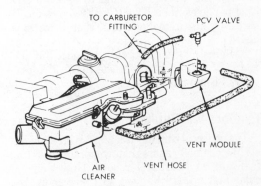

PCV system—2.2L engine

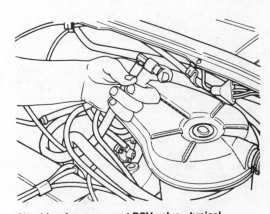

Checking for vacuum at PCV valve—typical

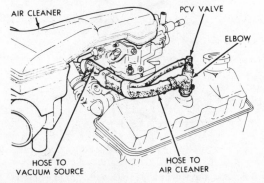

PVC system—1.6L engine

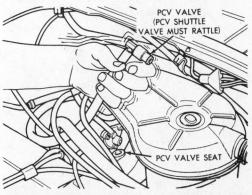

To be considered serviceable, the PCV valve must rattle when shaken

uum is not felt, replace or clean the ventilation line and clean the passage in the lower part of the carburetor. The carburetor does not have to be disassembled.

1. Remove the connecting line and either replace it or clean the line in combustion chamber conditioner or a similar solvent. The hose should not remain in solvent more than ½ hour and should be allowed to air dry until thoroughly dry.

2. Remove the carburetor. Turn a ¼" drill through the passage by hand to dislodge any solid particles, then blow the passage clean. If necessary, use a smaller drill so that no metal is dislodged.

3. Reinstall the carburetor, connect the line and PCV valve and repeat the PCV valve test under "Engine Idling."

Evaporative Canister

The charcoal canister is a feature on all models to store fuel vapors that evaporate from the fuel tank and carburetor bowl. Note that on some fuel bowls, the vent to the evaporative canister is capped since the fuel bowl is vented internally.

The only service is to replace the canister filter every 30,000 miles, if the car is driven in particularly dusty areas. Otherwise, no service is necessary.

All hoses used with this system should be inspected periodically and replaced if cracked or leaking. These hoses are of special fuel resistant material and must be replaced with the same type and quality. The OEM (Original Equipment Manufactured) clamps are "Keystone" type and will be destroyed when they are removed. Replacement types should be aircraft

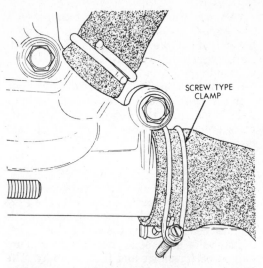

SCREW TYPE CLAMP

Spring and screw type hose clamps

type screw clamps if the original equipment is not available (spring type clamps are not recommended). Position the clamps so that no sharp edges contact adjacent hoses.

Battery

Loose, dirty, or corroded battery terminals are a major cause of "no-start." Every 3 months or so, remove the battery terminals and clean them, giving them a light coating of petroleum jelly when you are finished. This will help to retard corrosion.

Check the battery cables for signs of wear or chafing and replace any cable or terminal that looks marginal. Battery terminals can be easily

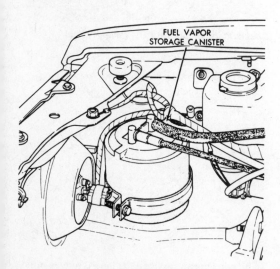

FUEL VAPOR STORAGE CANISTER

Fuel vapor storage canister

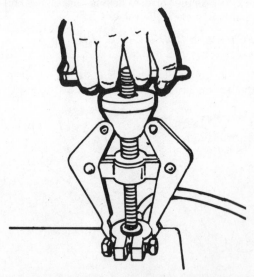

A small puller will easily remove the cable from the terminals

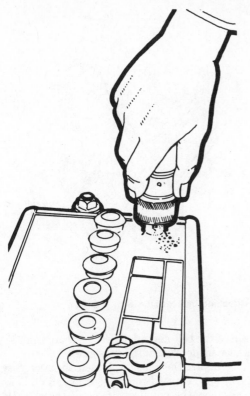

An inexpensive tool easily cleans the battery terminals

Clean the inside of the terminal clamp

cleaned and inexpensive terminal cleaning tools are an excellent investment that will pay for themselves many times over. They can usually be purchased from any well-equipped auto store or parts department. The accumulated white power and corrosion can be cleaned from the top of the battery with an old toothbrush and a solution of baking soda and water.

Unless you have a maintenance-free battery, check the electrolyte level (see Battery under Fluid Level Checks in this chapter) and check the specific gravity of each cell. Be sure that the vent holes in each cell cap are not blocked by grease or dirt. The vent holes allow hydrogen gas, formed by the chemical reaction in the battery, to escape safely.

REPLACEMENT BATTERIES

The cold power rating of a battery measures battery starting performance and provides an approximate relationship between battery size and engine size. The cold power rating of a replacement battery should match or exceed your engine size in cubic inches.

BATTERY FLUID LEVEL

Two types of batteries are used: Standard and Maintenance-Free. Both types are equipped with a Charge-Test Indicator, which is actually a miniature hydrometer built into the filler cap of the cell. The indicator will show green if the battery is above 75-80% charged, or dark if the battery needs recharging. Light yellow indicates the battery may be in need of water or replacement.

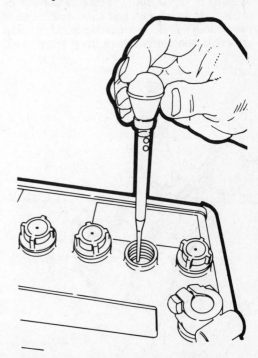

Check the specific gravity of the battery

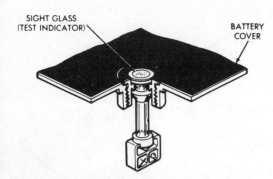

SIGHT GLASS
(TEST INDICATOR)

BATTERY COVER

Test indicator on maintenance free battery

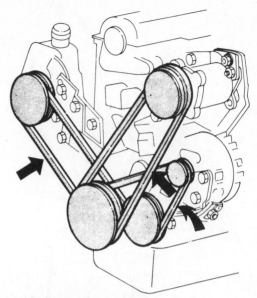

Checking belt tension with A/C

For standard batteries, check the level of the electrolyte every 2 months; more often on long trips or in extremely hot weather. If necessary add mineral free water to the bottom of the filler well.

At least once a year, check the specific gravity of a standard battery.

Checking and Adjusting Belt Tension

Your particular car may have as few as one or as many as 4 drive belts for the following accessories: alternator, A/C compressor, power steering pump, water pump, or air pump (California models only).

ALL BELTS EXCEPT ALTERNATOR BELT

Check the belt tension on any given belt by applying moderate thumb pressure midway in the longest span. The belt should deflect approximately ½". If the longest span is not easily accessible, you can also check the shortest span,

where the belt should deflect no more than ¼" under moderate thumb pressure.

To adjust the tension, loosen the accessory pivot bolt. On A/C compressor loosen all bolts shown on the compressor decal. Insert a ½" breaker bar in the accessory tensioning lug and move the accessory until the belt is properly tensioned. Tighten the pivot bolt.

ALTERNATOR BELT

Proper belt tension on the alternator belt is critical to proper alternator operation. For ease of adjusting alternator belt tension, a special tool has been developed that is easily fabricated or available from the tool company at about $10. The tool, when used with a torque wrench, assures proper belt tension with greater accessibility. Do not use the thumb pressure method on these belts.

It is essential that belt adjustment be performed from below the vehicle. The splash shield must be removed and on California models with an air pump, removing the horn will ease access to the adjustment bolt.

1. From underneath the vehicle, install a ½" drive torque wrench in the adjusting tool. Position the adjusting tool.

2. Loosen the alternator pivot bolt. If you don't do this, you'll break the alternator housing.

3. Adjust the belt tension to 70 ft. lbs. (new belt) or 50 ft. lbs. (used belt).

NOTE: *A belt is considered used after 15 minutes of running.*

4. Hold the alternator at the required torque. Tighten the adjusting bolt.

5. Reinstall the horn and splash shield.

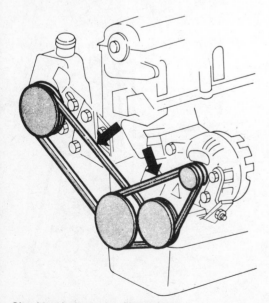

Checking belt tension without A/C

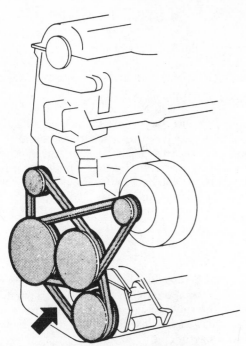

Checking belt tension with AIR pump

NOTE: *The air pump idler pulley is located behind the water pump pulley.*

3. The air pump drive belt is removed next. To remove this belt, the A/C compressor and the alternator belts MUST be removed.

4. The power steering pump drive belt is re-

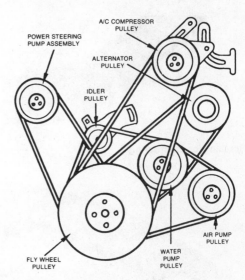

1.7L engine accessory drive belts

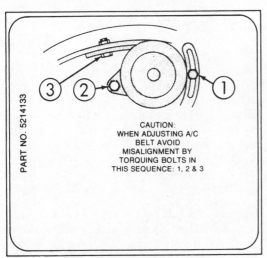

A/C compressor bolt tightening sequence

PART NO. 5214133

CAUTION:
WHEN ADJUSTING A/C
BELT AVOID
MISALIGNMENT BY
TORQUING BOLTS IN
THIS SEQUENCE: 1, 2 & 3

Belt Replacement

In most cases the car must be raised and supported, the splash shield removed and the horn removed from cars with air pumps.

1. The A/C compressor drive belt is removed first. Loosen the adjusting nut at the slotted bracket and push the compressor to its lowest position.

2. The alternator belt is removed second. Loosen the tension on the belt and use a ½" socket to remove the 3 bolts holding the water pump pulley. Remove the pulley.

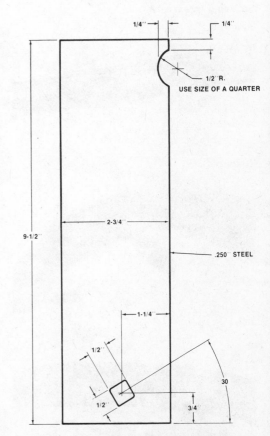

1.7L engine drive belt tension adjusting tool

HOW TO SPOT WORN V-BELTS

V-Belts are vital to efficient engine operation—they drive the fan, water pump and other accessories. They require little maintenance (occasional tightening) but they will not last forever. Slipping or failure of the V-belt will lead to overheating. If your V-belt looks like any of these, it should be replaced.

Cracking or weathering

This belt has deep cracks, which cause it to flex. Too much flexing leads to heat build-up and premature failure. These cracks can be caused by using the belt on a pulley that is too small. Notched belts are available for small diameter pulleys.

Softening (grease and oil)

Oil and grease on a belt can cause the belt's rubber compounds to soften and separate from the reinforcing cords that hold the belt together. The belt will first slip, then finally fail altogether.

Glazing

Glazing is caused by a belt that is slipping. A slipping belt can cause a run-down battery, erratic power steering, overheating or poor accessory performance. The more the belt slips, the more glazing will be built up on the surface of the belt. The more the belt is glazed, the more it will slip. If the glazing is light, tighten the belt.

Worn cover

The cover of this belt is worn off and is peeling away. The reinforcing cords will begin to wear and the belt will shortly break. When the belt cover wears in spots or has a rough jagged appearance, check the pulley grooves for roughness.

Separation

This belt is on the verge of breaking and leaving you stranded. The layers of the belt are separating and the reinforcing cords are exposed. It's just a matter of time before it breaks completely.

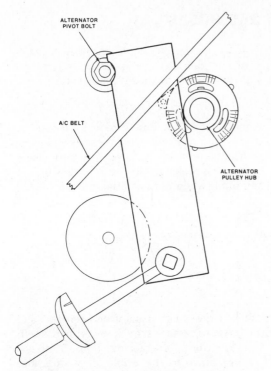

ALTERNATOR
PIVOT BOLT

A/C BELT

ALTERNATOR
PULLEY HUB

**Using the adjusting tool to adjust belt tension on
the 1.7L engine**

moved last. It is necessary to remove all other
belts, loosen the pump pivot bolt in the slotted
bracket and move the pump to its lowest
position.

5. New belts are installed in the reverse order. Tension all belts as outlined previously.
New belts will usually stretch, so they should be
checked after an hour's use.

Hoses

Hoses can be removed or installed with pliers
or a screwdriver. Some cars use spring type
clamps while others use screw type clamps. If
spring type clamps are used, it is recommended
to remove these with hose clamp pliers to avoid
pinching your fingers.

1. Drain the radiator.

CAUTION: *When draining the coolant, keep
in mind that cats and dogs are attracted by
the ethylene glycol antifreeze, and are quite
likely to drink any that is left in an uncovered
container or in puddles on the ground. This
will prove fatal in sufficient quantity. Always
drain the coolant into a sealable container.
Coolant should be reused unless it is contaminated or several years old.*

2. Remove the hose clamps.

3. Pull the hose off the fittings on the radiator and engine.

4. Install a new hose. A small amount of

soapy water on the inside of the hose end will
ease installation.

NOTE: *Radiator hoses should be routed
with no kinks and routed as the original. Use
of molded hoses is not recommended.*

5. Refill the cooling system and check the
level.

Air Conditioning

AIR-CONDITIONING SAFETY PRECAUTIONS

There are two particular hazards associated
with air conditioning systems and they both re-
late to the refrigerant gas.

First, the refrigerant gas is an extremely cold
substance. When exposed to air, it will instantly
freeze any surface it comes in contact with, including your eyes. The other hazard relates to
fire. Although normally non-toxic, refrigerant
gas becomes highly poisonous in the presence of
an open flame. One good whiff of the vapor
formed by burning refrigerant can be fatal.
Keep all forms of fire (including cigarettes) well
clear of the air-conditioning system.

Any repair work to an air conditioning system
should be left to a professional.

Checking for Oil Leaks

Refrigerant leaks show up as oily areas on the
various components because the compressor oil
is transported around the entire system along
with the refrigerant. Look for oily spots on all
the hoses and lines, and especially on the hose
and tubing connections. If there are oily deposits, the system may have a leak, and you should
have it checked by a qualified repairman.

NOTE: *A small area of oil on the front of the
compressor is normal and no cause for
alarm.*

Check the Compressor Belt

Refer to the section in this chapter on Drive
Belts.

Keep the Condenser Clear

Periodically inspect the front of the condenser for bent fins or foreign material (dirt, bugs,
leaves, etc.) If any cooling fins are bent,
straighten them carefully with needle nosed pliers. You can remove any debris with a stiff bris-
tle brush or hose.

Operate the A/C System Periodically

A lot of A/C problems can be avoided by simply running the air conditioner at least once a
week, regardless of the season. Simply let the
system run for at least 5 minutes a week (even
in the winter), and you'll keep the internal

HOW TO SPOT BAD HOSES

Both the upper and lower radiator hoses are called upon to perform difficult jobs in an inhospitable environment. They are subject to nearly 18 psi at under hood temperatures often over 280°F., and must circulate nearly 7500 gallons of coolant an hour—3 good reasons to have good hoses.

A good test for any hose is to feel it for soft or spongy spots. Frequently these will appear as swollen areas of the hose. The most likely cause is oil soaking. This hose could burst at any time, when hot or under pressure.

Swollen hose

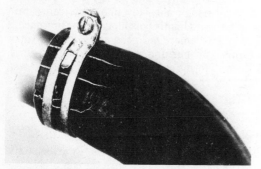

Cracked hoses can usually be seen but feel the hoses to be sure they have not hardened; a prime cause of cracking. This hose has cracked down to the reinforcing cords and could split at any of the cracks.

Cracked hose

Weakened clamps frequently are the cause of hose and cooling system failure. The connection between the pipe and hose has deteriorated enough to allow coolant to escape when the engine is hot.

Frayed hose end (due to weak clamp)

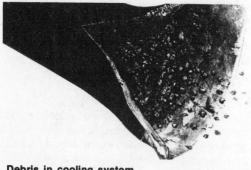

Debris, rust and scale in the cooling system can cause the inside of a hose to weaken. This can usually be felt on the outside of the hose as soft or thinner areas.

Debris in cooling system

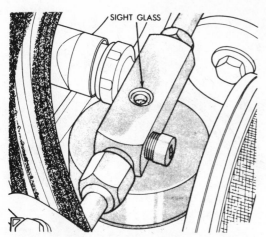

A/C sight glass in the top of the receiver/drier

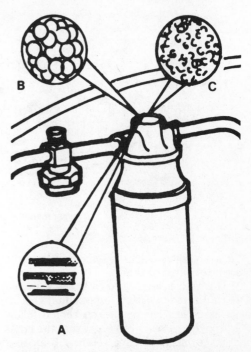

Oil streaks (A), constant bubbles (B) or foam (C) indicate there is not enough refrigerant in the system. Occasional bubbles during initial operation is normal. A clear sight glass indicates a proper charge of refrigerant or no refrigerant at all, which can be determined by the presence of cold air at the outlets in the car. If the glass is clouded with a milky white substance, have the receiver/drier checked professionally

parts lubricated as well as preventing the hoses from hardening.

Checking Refrigerant Level

The first order of business when checking the sight glass is to find it. It will be in the head of the receiver/drier. In some cases, it may be covered by a small rubber plug designed to keep it clean. Once you've found it, remove the cover, if necessary, wipe it clean and proceed as follows:

1. With the engine and the air conditioning system running, look for the flow of refrigerant through the sight glass. If the air conditioner is working properly, you'll be able to see a continuous flow of clear refrigerant through the sight glass, with perhaps an occasional bubble at very high outside temperatures.

2. Cycle the air conditioner on and off to make sure what you are seeing is a pure stream of liquid refrigerant. Since the refrigerant is clear, it is possible to mistake a completely discharged system for one that is fully charged. Turn the system off and watch the sight glass. If there is refrigerant in the system, you'll see bubbles during the off cycle. Also, the lines going into and out of the compressor will be at radically different temperatures (be careful about touching the line going forward to the condenser, which is in front of the radiator, as it will be very hot). If the bubbles disappear just after you start the compressor, there are no bubbles when the system is running, and the air flow from the unit in the car is cold, everything is O.K.

3. If you observe bubbles in the sight glass while the system is operating, the system is low on refrigerant. You may want to charge it yourself, as described later. Otherwise, have it checked by a professional.

4. If all you can see in the sight glass is oil streaks, this is an indication of trouble. This is true because there is no liquid refrigerant in the system (otherwise, the oil would mix with the refrigerant and would be invisible). Most of the time, if you see oil in the sight glass, it will appear as a series of streaks, although occasionally it may be a solid stream of oil. In either case, it means that part of the charge of refrigerant has been lost.

USING THE BAR GAUGE MANIFOLD

WARNING: *Refrigerant work is usually performed by highly trained technicians. Improper use of the gauges can result in a leakage of refrigerant liquid, damage to the compressor, or even explosion of a system part. The do-it-yourselfer must be very careful to insure that he proceeds with extreme care and understands what he is doing before proceeding. The best insurance for safety is a complete understanding of the system and proper techniques for servicing it. A careful study of a complete text such as CHILTON'S GUIDE TO AIR CONDITIONING SERVICE AND REPAIR, book part No. 7580, is the best insurance against either dangerous or system-damaging problems.*

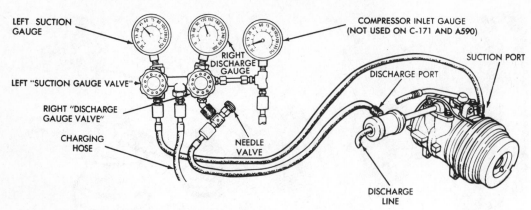

Typical manifold gauge set connections

To use the bar gauge manifold, follow the procedures outlined below.

1. It is first necessary to clear the manifold itself of air and moisture, especially if the fittings have been left open. You should follow this procedure, unless you know that the hoses and gauge manifold have recently been bled with refrigerant and capped off tightly. Otherwise, you may actually force air and moisture into the system when you are testing or charging it. Begin with both the service valves on the refrigerant gauge set *closed*.

  a. First, tap a can of refrigerant. To do this, first unscrew the tap's cutting tool all the way. Turn the rotatable locking lever so it leaves one side of the collar assembly open. Then, slide the tap onto the top of the can so the collar tabs fit over the rim that runs around the top of the can. Turn the locking lever so that it secures the collar. Then, turn the cutting tool all the way down to tap the can.

  b. Remove any plugs that may be present and then screw the *center* hose to the screw fitting on top of the tap. Now, slightly loosen the plugs in the ends of the other two lines.

  c. Sit the can of refrigerant down right side up on a flat surface. *Make sure the can does not get pulled up off the surface as you work, or you could be splattered by liquid refrigerant.* Then, open the tap by unscrewing the tapping tool handle all the way. Crack both of the bar gauge manifold valves just a little-- just until you hear a slight hiss at the plug at the end of the hose on either side. Allow the refrigerant to enter the system until you are sure it has reached the ends of the hoses (30 seconds). Tighten the plugs at the bottom of the hoses and then *immediately* turn off both manifold valves.

2. Using a wrench if the cap has flats, uncap the low and high pressure, Schrader valve type fittings for the system. The low pressure fitting

is located on the suction port of the compressor. In a typical mounting of the unit with the ports facing the front of the car, this is the lower port. You'll find that there is a line connecting with this port that comes from the evaporator (located behind the cowl). The high pressure fitting is located on the muffler, which, in turn is located on the line coming out of the commpressor and heading toward the condenser. There is a low pressure gauge on the left side of the manifold, which shows pressures up to about 100 psi *and* vacuum. Connect the line on this side to the low pressure side of the system. The gauge on the right or high pressure side of the manifold reads only pressure and, typically, the scale goes up to 500 psi. or higher. On some gauge sets sold for use with Chrysler systems, there is a third gauge, known as the compressor inlet gauge, to the right of the discharge or high pressure gauge. This gauge is for testing systems that use a special pressure regulating valve in the compressor. Since none of the front wheel drive cars covered by this guide use this type of compressor, you will not use this gauge. If you are shopping for gauges, you can use a conventional set which has only two gauges.

On many newer systems, the threads on high and low pressure Schrader valves are of different sizes to prevent improper hookup.

If you have an older set of gauges, you can get an adapter or a different hose that will convert your gauges to the new thread sizes. Consult a heating, air conditioning and refrigeration supply source.

WARNING: *When making connections, start the threads carefully and, once you are sure they are not crossthreaded, turn the fitting as fast as you can in order to avoid getting sprayed by refrigerant. Sometimes the Schrader valve will open early--before the fitting is tight, and this will cause a little refrigerant to be sprayed out.*

3. Use of the gauges once they are bled and

installed typically includes reading high and low side pressures with both valves closed, charging the system with the low side valve cracked partly open, and discharging it with both valves partly open. Refer to the section just below on "Charging the System" for specifics.

4. To disconnect the gauges, turn the fittings as quickly as possible so as to close the Schrader valves as quickly as possible. Note that liquid refrigerant and oil may be sprayed out for a short time as this is done, especially on the low pressure side. Turn the fittings by reaching down from above, as liquid will be sprayed out underneath the gauge connection. Less refrigerant will be sprayed out on the high side if the connection is broken a few minutes after the system is turned off. Cap the open ends of the gauges immediately. If, for any reason, the ends are left open for a minute or two, repeat the bleeding procedure above. Tightly cap the system openings right away.

DISCHARGING THE SYSTEM

NOTE: *Fluorocarbon refrigerants like that used in car air conditioners damage the upper atmosphere, destroying its ability to screen off dangerous solar radiation. For this reason, air conditioning service shops will soon be required to use special charging/evacuating stations to condense and recover refrigerants rather than releasing them to the atmosphere. While these environmental regulations may not apply to the do-it-yourselfer, you may wish to have your system discharged by a professional equipped to recover the refrigerant if you are concerned about the environment.*

1. Connect the gauges to the high and low sides of the system, as described above. Do not connect a refrigerant can to the center hose.

2. Insert the center hose into a glass bottle with an opening that is slightly larger in diameter than the hose. *Do not attempt to cap or seal the opening in the top of the bottle in any way.* This bottle will collect oil discharged from the system so that it can be measured and replaced when the system is recharged. Make sure you keep the bottle upright to avoid spilling any of this oil out.

3. Make sure the compressor is turned off and remains off throughout the procedure. Crack the low side manifold valve until refrigerant gas is expelled at a steady, moderate rate. Don't open the valve all the way, or too much refrigerant oil will be expelled from the system.

4. As refrigerant pressure drops and the gas begins to be expelled only very slowly, open the low side manifold valve more and more to compensate and keep the refrigerant moving out of the system.

5. Once *all* the pressure is discharged, slowly open the high side service valve, repeating Steps 3 and 4 until the system is clear. Close it after any pressure has escaped.

6. Disconnect the gauges and recap the openings. Retain the bottle of oil. If you have the system evacuated and recharged by a professional, give him the bottle of oil. He will measure the amount it contains and replace it with a like amount.

CHARGING THE SYSTEM

WARNING: *Charging the system can prove to be very dangerous. You must satisfy yourself that you are fully aware of all risks before starting. Although most systems use a high pressure cutoff switch for the compressor, overcharging the system, attempting to charge it when it contains air, or charging it when there is inadequate cooling of the condenser could cause dangerous pressures to develop if this switch should fail. Overcharging could also damage the compressor.*

The safest way to charge the system is with a set of gauges installed and reading both low and high side pressures so that you can monitor pressures throughout the procedure. It is best to refer to a text on refrigeration and air conditioning first, so that you understand what will happen. Using the simple hose sold for do-it-yourself charging of the system can be safe, provided three precautions are taken:

a. Make sure the system has been completely evacuated by a professional with a good vacuum pump. Eliminating air in the system is a vital step toward maintaining safe pressures during the charging process and ensuring reliable and effective operation later.

b. Charge the system with precisely the amount of refrigerant it is specified to use *and no more.* Consult the label on the compressor. Purchase the right number of cans. You can precisely estimate what percentage of a can has been charged into the system by noting the frost line on the can.

c. Run the engine at a moderate speed during charging (not too fast), valve the refrigerant into the system at a controlled rate, and keep a fan blowing across the condenser at all times.

Charge the system by following these steps:

1. Make sure the system has been completely evacuated with a good vacuum pump. This should be done with gauges connected and the pump must be able to create a vacuum of 28-29 in.Hg near sea level. Lower this specification

one in.Hg for each 1,000 feet above sea level at your location.

2. Connect the gauges as described above, including tapping in a new can of refrigerant. If you are using a gaugeless hose that is part of a charging kit, follow the directions on the package; in any case, make sure to hook up the hose to the low pressure side of the system--to the accumulator or POA valve.

3. Situate a fan in front of the condenser and use it to blow air through the condenser and radiator throughout the charging process.

4. Unless the system has a sight glass, get the exact refrigerant capacity off the compressor label. Make sure you have only the proper number of cans available to help avoid unnecessary overcharge.

5. It will speed the process to place the cans, top up, in warm water. Use a thermometer and make sure the water is *not over 120°F*. You will need to warm the water as the process goes on. Monitor the temperature to make sure it does not go too high, as warm water will almost immediately create excessive pressure inside the can — pressure that will not be reflected in gauge readings. Make sure the cans *always* stay top up. This requires a lot of attention because as the cans run low on refrigerant, they begin to float and may turn upside down. Charging the system with the can upside down may cause liquid refrigerant to enter the system, damaging the compressor. If the bar gauge manifold or charging line suddenly frosts up, check the position of the can immediately and rectify it, if necessary!

6. Start the process with the engine off. Open the charging valve (if you are using a kit) or the low side bar gauge manifold valve slightly until the pressures equalize. Then, close the charging valve or bar gauge manifold back off. Place an electric fan in front of the condenser. Then, start the engine and run it at idle speed or just very slightly above. Turn the blower to the lowest speed. Then, turn the air conditioner on in the normal operating mode. If the system has no refrigerant in it, the low pressure cutout switch on the compressor will keep it from starting until some pressure is created in the system.

7. If you're working with a charging kit, follow the manufacturer's instructions as to how far to open the charging valve. If you're working with a bar gauge manifold, and the system has a lot of refrigerant in it (you're just topping it off) follow the rest of this step. Otherwise, skip to 8. Note the operating pressure (the average if the compressor is cycling). Then, open the manifold valve until system low side pressure rises 10 psi. Throughout the charging procedure, maintain this pressure by opening or closing the valve to compensate for changes in the temperature of the refrigerant can. Also, keep your eye on the high side pressure and make sure it remains at a moderate level (usually less than 200 psi).

8. Gradually open the valve on the suction (left) side of the bar gauge manifold, as you watch the low side gauge. Allow the pressure to build until the compressor comes on and runs continuously. Keep permitting it to rise until it reaches 50 psi. Then, carefully control the position of the valve to maintain this pressure. You will have to change the position of the valve to compensate for cooling of the refrigerant can and surrounding water and to help empty the can.

9. When the first can runs out of refrigerant, close off the manifold valve or charging line valve. Tap in a new can, immerse it in liquid, keeping it right side up, and then open the charging line valve if you're working without gauges. If you are working with gauges, open the valve on the tap and then open the low side manifold valve as described in Step 8 to maintain the pressure as before.

10. Continue with the process until the last can is hooked up. Measure in a fraction of a can, if necessary, by watching the frost line on the can and stopping appropriately. Watch for the time when bubbles just disappear from the sight glass. If you're just topping off the system, stop charging just after this occurs. Otherwise, this is a sign that you should expect the system to be completely charged and find that you have just about measured the right amount of refrigerant in. Be ready to stop charging! If you're just topping off the system, turn off the charging valve or low side manifold valve and then run the system with the fan on high and the engine accelerated to about 1,500 rpm to check the charge. If bubbles appear, charge the system slightly more until just after all the bubbles disappear.

11. When charging is complete, turn off the manifold or charging line valves and any valve on the can. Disconnect the low side line *at the suction line and not at the gauges*, grabbing the connection from above, watching for liquid refrigerant to spray out, and unscrewing the connection as fast as you can. Turn off the engine and allow the pressure on the high side to drop until it stabilizes. Then, disconnect the high side gauge connection (if necessary) as quickly as possible. Cap both system openings and all gauge openings as soon as possible.

Windshield Wipers

Intense heat from the sun, snow and ice, road oils and the chemicals used in windshield wash-

Troubleshooting Basic Air Conditioning Problems

Problem	Cause	Solution
There's little or no air coming from the vents (and you're sure it's on)	• The A/C fuse is blown • Broken or loose wires or connections • The on/off switch is defective	• Check and/or replace fuse • Check and/or repair connections • Replace switch
The air coming from the vents is not cool enough	• Windows and air vent wings open • The compressor belt is slipping • Heater is on • Condenser is clogged with debris • Refrigerant has escaped through a leak in the system • Receiver/drier is plugged	• Close windows and vent wings • Tighten or replace compressor belt • Shut heater off • Clean the condenser • Check system • Service system
The air has an odor	• Vacuum system is disrupted • Odor producing substances on the evaporator case • Condensation has collected in the bottom of the evaporator housing	• Have the system checked/repaired • Clean the evaporator case • Clean the evaporator housing drains
System is noisy or vibrating	• Compressor belt or mountings loose • Air in the system	• Tighten or replace belt; tighten mounting bolts • Have the system serviced

Sight glass condition
  Constant bubbles, foam or oil streaks
  Clear sight glass, but no cold air
  Clear sight glass, but air is cold
  Clouded with milky fluid
	
	• Undercharged system
	
	• No refrigerant at all
	• System is OK
	• Receiver drier is leaking dessicant
		
		• Charge the system
		
		• Check and charge the system
		
		• Have system checked

Large difference in temperature of lines	• System undercharged	• Charge and leak test the system
Compressor noise	• Broken valves • Overcharged • Incorrect oil level • Piston slap • Broken rings • Drive belt pulley bolts are loose	• Replace the valve plate • Discharge, evacuate and install the correct charge • Isolate the compressor and check the oil level. Correct as necessary. • Replace the compressor • Replace the compressor • Tighten with the correct torque specification
Excessive vibration	• Incorrect belt tension • Clutch loose • Overcharged • Pulley is misaligned	• Adjust the belt tension • Tighten the clutch • Discharge, evacuate and install the correct charge • Align the pulley
Condensation dripping in the passenger compartment	• Drain hose plugged or improperly positioned • Insulation removed or improperly installed	• Clean the drain hose and check for proper installation • Replace the insulation on the expansion valve and hoses
Frozen evaporator coil	• Faulty thermostat • Thermostat capillary tube improperly installed • Thermostat not adjusted properly	• Replace the thermostat • Install the capillary tube correctly • Adjust the thermostat
Low side low—high side low	• System refrigerant is low • Expansion valve is restricted	• Evacuate, leak test and charge the system • Replace the expansion valve
Low side high—high side low	• Internal leak in the compressor—worn	• Remove the compressor cylinder head and inspect the compressor. Replace the valve plate assembly if necessary. If the compressor pistons, rings or

Troubleshooting Basic Air Conditioning Problems (cont.)

Problem	Cause	Solution
Low side high—high side low (cont.)		cylinders are excessively worn or scored replace the compressor
	• Cylinder head gasket is leaking	• Install a replacement cylinder head gasket
	• Expansion valve is defective	• Replace the expansion valve
	• Drive belt slipping	• Adjust the belt tension
Low side high—high side high	• Condenser fins obstructed	• Clean the condenser fins
	• Air in the system	• Evacuate, leak test and charge the system
	• Expansion valve is defective	• Replace the expansion valve
	• Loose or worn fan belts	• Adjust or replace the belts as necessary
Low side low—high side high	• Expansion valve is defective	• Replace the expansion valve
	• Restriction in the refrigerant hose	• Check the hose for kinks—replace if necessary
	• Restriction in the receiver/drier	• Replace the receiver/drier
	• Restriction in the condenser	• Replace the condenser
Low side and high side normal (inadequate cooling)	• Air in the system	• Evacuate, leak test and charge the system
	• Moisture in the system	• Evacuate, leak test and charge the system

er solvents combine to deteriorate the rubber wiper refills. The refills should be replaced about twice a year or whenever the blades begin to streak or chatter.

WIPER REFILL REPLACEMENT

Normally, if the wipers are not cleaning the windshield properly, only the refill has to be replaced. The blade and arm usually require replacement only in the vent of damage. It is not necessary (except on new Tridon refills) to remove the arm or the blade to replace the refill (rubber part), though you may have to position the arm higher on the glass. You can do this turning the ignition switch on and operating the wipers. When they are positioned where they are accessible, turn the ignition switch off.

There are several types of refills and your vehicle could have any kind, since aftermarket blades and arms may not use exactly the same type refill as the original equipment.

The original equipment wiper elements can be replaced as follows:

1. Lift the wiper arm off the glass.
2. Depress the release lever on the center bridge and remove the blade from the arm.

3. Lift the tab and pinch the end bridge to release it from the center bridge.
4. Slide the end bridge from the wiper blade and the wiper blade form the opposite end bridge.
5. Install a new element and be sure the tab on the end bridge is down to lock the element in place. Check each release point for positive engagement.

Most Trico styles uses a release button that is pushed down to allow the refill to slide out of the yoke jaws. The new refill slides in and locks in place. Some Trico refills are removed by locating where the metal backing strip or the refill is wider. Insert a small screwdriver blade between the frame and metal backing strip. Press down to release the refill from the retaining tab.

The Anco style is unlocked at one end by squeezing 2 metal tabs, and the refill is slid out of the frame jaws. When the new refill is installed, the tabs will click into place, locking the refill.

The polycarbonate type is held in place by a locking lever that is pushed downward out of the groove in the arm to free the refill. When the new refill is installed, it will lock in place automatically.

The Tridon refill has a plastic backing strip with a notch about an inch from the end. Hold the blade (frame) on a hard surface so that the frame is tightly bowed. Grip the tip of the backing strip and pull up while twisting counterclockwise. The backing strip will snap out of the retaining tab. Do this for the remaining tabs

Removing original equipment wiper blade and refill

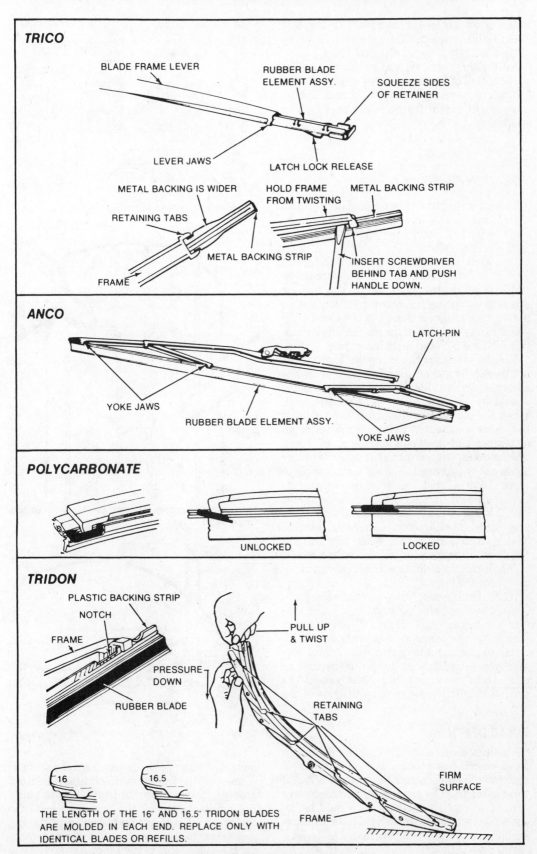

TRICO

BLADE FRAME LEVER

RUBBER BLADE ELEMENT ASSY.

SQUEEZE SIDES OF RETAINER

LEVER JAWS

LATCH LOCK RELEASE

METAL BACKING IS WIDER

RETAINING TABS

METAL BACKING STRIP

FRAME

HOLD FRAME FROM TWISTING

METAL BACKING STRIP

INSERT SCREWDRIVER BEHIND TAB AND PUSH HANDLE DOWN.

ANCO

LATCH-PIN

YOKE JAWS

RUBBER BLADE ELEMENT ASSY.

YOKE JAWS

POLYCARBONATE

UNLOCKED

LOCKED

TRIDON

PLASTIC BACKING STRIP

NOTCH

FRAME

PULL UP & TWIST

PRESSURE DOWN

RUBBER BLADE

RETAINING TABS

16

16.5

THE LENGTH OF THE 16" AND 16.5" TRIDON BLADES ARE MOLDED IN EACH END. REPLACE ONLY WITH IDENTICAL BLADES OR REFILLS.

FRAME

FIRM SURFACE

Replacing popular styles of wiper refills

until the refill is free of the arm. The length of these refills is molded into the end and they should be replaced with identical types.

No matter which type of refill you use, be sure that all of the frame claws engage the refill. Before operating the wipers, be sure that no part of the metal frame is contacting the windshield.

Tires

INFLATION PRESSURE

Tire inflation is the most ignored item of auto maintenance. Gasoline mileage can drop as much as 0.8% for every 1 pound per square inch (psi) of under inflation.

Two items should be a permanent fixture in every glove compartment; a tire pressure gauge and a tread depth gauge. Check the tire air pressure (including the spare) regularly with a pocket type gauge. Kicking the tires won't tell you a thing, and the gauge on the service station air hose is notoriously inaccurate.

The tire pressures recommended for your car are usually found on the door post or in the owner's manual. Ideally, inflation pressure should be checked when the tires are cool. When the air becomes heated it expands and the pressure increases. Every 10° rise (or drop) in temperature means a difference of 1 psi, which also explains why the tire appears to lose air on a very cold night. When it is impossible to check the tires "cold," allow for pressure build-up due to heat. If the "hot" pressure exceeds the "cold" pressure by more than 15 psi, reduce your speed, load or both. Otherwise internal heat is created in the tire. When the heat approaches the temperature at which the tire was cured, during manufacture, the tread can separate from the body.

WARNING: *Never counteract excessive pressure build-up by bleeding off air pressure (letting some air out). This will only further raise the tire operating temperature.*

Before starting a long trip with lots of luggage, you can add about 2-4 psi to the tires to make them run cooler, but never exceed the maximum inflation pressure on the side of the tire.

TREAD DEPTH

All tires made since 1968, have 8 built-in tread wear indicator bars that show up as ½" wide smooth bands across the tire when ¹⁄₁₆" of tread remains. The appearance of tread wear indicators means that the tires should be replaced. In fact, many states have laws prohibiting the use of tires with less than ¹⁄₁₆" tread.

You can check your own tread depth with an

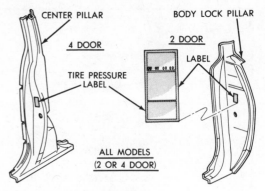

Tire pressure label location

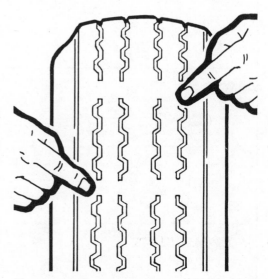

Tire wear indicators appear as ¹/₂″ wide bands when tread is less than ¹/₁₆″

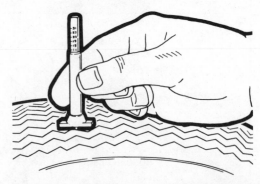

Check tire tread depth with an inexpensive gauge

inexpensive gauge or by using a Lincoln head penny. Slip the Lincoln penny into several tread grooves. If you can see the top of Lincoln's head in 2 adjacent grooves, the tires have less than ¹⁄₁₆" tread left and should be replaced. You can measure snow tires in the same manner by using the "tails" side of the Lincoln penny. If you

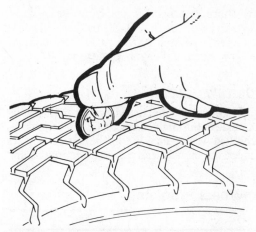

Tread depth can also be roughly checked with a Lincoln head penny. If the top of Lincoln's head is visible, replace the tires

can see the top of the Lincoln memorial, it's time to replace the snow tires.

TIRE ROTATION

Tire wear can be equalized by switching the position of the tires about every 6000 miles. Including a conventional spare in the rotation pattern can give up to 20% more tire life.

NOTE: *Do not include the Space-saver in the rotation pattern.*

There are certain exceptions to tire rotation, however. Studded snow tires should not be rotated, and radials should be kept on the same side of the car (maintain the same direction of rotation). The belt on radial tires get set in a pattern. If the direction of rotation is reversed, it can cause rough ride and vibration.

NOTE: *When radials or studded snows are taken off the car, mark them, so you can maintain the same direction of rotation.*

TIRE STORAGE

Store the tires at proper inflation pressures if they are mounted on wheels. All tires should be kept in a cool, dry place. If they are stored in the garage or basement, do not let them stand on a concrete floor; set them on strips of wood.

FLUIDS AND LUBRICANTS

Fuel Recommendations

Only gasolines with a 91 Research Octane Number (RON) or an octane value of 87 if using the (R + M)/2 method, should be used. Unleaded gasoline must be used in those cars with a catalytic converter. These cars have specially designed filler necks that prevent the direct insertion of the leaded gasoline pump nozzle.

Avoid the constant use of fuel system cleaning agents. Many of these materials contain highly active solvents that will deteriorate the gasket and diaphragm materials used on Omni and Horizon carburetors.

Engine

OIL RECOMMENDATION

Oils and lubricants are classified and graded according to standards established by the Society of Automotive Engineers (SAE), American Petroleum Institute (API), and the National Lubricating Grease Institute (NLGI).

Oils are classified by the SAE and API desig-

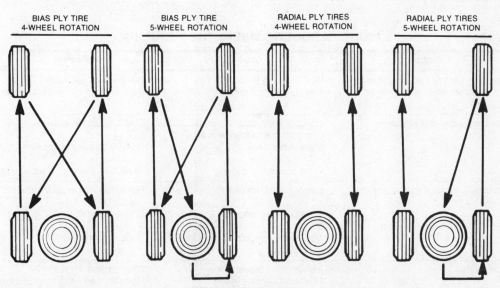

Tire rotation patterns

nations, found on the top of the oil can, such as SAE 5W-30, SAE 10W-30, etc. The SAE grade number indicates the viscosity of engine oils. Chrysler prefers the use of SAE 5W-30 for when minimum temperatures consistently fall below −10°F (−23°C). Chrysler does not recommend the use of SAE 5W-30 and 5W-40 in turbocharged engines in ambient temperatures above 60°F (15°C). or the use of SAE 10W-40 or SAE 10W-50 in any of their 1988-89 vehicles.

The API classification system defines oil performance in terms of usage. Only oils designed for service SF or SF/CD, SG or SG/CD should be used. These oils provide sufficient additives to give maximum engine protection.

OIL LEVEL CHECK

The engine oil dipstick is located on the radiator side of the engine. Engine oil level should be checked weekly as a matter of course. Always check the oil with the car on level ground and

Troubleshooting Basic Wheel Problems

Problem	Cause	Solution
The car's front end vibrates at high speed	• The wheels are out of balance • Wheels are out of alignment	• Have wheels balanced • Have wheel alignment checked/adjusted
Car pulls to either side	• Wheels are out of alignment • Unequal tire pressure • Different size tires or wheels	• Have wheel alignment checked/adjusted • Check/adjust tire pressure • Change tires or wheels to same size
The car's wheel(s) wobbles	• Loose wheel lug nuts • Wheels out of balance • Damaged wheel • Wheels are out of alignment • Worn or damaged ball joint • Excessive play in the steering linkage (usually due to worn parts) • Defective shock absorber	• Tighten wheel lug nuts • Have tires balanced • Raise car and spin the wheel. If the wheel is bent, it should be replaced • Have wheel alignment checked/adjusted • Check ball joints • Check steering linkage • Check shock absorbers
Tires wear unevenly or prematurely	• Incorrect wheel size • Wheels are out of balance • Wheels are out of alignment	• Check if wheel and tire size are compatible • Have wheels balanced • Have wheel alignment checked/adjusted

Troubleshooting Basic Tire Problems

Problem	Cause	Solution
The car's front end vibrates at high speeds and the steering wheel shakes	• Wheels out of balance • Front end needs aligning	• Have wheels balanced • Have front end alignment checked
The car pulls to one side while cruising	• Unequal tire pressure (car will usually pull to the low side) • Mismatched tires • Front end needs aligning	• Check/adjust tire pressure • Be sure tires are of the same type and size • Have front end alignment checked
Abnormal, excessive or uneven tire wear See "How to Read Tire Wear"	• Infrequent tire rotation • Improper tire pressure • Sudden stops/starts or high speed on curves	• Rotate tires more frequently to equalize wear • Check/adjust pressure • Correct driving habits
Tire squeals	• Improper tire pressure • Front end needs aligning	• Check/adjust tire pressure • Have front end alignment checked

after the engine has been shut off for about five minutes.

The oil level may read at the top of the Full range after the car has been standing for sever-al hours. When the engine is started, the level will drop, due to oil passages filling, but the level should never be allowed to remain below the ADD mark.

1. Remove the dipstick and wipe it clean.

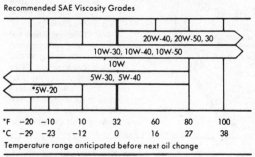

Recommended SAE Viscosity Grades

*SAE 5W-20 Not recommended for sustained high speed vehicle operation.

Oil viscosity chart—1978–87

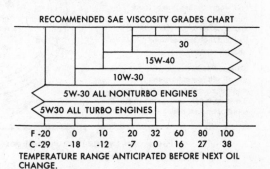

RECOMMENDED SAE VISCOSITY GRADES CHART

TEMPERATURE RANGE ANTICIPATED BEFORE NEXT OIL CHANGE.

Oil viscosity chart—1988–89

Tire Size Comparison Chart

"Letter" sizes			Inch Sizes	Metric-inch Sizes		
"60 Series"	"70 Series"	"78 Series"	1965–77	"60 Series"	"70 Series"	"80 Series"
		Y78-12	5.50-12, 5.60-12 6.00-12	165/60-12	165/70-12	155-12
		W78-13	5.20-13	165/60-13	145/70-13	135-13
		Y78-13	5.60-13	175/60-13	155/70-13	145-13
			6.15-13	185/60-13	165/70-13	155-13, P155/80-13
A60-13	A70-13	A78-13	6.40-13	195/60-13	175/70-13	165-13
B60-13	B70-13	B78-13	6.70-13	205/60-13	185/70-13	175-13
			6.90-13			
C60-13	C70-13	C78-13	7.00-13	215/60-13	195/70-13	185-13
D60-13	D70-13	D78-13	7.25-13			
E60-13	E70-13	E78-13	7.75-13			195-13
			5.20-14	165/60-14	145/70-14	135-14
			5.60-14	175/60-14	155/70-14	145-14
			5.90-14			
A60-14	A70-14	A78-14	6.15-14	185/60-14	165/70-14	155-14
	B70-14	B78-14	6.45-14	195/60-14	175/70-14	165-14
	C70-14	C78-14	6.95-14	205/60-14	185/70-14	175-14
D60-14	D70-14	D78-14				
E60-14	E70-14	E78-14	7.35-14	215/60-14	195/70-14	185-14
F60-14	F70-14	F78-14, F83-14	7.75-14	225/60-14	200/70-14	195-14
G60-14	G70-14	G77-14, G78-14	8.25-14	235/60-14	205/70-14	205-14
H60-14	H70-14	H78-14	8.55-14	245/60-14	215/70-14	215-14
J60-14	J70-14	J78-14	8.85-14	255/60-14	225/70-14	225-14
L60-14	L70-14		9.15-14	265/60-14	235/70-14	
	A70-15	A78-15	5.60-15	185/60-15	165/70-15	155-15
B60-15	B70-15	B78-15	6.35-15	195/60-15	175/70-15	165-15
C60-15	C70-15	C78-15	6.85-15	205/60-15	185/70-15	175-15
	D70-15	D78-15				
E60-15	E70-15	E78-15	7.35-15	215/60-15	195/70-15	185-15
F60-15	F70-15	F78-15	7.75-15	225/60-15	205/70-15	195-15
G60-15	G70-15	G78-15	8.15-15/8.25-15	235/60-15	215/70-15	205-15
H60-15	H70-15	H78-15	8.45-15/8.55-15	245/60-15	225/70-15	215-15
J60-15	J70-15	J78-15	8.85-15/8.90-15	255/60-15	235/70-15	225-15
	K70-15		9.00-15	265/60-15	245/70-15	230-15
L60-15	L70-15	L78-15, L84-15	9.15-15			235-15
	M70-15	M78-15				255-15
		N78-15				

Note: Every size tire is not listed and many size comparisons are approximate, based on load ratings. Wider tires than those supplied new with the vehicle, should always be checked for clearance.

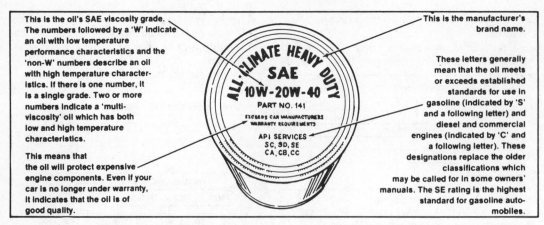

This is the oil's SAE viscosity grade. The numbers followed by a 'W' indicate an oil with low temperature performance characteristics and the 'non-W' numbers describe an oil with high temperature characteristics. If there is one number, it is a single grade. Two or more numbers indicate a 'multi-viscosity' oil which has both low and high temperature characteristics.

This means that the oil will protect expensive engine components. Even if your car is no longer under warranty, it indicates that the oil is of good quality.

This is the manufacturer's brand name.

These letters generally mean that the oil meets or exceeds established standards for use in gasoline (indicated by 'S' and a following letter) and diesel and commercial engines (indicated by 'C' and a following letter). These designations replace the older classifications which may be called for in some owners' manuals. The SE rating is the highest standard for gasoline automobiles.

The top of the oil can will tell you all you need to know about the oil

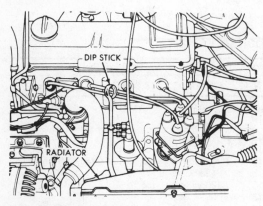

1.7L engine oil dipstick

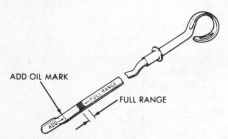

Engine oil dipstick markings

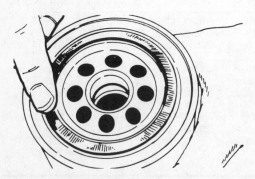

Lubricate the gasket on a new filter with clean engine oil

2. Reinsert the dipstick.

3. Remove the dipstick again. The oil level should be between the two marks. The difference between the marks is one quart.

4. Add oil through the capped opening on the top of the valve cover.

CHANGING OIL AND FILTER

Under normal service, the engine oil and filter should be changed every 12 months or 7500 miles, whichever comes first.

Under the following conditions, change the engine oil and filter every 3 months or 3000 miles, whichever comes first:

- Frequent driving in dusty conditions
- Frequent trailer pulling
- Extensive idling
- Frequent short trip driving (less than 10 miles)
- More than 50% operation at sustained high speeds (over 70 mph).

NOTE: *Drain the engine oil when the engine is at normal operating temperature.*

To change the oil, the vehicle should be on a level surface at normal operating temperature. This ensures that you will drain away the foreign matter in the oil, which will not happen if the engine is cold. Oil which is slightly dirty when drained is a good sign. This means that the contaminants are being drained away and not being left behind to form sludge.

You should have available some means to support the car, a 13 mm wrench, a filter wrench, 4 quarts of oil, a drain pan and some rags.

1. Jack up the front of the car and support it.

2. Position the drain pan under the drain plug, which is located at the rear of the oil pan.

CAUTION: *The EPA warns that prolonged contact with used engine oil may cause a number of skin disorders, including cancer! You should make every effort to minimize*

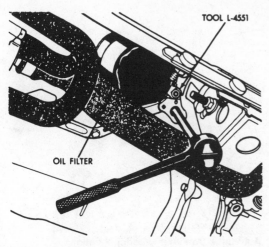

1.7L engine oil filter removal

Anticipated Temperature Range	Recommended SAE Grade
Above — 10° F.	90, 80W–90, 85W–90
As low as — 30° F.	80W, 80W–90, 85W–90
Below — 30° F.	75W

A412 transaxle lubricant recommendations

your exposure to used engine oil. Protective gloves should be worn when changing the oil. Wash your hands and any other exposed skin areas as soon as possible after exposure to used engine oil. Soap and water, or waterless hand cleaner should be used.

3. Loosen, but do not remove the drain plug. Cover your hand with a heavy rag and slowly unscrew the drain plug. Pushing the plug against the threads in the oil pan will prevent hot oil from running down your arm. As the drain plug comes to the end of the threads, quickly pull it away and allow all of the oil to drain into the pan.

4. When all the oil has drained, replace the drain plug and tighten it.

NOTE: *Be sure to dispose of the old oil in an environmentally safe manner.*

5. Remove the oil filter. It can only be removed with the tools shown, from below the car. Once the filter is loose, cover your hand with a thick rag and spin it off by hand.

NOTE: *On May 29, 1979, the assembly plant began installing 4" diameter oil filters in place of the previously used 3" diameter filters. The 4" filters are the same as those used on other Chrysler vehicles and should be used for service.*

6. Coat the rubber gasket on a new filter with clean engine oil and install the new filter. Tighten it by hand until the gasket contacts the mounting base and then ¾-1 turn further.

7. Refill the engine with 4 quarts of fresh oil of the proper viscosity according to the anticipated temperatures before the next oil change.

NOTE: *It requires 4 quarts of oil to fill the engine regardless of whether the filter was changed or not.*

8. Run the engine for a few minutes and check the oil level.

Manual Transaxle

FLUID RECOMMENDATIONS

The A-412 transaxle is a VW design and is the only model to use Hypoid gear lubricant. The A-412 transaxle can be easily identified from the Chrysler design models because the starter motor is located on the radiator side of the engine compartment. If it becomes necessary to add or change the fluid to the unit, lubricant conforming to API GL 4 specifications should be used. The recommended SAE grade should be selected from the chart.

All other manual transaxles through 1986, use only automatic transmission fluid labeled DEXRON®II. Starting in 1987, Chrysler recommends using SAE 5W-30 SF engine oil in all their manual transaxles.

LEVEL CHECK

The fluid level in the manual transaxle should be checked twice a year. Maintain the fluid level at the bottom of the filler plug opening.

To check the fluid level, position the car on a level surface and clean the dirt from around the transaxle filler plug. Remove the filler plug. The level should at least reach the bottom of the hole. You can check the level with your finger or a piece of bent wire.

DRAIN AND REFILL

Under normal conditions, the manual transaxle fluid will never need changing. Rare circumstances, such as the fluid becoming contaminated with water will necessitate fluid replacement.

It is relatively easy to change your own transaxle oil. The only equipment required is a drain pan, a wrench to fit the filler and drain plugs, and an oil suction gun. Gear oil and automatic transmission fluid can be purchased in both quart and gallon cans at automotive supply stores.

To change the oil:

1. Jack up the front of the car and support it safely on stands.

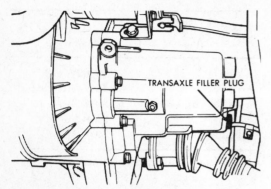

A-412 manual transaxle filler plug

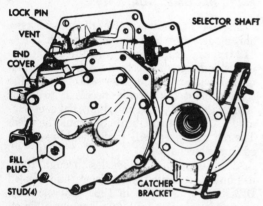

A-460, 465, and 525 manual transaxle filler plug

2. Slide drain pan under the transaxle.

3. Remove the filler plug and then the drain plug.

4. When the oil has been completely drained, install the drain plug. Tighten to 18 ft. lbs.

5. Using the suction gun, refill the transaxle up to the level of the filler plug.

6. Install and tighten the filler plug.

Automatic Transaxle

FLUID RECOMMENDATIONS

Dexron®II type transmission fluid is used in the Omni/Horizon automatic transaxles.

LEVEL CHECK

The automatic transaxle and differential are contained in the same housing, but the units are sealed from each other (1978-82 only). 1983 and later automatic transaxles are filled as one unit. The transmission does not have a conventional filler tube, but is filled through a die-cast opening in the case.

The filler hole is plugged during operation by the transmission dipstick.

The fluid level should be checked every 6 months when the engine and transmission fluid are warmed to normal operating temperature.

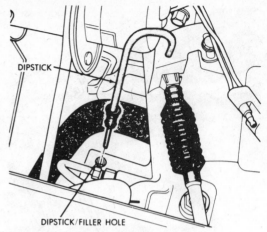

Automatic transaxle dipstick location

1. Position the car on a level surface.

2. Idle the engine and engage the parking brake.

3. Shift the lever through each gear momentarily and return the lever to PARK.

4. Remove the dipstick and wipe it clean.

5. Reinsert the dipstick and remove it again. The level should be between the ADD and FULL marks on the dipstick. If necessary, add DEXRON®II automatic transmission fluid. Do not overfill.

6. While you are checking the fluid level, check the condition of the fluid. The condition of the fluid will often reveal potential problems.

7. If the fluid level is consistently low, suspect a leak. The easiest way is to slip a piece of clean newspaper under the car overnight, but this is not always an accurate indication, since some leaks will occur only when the transmission is operating.

Other leaks can be located by driving the car. Wipe the underside of the transmission clean and drive the car for several miles to bring the fluid temperature to normal. Stop the car, shut off the engine and look for leakage, but remember, that where the fluid is located may not be the source of the leak. Airflow around the transmission while the car is moving may carry the fluid to other parts of the car.

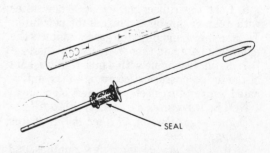

Automatic transaxle dipstick markings

8. Reinsert the dipstick and be sure it is properly seated. This is the only seal that prevents water or dirt entering the transmission through the filler opening.

DIFFERENTIAL (AUTOMATIC TRANSAXLE)

1978 through 1982 automatic transaxles have 2 separate reservoirs that require filling separately. 1983 and later models fill as one unit. Most models have a drain and fill plug in the differential cover; some models will have only a fill plug. Should it become necessary to drain the differential and the cover has only a fill plug, simply remove the cover to drain. A service gasket, should be formed from RTV sealant when the cover is installed. Use a $\frac{1}{16}''$ bead of RTV sealant on the cover.

To check the fluid level, remove the filler plug. The level should be at the bottom of the hole, which can be checked with your finger or a piece of bent wire.

If fluid is needed, use only Dexron®II®.

AUTOMATIC TRANSAXLE DRAIN AND REFILL

NOTE: *RTV silicone sealer is used in place of a pan gasket.*

Chrysler recommends no fluid or filter changes during the normal service life of the car. Severe usage requires a fluid and filter change every 15,000 miles. Severe usage is defined as:

● more than 50% heavy city traffic during 90° weather.

● police, taxi or commercial operation or trailer towing.

When changing the fluid, only Dexron®II fluid should be used. A filter change should be performed at every fluid change.

1. Raise the vehicle and support it on jackstands.

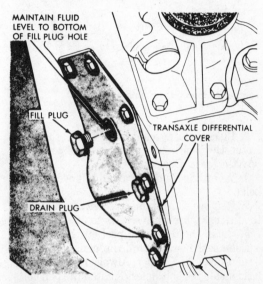

Automatic transaxle differential drain and fill plugs—1978–82 models

Transmission Fluid Indications

The appearance and odor of the transmission fluid can give valuable clues to the overall condition of the transmission. Always note the appearance of the fluid when you check the fluid level or change the fluid. Rub a small amount of fluid between your fingers to feel for grit and smell the fluid on the dipstick.

If the fluid appears:	It indicates:
Clear and red colored	● Normal operation
Discolored (extremely dark red or brownish) or smells burned	● Band or clutch pack failure, usually caused by an overheated transmission. Hauling very heavy loads with insufficient power or failure to change the fluid, often result in overheating. Do not confuse this appearance with newer fluids that have a darker red color and a strong odor (though not a burned odor).
Foamy or aerated (light in color and full of bubbles)	● The level is too high (gear train is churning oil). ● An internal air leak (air is mixing with the fluid). Have the transmission checked professionally.
Solid residue in the fluid	● Defective bands, clutch pack or bearings. Bits of band material or metal abrasives are clinging to the dipstick. Have the transmission checked professionally.
Varnish coating on the dipstick	● The transmission fluid is overheating.

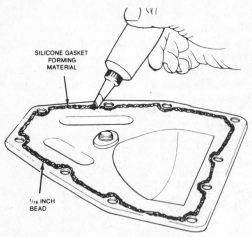

SILICONE GASKET
FORMING
MATERIAL

1/16 INCH
BEAD

Form a silicone gasket as shown

2. Place a large container under the pan, loosen the pan bolts and tap at one corner to break it loose. Drain the fluid.

3. When the fluid is drained remove the pan bolts.

4. Remove the retaining screws and replace the filter. Tighten the screws to 35 in. lbs.

5. Clean the fluid pan, peel off the old RTV silicone sealer and install the pan, using a 1/8" bead of new RTV sealer. Always run the sealer bead inside the bolt holes. Tighten the pan bolts to 10-12 ft. lbs.

6. Pour four quarts of Dexron®II fluid through the filler tube.

7. Start the engine and idle it for at least 2 minutes. Set the parking brake and move the selector through each position, ending in Park.

8. Add sufficient fluid to bring the level to the FULL mark on the dipstick. The level should be checked in Park, with the engine idling at normal operating temperature.

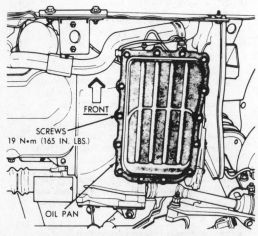

FRONT

SCREWS
19 N·m (165 IN. LBS.)

OIL PAN

Automatic transaxle oil pan

Cooling System

The cooling system should be inspected, flushed, and refilled with fresh coolant at the end of the first 2 years and every year thereafter. If the coolant is left in the system too long, it loses its ability to prevent rust and corrosion; if the coolant has too much water, it won't protect against freezing.

The pressure cap should be looked at for sign of age or deterioration. Fan belt and other drive belts should be inspected and adjusted to the proper tension. (See Checking Belt Tension).

Hose clamps should be tightened, and soft or cracked hoses replaced. Damp spots, or accumulations of rust or dye near hoses, water pump or other areas, indicate possible leakage, which must be corrected before filling the system with fresh coolant.

FLUID RECOMMENDATION

If additional coolant is needed, remove the cap from the reserve tank. DO NOT REMOVE THE RADIATOR CAP. Add a 50/50 mix of ethylene glycol coolant and water.

COOLANT LEVEL CHECK

The coolant reserve system provides a quick and easy way to verify proper coolant level. With the engine idling and at normal operating temperature, observe the level of the coolant in the plastic see-through tank. It should be between the minimum and maximum marks.

CHECK THE RADIATOR CAP

While you are checking the coolant level, check the radiator cap for a worn or cracked gasket. If the cap doesn't seal properly, fluid will be lost and the engine will overheat.

Worn caps should be replaced with a new one.

CLEAN RADIATOR OF DEBRIS

Periodically clean any debris — leaves, paper, insects, etc. — from the radiator fins. Pick the large pieces off by hand. The smaller pieces can be washed away with water pressure from a hose.

Carefully straighten any bent radiator fins with a pair of needle nosed pliers. Be careful, the fins are very soft! Don't wiggle the fins back and forth too much. Straighten them once and try not to move them again.

DRAIN AND REFILL THE COOLING SYSTEM

Completely draining and refilling the cooling system every year at least will remove accumulated rust, scale and other deposits. Coolant should be at least a 50/50 mixture of ethylene glycol and water for year round use. Use a good quality antifreeze with water pump lubricants.

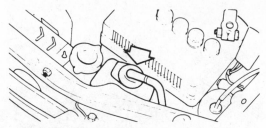

Coolant reserve bottle location

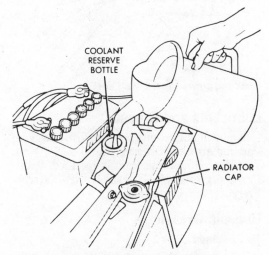

Add coolant to the coolant reserve bottle

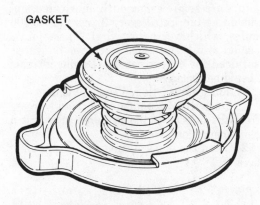

Check the radiator cap gasket

rust inhibitors and other corrosion inhibitors along with acid neutralizers.

1. Drain the existing antifreeze and coolant. Open the radiator and engine drain petcocks, or disconnect the bottom radiator hose, at the radiator outlet.

NOTE: *Before opening the radiator petcock, spray it with some penetrating lubricant.*

2. Close the petcock or re-connect the lower hose and fill the system with water.

CAUTION: *When draining the coolant, keep in mind that cats and dogs are attracted by*

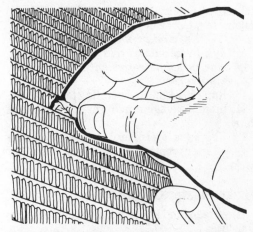

Remove debris from the radiator cooling fins

the ethylene glycol antifreeze, and are quite likely to drink any that is left in an uncovered container or in puddles on the ground. This will prove fatal in sufficient quantity. Always drain the coolant into a sealable container. Coolant should be reused unless it is contaminated or several years old.

3. Add a can of quality radiator flush.

4. Idle the engine until the upper radiator hose gets hot.

5. Drain the system again.

6. Repeat this process until the drained water is clear and free of scale.

7. Close all petcocks and connect all the hoses.

8. If equipped with a coolant recovery system, flush the reservoir with water and leave empty.

9. Determine the capacity of your cooling system (see Capacities specifications). Add a 50/

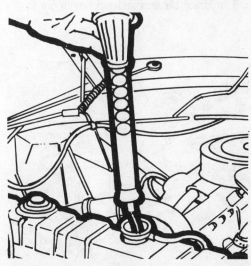

Check the anti-freeze protection

50 mix of quality antifreeze (ethylene glycol) and water to provide the desired protection.

NOTE: *Use a minimum of 50% ethylene glycol anti-freeze and water. This is necessary to provide adequate corrosion protection with aluminum parts.*

10. Run the engine to operating temperature.

11. Stop the engine and check the coolant level.

12. Check the level of protection with an antifreeze tester, replace the cap and check for leaks.

Brake Master Cylinder

The brake fluid level should be checked every 6 months.

1. Wipe the area around the master cylinder clean.

2. Remove the master cylinder cap. The fluid level should be within ¼″ of the top of the reservoir.

3. If necessary, add brake fluid identified on the container as conforming to DOT 3 specifications.

Power Steering Reservoir

The power steering reservoir fluid level should be checked with the engine OFF to prevent accidents. Check the level every 6 months.

1. Position the car on a level surface.

2. Wipe the area around the power steering reservoir cap clean and remove the cap.

3. The power steering pump cap has a dipstick attached. Fluid level should be kept at the level indicated on the dipstick.

4. If it is necessary to add fluid, use only MOPAR Power Steering Fluid or the equivalent. DO NOT USE AUTOMATIC TRANSMISSION FLUID.

5. Replace the cap and tighten in place.

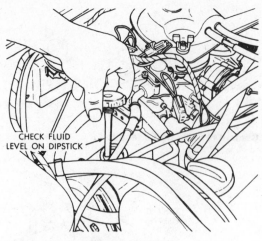

Checking power steering fluid level

Lubricants and Greases

Semi-solid lubricants bear an NLGI designation and are classified as grades 0, 1, 2, 3 or 4. Whenever chassis lubricant is specified, Multi-Purpose grease, NLGI grade 2, EP (Extreme Pressure) is recommended.

Chassis Greasing

Tie Rod Ends

There are only 2 points on the car that require periodic greasing. The tie-rod end ball joints are semi-permanently lubricated and should be lubricated every 3 years or 30,000 miles, whichever occurs first. These joints should also be inspected whenever the car is serviced for other reasons. Damaged seals should be replaced.

To lubricate the tie rod end ball joints:

1. Clean the accumulated dirt and grease from the outside of the seal area to permit a close inspection.

2. Clean the grease fitting and surrounding area.

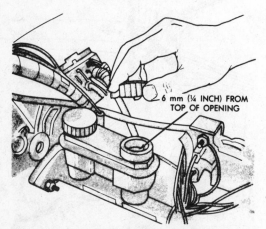

Check master cylinder fluid level

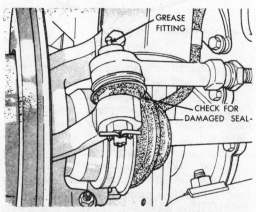

Check the tie-rod end ball joint seals

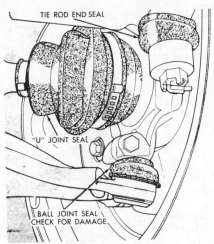

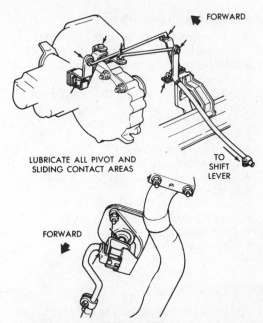

Check ball joints for damaged seals

3. Using a grease gun fill the joint with fresh grease.

4. Stop filling when the grease begins to flow freely from the areas at the base of the seal or when the seal begins to balloon.

5. Wipe off the excess grease.

Steering Shaft Seal

The steering shaft seal where the steering shaft passes through the dash is lubricated at manufacture. If the seal becomes noisy when the steering shaft is turned, it should be relubricated with multi-purpose chassis grease, NLGI Grade 2 EP.

Front Suspension Ball Joints

The 2 lower front suspension ball joints are permanently lubricated at the factory. Inspect the joints whenever the car is serviced for other reasons. Damaged seals should be replaced to prevent leakage of grease.

Clutch Cable

If the clutch cable begins to make odd noises or if the effort to depress the clutch becomes excessive, lubricate the clutch cable ball end with multi-purpose chassis grease NLGI Grade 2 EP.

Lubricate the floor shift linkage

Floorshift Control Linkage

The gearshift control linkage should be lubricated whenever the shifting effort becomes excessive or if the linkage exhibits a rattling noise. Use a multi-purpose chassis grease NLGI Grade 2 EP. Remove the unit and lubricate the spherical balls, metal caps and shaft and lubricate each plastic grommet or bushing.

Driveshaft U-Joints

The car has 4 constant velocity U-joints. No periodic lubrication is required, but the joint seals should be inspected for damage or leakage whenever the car is serviced. If damage is found, replace the U-joint boot and seal and fill with fresh grease immediately. Failure to do so will eventually require complete replacement of the constant velocity joint.

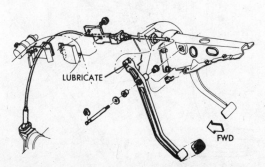

Lubricate the ball end of the clutch cable

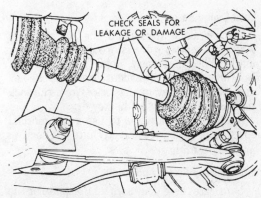

Inspect U-joint seals for leakage

Parts Requiring No Lubrication

Some components are permanently lubricated. Some parts will be adversely affected by lubricants. In particular, rubber bushings should not be lubricated, since it will destroy their frictional characteristics. Parts that should not be lubricated are:

- Alternator bearings
- Drive belts
- Fan idler belt pulley
- Front wheel bearings
- Rubber bushings
- Starter bearings
- Suspension strut bearing
- Throttle cable control
- Throttle linkage
- Water pump bearings

Body Lubrication

Operating mechanisms of the body should be inspected, cleaned and lubricated as necessary. This will provide maximum protection against rust and wear.

Prior to lubricating, wipe the parts clean of dirt and old lubricant. When Lubriplate is specified, use a smooth, white body lubricant of NLGI Grade 1. When Door-Ease is specified, use a stainless, wax-type lubricant.

Hood Latch And Release

Apply Lubriplate, or the equivalent to all pivot and sliding contact areas. Work the lubricant into the lock mechanism. Apply a thin film of the same lubricant to the safety catch.

Body Hinges

These parts should be lubricated with engine oil at the points shown.

Door Check Straps

Apply Lubriplate or the equivalent whenever the car is serviced.

Lock Cylinders

Pay particular attention to the lock cylinders when the temperature is around the freezing mark. When necessary, apply a thin film of Lubriplate, or the equivalent directly to the key and insert the key in the lock. Work the lock several times and wipe the key dry.

Another alternative is to use a commercial spray that is sprayed directly into the lock to prevent freezing.

Liftgate Prop Pivots And Latch

Lubricate these points with Lubriplate or the equivalent.

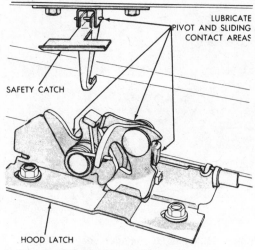

Lubricate the hood latch release

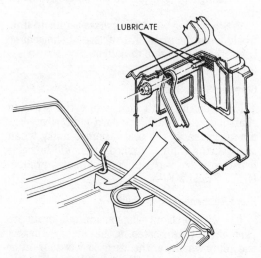

Lubricate the hood hinges

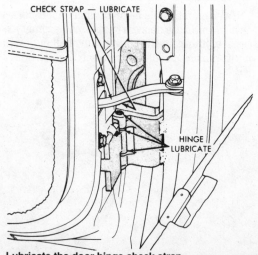

Lubricate the door hinge check strap

Door Latch, Lock Control, Linkage And Window Regulator

To lubricate these parts it is necessary to remove the trim panel. Lubricate all pivot and sliding contact areas with Lubriplate or the equivalent.

Parking Brake Mechanism

Lubricate all parking brake sliding and pivot contact areas with Lubriplate or the equivalent.

Door Latch and Striker Plate

Lubricate the striker plate contact area and the ratchet pivot areas with a stainless, wax-type lubricant such as Door Ease.

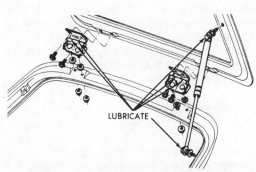

Lubricate the liftgate hinges and prop pivots

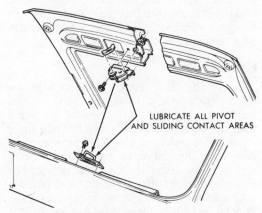

Lubricate the liftgate latch

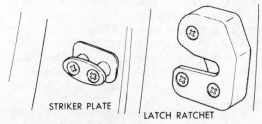

Lubricate the door latches

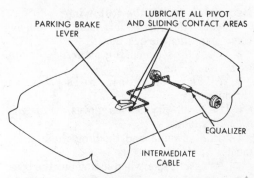

Lubricate the parking brake

Wheel Bearings

Front Wheel Bearings

The front wheel bearings are permanently sealed and require no periodic lubrication.

Rear Wheel Bearings

The rear wheel bearings should be inspected and relubricated whenever the rear brakes are serviced or at least every 30,000 miles. Repack the bearings with high temperature multi-purpose grease.

Check the lubricant to see if it is contaminated. If it contains dirt or has a milky appearance indicating the presence of water, the bearings should be cleaned and repacked.

Clean the bearings in kerosene, mineral spirits or other suitable cleaning fluid. Do not dry them by spinning the bearings. Allow them to air dry.

NOTE: *Sodium-based grease is not compatible with lithium-based grease. Read the package labels and be careful not to mix the two types. If there is any doubt as to the type of grease used, completely clean the old grease from the bearing and hub before replacing.*

Before handling the bearings, there are a few things that you should remember to do and not to do.

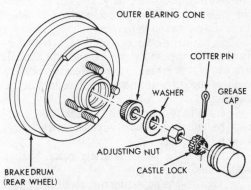

Exploded view of rear wheel bearing

Remember to DO the following:
- Remove all outside dirt from the housing before exposing the bearing.
- Treat a used bearing as gently as you would a new one.
- Work with clean tools in clean surroundings.
- Use clean, dry canvas gloves, or at least clean, dry hands.
- Clean solvents and flushing fluids are a must.
- Use clean paper when laying out the bearings to dry.
- Protect disassembled bearings from rust and dirt. Cover them up.
- Use clean rags to wipe bearings.
- Keep the bearings in oil-proof paper when they are to be stored or are not in use.
- Clean the inside of the housing before replacing the bearing.

Do NOT do the following:
- Don't work in dirty surroundings.
- Don't use dirty, chipped or damaged tools.
- Try not to work on wooden work benches or use wooden mallets.
- Don't handle bearings with dirty or moist hands.
- Do not use gasoline for cleaning; use a safe solvent.
- Do not spin-dry bearings with compressed air. They will be damaged.
- Do not spin dirty bearings.
- Avoid using cotton waste or dirty cloths to wipe bearings.
- Try not to scratch or nick bearing surfaces.
- Do not allow the bearing to come in contact with dirt or rust at any time.

1. Raise and support the car with the rear wheels off the floor.
2. Remove the wheel grease cap, cotter pin, nut-lock and bearing adjusting nut.
3. Remove the thrust washer and bearing.
4. Remove the drum from the spindle.
5. Thoroughly clean the old lubricant from the bearings and hub cavity. Inspect the bearing rollers for pitting or other signs of wear. Light discoloration is normal.
6. Repack the bearings with high temperature multi-purpose EP grease and add a small amount of new grease to the hub cavity. Be sure to force the lubricant between all rollers in the bearing.
7. Install the drum on the spindle after coating the polished spindle surfaces with wheel bearing lubricant.
8. Install the outer bearing cone, thrust washer and adjusting nut.
9. Tighten the adjusting nut to 20-25 ft. lbs. while rotating the wheel.

10. Back off the adjusting nut to completely release the preload from the bearing.
11. Tighten the adjusting nut finger-tight.
12. Position the nut-lock with one pair of slots in line with the cotter pin hole. Install the cotter pin.
13. Clean and install the grease cap and wheel.
14. Lower the car.

TRAILER TOWING

General Recommendations

Your car was primarily designed to carry passengers and cargo. It is important to remember that towing a trailer will place additional loads on your vehicle's engine, drive train, steering, braking and other systems. However, if you find it necessary to tow a trailer, using the proper equipment is a must.

Local laws may require specific equipment such as trailer brakes or fender mounted mirrors. Check your local laws.

Trailer Weight

The weight of the trailer is the most important factor. A good weight-to-horsepower ratio is about 35:1, 35 lbs. of GCW (Gross Combined Weight) for every horsepower your engine develops. Multiply the engine's rated horsepower by 35 and subtract the weight of the car passengers and luggage. The result is the approximate ideal maximum weight you should tow, although a a numerically higher axle ratio can help compensate for heavier weight.

Hitch Weight

Figure the hitch weight to select a proper hitch. Hitch weight is usually 9-11% of the trailer gross weight and should be measured with the trailer loaded. Hitches fall into three types: those that mount on the frame and rear bumper or the bolt-on or weld-on distribution type used for larger trailers. Axle mounted or clamp-on bumper hitches should never be used.

Check the gross weight rating of your trailer. Tongue weight is usually figured as 10% of gross trailer weight. Therefore, a trailer with a maximum gross weight of 2,000 lb. will have a maximum tongue weight of 200 lb. Class I trailers fall into this category. Class II trailers are those with a gross weight rating of 2,000-3,500 lb., while Class III trailers fall into the 3,500-6,000 lb. category. Class IV trailers are those over 6,000 lb. and are for use with fifth wheel trucks, only.

When you've determined the hitch that you'll need, follow the manufacturer's installation instructions, exactly, especially when it comes to fastener torques. The hitch will subjected to a lot of stress and good hitches come with hardened bolts. Never substitute an inferior bolt for a hardened bolt.

Cooling
ENGINE

One of the most common, if not THE most common, problems associated with trailer towing is engine overheating.

If you have a standard cooling system, without an expansion tank, you'll definitely need to get an aftermarket expansion tank kit, preferably one with at least a 2 quart capacity. These kits are easily installed on the radiator's overflow hose, and come with a pressure cap designed for expansion tanks.

Another helpful accessory is a Flex Fan. These fan are large diameter units are designed to provide more airflow at low speeds, with blades that have deeply cupped surfaces. The blades then flex, or flatten out, at high speed, when less cooling air is needed. These fans are far lighter in weight than stock fans, requiring less horsepower to drive them. Also, they are far quieter than stock fans.

If you do decide to replace your stock fan with a flex fan, note that if your car has a fan clutch, a spacer between the flex fan and water pump hub will be needed.

Aftermarket engine oil coolers are helpful for prolonging engine oil life and reducing overall engine temperatures. Both of these factors increase engine life.

While not absolutely necessary in towing Class I and some Class II trailers, they are recommended for heavier Class II and all Class III towing.

Engine oil cooler systems consist of an adapter, screwed on in place of the oil filter, a remote filter mounting and a multi-tube, finned heat exchanger, which is mounted in front of the radiator or air conditioning condenser.

TRANSMISSION

An automatic transmission is usually recommended for trailer towing. Modern automatics have proven reliable and, of course, easy to operate, in trailer towing.

The increased load of a trailer, however, causes an increase in the temperature of the automatic transmission fluid. Heat is the worst enemy of an automatic transmission. As the temperature of the fluid increases, the life of the fluid decreases.

It is essential, therefore, that you install an automatic transmission cooler.

The cooler, which consists of a multi-tube,

finned heat exchanger, is usually installed in front of the radiator or air conditioning compressor, and hooked inline with the transmission cooler tank inlet line. Follow the cooler manufacturer's installation instructions.

Select a cooler of at least adequate capacity, based upon the combined gross weights of the car and trailer.

Cooler manufacturers recommend that you use an aftermarket cooler in addition to, and not instead of, the present cooling tank in your radiator. If you do want to use it in place of the radiator cooling tank, get a cooler at least two sizes larger than normally necessary.

NOTE: *A transmission cooler can, sometimes, cause slow or harsh shifting in the transmission during cold weather, until the fluid has a chance to come up to normal operating temperature. Some coolers can be purchased with or retrofitted with a temperature bypass valve which will allow fluid flow through the cooler only when the fluid has reached operating temperature, or above.*

Handling A Trailer

Towing a trailer with ease and safety requires a certain amount of experience. It's a good idea to learn the feel of a trailer by practicing turning, stopping and backing in an open area such as an empty parking lot.

PUSHING AND TOWING

If your car is equipped with a manual transaxle, it may be push started in an extreme emergency, but there is the possibility of damaging dumpers and/or fenders of both cars. Make sure that the bumpers of both cars are evenly matched. Depress the clutch pedal, select Second or Third gear, and switch the ignition On. When the car reaches a speed of approximately 10 or 15 mph, release the clutch to start the engine. DO NOT ATTEMPT TO PUSH START AN AUTOMATIC OMNI OR HORIZON.

Manual transaxle models may be flat-towed short distances. Attach tow lines to the towing eye on the front suspension or the left or right bumper bracket at the rear. Flat-towing automatic transaxle models is not recommended more than 15 miles at more than 30 mph, and this only in an emergency. Cars equipped with t he automatic should only be towed from the rear when the front wheels are on towing dollies.

If you plan on towing a trailer, don't exceed 1000 lbs. (trailer without brakes). Towing a trailer with an automatic equipped car places an extra load on the transmission and a few items should be made note of here. Make doubly sure that the transmission fluid is at the correct level. Change the fluid more frequently if you're doing much trailer hauling. Start out in 1 or 2 and use the lower ranges when climbing hills. Aftermarket transmission coolers are available which greatly ease the load on your automatic and one should be considered if you often pull a trailer.

JUMP STARTING

Jump starting is the favored method of starting a car with a dead battery. Make sure that the cables are properly connected, negative-to-negative and positive-to-positive, or you stand a chance of damaging the electrical systems of both cars. Keep the engine running in the donor car. If the car still fails to start, call a garage. Continual grinding on the starter will overheat the unit and make repair or replacement necessary.

JACKING

Floor jacks can be used to raise the car at the locations shown. In addition a front jacking point is located at the center of the front cross-

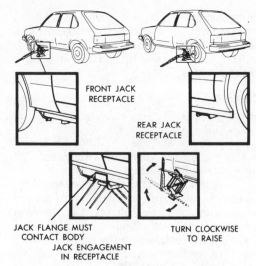

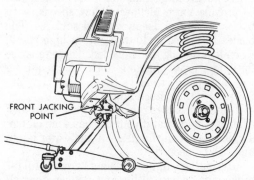
Jacking locations with tire changing jack

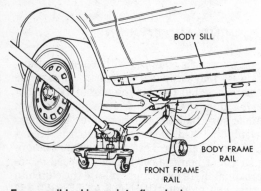
Front jacking point—floor jack

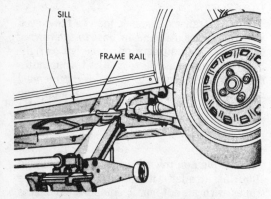
Frame rail jacking point—floor jack

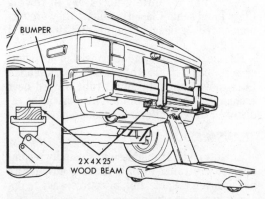
4-door model rear jacking point—floor jack

Rear frame rail jacking point—floor jack

member. Four door models only can be jacked at the extreme rear provided a 2″ × 4″ × 25″ (minimum dimensions) wood spacer is positioned as shown against the ledge of the rear bumper.

Jack receptacles are located at the front and rear of the body sill for use with jack supplied with a car. Do not use these lift points as bearing points for a floor jack.

JUMP STARTING A DEAD BATTERY

The chemical reaction in a battery produces explosive hydrogen gas. This is the safe way to jump start a dead battery, reducing the chances of an accidental spark that could cause an explosion.

Jump Starting Precautions

1. Be sure both batteries are of the same voltage.
2. Be sure both batteries are of the same polarity (have the same grounded terminal).
3. Be sure the vehicles are not touching.
4. Be sure the vent cap holes are not obstructed.
5. Do not smoke or allow sparks around the battery.
6. In cold weather, check for frozen electrolyte in the battery.
7. Do not allow electrolyte on your skin or clothing.
8. Be sure the electrolyte is not frozen.

Jump Starting Procedure

1. Determine voltages of the two batteries; they must be the same.
2. Bring the starting vehicle close (they must not touch) so that the batteries can be reached easily.
3. Turn off all accessories and both engines. Put both cars in Neutral or Park and set the handbrake.
4. Cover the cell caps with a rag -- do not cover terminals.
5. If the terminals on the run-down battery are heavily corroded, clean them.
6. Identify the positive and negative posts on both batteries and connect the cables in the order shown.
7. Start the engine of the starting vehicle and run it at fast idle. Try to start the car with the dead battery. Crank it for no more than 10 seconds at a time and let it cool off for 20 seconds in between tries.
8. If it doesn't start in 3 tries, there is something else wrong.
9. Disconnect the cables in the reverse order.
10. Replace the cell covers and dispose of the rags.

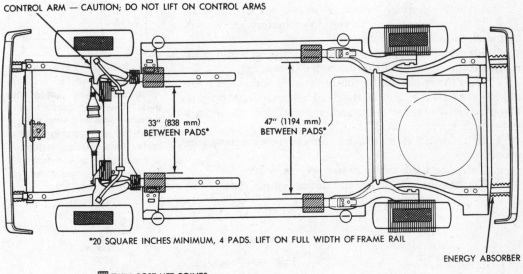

CONTROL ARM — CAUTION; DO NOT LIFT ON CONTROL ARMS

33" (838 mm) BETWEEN PADS*

47" (1194 mm) BETWEEN PADS*

*20 SQUARE INCHES MINIMUM, 4 PADS. LIFT ON FULL WIDTH OF FRAME RAIL

ENERGY ABSORBER

▦ TWIN POST LIFT POINTS
▨ FRAME CONTACT OR FLOOR JACK
▩ DRIVE ON HOIST
O SCISSORS JACK (EMERGENCY) LOCATIONS

Jacking and hoisting contact locations

JUMP STARTING A DEAD BATTERY

The chemical reaction in a battery produces explosive hydrogen gas. This is the safe way to jump start a dead battery, reducing the chances of an accidental spark that could cause an explosion.

Jump Starting Precautions

1. Be sure both batteries are of the same voltage.
2. Be sure both batteries are of the same polarity (have the same grounded terminal).
3. Be sure the vehicles are not touching.
4. Be sure the vent cap holes are not obstructed.
5. Do not smoke or allow sparks around the battery.
6. In cold weather, check for frozen electrolyte in the battery.
7. Do not allow electrolyte on your skin or clothing.
8. Be sure the electrolyte is not frozen.

Jump Starting Procedure

1. Determine voltages of the two batteries; they must be the same.
2. Bring the starting vehicle close (they must not touch) so that the batteries can be reached easily.
3. Turn off all accessories and both engines. Put both cars in Neutral or Park and set the handbrake.
4. Cover the cell caps with a rag—do not cover terminals.
5. If the terminals on the run-down battery are heavily corroded, clean them.
6. Identify the positive and negative posts on both batteries and connect the cables in the order shown.
7. Start the engine of the starting vehicle and run it at fast idle. Try to start the car with the dead battery. Crank it for no more than 10 seconds at a time and let it cool off for 20 seconds in between tries.
8. If it doesn't start in 3 tries, there is something else wrong.
9. Disconnect the cables in the reverse order.
10. Replace the cell covers and dispose of the rags.

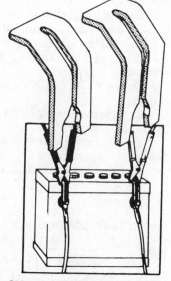

Side terminal batteries occasionally pose a problem when connecting jumper cables. There frequently isn't enough room to clamp the cables without touching sheet metal. Side terminal adaptors are available to alleviate this problem and should be removed after use.

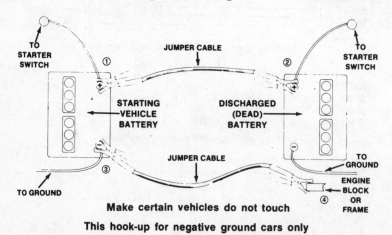

Make certain vehicles do not touch

This hook-up for negative ground cars only

Maintenance Intervals

General Maintenance		Miles—in thousands					
		7.5	15	22.5	30	37.5	45
Brake Linings	Inspect front brakes		●		●		●
	Inspect rear brakes				●		
*Cooling System	First drain, flush and refill at 24 months or				●		
	Subsequent drain, flush and refill every 12 months or						●
	Check and service system every 12 months or		●		●		●
*Drive Belts	Check tension and condition	●	●	●	●	●	●
*Engine Oil	Change every 12 months or	●	●	●	●	●	●
*Engine Oil Filter	Change every 12 months or	●		●		●	
Rear Wheel Bearings	Inspect or				●		●
Clutch Pedal Free Play	Adjust every 6 months or	●	●	●	●	●	●
Steering Linkage Tie Rod Ends	Lubricate every 6 months or				●		

* Also an emission control service.

Emission Control System Maintenance		Miles—in thousands					
		7.5	15	22.5	30	37.5	45
Automatic Choke	Check and adjust		●		●		●
Carburetor Choke Shaft	Apply solvent every six months or	●	●	●	●	●	●
Carburetor Air Filter	Replace at				●		
Fast Idle Cam and Pivot Pin	Apply solvent every six months or	●	●	●	●	●	●
Fuel Filter	Replace at	●		●		●	
Idle Speed Air-Fuel Mixture	Check and adjust at		●		●		●
Ignition Cables	Check and replace as required at time of spark replacement						
Ignition Timing	Check and adjust if necessary		●		●		●
PCV Valve	Check and adjust if necessary		●		●		●
PCV Valve	Replace				●		
Spark Plugs	Replace		●		●		●
Valve Lash	Check and adjust if necessary at		●		●		●
Underhood Rubber & Plastic Components (Emission Hoses)	Inspect and replace at		●		●		●

Inspect and Service should also be performed any time a malfunction is observed or suspected.

Maintenance Intervals (cont.)

Severe Service Maintenance			Miles—in thousands																
			3	6	9	12	15	18	21	24	27	30	33	36	39	42	45	48
Brake Linings	Inspect	Front		●		●		●		●		●		●		●		●
		Rear				●				●				●				●
Change Oil	Change every 3 months	or	●	●	●	●	●	●	●	●	●	●	●	●	●	●	●	●
Engine Oil Filter	Change at initial oil change and every second oil change thereafter																		
Rear Wheel Bearings	Inspect and Relubricate whenever drums are removed to inspect or service brakes or every				●			●			●				●			●	
Front Suspension Ball Joints	Inspect at every oil change																		
Steering Linkage Tie Rod Ends	Lubricate every 18 months	or					●					●					●	
Transmission Fluid "Automatic"	Change						●					●					●	
Constant Velocity Universal Joints	Inspect at every oil change																		

*Driving under any of the following operating conditions: Stop and go driving, driving in dusty conditions, extensive idling, frequent short trips, operating at sustained high speeds during hot weather (above +90°F, +32°C).

Capacities

Year	Model	Engine Displacement	Crankcase Incl. Filter (qts)	Transmission Pints to Refill after Draining		Final Drive (pts)	Gasoline Tank (gals)	Cooling System (qts)	
				Manual	Automatic			W/AC	WO/AC
'78	All	1.7L	4	2.65	13.0	2.0	13	6.5	8.0
'79	All	1.7L	4	2.65	13.0	2.0	13	6.0	6.0
'80	All	1.7L	4	2.65	13.0	2.0	13	6.0	6.0
'81–'82	All	1.7L	4	2.65	14.5	2.37	13	6.0	6.0
	All	2.2L	4	3.75	15.0	2.37	13	8.7	8.7
'83–'86	All	1.6L	3.5	①	18.0	—	13	6.8	6.8
	All	1.7L	4	①	16.8	—	13	6.0	6.0
	All	2.2L	4 ②	①	18.0	—	13	9.0	9.0
'87–'89	All	2.2L	4 ②	③	18.0	—	13	9.0	9.0

① 4-speed; 3.75
   5-speed; 4.55
② turbo: 5 qts
③ A525: 4.6
   A520, A555: 5.0

Engine Performance and Tune-Up

2

TUNE-UP PROCEDURES

An engine tune-up is a service designed to restore the maximum capability of power, performance, economy and reliability in an engine, and, at the same time, assure the owner of a complete check and more lasting results in efficiency and trouble-free performance. Engine tune-up becomes increasingly important each year, to ensure that pollutant levels are in compliance with federal emissions standards.

It is advisable to follow a definite and thorough tune-up procedure. Tune-up consists of three separate steps: Analysis, the process of determining whether normal wear is responsible for performance loss, and whether parts require replacement or service; Parts Replacement or Service; and Adjustment, where engine adjustments are returned to the original factory specifications.

The extent of an engine tune-up is usually determined by the length of time since the previous service, although the type of driving and the general mechanical condition of the engine must be considered. Specific maintenance should also be performed at regular intervals, depending on operating conditions.

Troubleshooting is a logical sequence of procedures designed to lead the owner or service man to the particular cause of trouble. The troubleshooting chapter of this manual is general in nature, yet specific enough to locate the problem. Service usually comprises two areas; diagnosis and repair. While the apparent cause of trouble, in many cases, is worn or damaged parts, performance problems are less obvious. The first job is to locate the problem and cause. Once the problem has been isolated, refer to the appropriate section for repair, removal or adjustment procedures.

It is advisable to read the entire chapter before beginning a tune-up, although those who are more familiar with tune-up procedures may wish to go directly to the instructions.

Spark Plugs

Spark plugs ignite the air and fuel mixture in the cylinder as the piston reaches the top of the compression stroke. The controlled explosion that results forces the piston down, turning the crankshaft and the rest of the drive train.

The average life of a spark plug is dependent on a number of factors: the mechanical condition of the engine; the type of engine; the type of fuel; driving conditions; and the driver.

When you remove the spark plugs, check their condition. They are a good indicator of the condition of the engine. It it a good idea to remove the spark plugs at regular intervals, such as every 2,000 or 3,000 miles, just so you can keep an eye on the mechanical state of your engine.

A small deposit of light tan or gray material on a spark plug that has been used for any period of time is to be considered normal.

The gap between the center electrode and the side or ground electrode can be expected to increase not more than 0.001″ every 1,000 miles under normal conditions.

When a spark plug is functioning normally or, more accurately, when the plug is installed in an engine that is functioning properly, the plugs can be taken out, cleaned, regapped, and reinstalled in the engine without doing the engine any harm.

When, and if, a plug fouls and beings to misfire, you will have to investigate, correct the cause of the fouling, and either clean or replace the plug.

There are several reasons why a spark plug will foul and you can learn which is at fault by just looking at the plug. A few of the most common reasons for plug fouling, and a description of the fouled plug's appearance, are listed in the

Tune-Up Specifications

Part numbers listed in this reference are not recommendations by Chilton for any product by brand name. They are references that can be used with interchange manuals and after market supplier catalogs to locate each brand supplier's discrete part number. NOTE: When analyzing compression test results, look for uniformity among cylinders rather than specfic pressures. The lowest reading cylinder should be within 20% of the highest.

Year	Displ	Spark Plugs		Ignition Timing (deg)▲		Intake Valve Opens (deg)■	Fuel Pump Pressure (psi)	Idle Speed (rpm)▲		Valve Lash (in.)▲	
		Orig Type	Gap (in.)	Man Trans	Auto Trans			Man Trans	Auto Trans	Intake	Exhaust
'78	1.7L	RN-12Y	.035	15B	15B	23	4.5–6	900	900	.008–.012H	.016–.020H
'79	1.7L	RN-12Y	.035	15B	15B	14	4.4–5.8	900	900	.008–.012H	.016–.020H
'80	1.7L	RN-12Y	.035	12B⑤	12B⑤	14	4.4–5.8	900	900	.008–.012H	.016–.020H
'81	1.7L	P65-PR4①	.048②	12B③	10B④	14	4.4–5.8	900	900	.008–.012H	.016–.020H
	2.2L	P65-PR	.035	10B	10B	12	4.5–6.0	900	900	Hyd.	Hyd.
'82	1.7L	P65-PR	.035	20B	12B	14	4.4–5.8	900	900	.008–.012H	.016–.020H
	2.2L	P65-PR	.035	12B	12B	12	4.5–6.0	900	900	Hyd.	Hyd.
'83	1.7L	RN-12YC⑥	.035	20°	12°	14	4.4–5.8	850	900	.008–.012H	.016–.020H
	2.2L	RN-12YC⑥	.035	12°⑦	12°⑦	12	4.5–6.0	850	900	Hyd.	Hyd.
'84–'86	1.6L	RN-12YC⑥	.035	12°	12°	16	4.5–6.0	850	1000	.012C	.014C
	2.2L	RN-12YC⑥	.035	10°⑧	10°⑧	12	4.5–6.0	900⑧	900⑧	Hyd.	Hyd.
'87	2.2L	RN12YC⑥	.035	12°	12°	16°⑩		900	700⑨	Hyd.	Hyd.
'88–'89	2.2L	RN12YC⑥	.035	12°	12°	0°		850	850	Hyd.	Hyd.

NOTE: The underhood specifications sticker often reflects tune-up specification changes made in production. Sticker figures must be used if they disagree with those in this chart.

▲ See text for procedure
■ Before Top Dead Center
① Canada: P65-PR
② Canada: .035
③ Canada: 5B
④ Canada: 10B
⑤ California: 10B
⑥ Replacement plug: RN-12Y
⑦ High-altitude: 6B
⑧ High-performance engine: 15°B @ 850 RPM—refer to VECI label under hood.
⑨ Turbocharged: 800

Troubleshooting Engine Performance

Problem	Cause	Solution
Hard starting (engine cranks normally)	• Binding linkage, choke valve or choke piston	• Repair as necessary
	• Restricted choke vacuum diaphragm	• Clean passages
	• Improper fuel level	• Adjust float level
	• Dirty, worn or faulty needle valve and seat	• Repair as necessary
	• Float sticking	• Repair as necessary
	• Faulty fuel pump	• Replace fuel pump
	• Incorrect choke cover adjustment	• Adjust choke cover
	• Inadequate choke unloader adjustment	• Adjust choke unloader
	• Faulty ignition coil	• Test and replace as necessary
	• Improper spark plug gap	• Adjust gap
	• Incorrect ignition timing	• Adjust timing
	• Incorrect valve timing	• Check valve timing; repair as necessary
Rough idle or stalling	• Incorrect curb or fast idle speed	• Adjust curb or fast idle speed
	• Incorrect ignition timing	• Adjust timing to specification
	• Improper feedback system operation	• Refer to Chapter 4
	• Improper fast idle cam adjustment	• Adjust fast idle cam
	• Faulty EGR valve operation	• Test EGR system and replace as necessary
	• Faulty PCV valve air flow	• Test PCV valve and replace as necessary
	• Choke binding	• Locate and eliminate binding condition
	• Faulty TAC vacuum motor or valve	• Repair as necessary
	• Air leak into manifold vacuum	• Inspect manifold vacuum connections and repair as necessary
	• Improper fuel level	• Adjust fuel level
	• Faulty distributor rotor or cap	• Replace rotor or cap
	• Improperly seated valves	• Test cylinder compression, repair as necessary
	• Incorrect ignition wiring	• Inspect wiring and correct as necessary
	• Faulty ignition coil	• Test coil and replace as necessary
	• Restricted air vent or idle passages	• Clean passages
	• Restricted air cleaner	• Clean or replace air cleaner filler element
	• Faulty choke vacuum diaphragm	• Repair as necessary
Faulty low-speed operation	• Restricted idle transfer slots	• Clean transfer slots
	• Restricted idle air vents and passages	• Clean air vents and passages
	• Restricted air cleaner	• Clean or replace air cleaner filter element
	• Improper fuel level	• Adjust fuel level
	• Faulty spark plugs	• Clean or replace spark plugs
	• Dirty, corroded, or loose ignition secondary circuit wire connections	• Clean or tighten secondary circuit wire connections
	• Improper feedback system operation	• Refer to Chapter 4
	• Faulty ignition coil high voltage wire	• Replace ignition coil high voltage wire
	• Faulty distributor cap	• Replace cap
Faulty acceleration	• Improper accelerator pump stroke	• Adjust accelerator pump stroke
	• Incorrect ignition timing	• Adjust timing
	• Inoperative pump discharge check ball or needle	• Clean or replace as necessary
	• Worn or damaged pump diaphragm or piston	• Replace diaphragm or piston

Troubleshooting Engine Performance (cont.)

Problem	Cause	Solution
Faulty acceleration (cont.)	• Leaking carburetor main body cover gasket	• Replace gasket
	• Engine cold and choke set too lean	• Adjust choke cover
	• Improper metering rod adjustment (BBD Model carburetor)	• Adjust metering rod
	• Faulty spark plug(s)	• Clean or replace spark plug(s)
	• Improperly seated valves	• Test cylinder compression, repair as necessary
	• Faulty ignition coil	• Test coil and replace as necessary
	• Improper feedback system operation	• Refer to Chapter 4
Faulty high speed operation	• Incorrect ignition timing	• Adjust timing
	• Faulty distributor centrifugal advance mechanism	• Check centrifugal advance mechanism and repair as necessary
	• Faulty distributor vacuum advance mechanism	• Check vacuum advance mechanism and repair as necessary
	• Low fuel pump volume	• Replace fuel pump
	• Wrong spark plug air gap or wrong plug	• Adjust air gap or install correct plug
	• Faulty choke operation	• Adjust choke cover
	• Partially restricted exhaust manifold, exhaust pipe, catalytic converter, muffler, or tailpipe	• Eliminate restriction
	• Restricted vacuum passages	• Clean passages
	• Improper size or restricted main jet	• Clean or replace as necessary
	• Restricted air cleaner	• Clean or replace filter element as necessary
	• Faulty distributor rotor or cap	• Replace rotor or cap
	• Faulty ignition coil	• Test coil and replace as necessary
	• Improperly seated valve(s)	• Test cylinder compression, repair as necessary
	• Faulty valve spring(s)	• Inspect and test valve spring tension, replace as necessary
	• Incorrect valve timing	• Check valve timing and repair as necessary
	• Intake manifold restricted	• Remove restriction or replace manifold
	• Worn distributor shaft	• Replace shaft
	• Improper feedback system operation	• Refer to Chapter 4
Misfire at all speeds	• Faulty spark plug(s)	• Clean or replace spark plug(s)
	• Faulty spark plug wire(s)	• Replace as necessary
	• Faulty distributor cap or rotor	• Replace cap or rotor
	• Faulty ignition coil	• Test coil and replace as necessary
	• Primary ignition circuit shorted or open intermittently	• Troubleshoot primary circuit and repair as necessary
	• Improperly seated valve(s)	• Test cylinder compression, repair as necessary
	• Faulty hydraulic tappet(s)	• Clean or replace tappet(s)
	• Improper feedback system operation	• Refer to Chapter 4
	• Faulty valve spring(s)	• Inspect and test valve spring tension, repair as necessary
	• Worn camshaft lobes	• Replace camshaft
	• Air leak into manifold	• Check manifold vacuum and repair as necessary
	• Improper carburetor adjustment	• Adjust carburetor
	• Fuel pump volume or pressure low	• Replace fuel pump
	• Blown cylinder head gasket	• Replace gasket
	• Intake or exhaust manifold passage(s) restricted	• Pass chain through passage(s) and repair as necessary
	• Incorrect trigger wheel installed in distributor	• Install correct trigger wheel

Troubleshooting Engine Performance (cont.)

Problem	Cause	Solution
Power not up to normal	• Incorrect ignition timing	• Adjust timing
	• Faulty distributor rotor	• Replace rotor
	• Trigger wheel loose on shaft	• Reposition or replace trigger wheel
	• Incorrect spark plug gap	• Adjust gap
	• Faulty fuel pump	• Replace fuel pump
	• Incorrect valve timing	• Check valve timing and repair as necessary
	• Faulty ignition coil	• Test coil and replace as necessary
	• Faulty ignition wires	• Test wires and replace as necessary
	• Improperly seated valves	• Test cylinder compression and repair as necessary
	• Blown cylinder head gasket	• Replace gasket
	• Leaking piston rings	• Test compression and repair as necessary
	• Worn distributor shaft	• Replace shaft
	• Improper feedback system operation	• Refer to Chapter 4
Intake backfire	• Improper ignition timing	• Adjust timing
	• Faulty accelerator pump discharge	• Repair as necessary
	• Defective EGR CTO valve	• Replace EGR CTO valve
	• Defective TAC vacuum motor or valve	• Repair as necessary
	• Lean air/fuel mixture	• Check float level or manifold vacuum for air leak. Remove sediment from bowl
Exhaust backfire	• Air leak into manifold vacuum	• Check manifold vacuum and repair as necessary
	• Faulty air injection diverter valve	• Test diverter valve and replace as necessary
	• Exhaust leak	• Locate and eliminate leak
Ping or spark knock	• Incorrect ignition timing	• Adjust timing
	• Distributor centrifugal or vacuum advance malfunction	• Inspect advance mechanism and repair as necessary
	• Excessive combustion chamber deposits	• Remove with combustion chamber cleaner
	• Air leak into manifold vacuum	• Check manifold vacuum and repair as necessary
	• Excessively high compression	• Test compression and repair as necessary
	• Fuel octane rating excessively low	• Try alternate fuel source
	• Sharp edges in combustion chamber	• Grind smooth
	• EGR valve not functioning properly	• Test EGR system and replace as necessary
Surging (at cruising to top speeds)	• Low carburetor fuel level	• Adjust fuel level
	• Low fuel pump pressure or volume	• Replace fuel pump
	• Metering rod(s) not adjusted properly (BBD Model Carburetor)	• Adjust metering rod
	• Improper PCV valve air flow	• Test PCV valve and replace as necessary
	• Air leak into manifold vacuum	• Check manifold vacuum and repair as necessary
	• Incorrect spark advance	• Test and replace as necessary
	• Restricted main jet(s)	• Clean main jet(s)
	• Undersize main jet(s)	• Replace main jet(s)
	• Restricted air vents	• Clean air vents
	• Restricted fuel filter	• Replace fuel filter
	• Restricted air cleaner	• Clean or replace air cleaner filter element
	• EGR valve not functioning properly	• Test EGR system and replace as necessary
	• Improper feedback system operation	• Refer to Chapter 4

Color Section, which also offers solutions to the problems.

SPARK PLUG HEAT RANGE

Spark plug heat range is the ability of the plug to dissipate heat. The longer the insulator (or the farther it extends into the engine), the hotter the plug will operate; the shorter the insulator the cooler it will operate. A plug that absorbs little heat and remains too cool will quickly accumulate deposits of oil and carbon since it is not hot enough to burn them off. This leads to plug fouling and consequently to misfiring. A plug that absorbs too much heat will have no deposits, but, due to the excessive heat, the electrodes will burn away quickly and in some instances, preignition may result. Preignition takes place when plug tips get so hot that they glow sufficiently to ignite the fuel/air mixture before the actual spark occurs. This early ignition will usually cause a pinging during low speeds and heavy loads.

The general rule of thumb for choosing the correct heat range when picking a spark plug is: if most of your driving is long distance, high speed travel, use a colder plug; if most of your driving is stop and go, use a hotter plug. Original equipment plugs are compromise plugs, but most people never have occasion to change their plugs from the factory recommended heat range.

REPLACING SPARK PLUGS

A set of spark plugs usually requires replacement after about 10,000 miles on cars with conventional ignition systems and after about 20,000 to 30,000 miles on cars with electronic ignition, depending on your style of driving. In normal operation, plug gap increases about 0.025mm for every 1,000-2,500 miles. As the gap increases, the plug's voltage requirement also increases. It requires a greater voltage to jump the wider gap and about two to three times as much voltage to fire a plug at high speeds than at idle.

When you're removing spark plugs, you should work on one at a time. Don't start by removing the plug wires all at once, because unless you number them, they may become mixed up. Take a minute before you begin and number the wires with tape. The best location for numbering is near where the wires come out of the cap.

REMOVAL

1. Twist the spark plug boot and remove the boot and wire from the plug. Do not pull on the wire itself as this will ruin the wire.
2. If possible, use a brush or rag to clean the area around the spark plug. Make sure that all the dirt is removed so that none will enter the cylinder after the plug is removed.
3. Remove the spark plug using the proper size socket. Turn the socket counterclockwise to remove the plug. Be sure to hold the socket straight on the plug to avoid breaking the plug, or rounding off the hex on the plug.

INSPECTION

Check the plugs for deposits and wear. If they are not going to be replaced, clean the plugs thoroughly. Remember that any kind of deposit will decrease the efficiency of the plug. Plugs can be cleaned on a spark plug cleaning machine, which can sometimes be found in service stations, or you can do an acceptable job of cleaning with a stiff brush.

Check spark plug gap before installation. The ground electrode must be aligned with the center electrode and the specified size wire gauge should pass through the gap with a slight drag. If the electrodes are worn, it is possible to file them level.

INSTALLATION

1. Use a round wire feeler gauge to check the plug gap. The correct size gauge should pass

GASKET TYPE PLUGS

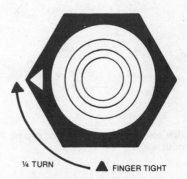

¼ TURN   ▲ FINGER TIGHT

TAPERED SEAT PLUGS (NO GASKET)

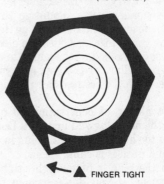

▲ FINGER TIGHT

¹⁄₁₆ TURN

Tighten the plugs as shown in the absence of a specified torque

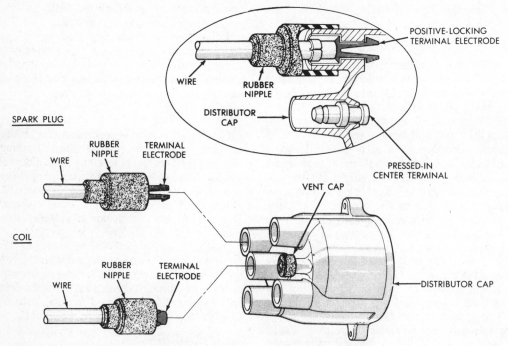

POSITIVE-LOCKING
TERMINAL ELECTRODE

WIRE

RUBBER
NIPPLE

DISTRIBUTOR
CAP

PRESSED-IN
CENTER TERMINAL

SPARK PLUG

RUBBER
NIPPLE

TERMINAL
ELECTRODE

WIRE

COIL

VENT CAP

RUBBER
NIPPLE

TERMINAL
ELECTRODE

WIRE

DISTRIBUTOR CAP

Coil and spark plug wires—1980 and later models

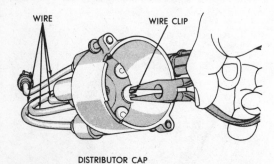

WIRE

WIRE CLIP

DISTRIBUTOR CAP

Removing the spark plug wires from the cap on 1980 and later models.

through the electrode gap with a slight drag. If you're in doubt, try one size smaller and one larger. The smaller gauge should go through easily while the larger one shouldn't go through at all. If the gap is incorrect, use the electrode bending tool on the end of the gauge to adjust the gap. When adjusting the gap, always bend the side electrode. The center electrode is non-adjustable.

2. Squirt a drop of penetrating oil on the threads of the new plug and install it. Don't oil the threads too heavily. Turn the plug in clockwise by hand until it is snug.

3. When the plug is finger tight, tighten it with a wrench. If you don't have a torque wrench, tighten the plug as shown.

4. Install the plug boot firmly over the plug. Proceed to the next plug.

CHECKING AND REPLACING SPARK PLUG CABLES

NOTE: *On 1980 and later models, to maintain proper sealing between the towers and the nipples, the cable and nipple assemblies should not be removed from the distributor cap or coil towers unless the nipple are damaged or the cables require replacement. Plug wires on 1980 and later models. DO NOT pull from the distributor cap, they must be released from inside the cap.*

Visually inspect the spark plug cables for burns, cuts, or breaks in the insulation. Check the spark plug boots and the nipples on the distributor cap and coil. Replace any damaged wiring. If no physical damage is obvious, the wires can be checked with an ohmmeter for excessive resistance. (See the tune-up and troubleshooting section).

When installing a new set of spark plug cables, replace the cables one at a time so there will be no mixup. Start by replacing the longest cable first. Install the boot firmly over the spark plug. Route the wire exactly the same as the original. Insert the nipple firmly into the tower on the distributor cap. Repeat the process for each cable.

FIRING ORDERS

To avoid confusion, replace spark plug wires or spark plugs one at a time.

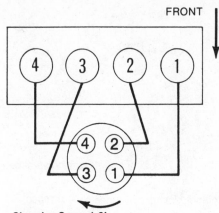

FRONT

Chrysler Corp: 1.6L
Engine Firing Order: 1-3-4-2
Distributor Rotation: Clockwise

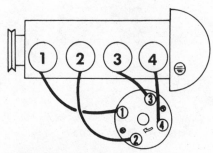

Chrysler Corp. 1.7L
Engine Firing Order: 1-3-4-2
Distributor Rotation: Clockwise

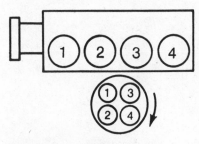

Chrysler Corp. 2.2L
Engine Firing Order: 1-3-4-2
Distributor Rotation: Clockwise

CHRYSLER CORPORATION ELECTRONIC IGNITION

Omni and Horizon are equipped with the "Electronic Fuel Control System". This consists of a Spark Control Computer, various engine sensors, and a specially calibrated carburetor with an electronically controlled fuel metering system. On fuel injected engines, the computer controls the total amount of fuel injected by slightly modifying the pulses that operate the injectors. The function of this system is to provide a way for the engine to burn a correct air-fuel mixture.

The Spark Control Computer is the heart of the entire system. It has the capability of igniting the fuel mixture according to different models of engine operation by delivering an infinite number of different variable advance curves. The computer consists of one electronic printed circuit board, which simultaneously received signals from all the sensors and within milliseconds, analyzes them to determine how the engine is operating and then advances or retards the timing.

For 1988, this system has been renamed the SMEC ("Single Module Engine Controller") system. It functions similarly to the Electronic Fuel Control System, using coolant temperature, engine rpm, and available manifold vacuum for inputs. On turbo engines, it synchronizes the injection pulses with the ignition pulses by reading signals from the Hall Effect pickup in the distributor. Both systems use the oxygen sensor to fine-tune the mixture to actual operating conditions.

SYSTEM TESTS

The electronic ignition system is controlled by the "Chrysler Corporation Lean Burn System," which is actually an emission control system.

The ignition coil can be tested on a conventional coil tester. The ballast resistor, mounted on the firewall, must be included in all tests. Refer to the beginning of Chapter 3 for coil testing.

Equipment

Some of the procedures in this section refer to an adjustable timing light. This is also known as a spark advance tester, i.e., a device that will measure how much spark advance is present going from one point, a base figure, to another. Since precise timing is very important to the Lean Burn System, do not attempt to perform any of the tests calling for an adjustable timing light without one.

Troubleshooting Carbureted Engines

1. Remove the coil wire from the distributor cap and hold it cautiously about ¼" away from an engine ground, then have someone crank the engine while you check for spark.

2. If you have a good spark, slowly move the coil wire away from the engine and check for arcing at the coil while cranking.

3. If you have good spark and it is not arcing at the coil, check the rest of the parts of the ignition system.

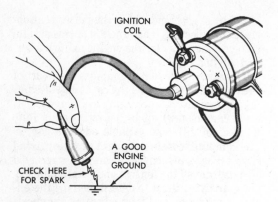

Testing the ignition coil

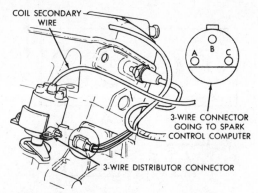

Distributor pick-up coil connector—1978–80

Engine Not Running
Will Not Start

1978-80 MODELS

1. Before performing this test, be sure the "Troubleshooting" test has been performed. Measure the battery specific gravity: it must be at least 1.220, temperature corrected. Measure the battery voltage and make a note of it.

2. Disconnect the thin wire from the negative coil terminal.

3. Remove the coil high tension lead at the distributor cap.

4. Turn the ignition On. While holding the coil high tension lead ¼" from a ground, connect a jumper wire from the negative coil terminal to a ground. A spark should be obtained from the high tension lead.

5. If there is no spark, use a voltmeter to test for at least 9 volts at the positive coil terminal (ignition On). If so, the coil must be replaced. If less than 9 volts is obtained, check the ballast resistor, wiring, and connections. If the car still won't start, proceed to Step 6.

6. If there was a spark in Step 4, turn the ignition Off, reconnect the wire to the negative coil terminal, and disconnect the distributor pick-up coil connector.

7. Turn the ignition On, and measure voltage between pin **B** of the pick-up coil connector on the spark control computer side, and a good engine ground. Voltage should be the same as the battery voltage measured in Step 1. If so, go to Step 11. If not, go to the next Step.

NOTE: *Malfunction of the distributor pick-up coil can be the result of the rotor not properly grounded to the distributor shaft. Remove the rotor and check the metal grounding tab to be sure it is not covered with plastic. If so, replace the rotor with a new one. Clean the top of the distributor shaft and install the rotor, pushing it onto the shaft so the metal tab contacts the shaft. Check for continuity between the interrupter vane and distributor*

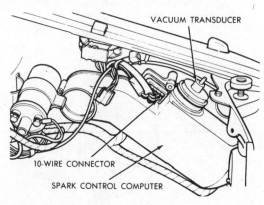

Spark control computer location

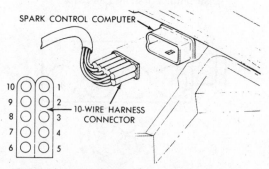

10-terminal wire harness

housing. Do not try to start the engine with no continuity.

8. Turn the ignition Off and disconnect the terminal connector at the spark control computer.

NOTE: *Do not remove grease from the 10-wire harness connector.*

9. Check for continuity between pin **B** of the pick-up coil connector on the computer side, and terminal **3** of the computer connector. If there is no continuity, the wire must be replaced. If continuity exists, go to the next step.

10. With the ignition On, connect a voltmeter

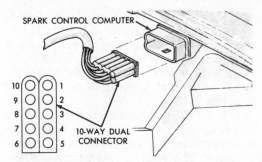

Removing the 10-way connector from the computer

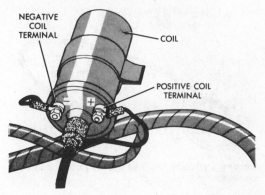

Coil terminal location

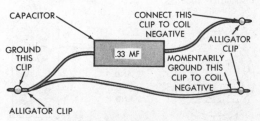

Construct this special jumper wire to perform the no-start test on 1981 and later models

between terminals **2** and **10** of the computer connector. Voltage should be the same as measured in Step 1. If so, the computer is defective and must be replaced.

11. Reconnect the 10 wire computer connector. Turn the ignition On. Hold the coil high tension lead (disconnected at the distributor cap) about ¼" from a ground. Connect a jumper wire between pins **A** and **C** of the distributor pick-up coil connector. If a spark is obtained, the distributor pick-up is defective and must be replaced. If not, go to the next step.

12. Turn the ignition Off. Disconnect the 10 wire computer connector.

13. Check for continuity between pin **C** of the distributor connector and terminal **9** of the computer connector. Also check for continuity between pin **A** of the distributor connector and terminal **5** of the computer connector. If continuity exists, the computer is defective and must be replaced. If not, the wires are damaged. Repair them and recheck, starting at Step 11.

1981 AND LATER

1. Perform the "Troubleshooting" test before proceeding with the following. Make sure the battery is fully charged, then measure and record the battery voltage.

2. Remove the coil secondary wire from the distributor cap.

3. With the key on, use the special jumper wire and momentarily connect the negative terminal of the ignition coil to ground while holding the coil secondary wire (using insulated pliers and heavy gloves) about ¼" from a good ground. A spark should fire.

4. If spark was obtained, go to Step 9.

5. If no spark was obtained, turn off the ignition and disconnect the 10-wire harness going into the Spark Control Computer. Do not remove the grease from the connector.

6. With the ignition key on, use the special jumper wire and momentarily connect the negative terminal of the ignition coil to ground while holding the coil wire ¼" from a good engine ground. A spark should fire.

7. If a spark is present, the computer output is shorted: replace the computer.

8. If no spark is obtained, measure the voltage at the coil positive terminal. It should be within 1 volt of battery voltage. If voltage is present but no spark is available when shorting negative terminal, replace the coil. If no voltage is present, replace the coil or check the primary wiring.

9. If voltage was obtained but the engine will not start, hold the carburetor switch open with a thin cardboard insulator and measure the voltage at the switch. It should be at least 5 volts. If voltage is present, go to Step 16.

10. If no voltage is present, turn the ignition switch off and disconnect the 10 terminal wire harness going into the computer.

11. Turn the ignition switch on and measure the voltage at terminal **2** of the harness. It should be within 1 volt of battery voltage.

12. If no battery voltage is present, check for continuity between the battery and terminal **2** of the harness. If no continuity, repair fault and repeat Step 11.

13. If voltage is present turn ignition switch off and check for continuity between the carburetor switch and terminal **7** on connector. If no continuity is present, check for open wire between terminal **7** and the carburetor switch.

14. If continuity is present, check continuity between terminal **10** and ground. If continuity is present here, replace the computer. Repeat Step 9.

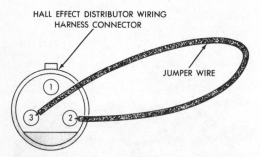

HALL EFFECT DISTRIBUTOR WIRING
HARNESS CONNECTOR

JUMPER WIRE

1

3   2

Jumping cavities 2 and 3 of the distributor harness connector

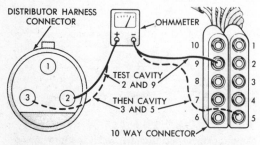

DISTRIBUTOR HARNESS
CONNECTOR

OHMMETER

1

3   2

TEST CAVITY
2 AND 9

THEN CAVITY
3 AND 5

10 WAY CONNECTOR

10   1
9   2
8   3
7   4
6   5

Testing cavities 2 and 9 then cavities 3 and 5 for continuity

15. If no continuity is present, check for an open wire. If wiring is OK but the engine still won't start, go to next step.

16. Plug the 10 terminal dual connector back into the computer and turn the ignition switch on, hold the secondary coil wire near a good ground and disconnect the distributor harness connector. Using a regular jumper wire (not the special one mentioned earlier), jump terminal **2** to terminal **3** of the connector: a spark should fire at the coil wire. Make and break the connection at terminal **2** or **3** several times and check for good spark at the coil wire.

17. If spark is present at the coil wire but the engine won't start, replace the Hall Effect pickup and check the rotor for cracks or burning. Replace as necessary.

NOTE: *When replacing a pick-up, always make sure rotor blades are grounded using an ohmmeter.*

18. If no spark is present at the coil wire, measure the voltage at terminal 1 of the distributor harness connector: it should be within 1 volt of battery voltage.

19. If correct, disconnect the 10 terminal dual connector from the computer and check for continuity between terminal **2** of distributor harness and terminal **9** of the dual connector. Repeat test on terminal **3** of distributor harness and terminal **5** of dual connector. If no continuity, repair the harness. If continuity is present, replace the computer and repeat Step 16.

20. If no battery voltage is present in Step 18, turn off the ignition switch, disconnect the 10 terminal dual connector from the computer and check for continuity between terminal **1** of distributor harness and terminal **3** of dual connector. If no continuity, repair wire and repeat Step 16.

21. If continuity is present, turn the ignition switch on and check for battery voltage between terminal **2** and terminal **10** of the dual connector. If voltage is present, replace the computer and repeat Step 16. If no battery voltage is present, the computer is not grounded. Check and repair the ground wire and repeat Step 16.

Poor Engine Performance

Before proceeding with these tests, be sure the ignition timing and idle speed are as specified.

CARBURETOR SWITCH TEST

1. With the key OFF, disconnect the 10-wire harness from the Spark Control Computer.

2. With the throttle completely closed, check for continuity between pin **7** of the harness connector and a good ground. If there is no continuity, check the carburetor switch and wire. Recheck the timing.

3. With the throttle open, check for continuity between pin **7** of the harness connector and a good ground. There should be no continuity.

COOLANT SWITCH TEST

1. With the key OFF, disconnect the wire from the coolant switch.

2. Connect one lead of an ohmmeter to a good ground, on the engine.

3. Connect the other lead to the terminal of the coolant switch. On a cold engine, (below 150°F [66°C]) continuity should be present at the coolant switch. If not, replace the switch.

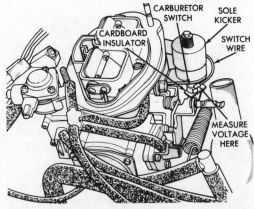

CARBURETOR
SWITCH

SOLE
KICKER

CARDBOARD
INSULATOR

SWITCH
WIRE

MEASURE
VOLTAGE
HERE

Carburetor switch insulator positioning—1.7L shown, 1.6L and 2.2L similar

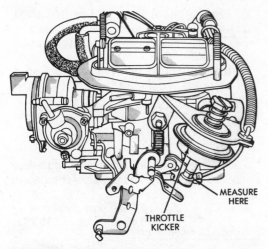

Carburetor switch continuity test—2.2L engine shown, 1.6L and 1.7L similar

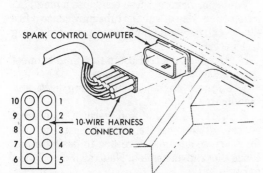

Carburetor switch continuity check

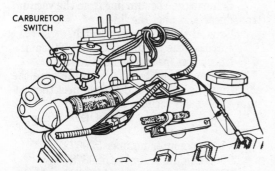

Carburetor switch location—1.6L engine

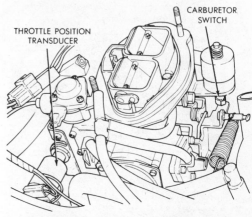

Carburetor switch location—1.7L engine

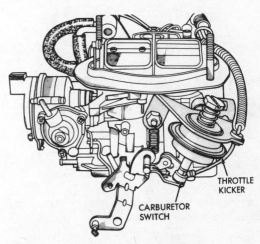

Carburetor switch location—2.2L engine

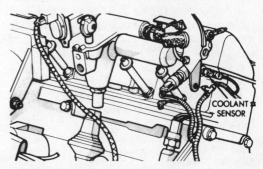

Coolant sensor location—1.6L engine

On a warm engine (above 150°F [66°C]) or on an engine at operating temperature (thermostat open), the ohmmeter should show no continuity. If it does, replace the coolant switch.

START-UP ADVANCE TEST
1978-79 MODELS

1. Connect an adjustable timing light to the engine so that the total timing advance can be checked.

2. Connect a jumper wire from the carburetor switch to a ground.

3. Start the engine and immediately adjust the timing light so that the basic timing light is seen on the timing plate of the engine. The meter (on the timing light) should show an 8° advance. Continue to observe the mark for 90 seconds, adjusting the light as necessary. The basic timing signal over a period of about one minute. If not, replace the Spark Control Computer and recheck. If it is ok, go on to the next test. Do not

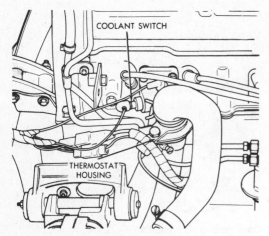

Coolant sensor location—1.7L engine

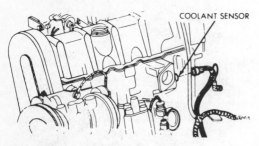

Coolant sensor location—2.2L engine

remove the timing light or jumper wire. They will be used for the next test.

SPEED ADVANCE TEST
1978-80 MODELS

1. Start and run the engine for 2 minutes.
2. Adjust the timing light so that the basic timing is shown at the timing indicator. Additional advance shown on the timing light meter should be:
- 0-3° @ 1100 rpm
- 8-12° a 2000 rpm

If not, replace the spark control computer and repeat the test. If as specified, go to the next test.

SPARK ADVANCE TEST
1981 AND LATER

1. Check basic ignition timing and adjust if necessary.
2. Run the engine to obtain normal operating temperature. Check the operation of the coolant temperature sensor, refer to "coolant switch test" in this section.
3. Remove and plug the vacuum hose at the vacuum transducer.
4. Connect an auxiliary vacuum pump to the vacuum transducer and apply 16 in.Hg of vacuum.

5. Increase the engine speed to 2000 RPM, wait one minute and check specifications.
NOTE: *The advance specifications are in addition to the basic advance.*
6. If the computer fails to obtain the specified settings, replace the Spark Control Computer.

VACUUM ADVANCE TEST
1979-80 MODELS

The program for each computer is different. Specifications for individual computer numbers are:
- 18-22° @ 2000 rpm (all part numbers)
- 23-27° @ 3000 rpm (nos. 5206721, 5206784 and 5206793)
- 28-32° @ 3000 rpm (nos. 5206785 and 5206790)

While performing these tests, use a metal exhaust tube. Use of rubber tube may cause a fire due to extremely high temperatures and a long test period.

If the spark control computer fails to meet these tests, it should be replaced.

1. Connect an adjustable timing light and tachometer.
2. Start the engine and warm it to normal operating temperature. Wait at least 1 minute for start up advance to return to basic timing. Place the transmission in Neutral and apply the parking brake.
3. Check, and, if necessary, adjust the basic timing.
4. Remove the vacuum line from the vacuum transducer and plug the line.
5. Ground the carburetor switch.
6. Increase the engine speed to 1100 rpm.
7. Check the speed advance timing.
8. Increase speed to 2000 rpm. Remove the carburetor switch ground and connect the vacuum line to the vacuum transducer.
9. Check the Zero Time Offset. Timing should be:
- 6-10°: computer number 5206721
- 2-6°: computer number 5206784
- 3-7°: computer number 5206785
- 0-3°: computer number 5206790, 5206793

10. Allow the accumulator in the computer to "clock-up" for 8 minutes.
11. With the accumulator "clocked-up" and the speed at 1100 rpm, check the vacuum advance. It should be 0-3° at 1100 rpm.
12. Disconnect and plug the vacuum line from the transducer and increase the engine speed to 3000 rpm. Note the speed advance timing.
13. Reconnect the vacuum line to the transducer and recheck the vacuum advance.
14. Return the engine to curb idle. Connect the wire to the carburetor switch if applicable.

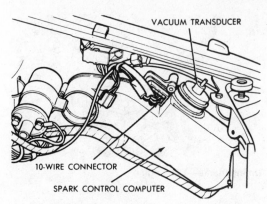

Spark control computer removal and installation

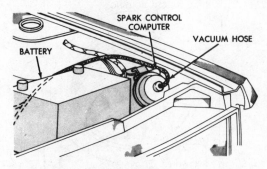

Spark control computer vacuum hose connection

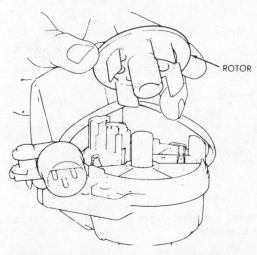

Removing or installing the Hall-effect distributor rotor

REMOVAL AND OVERHAUL

None of the components of the Lean Burn System (except the carburetor) may be taken apart and repaired. When a part is known to be bad, it should be replaced.

The Spark Control Computer is held on by mounting screws. First remove the battery, then disconnect the 10 terminal connectors and

the air duct from the computer. Next remove the vacuum line from the transducer. Remove the three screws securing the computer to the left front fender, and remove the computer. To remove the vacuum transducer, replace the spark control computer.

NOTE: *When disconnecting the Spark Control Computer, check the following:*

1. Discard any foam gasket found inside the connector cavity.

2. Be sure there is at least ¼" silicone grease in the cavity connector.

3. Computers built after 1/78 have a piece of Butyl tape. If neither is present, clean the connector and cover the slotted latch with ¾" wide electrical tape.

If it becomes necessary to replace the carburetor switch, replace the bracket and solenoid assembly.

HALL EFFECT PICKUP REPLACEMENT

1. Loosen the distributor cap retaining screws and remove the cap.

2. Pull straight up on the rotor and remove it from the shaft.

3. Disconnect the pickup assembly lead.

4. Remove the pickup lead hold down screw.

5. Remove the pickup assembly lock springs and lift off the pickup.

6. Install the new pickup assembly onto the distributor housing and fasten it into place with the lock springs.

7. Fasten the pickup lead to the housing with the hold down screw.

8. Reconnect the lead to the harness.

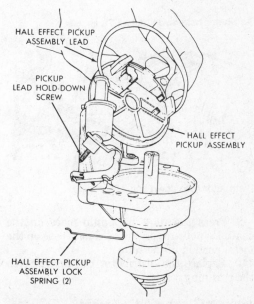

Removing or installing the Hall-effect pick-up assembly

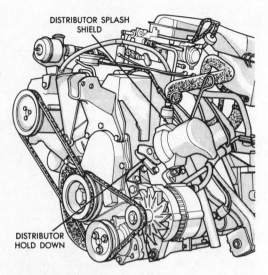

Loosen the distributor hold-down bolt to adjust the timing—1.6L engine shown

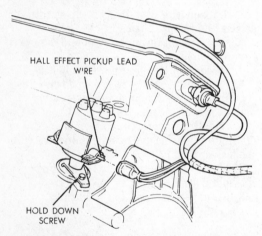

Distributor hold-down bolt—1.7L engine

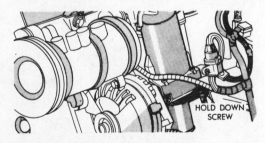

Distributor hold-down bolt 2.2L engine

9. Press the rotor back into place on the shaft. Do not wipe off the silicone grease on the metal portion of the rotor.

10. Replace the distributor cap and tighten the retaining screws.

Ignition Timing Adjustment

The engine is timed on No. 1 cylinder, which is the passenger's side of the car.

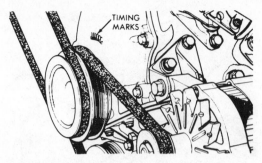

Timing marks—1.6L engine

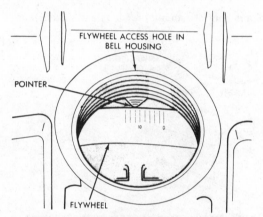

Timing marks—A-412 transaxle

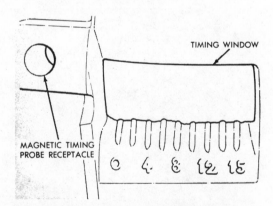

Timing marks—all models except A-412 transaxle and 1.6L engine

1. Connect a timing light according to the manufacturer's instructions.

2. Run the engine to normal operating temperature.

3. Make sure the idle speed is correct.

4. Loosen the distributor holddown screw just enough so that the distributor can be rotated.

5. Ground the carburetor switch on models so equipped.

6. Disconnect and plug the vacuum line at the Spark Control Computer (if so equipped).

7. Remove the timing hole access cover and aim the timing light at the hole in the clutch housing. Carefully rotate the distributor until the mark is aligned with the pointer on the flywheel housing.

8. Tighten the distributor and recheck the timing.

9. Check, and if necessary adjust, the idle speed.

VALVE ADJUSTMENT

Valve adjustment is not required as a matter of routine maintenance on the 1.6L and 1.7L engines. It is, however, necessary to check the valve clearance periodically. The 1.6L engine is an overhead valve design with adjustable rocker arms. The 1.7L engine clearance is adjusted by substituting discs located at the top of the cam followers. The discs are available in 0.05mm increments from 3.00 to 4.25mm. One disc is located in each cam follower. A special tool is required for the disc removal and installation. The 2.2L engine uses hydraulic valve lifters and does not require valve adjustment.

CHECKING/ADJUSTING VALVE CLEARANCE

1.6L Engine

The valve clearance should be checked with the engine cold and the piston at TDC (top dead center) on the compression stroke. The valves should be checked in the firing order 1-3-4-2.

1. Remove the valve cover.

2. Turn the crankshaft and watch the movement of the exhaust valves. When one is closing (moving upward) continue turning slowly until the inlet valve on the same cylinder just begins to open. This is called the "valve rocking" position. The piston in the opposite cylinder is then at TDC on the compression stroke, and its valve clearance can be checked and adjusted.

3. After checking both valve clearances, rotate the crankshaft one half turn, the next cyl-

VALVES 'ROCKING' ON CYLINDER NUMBER	ADJUST VALVES ON CYLINDER NUMBER
4	1
2	3
1	4
3	2

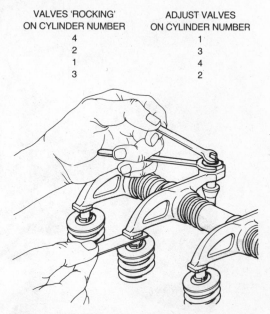

Making valve adjustment—1.6L engine

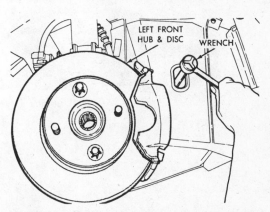

Rotate the 1.7L engine by inserting a wrench through the access hole

inder in the firing order should have its valves "rocking" and the pared cylinder can be adjusted.

4. To make an adjustment, loosen the locknut and turn the adjusting screw until the correct size feeler gauge is a sliding fit between the valve stem and the rocker arm. The cold clearance should be 0.25mm intake and 0.35mm exhaust.

5. When the correct clearance has been obtained, tighten the locknut securely while holding the adjusting screw.

6. Reinstall the valve cover.

1.7L Engine

The valve should be checked with the engine warm and be checked in the firing order 1-3-4-2.

1. Run the engine to normal operating temperature.

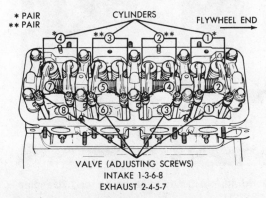

Valve adjustment locations—1.6L engine

1.7L engine valve cover removal

The valves of cylinders 1, 3, 4, can be adjusted when No. 1 is positioned as shown on the 1.7L engine

Checking valve clearance with a feeler gauge on the 1.7L engine

On the 1.7L engine, depress the cam followers with the special tool shown

On the 1.7L engine; remove the valve adjusting disc with special tools shown.

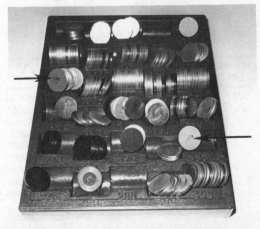

Typical valve adjustment disc assortment for the 1.7L engine

2. Remove the valve cover.

3. Use a socket wrench on the crankshaft pulley or bump the engine around until the camshaft lobes of No. 1 cylinder are positioned as shown. Due to the design of the camshaft lobes, it is not necessary that the lobes be pointing directly away (perpendicular) to the adjusting disc.

WARNING: *Do not turn the engine using the camshaft pulley, and only turn the engine in the direction of normal rotation.*

4. Using a feeler gauge, check the valve clearance between the camshaft lobe and the valve adjusting disc.

Cold clearance should be 0.15-0.25mm intake and 0.35-0.45mm exhaust; warm clearance is 0.20-0.30mm intake and 0.40-0.50mm exhaust.

5. If the measure clearance is not as specified, the valve adjusting disc can be removed and replaced with another of the proper size to give the correct valve clearance.

6. To remove the disc:

a. Depress the cam follower with Tool L-4417. This tool is necessary to remove the disc without damaging the camshaft or cylinder head.

b. Remove the valve adjusting disc with special removal pliers as shown in the illustration.

c. Calculate the thickness of a new disc and install one of the proper size. Be sure the number indicating the thickness of the disc (mm) faces down when installed.

d. Recheck the valve clearance.

7. Recheck or adjust all other valves in the same manner.

NOTE: *When the camshaft is in position to check the valves of No. 1 cylinder, cylinders No. 3 and 4 can also be checked or adjusted. It is only necessary to turn the engine one*

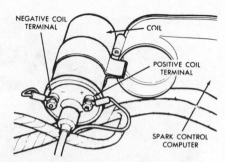

Tachometer connections

time to position the camshaft to check No. 2 cylinder.

8. Reinstall the camshaft cover.

2.2L Engine

This engine has hydraulic valve lifter and no adjustment is required.

IDLE SPEED AND MIXTURE

TACHOMETER HOOKUP

1. Connect the red lead of the test tachometer to the negative primary terminal of the coil and the black lead to a good ground.

2. Turn the selector switch to the appropriate cylinder position and read the idle on the 1000 rpm scale, if so equipped.

3. With the engine at normal operating temperature momentarily open the throttle to check for binding in the linkage. Make sure that the idle screw is against its stop.

4. Adjust the idle speed to specifications. If the engine is equipped with an idle solenoid, the solenoid must be energized and the adjusting screw must be resting on the solenoid plunger.

IDLE SPEED AND MIXTURE ADJUSTMENT

Carbureted Engines

Chrysler recommends the use of a propane enrichment procedure to adjust the mixture. The equipment needed for this procedure is not readily available to the general public. An alternate method recommended by Chrysler is with the use of an exhaust gas analyzer. If this equipment is not available, and a mixture adjustment must be performed, follow this procedure:

1. Run the engine to normal operating temperature.

2. Place the transmission in Neutral (MT) or Drive (AT), turn off the lights and air conditioning and make certain that the electric cooling fan is operating.

3. Disconnect the EGR vacuum line, disconnect the distributor electrical advance connec-

Valve Adjusting Discs, 1.7

Thickness (mm)	Part Number	Thickness (mm)	Part Number
3.00	5240946	3.65	5240580
3.05	5240945	3.70	5240581
3.10	5240944	3.75	5240582
3.15	5240943	3.80	5240583
3.20	5240942	3.85	5240584
3.25	5240941	3.90	5240585
3.30	5240573	3.95	5240586
3.35	5240574	4.00	5240587
3.40	5240575	4.05	5240588
3.45	5240576	4.10	5240589
3.50	5240577	4.15	5240590
3.55	5240578	4.20	5240591
3.60	5240579	4.25	5240592

tor, and ground the carburetor idle stop switch (if equipped) with a jumper wire.

4. Connect tachometer according to the manufacturer's specifications. (See previous procedure).

5. Adjust the idle screw to achieve the curb idle figure listed on the underhood sticker.

6. Back out the mixture screw to achieve the fastest possible idle.

7. Adjust the idle screw to the specified curb idle speed.

Fuel Injected Engines

The idle speed is controlled by the automatic idle speed (AIS) motor which is controlled by the logic module. The logic module gathers data from the various sensors and switches in the system and adjusts the engine idle to a predetermined speed. Idle specifications can be found on the vehicle emission control information (VECI) label located in the engine compartment.

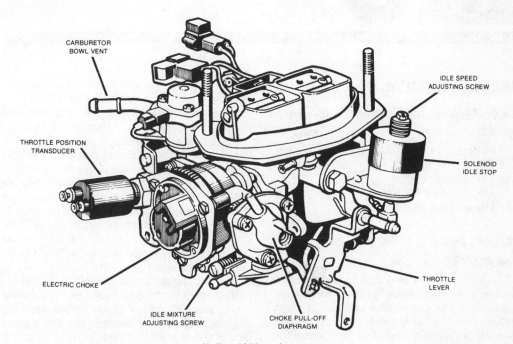

Holley 5220 carburetor

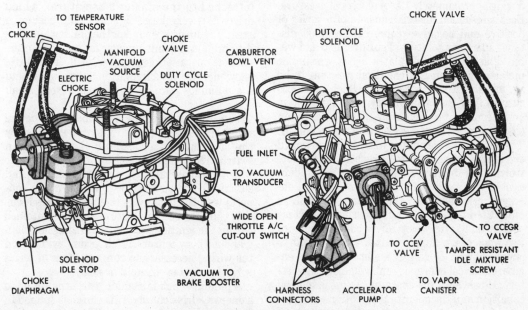

Holley 6520 carburetor, with air conditioning

Engine and Engine Overhaul

3

ENGINE ELECTRICAL

Understanding the Engine Electrical System

The engine electrical system can be broken down into three separate and distinct systems:
1. The starting system.
2. The charging system.
3. The ignition system.

BATTERY AND STARTING SYSTEM

Basic Operating Principles

The battery is the first link in the chain of mechanisms which work together to provide cranking of the automobile engine. In most modern cars, the battery is a lead/acid electrochemical device consisting of six 2v subsections connected in series so the unit is capable of producing approximately 12v of electrical pressure. Each subsection, or cell, consists of a series of positive and negative plates held a short distance apart in a solution of sulfuric acid and water. The two types of plates are of dissimilar metals. This causes a chemical reaction to be set up, and it is this reaction which produces current flow from the battery when its positive and negative terminals are connected to an electrical appliance such as a lamp or motor. The continued transfer of electrons would eventually convert the sulfuric acid in the electrolyte to water, and make the two plates identical in chemical composition. As electrical energy is removed from the battery, its voltage output tends to drop. Thus, measuring battery voltage and battery electrolyte composition are two ways of checking the ability of the unit to supply power. During the starting of the engine, electrical energy is removed from the battery. However, if the charging circuit is in good condition and the operating conditions are normal, the power removed from the battery will be replaced by the generator (or alternator) which will force electrons back through the battery, reversing the normal flow, and restoring the battery to its original chemical state.

The battery and starting motor are linked by very heavy electrical cables designed to minimize resistance to the flow of current. Generally, the major power supply cable that leaves the battery goes directly to the starter, while other electrical system needs are supplied by a smaller cable. During starter operation, power flows from the battery to the starter and is grounded through the car's frame and the battery's negative ground strap.

The starting motor is a specially designed, direct current electric motor capable of producing a very great amount of power for its size. One thing that allows the motor to produce a great deal of power is its tremendous rotating speed. It drives the engine through a tiny pinion gear (attached to the starter's armature), which drives the very large flywheel ring gear at a greatly reduced speed. Another factor allowing it to produce so much power is that only intermittent operation is required of it. This, little allowance for air circulation is required, and the windings can be built into a very small space.

The starter solenoid is a magnetic device which employs the small current supplied by the starting switch circuit of the ignition switch. This magnetic action moves a plunger which mechanically engages the starter and electrically closes the heavy switch which connects it to the battery. The starting switch circuit consists of the starting switch contained within the ignition switch, a transmission neutral safety switch or clutch pedal switch, and the wiring necessary to connect these in series with the starter solenoid or relay.

A pinion, which is a small gear, is mounted to a one-way drive clutch. This clutch is splined to the starter armature shaft. When the ignition switch is moved to the **start** position, the solenoid plunger slides the pinion toward the flywheel ring gear via a collar and spring. If the teeth on the pinion and flywheel match properly, the pinion will engage the flywheel immediately. If the gear teeth butt one another, the spring will be compressed and will force the gears to mesh as soon as the starter turns far enough to allow them to do so. As the solenoid plunger reaches the end of its travel, it closes the contacts that connect the battery and starter and then the engine is cranked.

As soon as the engine starts, the flywheel ring gear begins turning fast enough to drive the pinion at an extremely high rate of speed. At this point, the one-way clutch begins allowing the pinion to spin faster than the starter shaft so that the starter will not operate at excessive speed. When the ignition switch is released from the starter position, the solenoid is de-energized, and a spring contained within the solenoid assembly pulls the gear out of mesh and interrupts the current flow to the starter.

Some starter employ a separate relay, mounted away from the starter, to switch the motor and solenoid current on and off. The relay thus replaces the solenoid electrical switch, buy does not eliminate the need for a solenoid mounted on the starter used to mechanically engage the starter drive gears. The relay is used to reduce the amount of current the starting switch must carry.

THE CHARGING SYSTEM

Basic Operating Principles

The automobile charging system provides electrical power for operation of the vehicle's ignition and starting systems and all the electrical accessories. The battery services as an electrical surge or storage tank, storing (in chemical form) the energy originally produced by the engine driven generator. The system also provides a means of regulating generator output to protect the battery from being overcharged and to avoid excessive voltage to the accessories.

The storage battery is a chemical device incorporating parallel lead plates in a tank containing a sulfuric acid/water solution. Adjacent plates are slightly dissimilar, and the chemical reaction of the two dissimilar plates produces electrical energy when the battery is connected to a load such as the starter motor. The chemical reaction is reversible, so that when the generator is producing a voltage (electrical pressure) greater than that produced by the battery, electricity is forced into the battery, and the battery is returned to its fully charged state.

The vehicle's generator is driven mechanically, through V-belts, by the engine crankshaft. It consists of two coils of fine wire, one stationary (the stator), and one movable (the rotor). The rotor may also be known as the armature, and consists of fine wire wrapped around an iron core which is mounted on a shaft. The electricity which flows through the two coils of wire (provided initially by the battery in some cases) creates an intense magnetic field around both rotor and stator, and the interaction between the two fields creates voltage, allowing the generator to power the accessories and charge the battery.

There are two types of generators: the earlier is the direct current (DC) type. The current produced by the DC generator is generated in the armature and carried off the spinning armature by stationary brushes contacting the commutator. The commutator is a series of smooth metal contact plates on the end of the armature. The commutator is a series of smooth metal contact plates on the end of the armature. The commutator plates, which are separated from one another by a very short gap, are connected to the armature circuits so that current will flow in one directions only in the wires carrying the generator output. The generator stator consists of two stationary coils of wire which draw some of the output current of the generator to form a powerful magnetic field and create the interaction of fields which generates the voltage. The generator field is wired in series with the regulator.

Newer automobiles use alternating current generators or alternators, because they are more efficient, can be rotated at higher speeds, and have fewer brush problems. In an alternator, the field rotates while all the current produced passes only through the stator winding. The brushes bear against continuous slip rings rather than a commutator. This causes the current produced to periodically reverse the direction of its flow. Diodes (electrical one-way switches) block the flow of current from traveling in the wrong direction. A series of diodes is wired together to permit the alternating flow of the stator to be converted to a pulsating, but unidirectional flow at the alternator output. The alternator's field is wired in series with the voltage regulator.

The regulator consists of several circuits. Each circuit has a core, or magnetic coil of wire, which operates a switch. Each switch is connected to ground through one or more resistors. The coil of wire responds directly to system voltage. When the voltage reaches the required level, the magnetic field created by the winding of wire closes the switch and inserts a resistance into the generator field circuit, thus reducing the output. The contacts of the switch cycle open and close many times each second to precisely control voltage.

While alternators are self-limiting as far as maximum current is concerned, DC generators employ a current regulating circuit which responds directly to the total amount of current flowing through the generator circuit rather than to the output voltage. The current regulator is similar to the voltage regulator except that all system current must flow through the energizing coil on its way to the various accessories.

Ignition Coil

TESTING

NOTE: *To perform a reliable test of the coil, you must make up several jumper wires. You'll need two simple wires several feet long with alligator clips on the ends. A third wire must incorporate a capacitor of 0.33 MicroFarad capacitance. The materials and components needed to make up such jumpers should be available at a reasonable price in a local electronics store.*

1. Turn the ignition key off. Disconnect the negative battery cable. Then, carefully remove the retaining nuts and disconnect the two coil primary leads. Wrap the positive (+) lead in electrician's tape or otherwise ensure that it cannot accidentally ground during the test.

2. Run a jumper wire from the battery positive (+) terminal directly to the coil positive (÷) terminal. Run the jumper wire incorporating the capacitor from the coil negative terminal to a good ground. Reconnect the battery negative cable and turn on the ignition switch. Fasten one end of the remaining standard jumper wire in a position where the clip cannot ground. Then connect the other end of it to the coil negative terminal. Turn on the ignition key.

3. Unclip the coil high tension lead from inside the distributor cap and pull it out. Hold the distributor end of the lead ¼" from a good ground. Ground the standard jumper wire coming from the coil negative terminal.

4. Break the ground in the standard lead coming from the coil negative as you watch for spark. The coil should produce a hot, blue-white spark. Repeat the test looking at the coil tower. If sparks are visible there, replace the ignition wires if the rubber boots are deteriorated, or the coil, if the tower is burned and tracked.

5. If the coil tower and wire boots are okay, and this test fails to produce a spark, replace the coil.

On 1987-89 cars, you can confirm the problem with an ohmmeter. Turn off the ignition switch, and disconnect the negative battery cable. With the coil primary wires still disconnected, test the resistance between positive and negative primary terminals. It must be 1.35-1.55Ω. For secondary resistance, first determine whether the coil is a Chrysler Prestolite, Chrysler Essex, or Diamond brand coil by wiping off the coil and looking for appropriate lettering. Then, pull the high tension lead out of the coil tower and run the ohmmeter lead between the coil negative primary terminal and the brass connector down inside the tower. Resistance ranges must be as follows:

- Chrysler Prestolite – 9,400-11,700Ω
- Chrysler Essex – 9,000-12,200Ω
- Diamond – 15,000-19,000Ω

WARNING: *If the coil tests okay, you must be sure to turn off the ignition switch and have the battery negative cable disconnected before reconnecting the primary leads.*

Ignition Computer/Power Module (1981-87)

REMOVAL AND INSTALLATION

WARNING: *The grease located in the 10 or 14 way connector cavity in the computer is necessary to prevent moisture from corroding the terminals. Not only should this grease be left in place, but if the layer is less than ⅛" thick, spread Mopar Multi-purpose grease Part No. 2932524 or an equivalent available in the aftermarket in an even layer over the end of each connector plug before reconnecting them.*

1. Disconnect the negative battery cable. Then, disconnect the 10- and 14-way dual connectors.

2. Disconnect the outside air duct at the computer housing. Disconnect the vacuum line at the vacuum transducer on top of the housing.

3. Remove the 3 mounting screws that fas-

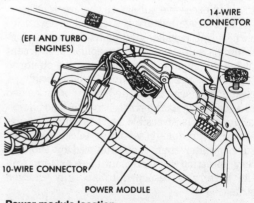

Power module location

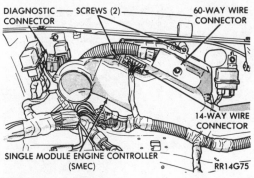

SMEC mounting location

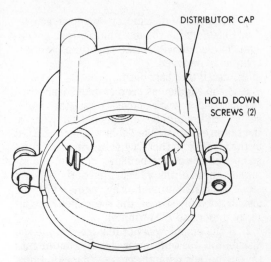

1980 and later distributor cap showing plug wire retaining clips. These clips double as rotor contacts.

ten the computer to the inside of the left front fender and remove it.

4. Installation is the reverse of removal.

SMEC Controller
1988-89

1. Disconnect both battery cables (negative first).

2. Disconnect the air cleaner duct at the SMEC.

3. Remove the two mounting screws by which the module hangs onto the fender well.

4. Move the unit out slightly for access and then disconnect both the 14- and 60-way wiring connectors. Remove the SMEC from the engine compartment.

5. Install the module in reverse order, making sure to connect the electrical connectors before attempting to mount it.

Distributor

WARNING: *1980 and later models have a different distributor cap. Never pull the wire from the cap. The wires are retained in the cap by means of internal clips in the wire towers. To remove a wire, first remove the distributor cap, then squeeze the clips ends together while gently removing the wire from the cap. Failure to follow this procedure will damage the core of the wire.*

Chrysler recommends that the wires not be removed from the cap for any reason other than replacement of a damaged wire or a wire that shows too much resistance.

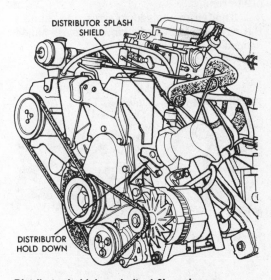

Distributor hold down bolt—1.6L engine

REMOVAL AND INSTALLATION

1. Disconnect the distributor pickup lead wire at the harness connector and remove the splash shield (if so equipped).

2. Remove the distributor cap.

3. Rotate the engine crankshaft until the rotor is pointing toward the cylinder block. Make a mark on the block at this point for installation reference.

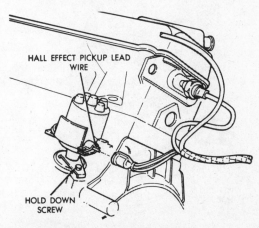

Distributor hold-down bolt—1.7L engine

4. Remove the distributor holddown screw.

5. Carefully lift the distributor from the engine. The shaft will rotate slightly as the distributor is removed.

To install the distributor:

1. If the engine has been cranked over while the distributor was removed, rotate the crankshaft until the number one piston is at TDC on the compression stroke. This will be indicated by the O mark on the flywheel aligning with the pointer on the clutch housing. Position the rotor just ahead of the #1 terminal of the cap and lower the distributor into the engine. With the distributor fully seated, the rotor should be directly under the #1 terminal.

2. If the engine was not disturbed while the distributor was out, lower the distributor into the engine, engaging the gears and making sure that the gasket is properly seated in the block. The rotor should line up with the mark made before removal.

3. Tighten the holddown screw and connect the wires. Install the distributor splash shield on models so equipped.

4. Check and adjust the ignition timing.

Distributor hold down bolt—2.2L engine

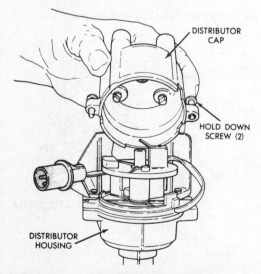

Removing or installing the distributor cap

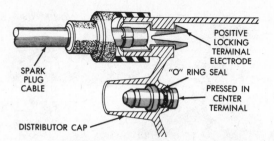

Coil and spark plug terminals—1980 and later models

Alternator

A conventional alternator is used. It has six built-in rectifiers which convert AC current to DC current. Current at the output terminal is DC. The main components of the alternator are: the rotor, stator, rectifiers, end shields and the drive pulley.

The electronic voltage regulator is a device which regulates the vehicle electrical system voltage by limiting the output voltage that is generated by the alternator. This is accomplished by controlling the amount of current that is allowed to pass through the alternator field windings. The regulator has no moving parts and requires no adjustment.

Ammeter fluctuation may be caused by an intermittent loss of alternator ground, which is easily corrected.

1. Do not remove the alternator from the car.

2. Remove the forward (black) through-bolt from the alternator and discard.

3. Assemble the ground strap (Part No. 5211756) under the head of the cadmium plated (silver) replacement through-bolt (Part No. 5206804).

4. Route the ground strap as shown.

5. Remove the bolt from the thermostat housing and assemble the other end of the ground strap under the bolt.

6. Tighten the bolt.

ALTERNATOR PRECAUTIONS

To prevent damage to the alternator and regulator, the following precautions should be taken when working with the electrical system.

1. Never reverse the battery connections.

2. Booster batteries for starting must be connected properly: positive-to-positive and negative-to-negative.

3. Disconnect the battery cables before using a fast charger; the charger has a tendency to force current through the diodes in the opposite direction for which they were designed. This burns out the diodes.

4. Never use a fast charger as a booster for starting the vehicle.

5. Never disconnect the voltage regulator while the engine is running.

6. Avoid long soldering times when replacing diodes or transistors. Prolonged heat is damaging to AC generators.

7. Do not use test lamps of more than 12 volts (V) for checking diode continuity.

8. Do not short across or ground any of the terminals on the AC generator.

9. The polarity of the battery, generator, and regulator must be matched and considered before making any electrical connections within the system.

10. Never operate the alternator on an open circuit. Make sure that all connections within the circuit are clean and tight.

11. Disconnect the battery terminals when performing any service on the electrical system. This will eliminate the possibility of accidental reversal of polarity.

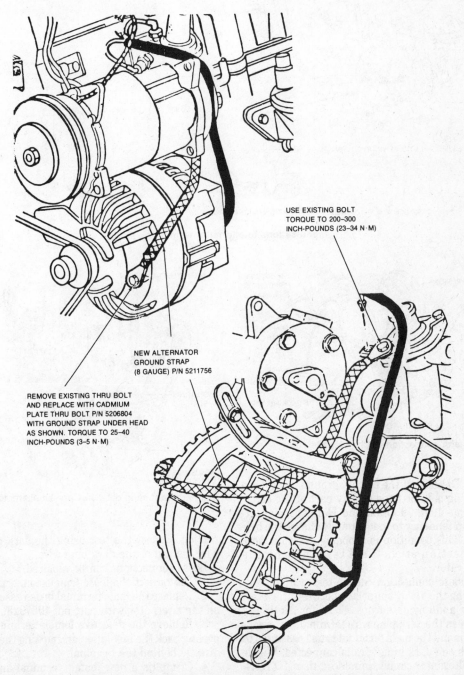

USE EXISTING BOLT TORQUE TO 200–300 INCH-POUNDS (23–34 N·M)

NEW ALTERNATOR GROUND STRAP (8 GAUGE) P/N 5211756

REMOVE EXISTING THRU BOLT AND REPLACE WITH CADMIUM PLATE THRU BOLT P/N 5206804 WITH GROUND STRAP UNDER HEAD AS SHOWN. TORQUE TO 25–40 INCH-POUNDS (3–5 N·M)

Modifications to improve alternator grounding on the 1.7L engine

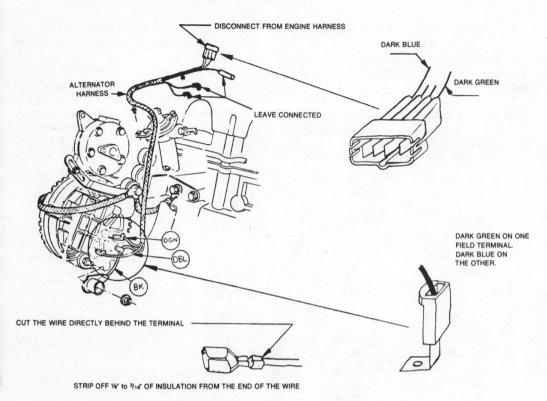

DISCONNECT FROM ENGINE HARNESS

DARK BLUE

DARK GREEN

ALTERNATOR HARNESS

LEAVE CONNECTED

DGN

DBL

BK

DARK GREEN ON ONE FIELD TERMINAL. DARK BLUE ON THE OTHER.

CUT THE WIRE DIRECTLY BEHIND THE TERMINAL

STRIP OFF ⅛" to ³/₁₆" OF INSULATION FROM THE END OF THE WIRE

Modifications to alternator terminals

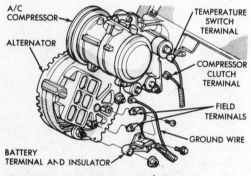

A/C COMPRESSOR

ALTERNATOR

BATTERY TERMINAL AND INSULATOR

TEMPERATURE SWITCH TERMINAL

COMPRESSOR CLUTCH TERMINAL

FIELD TERMINALS

GROUND WIRE

Alternator connections—Chrysler alternator

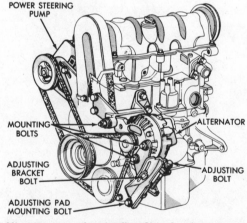

POWER STEERING PUMP

MOUNTING BOLTS

ALTERNATOR

ADJUSTING BRACKET BOLT

ADJUSTING BOLT

ADJUSTING PAD MOUNTING BOLT

Alternator mounting details—Chrysler alternator

12. Disconnect the battery ground cable if arc welding is to be done on any part of the car.

Some 1978-79 Omni and Horizons may exhibit a tendency to inadequately charge the battery. This condition is probably due to a loose connection at the field terminals on the alternator.

A loose connection can be tested by disconnecting the 4-way connector between the alternator and engine harness. Test for continuity between the dark blue wire terminal in the connector and the male terminal brush assembly to which the dark blue wire is connected. Wiggle the alternator connection. More than 1Ω resistance or an erratic reading indicates a loose con-

nection. Repeat the test using the dark green wire instead of the dark blue wire.

Loose connections can be repaired.

1. Disconnect the loose female connections.

2. Replace the male terminal brush assembly on the alternator with part no. 4057928.

3. Remove the defective female terminal by peeling back the insulation and cutting the wire directly behind the terminal.

4. Crimp on a new female terminal and replace the connections.

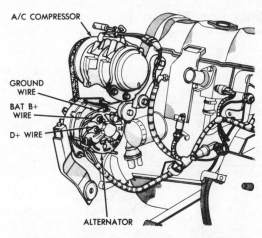

Alternator connections—bosch alternator w/internal regulator

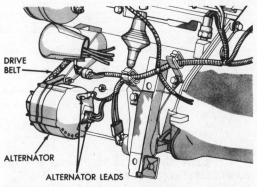

Alternator connections—Bosch alternator w/external regulator

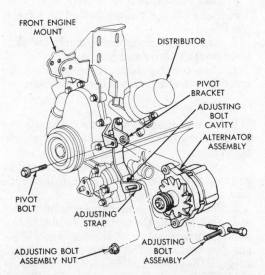

Alternator mounting details—Bosch alternator, typical

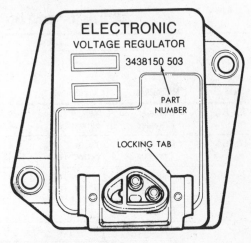

Electronic voltage regulator

REMOVAL AND INSTALLATION

1. Disconnect the battery ground cable.
2. Remove the wires from the alternator.
3. Support the alternator, remove the mounting bolts and lift out the unit.
4. Reverse the procedure for installation.

Regulator

REMOVAL AND INSTALLATION

1. Disconnect the battery ground cable.
2. Remove the wires from the regulator.
3. Remove the two sheet metal screws securing the regulator to the right side fender skirt.
4. Installation is the reverse of removal.

Starter

The starter is an overrunning clutch drive type with a solenoid mounted on the starter motor. Six different type starters are used on Omni/Horizon models. Two each are built by Nippondenso, Bosch and Mitsubishi for manual and automatic transmission applications. Removal and installation procedures are the same for all units.

Some early production models may experience starter motor damage due to improper fit of the upper and lower steering column shrouds. Irregularities in the mating surface of the key cylinder area may cause the ignition key to bind, causing the starter to be continuously engaged. The condition can be corrected by loosening the shroud cover screws about 1 ½ turns.

If loosening the screws does not solve the problem, the covers will have to be replaced with new parts, which are available only in black and must be painted to match interior trim.

Alternator and Regulator Specifications

Year	Alternator		Field Current @ 12v (amp)	Output (amps)	Regulator	Volts @ 75°F
	Manufacturer	Identification			Manufacturer	
'79–'81	Chrysler	Yellow Tag	4.5–6.5	60	Chrysler Electronic	13.9
	Chrysler	Brown Tag	4.5–6.5	65	Chrysler Electronic	13.9
'82–'83	Chrysler	Yellow Tag	4.5–6.5	60	Chrysler Electronic	13.9
	Chrysler	Brown Tag	4.5–6.5	78	Chrysler Electronic	13.9
'84–'86	Chrysler	Yellow Tag	2.5–5.0	60	Chrysler Electronic	13.9
	Chrysler	Brown Tag	2.5–5.0	78	Chrysler Electronic	13.9
	Bosch	K1	2.5–5.0	65	Chrysler Electronic	13.9
	Bosch	N1	—	90	Bosch Integral	14.1
'87	Chrysler	5213763	2.5–5.0	78	Chrysler Electronics	13.9
	Chrysler	5226135	2.5–5.0	78	——— ① ———	
	Chrysler	5227100	2.5–5.0	40/90	——— ① ———	
	Bosch	522600	2.5–5.0	40/90	——— ① ———	
'88–'89	Bosch	5227469	2.5–5.0	35/75	——— ① ———	
	Bosch	5227474	2.5–5.0	40/90	——— ① ———	
	Bosch	5227749	2.5–5.0	40/90	——— ① ———	
	Chrysler	5233474	2.5–5.0	40/90	——— ① ———	
	Chrysler	5233508	2.5–5.0	50/120	——— ① ———	

① Contained within engine electronics Power Module and Logic Module

REMOVAL AND INSTALLATION

1. Disconnect the battery ground cable.
2. Remove the wires from the starter and solenoid.
3. Support the starter, remove the bolts and lift the unit out from the flywheel housing.
4. Installation is the reverse of removal.

OVERHAUL

Service procedures are similar for the Bosch, Mitsubishi and Nippondenso starters. The starter drive is an over-running clutch type with a solenoid mounted externally on the motor.

Disassembly

1. Disconnect the field coil wire from the solenoid terminal.
2. Remove the solenoid mounting screws and work the solenoid off the shift fork.
3. On Nippondenso units, remove the bearing cover, armature shaft lock, washer, spring, and seal.
4. On Bosch units, remove the bearing cover, armature shaft lock, and shim.

5. Remove the two through-bolts and the commutator end frame cover.
6. Remove the two brushes and the brush holder.
7. Slide the field frame off over the armature.
8. Take out the shift lever pivot bolt.
9. Take off the rubber gasket and metal plate.
10. Remove the armature assembly and shift lever from the drive end housing.
11. Press the stop collar off the snap ring. Remove the snapring, stop collar, and clutch.

Inspection

1. Brushes that are worn more than ½ the length of new brushes, or are oil-soaked, should be replaced.
2. Do not immerse the starter clutch unit in cleaning solvent. Solvent will wash the lubricant from the clutch.
3. Place the drive unit on the armature shaft and, while holding the armature, rotate the pinion. The drive pinion should rotate smoothly in one direction only. The pinion may not rotate easily. If the clutch unit does not function properly, or if the pinion is worn, chipped, or burred, replace the unit.

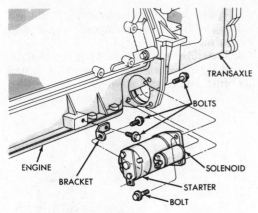

1.6L engine starter mounting

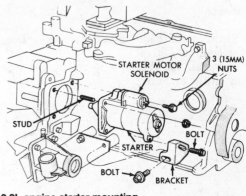

2.2L engine starter mounting

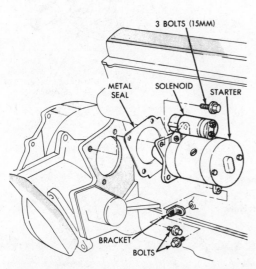

1.7L engine except w/A-412 manual transaxle—starter mounting

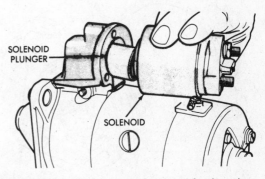

Solenoid removal (automatic transaxle shown)

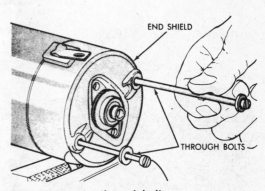

Removing starter through bolts

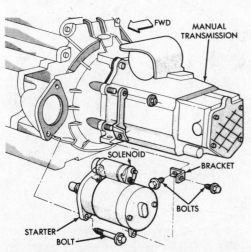

1.7L engine w/A-412 manual transaxle—starter mounting

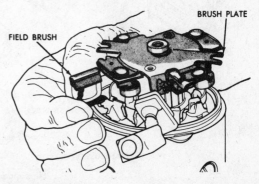

Brush assembly

Assembly

1. Lubricate the armature shaft and splines with SAE 10W-30 oil.

2. Install the clutch, stop collar, and lock ring on the armature.

3. Place the armature assembly and shift fork in the drive end housing. Install the shift lever pivot bolt.

4. Install the rubber gasket and metal plate.

5. Slide the field frame into position. Install the brush holder and brushes.

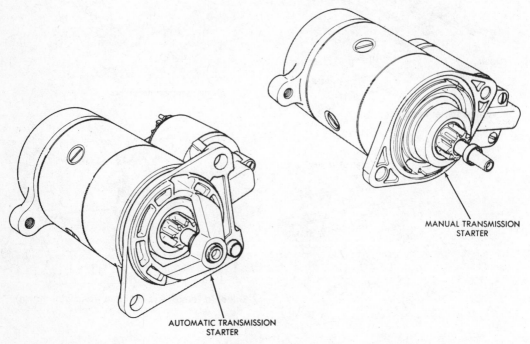

MANUAL TRANSMISSION STARTER

AUTOMATIC TRANSMISSION STARTER

Bosch Starters

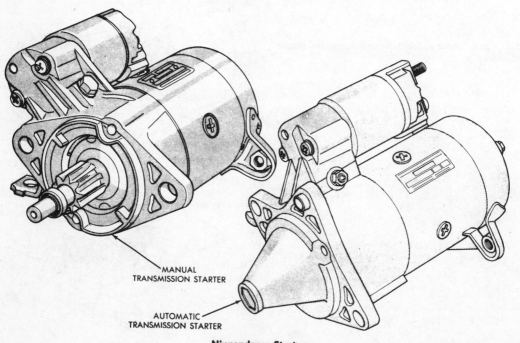

MANUAL TRANSMISSION STARTER

AUTOMATIC TRANSMISSION STARTER

Nippondenso Starters

Starter identification

6. Position the commutator end frame cover and install the through bolts.

7. On Nippondenso units, install the seal, spring, washer, armature shaft lock, and bearing cover.

8. On Bosch units, install the shim and armature shaft lock. Check that end play is 0.05-0.30mm. Install the bearing cover.

9. Assemble the solenoid to the shift fork and install the mounting screws.

10. Connect the field coil wire to the solenoid.

Battery

The battery is located conventionally, under the hood. It can be easily removed by discon-

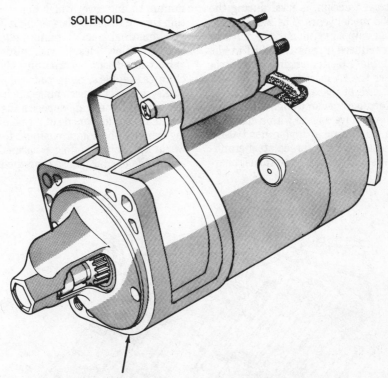

SOLENOID

Manual and Automatic transmission starter Mitsubishi Starter

Starter Specifications

Year	Engine	Trans.	Manufacturer	Load Test*		Torque (ft. lb.)	No-Load Test		
				Amps	Volts		Amps	Volts	RPM
'78–'83	All	All	Bosch or Nippondenso	120–160	12	—	47	11	6600
'84–'86	1.6	All	Mitsubishi	120–160	12	—	47	11	6600
	2.2	All	Bosch or Nippondenso	120–160	12	—	47	11	6600
'87	2.2	All	Bosch ①	120–160	12	—	47	11	6600
	2.2	All	Bosch ②	150–210	12	—	75	11	4020
	2.2	All	Nippondenso ②	150–210	12	—	75	11	4020
'88–'89	2.2	All	Nippondenso ②	150–220	12	—	82	11	3625

*To perform the load test, the engine should be up to operating temperature. Extremely heavy oil or tight engine will increase starter amperage draw.
① Direct Drive starter
② Reduction Gear starter

necting the battery cables and removing the holddown bolts from the battery tray. Coat the terminals with a small amount of petroleum jelly after installation.

ENGINE MECHANICAL

There are three different engines used in the Omni/Horizon body styles. The 1.7 liter, basically a Volkswagen design, is used during the 1978 thru 1983 model years. The 2.2 liter engine, a Chrysler refined version of the 1.7 liter engine was introduced during the 1981 model year. In 1984 the 1.6 liter engine was introduced to replace the 1.7 liter engine. Below is a description of each of these engines.

The 1.6 Liter displacement engine is a four cylinder overhead valve engine with a cast iron block and an aluminum cylinder head. Five main bearings support the forged steel crankshaft with number three being the thrust bear-

ing. The cast iron dual timing chain sprocket on the crankshaft, not only provides power for the timing chains, but it also acts as a vibration damper. The cast iron camshaft is mounted on three babbitt bearings and a thrust plate located at the front bearing controls the camshaft end play. The camshaft itself is positioned left of the crankshaft, or toward the front of the car. The camshaft is driven by dual timing chains. These chains are enclosed by a cast aluminum timing cover which has the strobe ignition timing marks embossed on it. The cylinder head material is an aluminum alloy. The head is a "crossflow" design with inline valves. The valve train design incorporates the use of mechanical tappets, push rods, and adjustable rocker arms. The spark plugs are located on the left side of the engine opposite the valves. The intake manifold is made of a cast aluminum alloy, cored with coolant passages for carburetor warm up. This manifold is located on the left side of the head. Embossed on the intake mani-

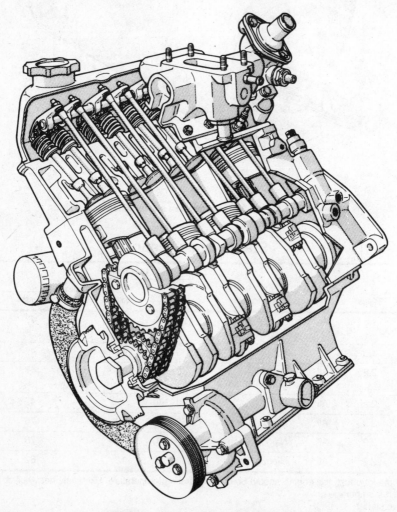

1.6L four cylinder engine—cut-away view

fold is the cylinder number identification, firing order, and the direction of the distributor rotation. The exhaust manifold is made of nodular iron and is attached to the right side of the head (towards the rear of the car) and is held on by eight bolts.

The 1.7 Liter displacement engine is a four cylinder, overhead camshaft engine. The block is cast iron and the head is aluminum. A five main bearing forged steel crankshaft using no vibration damper is employed, rotated by cast aluminum pistons. A sintered iron timing belt sprocket is mounted on the end of the crank-

shaft. The intake manifold and oil filter base are aluminum. A steel reinforced belt drives the intermediate shaft and camshaft. The intermediate shaft drives the oil pump, distributor, and fuel pump. The cylinder head is lightweight aluminum alloy. The intake and exhaust manifolds are mounted on the same side of the cylinder head. The valves are opened and closed by the camshaft lobes operating on cupped cam followers which fit over the valves and springs. This design results in lighter valve train weight and fewer moving parts.

The 2.2 Liter displacement engine is a four

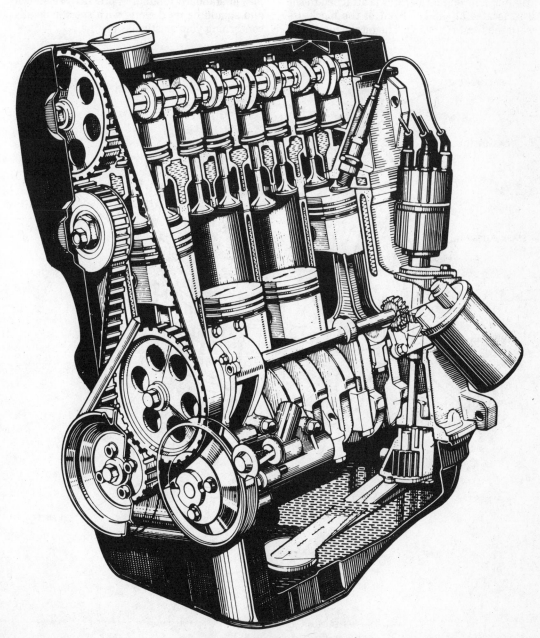

1.7L four cylinder engine—cut-away view

cylinder, overhead camshaft design powerplant with a cast iron block and an aluminum cylinder head. The cast iron crankshaft is supported by five main bearings. No vibration dampener is used. The iron camshaft also has five bearing journals and there are flanges at the rear journal to control the camshaft end play. Sintered iron timing sprockets are mounted on both the camshaft and the crankshaft which are driven by the timing belt. The timing belt also drives an accessory shaft, housed in the forward facing side of the block. The accessory shaft, in turn drives the fuel pump, oil pump and the distributor. The engine oil filter is attached to the base located at the left front of the block, toward the front of the car. The intake manifolds are cast aluminum and the exhaust manifolds are iron, both of which face the rear of the vehicle. The distributor, spark plugs and oil filter are all located on the forward facing side of the engine.

Engine Overhaul Tips

Most engine overhaul procedures are fairly standard. In addition to specific parts replacement procedures and complete specifications for your individual engine, this chapter also is a guide to accept rebuilding procedures. Examples of standard rebuilding practice are shown and should be used along with specific details concerning your particular engine.

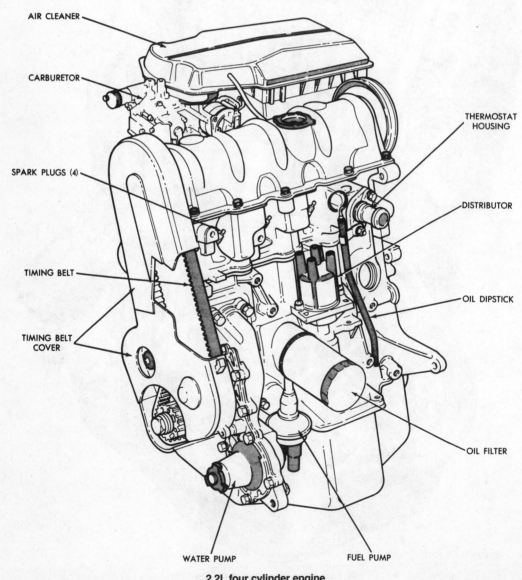

2.2L four cylinder engine

Competent and accurate machine shop services will ensure maximum performance, reliability and engine life.

In most instances it is more profitable for the do-it-yourself mechanic to remove, clean and inspect the component, buy the necessary parts and deliver these to a shop for actual machine work.

On the other hand, much of the rebuilding work (checking crankshaft, block, piston, rods, and other components and fitting new bearings) is well within the scope of the do-it-yourself mechanic.

TOOLS

The tools required for an engine overhaul or parts replacement will depend on the depth of your involvement. With a few exceptions, they will be the tools found in a mechanic's tool kit (see Chapter 1). More in-depth work will require any or all of the following:

• a dial indicator (reading in thousandths) mounted on a universal base
• micrometers and telescope gauges
• jaw and screw-type pullers
• scraper
• valve spring compressor
• ring groove cleaner
• piston ring expander and compressor
• ridge reamer
• cylinder hone or glaze breaker
• Plastigage®
• engine stand

The use of most of these tools is illustrated in this chapter. Many can be rented for a one-time use from a local parts jobber or tool supply house specializing in automotive work.

Occasionally, the use of special tools is called for. See the information on Special Tools and the Safety Notice in the front of this book before substituting another tool.

INSPECTION TECHNIQUES

Procedures and specifications are given in this chapter for inspecting, cleaning and assessing the wear limits of most major components. Other procedures such as Magnaflux® and Zyglo® can be used to locate material flaws and stress cracks. Magnaflux® is a magnetic process applicable only to ferrous materials. The Zyglo® process coats the material with a fluorescent dye penetrant and can be used on any material Check for suspected surface cracks can be more readily made using spot check dye. The dye is sprayed onto the suspected area, wiped off and the area sprayed with a developer. Cracks will show up brightly.

OVERHAUL TIPS

Aluminum has become extremely popular for use in engines, due to its low weight. Observe the following precautions when handling aluminum parts:

• Never hot tank aluminum parts (the caustic hot tank solution will eat the aluminum.
• Remove all aluminum parts (identification tag, etc.) from engine parts prior to the tanking.
• Always coat threads lightly with engine oil or anti-seize compounds before installation, to prevent seizure.
• Never overtorque bolts or spark plugs especially in aluminum threads.

Stripped threads in any component can be repaired using any of several commercial repair kits (Heli-Coil®, Microdot®, Keenserts®, etc.).

When assembling the engine, any parts that will be frictional contact must be prelubed to provide lubrication at initial start-up. Any product specifically formulated for this purpose can be used, but engine oil is not recommended as a prelube, as it will not be retained on the wearing surfaces in sufficient quantities to provide adequate lubrication for new parts.

When semi-permanent (locked, but removable) installation of bolts or nuts is desired, threads should be cleaned and coated with Loctite® or other similar, commercial non-hardening sealant.

REPAIRING DAMAGED THREADS

Several methods of repairing damaged threads are available. Heli-Coil® (shown here), Keenserts® and Microdot® are among the most widely used. All involve basically the same principle—drilling out stripped threads, tapping the hole and installing a prewound insert—making welding, plugging and oversize fasteners unnecessary.

Two types of thread repair inserts are usually supplied: a standard type for most Inch Coarse, Inch Fine, Metric Course and Metric Fine thread sizes and a spark lug type to fit most spark plug port sizes. Consult the individual manufacturer's catalog to determine exact applications. Typical thread repair kits will contain a selection of prewound threaded inserts, a tap (corresponding to the outside diameter threads of the insert) and an installation tool. Spark plug inserts usually differ because they

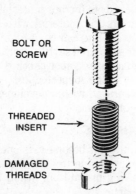

Damaged bolt holes can be repaired with thread repair inserts

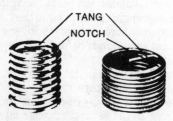

Standard thread repair insert (left) and spark plug thread insert (right)

Drill out the damaged threads with specified drill. Drill completely through the hole or to the bottom of a blind hole

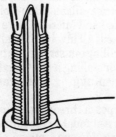

With the tap supplied, tap the hole to receive the thread insert. Keep the tap well oiled and back it out frequently to avoid clogging the threads

require a tap equipped with pilot threads and a combined reamer/tap section. Most manufacturers also supply blister-packed thread repair inserts separately in addition to a master kit

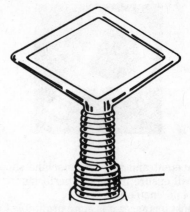

Screw the threaded insert onto the installation tool until the tang engages the slot. Screw the insert into the tapped hole until it is ¼–½ turn below the top surface. After installation break off the tang with a hammer and punch

containing a variety of taps and inserts plus installation tools.

Before effecting a repair to a threaded hole, remove any snapped, broken or damaged bolts or studs. Penetrating oil can be used to free frozen threads. The offending item can be removed with locking pliers or with a screw or stud extractor. After the hole is clear, the thread can be repaired, as shown in the series of accompanying illustrations.

Checking Engine Compression

A noticeable lack of engine power, excessive oil consumption and/or poor fuel mileage measured over an extended period are all indicators of internal engine wear. Worn piston rings, scored or worn cylinder bores, blown head gaskets, sticking or burnt valves and worn valve seats are all possible culprits here. A check of each cylinder's compression will help you locate the problems.

As mentioned in the Tools and Equipment section of Chapter 1, a screw-in type compres-

The screw-in type compression gauge is more accurate

Standard Torque Specifications and Fastener Markings

In the absence of specific torques, the following chart can be used as a guide to the maximum safe torque of a particular size/grade of fastener.

- There is no torque difference for fine or coarse threads.
- Torque values are based on clean, dry threads. Reduce the value by 10% if threads are oiled prior to assembly.
- The torque required for aluminum components or fasteners is considerably less.

U.S. Bolts

SAE Grade Number	1 or 2			5			6 or 7		
Number of lines always 2 less than the grade number.									
Bolt Size (Inches)—(Thread)	Ft./Lbs.	Kgm	Nm	Ft./Lbs.	Kgm	Nm	Ft./Lbs.	Kgm	Nm
¼—20	5	0.7	6.8	8	1.1	10.8	10	1.4	13.5
—28	6	0.8	8.1	10	1.4	13.6			
⁵⁄₁₆—18	11	1.5	14.9	17	2.3	23.0	19	2.6	25.8
—24	13	1.8	17.6	19	2.6	25.7			
⅜—16	18	2.5	24.4	31	4.3	42.0	34	4.7	46.0
—24	20	2.75	27.1	35	4.8	47.5			
⁷⁄₁₆—14	28	3.8	37.0	49	6.8	66.4	55	7.6	74.5
—20	30	4.2	40.7	55	7.6	74.5			
½—13	39	5.4	52.8	75	10.4	101.7	85	11.75	115.2
—20	41	5.7	55.6	85	11.7	115.2			
⁹⁄₁₆—12	51	7.0	69.2	110	15.2	149.1	120	16.6	162.7
—18	55	7.6	74.5	120	16.6	162.7			
⅝—11	83	11.5	112.5	150	20.7	203.3	167	23.0	226.5
—18	95	13.1	128.8	170	23.5	230.5			
¾—10	105	14.5	142.3	270	37.3	366.0	280	38.7	379.6
—16	115	15.9	155.9	295	40.8	400.0			
⅞—9	160	22.1	216.9	395	54.6	535.5	440	60.9	596.5
—14	175	24.2	237.2	435	60.1	589.7			
1—8	236	32.5	318.6	590	81.6	799.9	660	91.3	894.8
—14	250	34.6	338.9	660	91.3	849.8			

Metric Bolts

Relative Strength Marking	4.6, 4.8			8.8		
Bolt Markings						
Bolt Size Thread Size x Pitch (mm)	Ft./Lbs.	Kgm	Nm	Ft./Lbs.	Kgm	Nm
6 x 1.0	2–3	.2–.4	3–4	3–6	.4–.8	5–8
8 x 1.25	6–8	.8–1	8–12	9–14	1.2–1.9	13–19
10 x 1.25	12–17	1.5–2.3	16–23	20–29	2.7–4.0	27–39
12 x 1.25	21–32	2.9–4.4	29–43	35–53	4.8–7.3	47–72
14 x 1.5	35–52	4.8–7.1	48–70	57–85	7.8–11.7	77–110
16 x 1.5	51–77	7.0–10.6	67–100	90–120	12.4–16.5	130–160
18 x 1.5	74–110	10.2–15.1	100–150	130–170	17.9–23.4	180–230
20 x 1.5	110–140	15.1–19.3	150–190	190–240	26.2–46.9	160–320
22 x 1.5	150–190	22.0–26.2	200–260	250–320	34.5–44.1	340–430
24 x 1.5	190–240	26.2–46.9	260–320	310–410	42.7–56.5	420–550

Troubleshooting Engine Mechanical Problems

Problem	Cause	Solution
External oil leaks	• Fuel pump gasket broken or improperly seated	• Replace gasket
	• Cylinder head cover RTV sealant broken or improperly seated	• Replace sealant; inspect cylinder head cover sealant flange and cylinder head sealant surface for distortion and cracks
	• Oil filler cap leaking or missing	• Replace cap
	• Oil filter gasket broken or improperly seated	• Replace oil filter
	• Oil pan side gasket broken, improperly seated or opening in RTV sealant	• Replace gasket or repair opening in sealant; inspect oil pan gasket flange for distortion
	• Oil pan front oil seal broken or improperly seated	• Replace seal; inspect timing case cover and oil pan seal flange for distortion
	• Oil pan rear oil seal broken or improperly seated	• Replace seal; inspect oil pan rear oil seal flange; inspect rear main bearing cap for cracks, plugged oil return channels, or distortion in seal groove
	• Timing case cover oil seal broken or improperly seated	• Replace seal
	• Excess oil pressure because of restricted PCV valve	• Replace PCV valve
	• Oil pan drain plug loose or has stripped threads	• Repair as necessary and tighten
	• Rear oil gallery plug loose	• Use appropriate sealant on gallery plug and tighten
	• Rear camshaft plug loose or improperly seated	• Seat camshaft plug or replace and seal, as necessary
	• Distributor base gasket damaged	• Replace gasket
Excessive oil consumption	• Oil level too high	• Drain oil to specified level
	• Oil with wrong viscosity being used	• Replace with specified oil
	• PCV valve stuck closed	• Replace PCV valve
	• Valve stem oil deflectors (or seals) are damaged, missing, or incorrect type	• Replace valve stem oil deflectors
	• Valve stems or valve guides worn	• Measure stem-to-guide clearance and repair as necessary
	• Poorly fitted or missing valve cover baffles	• Replace valve cover
	• Piston rings broken or missing	• Replace broken or missing rings
	• Scuffed piston	• Replace piston
	• Incorrect piston ring gap	• Measure ring gap, repair as necessary
	• Piston rings sticking or excessively loose in grooves	• Measure ring side clearance, repair as necessary
	• Compression rings installed upside down	• Repair as necessary
	• Cylinder walls worn, scored, or glazed	• Repair as necessary
	• Piston ring gaps not properly staggered	• Repair as necessary
	• Excessive main or connecting rod bearing clearance	• Measure bearing clearance, repair as necessary
No oil pressure	• Low oil level	• Add oil to correct level
	• Oil pressure gauge, warning lamp or sending unit inaccurate	• Replace oil pressure gauge or warning lamp
	• Oil pump malfunction	• Replace oil pump
	• Oil pressure relief valve sticking	• Remove and inspect oil pressure relief valve assembly
	• Oil passages on pressure side of pump obstructed	• Inspect oil passages for obstruction

Troubleshooting Engine Mechanical Problems (cont.)

Problem	Cause	Solution
No oil pressure (cont.)	• Oil pickup screen or tube obstructed	• Inspect oil pickup for obstruction
	• Loose oil inlet tube	• Tighten or seal inlet tube
Low oil pressure	• Low oil level	• Add oil to correct level
	• Inaccurate gauge, warning lamp or sending unit	• Replace oil pressure gauge or warning lamp
	• Oil excessively thin because of dilution, poor quality, or improper grade	• Drain and refill crankcase with recommended oil
	• Excessive oil temperature	• Correct cause of overheating engine
	• Oil pressure relief spring weak or sticking	• Remove and inspect oil pressure relief valve assembly
	• Oil inlet tube and screen assembly has restriction or air leak	• Remove and inspect oil inlet tube and screen assembly. (Fill inlet tube with lacquer thinner to locate leaks.)
	• Excessive oil pump clearance	• Measure clearances
	• Excessive main, rod, or camshaft bearing clearance	• Measure bearing clearances, repair as necessary
High oil pressure	• Improper oil viscosity	• Drain and refill crankcase with correct viscosity oil
	• Oil pressure gauge or sending unit inaccurate	• Replace oil pressure gauge
	• Oil pressure relief valve sticking closed	• Remove and inspect oil pressure relief valve assembly
Main bearing noise	• Insufficient oil supply	• Inspect for low oil level and low oil pressure
	• Main bearing clearance excessive	• Measure main bearing clearance, repair as necessary
	• Bearing insert missing	• Replace missing insert
	• Crankshaft end play excessive	• Measure end play, repair as necessary
	• Improperly tightened main bearing cap bolts	• Tighten bolts with specified torque
	• Loose flywheel or drive plate	• Tighten flywheel or drive plate attaching bolts
	• Loose or damaged vibration damper	• Repair as necessary
Connecting rod bearing noise	• Insufficient oil supply	• Inspect for low oil level and low oil pressure
	• Carbon build-up on piston	• Remove carbon from piston crown
	• Bearing clearance excessive or bearing missing	• Measure clearance, repair as necessary
	• Crankshaft connecting rod journal out-of-round	• Measure journal dimensions, repair or replace as necessary
	• Misaligned connecting rod or cap	• Repair as necessary
	• Connecting rod bolts tightened improperly	• Tighten bolts with specified torque
Piston noise	• Piston-to-cylinder wall clearance excessive (scuffed piston)	• Measure clearance and examine piston
	• Cylinder walls excessively tapered or out-of-round	• Measure cylinder wall dimensions, rebore cylinder
	• Piston ring broken	• Replace all rings on piston
	• Loose or seized piston pin	• Measure piston-to-pin clearance, repair as necessary
	• Connecting rods misaligned	• Measure rod alignment, straighten or replace
	• Piston ring side clearance excessively loose or tight	• Measure ring side clearance, repair as necessary
	• Carbon build-up on piston is excessive	• Remove carbon from piston

Troubleshooting Engine Mechanical Problems (cont.)

Problem	Cause	Solution
Valve actuating component noise	• Insufficient oil supply	• Check for: 　(a) Low oil level 　(b) Low oil pressure 　(c) Plugged push rods 　(d) Wrong hydraulic tappets 　(e) Restricted oil gallery 　(f) Excessive tappet to bore clearance
	• Push rods worn or bent	• Replace worn or bent push rods
	• Rocker arms or pivots worn	• Replace worn rocker arms or pivots
	• Foreign objects or chips in hydraulic tappets	• Clean tappets
	• Excessive tappet leak-down	• Replace valve tappet
	• Tappet face worn	• Replace tappet; inspect corresponding cam lobe for wear
	• Broken or cocked valve springs	• Properly seat cocked springs; replace broken springs
	• Stem-to-guide clearance excessive	• Measure stem-to-guide clearance, repair as required
	• Valve bent	• Replace valve
	• Loose rocker arms	• Tighten bolts with specified torque
	• Valve seat runout excessive	• Regrind valve seat/valves
	• Missing valve lock	• Install valve lock
	• Push rod rubbing or contacting cylinder head	• Remove cylinder head and remove obstruction in head
	• Excessive engine oil (four-cylinder engine)	• Correct oil level

sion gauge is more accurate that the type you simply hold against the spark plug hole, although it takes slightly longer to use. It's worth it to obtain a more accurate reading. Follow the procedures below.

1. Warm up the engine to normal operating temperature.

2. Remove all the spark plugs.

3. Disconnect the high tension lead from the ignition coil.

4. Fully open the throttle either by operating the carburetor throttle linkage by hand or by having an assistant floor the accelerator pedal.

5. Screw the compression gauge into the no.1 spark plug hole until the fitting is snug.

WARNING: *Be careful not to crossthread the plug hole. On aluminum cylinder heads use extra care, as the threads in these heads are easily ruined.*

6. Ask an assistant to depress the accelerator pedal fully on both carbureted and fuel injected vehicles. Then, while you read the compression gauge, ask the assistant to crank the engine two or three times in short bursts using the ignition switch.

7. Read the compression gauge at the end of each series of cranks, and record the highest of these readings. Repeat this procedure for each of the engine's cylinders. Compare the highest reading of each cylinder to the compression pressure specification in the Tune-Up Specifi-

cations chart in Chapter 2. The specs in this chart are maximum values.

A cylinder's compression pressure is acceptable on these cars if it is not less than 75% of maximum. The minimum pressure for these engines is 100 psi.

8. If a cylinder is unusually low, pour a tablespoon of clean engine oil into the cylinder through the spark plug hole and repeat the compression test. If the compression comes up after adding the oil, it appears that the cylinder's piston rings or bore are damaged or worn. If the pressure remains low, the valves may not be seating properly (a valve job is needed), or the head gasket may be blown near that cylinder. If compression in any two adjacent cylinders is low, and if the addition of oil doesn't help the compression, there is leakage past the head gasket. Oil and coolant water in the combustion chamber can result from this problem. There may be evidence of water droplets in the oil film on the engine dipstick when a head gasket has blown.

Engine

REMOVAL

1. Disconnect the battery.

2. Mark the hood hinge outline and remove the hood.

Troubleshooting the Cooling System

Problem	Cause	Solution
High temperature gauge indication—overheating	• Coolant level low	• Replenish coolant
	• Fan belt loose	• Adjust fan belt tension
	• Radiator hose(s) collapsed	• Replace hose(s)
	• Radiator airflow blocked	• Remove restriction (bug screen, fog lamps, etc.)
	• Faulty radiator cap	• Replace radiator cap
	• Ignition timing incorrect	• Adjust ignition timing
	• Idle speed low	• Adjust idle speed
	• Air trapped in cooling system	• Purge air
	• Heavy traffic driving	• Operate at fast idle in neutral intermittently to cool engine
	• Incorrect cooling system component(s) installed	• Install proper component(s)
	• Faulty thermostat	• Replace thermostat
	• Water pump shaft broken or impeller loose	• Replace water pump
	• Radiator tubes clogged	• Flush radiator
	• Cooling system clogged	• Flush system
	• Casting flash in cooling passages	• Repair or replace as necessary. Flash may be visible by removing cooling system components or removing core plugs.
	• Brakes dragging	• Repair brakes
	• Excessive engine friction	• Repair engine
	• Antifreeze concentration over 68%	• Lower antifreeze concentration percentage
	• Missing air seals	• Replace air seals
	• Faulty gauge or sending unit	• Repair or replace faulty component
	• Loss of coolant flow caused by leakage or foaming	• Repair or replace leaking component, replace coolant
	• Viscous fan drive failed	• Replace unit
Low temperature indication—undercooling	• Thermostat stuck open	• Replace thermostat
	• Faulty gauge or sending unit	• Repair or replace faulty component
Coolant loss—boilover	• Overfilled cooling system	• Reduce coolant level to proper specification
	• Quick shutdown after hard (hot) run	• Allow engine to run at fast idle prior to shutdown
	• Air in system resulting in occasional "burping" of coolant	• Purge system
	• Insufficient antifreeze allowing coolant boiling point to be too low	• Add antifreeze to raise boiling point
	• Antifreeze deteriorated because of age or contamination	• Replace coolant
	• Leaks due to loose hose clamps, loose nuts, bolts, drain plugs, faulty hoses, or defective radiator	• Pressure test system to locate source of leak(s) then repair as necessary
	• Faulty head gasket	• Replace head gasket
	• Cracked head, manifold, or block	• Replace as necessary
	• Faulty radiator cap	• Replace cap
Coolant entry into crankcase or cylinder(s)	• Faulty head gasket	• Replace head gasket
	• Crack in head, manifold or block	• Replace as necessary
Coolant recovery system inoperative	• Coolant level low	• Replenish coolant to FULL mark
	• Leak in system	• Pressure test to isolate leak and repair as necessary
	• Pressure cap not tight or seal missing, or leaking	• Repair as necessary
	• Pressure cap defective	• Replace cap
	• Overflow tube clogged or leaking	• Repair as necessary
	• Recovery bottle vent restricted	• Remove restriction

Troubleshooting the Cooling System (cont.)

Problem	Cause	Solution
Noise	• Fan contacting shroud	• Reposition shroud and inspect engine mounts
	• Loose water pump impeller	• Replace pump
	• Glazed fan belt	• Apply silicone or replace belt
	• Loose fan belt	• Adjust fan belt tension
	• Rough surface on drive pulley	• Replace pulley
	• Water pump bearing worn	• Remove belt to isolate. Replace pump.
	• Belt alignment	• Check pulley alignment. Repair as necessary.
No coolant flow through heater core	• Restricted return inlet in water pump	• Remove restriction
	• Heater hose collapsed or restricted	• Remove restriction or replace hose
	• Restricted heater core	• Remove restriction or replace core
	• Restricted outlet in thermostat housing	• Remove flash or restriction
	• Intake manifold bypass hole in cylinder head restricted	• Remove restriction
	• Faulty heater control valve	• Replace valve
	• Intake manifold coolant passage restricted	• Remove restriction or replace intake manifold

NOTE: *Immediately after shutdown, the engine enters a condition known as heat soak. This is caused by the cooling system being inoperative while engine temperature is still high. If coolant temperature rises above boiling point, expansion and pressure may push some coolant out of the radiator overflow tube. If this does not occur frequently it is considered normal.*

Troubleshooting the Serpentine Drive Belt

Problem	Cause	Solution
Tension sheeting fabric failure (woven fabric on outside circumference of belt has cracked or separated from body of belt)	• Grooved or backside idler pulley diameters are less than minimum recommended	• Replace pulley(s) not conforming to specification
	• Tension sheeting contacting (rubbing) stationary object	• Correct rubbing condition
	• Excessive heat causing woven fabric to age	• Replace belt
	• Tension sheeting splice has fractured	• Replace belt
Noise (objectional squeal, squeak, or rumble is heard or felt while drive belt is in operation)	• Belt slippage	• Adjust belt
	• Bearing noise	• Locate and repair
	• Belt misalignment	• Align belt/pulley(s)
	• Belt-to-pulley mismatch	• Install correct belt
	• Driven component inducing vibration	• Locate defective driven component and repair
	• System resonant frequency inducing vibration	• Vary belt tension within specifications. Replace belt.
Rib chunking (one or more ribs has separated from belt body)	• Foreign objects imbedded in pulley grooves	• Remove foreign objects from pulley grooves
	• Installation damage	• Replace belt
	• Drive loads in excess of design specifications	• Adjust belt tension
	• Insufficient internal belt adhesion	• Replace belt
Rib or belt wear (belt ribs contact bottom of pulley grooves)	• Pulley(s) misaligned	• Align pulley(s)
	• Mismatch of belt and pulley groove widths	• Replace belt
	• Abrasive environment	• Replace belt
	• Rusted pulley(s)	• Clean rust from pulley(s)
	• Sharp or jagged pulley groove tips	• Replace pulley
	• Rubber deteriorated	• Replace belt

Troubleshooting the Serpentine Drive Belt (cont.)

Problem	Cause	Solution
Longitudinal belt cracking (cracks between two ribs)	• Belt has mistracked from pulley groove	• Replace belt
	• Pulley groove tip has worn away rubber-to-tensile member	• Replace belt
Belt slips	• Belt slipping because of insufficient tension	• Adjust tension
	• Belt or pulley subjected to substance (belt dressing, oil, ethylene glycol) that has reduced friction	• Replace belt and clean pulleys
	• Driven component bearing failure	• Replace faulty component bearing
	• Belt glazed and hardened from heat and excessive slippage	• Replace belt
"Groove jumping" (belt does not maintain correct position on pulley, or turns over and/or runs off pulleys)	• Insufficient belt tension	• Adjust belt tension
	• Pulley(s) not within design tolerance	• Replace pulley(s)
	• Foreign object(s) in grooves	• Remove foreign objects from grooves
	• Excessive belt speed	• Avoid excessive engine acceleration
	• Pulley misalignment	• Align pulley(s)
	• Belt-to-pulley profile mismatched	• Install correct belt
	• Belt cordline is distorted	• Replace belt
Belt broken (Note: identify and correct problem before replacement belt is installed)	• Excessive tension	• Replace belt and adjust tension to specification
	• Tensile members damaged during belt installation	• Replace belt
	• Belt turnover	• Replace belt
	• Severe pulley misalignment	• Align pulley(s)
	• Bracket, pulley, or bearing failure	• Replace defective component and belt
Cord edge failure (tensile member exposed at edges of belt or separated from belt body)	• Excessive tension	• Adjust belt tension
	• Drive pulley misalignment	• Align pulley
	• Belt contacting stationary object	• Correct as necessary
	• Pulley irregularities	• Replace pulley
	• Improper pulley construction	• Replace pulley
	• Insufficient adhesion between tensile member and rubber matrix	• Replace belt and adjust tension to specifications
Sporadic rib cracking (multiple cracks in belt ribs at random intervals)	• Ribbed pulley(s) diameter less than minimum specification	• Replace pulley(s)
	• Backside bend flat pulley(s) diameter less than minimum	• Replace pulley(s)
	• Excessive heat condition causing rubber to harden	• Correct heat condition as necessary
	• Excessive belt thickness	• Replace belt
	• Belt overcured	• Replace belt
	• Excessive tension	• Adjust belt tension

3. Drain the cooling system.

CAUTION: *When draining the coolant, keep in mind that cats and dogs are attracted by the ethylene glycol antifreeze, and are quite likely to drink any that is left in an uncovered container or in puddles on the ground. This will prove fatal in sufficient quantity. Always drain the coolant into a sealable container. Coolant should be reused unless it is contaminated or several years old.*

4. Remove the radiator hoses and remove the radiator and shroud assembly.

5. Remove the air cleaner and hoses.

6. On cars equipped with air conditioning, the compressor does not have to be disconnected. Remove it from its bracket and position it out of the way. Securing it with a piece of wire is the best method.

NOTE: *On air conditioned, cars do not disconnect any hoses from the air conditioning system. Disconnect the compressor from the bracket with the hoses attached.*

7. Remove the power steering pump and position it out of the way.

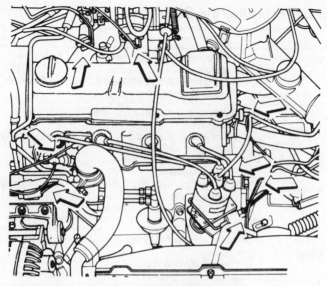

Engine electrical connections

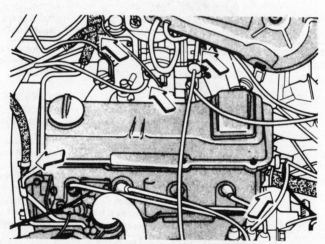

Fuel, heater and accelerator connections

8. Drain the engine oil and remove the oil filter.

CAUTION: *The EPA warns that prolonged contact with used engine oil may cause a number of skin disorders, including cancer! You should make every effort to minimize your exposure to used engine oil. Protective gloves should be worn when changing the oil. Wash your hands and any other exposed skin areas as soon as possible after exposure to used engine oil. Soap and water, or waterless hand cleaner should be used.*

9. Disconnect all the wiring from the engine and alternator.

10. Disconnect the fuel line, heater hose and the accelerator cable.

11. Remove the alternator.

12. On Manual Transaxle models:

    a. disconnect the clutch cable.

    b. Remove the transaxle case lower cover.

    c. Disconnect the exhaust pipe at the manifold.

    d. Remove the starter.

    e. Install a transaxle holding fixture to support the transaxle when the engine is removed.

13. On Automatic Transaxle models:

    a. Disconnect the exhaust pipe at the manifold.

    b. Remove the starter.

    c. Remove the transaxle case lower cover.

    d. Mark the flex plate to the torque converter for reassembly.

    e. Attach a "C" clamp on the front bottom of the torque converter housing to prevent the torque converter from coming out.

    f. Install a transaxle holding fixture to support the transaxle when the engine is removed.

14. Attach a lifting fixture and a shop crane to

the engine. Raise the engine slightly to take up the weight of the engine.

CAUTION: *On models with the A-460 transaxle, the left front engine mount is attached with two different types of mounting bolts. Two of the three bolts are of the pilot type with extended tips. These bolts must be installed in the positions shown in the accompanying illustration. Damage to the shift cover or difficult shifting may occur if the bolts are incorrectly installed.*

15. Remove the right inner splash shield.
16. Remove the ground strap.
17. To raise the engine remove the long bolts through the yoke and insulator.

NOTE: *If the insulator screws are to be re-*

General Engine Specifications

Engine	Year	Carb. Type	Horsepower @ rpm	Torque ft. lb. @ rpm	Bore x Stroke	Comp. Ratio	Oil. Press. (psi.) @ 2000 rpm
1.6L	'84	2 bbl.	64 @ 4800	87 @ 2800	3.17 x 3.07	8.8:1	58–87
1.7L	'78	2 bbl.	75 @ 5600	90 @ 3200	3.13 x 3.40	8.2:1	60–90
	'79	2 bbl.	70 @ 5200	85 @ 2800	3.13 x 3.40	8.2:1	60–90
	'80	2 bbl.	65 @ 5200	85 @ 2400	3.13 x 3.40	8.2:1	60–90
	'81–'82	2 bbl	63 @ 5200	83 @ 2400	3.13 x 3.40	8.2:1	60–90
	'83	2 bbl.	63 @ 4800	83 @ 2400	3.13 x 3.40	8.2:1	60–90
2.2L	'81–'82	2 bbl.	84 @ 4800	111 @ 2800	3.44 x 3.62	8.5:1	50
	'83	2 bbl.	94 @ 5200	117 @ 3200	3.44 x 3.62	9.0:1	50
	①	2 bbl.	100 @ 5200	122 @ 3200	3.44 x 3.62	9.0:1	50
	②	2 bbl.	107 @ 5600	126 @ 3600	3.44 x 3.62	9.6:1	50
	'84–'86	2 bbl.	96 @ 5200	119 @ 3200	3.44 x 3.62	9.0:1	50
	①	2 bbl.	101 @ 5200	124 @ 3200	3.44 x 3.62	9.0:1	50
	②	2 bbl.	110 @ 5600	129 @ 3600	3.44 x 3.62	9.6:1	50
	③	EFI	110 @ 5600	129 @ 3600	3.44 x 3.62	—	50
	④	Turbo	146 @ 5200	170 @ 3600	3.44 x 3.62	—	50
	'87	2 bbl.	96 @ 5200	119 @ 3200	3.44 x 3.62	9.0:1	50
		Turbo.	146 @ 5200	170 @ 3600	3.44 x 3.62	8.0:1	50
	'88–'89	EFI	93 @ 4800	121 @ 3200	3.44 x 3.62	9.5:1	50

① Standard engine in the Charger & Turismo 2.2 models
② High output engine used in the Shelby Charger
③ High output GLH
④ Turbo GLH

Valve Specifications

Engine	Seat Angle (deg)	Face Angle (deg)	Spring Test Pressure (lbs. @ in.)	Spring Installed Height (in.)	Stem to Guide Clearance (in.) Intake	Exhaust	Stem Diameter (in.) Intake	Exhaust
1.6L	46	45	—	—	.0015–.0027	.0022–.0035	.3137–.3143	.3129–.3136
1.7L	45	①	②	③	.020 ④ max	.027 ④ max	.3140	.3140
2.2L (1981–82)	45	45.5	⑤	1.65	.001–.003	.002–.004	.312–.313	.311–.312
2.2L (1983–89)	45	45	⑤	1.65	.0009–.0026	.0030–.0047	.3124	.3103

① Intake: 45° 33′ Exhaust: 43° 33′
② Outer: 101 @ .878 Inner: 49 @ .720
③ Outer: 1.28 Inner: 1.13
④ Measurement is made with the valve in the cylinder head positioned .400 in. above the cylinder head gasket surface.
⑤ Standard: 150 lbs. @ 122. Turbo: 175 @ 1.22

Crankshaft and Connecting Rod Specifications

Engine	Crankshaft				Connecting Rod		
	Main Bearing Journal Dia.	Main Bearing Oil Clearance	Shaft End Play	Thrust on No.	Journal Dia.	Oil Clearance	Side Clearance
1.6L	2.046–2.047	.0009–.0031	.003–.011	3	1.612–1.613	.0010–.0025	.006–.009
1.7L	2.124–2.128	.0008–.0030	.003–.007	3	1.809–1.813	.0011–.0034	.015
2.2L	2.362–2.363	.0003–.0031	.002–.007	3	1.968–1.969	.0008–.0034 ①	.005–.013

① Turbocharged: .0008–.0031

Piston and Ring Specifications

Engine	Year	Ring Gap			Ring Side Clearance			Piston Clearance
		Top Compr.	Bottom Compr.	Oil Control	Top Compr.	Bottom Compr.	Oil Control	
1.6L	'84	.012–.018	.012–.018	.010–.016	.0018–.0028	.0018–.0028	.008 max	.0016–.0020
1.7L	'78–'79	.012–.018	.012–.018	.010–.016	.0008–.0020	.0008–.0020	.0008–.0020	.0011–.0270
	'80	.012–.018	.012–.018	.016–.045	.0016–.0028	.0008–.0020	.0008–.0020	.0004–.0015
	'81–'83	.012–.018	.012–.018	.016–.055	.0016–.0028	.0008–.0020	.008 max	.0004–.0015
2.2L	'81–'83	.011–.021	.011–.021	.015–.055	.0015–.0031	.0015–.0037	.008 max	.0005–.0015
2.2L	'84–'89	.010–.020	.009–.019	.015–.055	.0015–.0031	.0015–.0037	.008 max	.0015–.0025

Torque Specifications
(ft. lbs.)

Engine	Cyl. Head	Conn. Rod	Main Bearing	Crankshaft Bolt	Flywheel	Camshaft Cap Bolts	Camshaft Sprocket Bolts
1.6L	52	28	48	110	—	—	—
1.7L	60 ①	35 ③	47	58	55 ②	14	58
2.2L	45 ①	40 ①	30 ①	50	65	14	65

① Thru 1986; 4 step sequence: 30, 45, 45 plus ¼ turn more
  1987–89: 4 step sequence: 45, 65, 65 plus ½ turn more
② 50 ft. lbs. with auto. trans.
③ 1978 33 ft. lbs.
④ 1986–89 all transaxles: 70 ft. lbs.

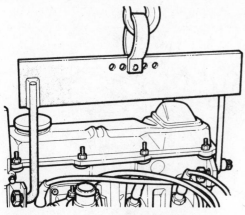

Attach a lifting sling to the engine

house) or the insulator bracket to transmission screws.

23. Lift the engine out of the vehicle.

INSTALLATION

1. Carefully lower the engine into place and loosely install all the mounting bolts. When all the mounting bolts have been hand tightened, then torque each to 40 ft. lbs.

2. Install the transaxle case to the engine and torque the mounting bolts to 70 ft. lbs.

3. Remove the engine sling and the transaxle holding fixture.

4. Install the ground strap.

5. Install the right inner splash shield.

6. Install the starter.

7. Connect the exhaust pipe to the manifold.

8. On manual transaxle models, install the lower case cover and connect the clutch cable.

9. On automatic transaxle models, remove the "C" clamp from the torque converter housing. Align the flex plate to the torque converter, install the mounting screws and tighten to 40 ft. lbs.

10. Reinstall the power steering pump and alternator.

11. Connect the fuel line, heater hose and the accelerator cable.

12. Connect all wiring.

moved, mark the insulator position on the side rail to insure an exact reinstallation.

18. Remove the transaxle case to engine mounting screws.

19. Disconnect the clutch cable.

20. Remove the screw and nut from the front engine mount.

21. Remove the manual transaxle anti-roll strut.

22. Remove the left engine mount insulator through bolt (from the inside of the wheel-

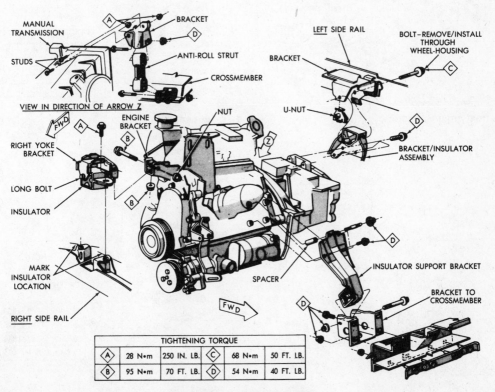

TIGHTENING TORQUE					
A	28 N•m	250 IN. LB.	C	68 N•m	50 FT. LB.
B	95 N•m	70 FT. LB.	D	54 N•m	40 FT. LB.

1.6L engine mounting brackets

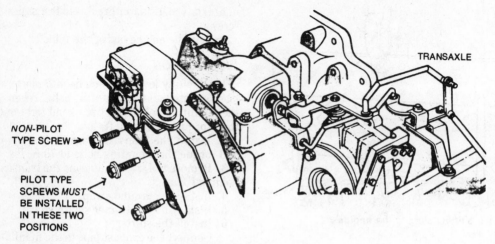

NON-PILOT
TYPE SCREW →

PILOT TYPE
SCREWS *MUST*
BE INSTALLED
IN THESE TWO
POSITIONS

TRANSAXLE

Left front engine mount—1.7L

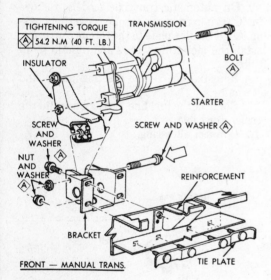

TIGHTENING TORQUE	
Ⓐ	54.2 N.M (40 FT. LB.)

INSULATOR
TRANSMISSION
BOLT Ⓐ
STARTER
SCREW AND WASHER Ⓐ
SCREW
AND
WASHER
NUT
AND
WASHER Ⓐ
Ⓐ
REINFORCEMENT
BRACKET
TIE PLATE
FRONT — MANUAL TRANS.

1.7L front engine mount

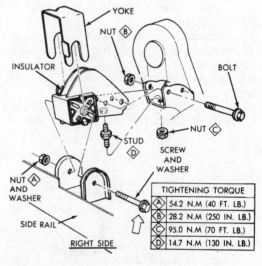

YOKE
NUT Ⓑ
BOLT
INSULATOR
NUT Ⓒ
STUD Ⓓ
SCREW
AND
WASHER
NUT
AND
WASHER
SIDE RAIL
RIGHT SIDE

TIGHTENING TORQUE	
Ⓐ	54.2 N.M (40 FT. LB.)
Ⓑ	28.2 N.M (250 IN. LB.)
Ⓒ	95.0 N.M (70 FT. LB.)
Ⓓ	14.7 N.M (130 IN. LB.)

1.7L right engine mount

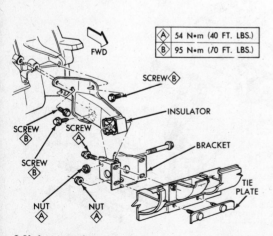

FWD

Ⓐ	54 N•m (40 FT. LBS.)
Ⓑ	95 N•m (70 FT. LBS.)

SCREW Ⓑ
INSULATOR
SCREW Ⓑ SCREW Ⓐ
SCREW
Ⓑ
BRACKET
TIE PLATE
NUT Ⓐ   NUT Ⓐ

2.2L front engine mount

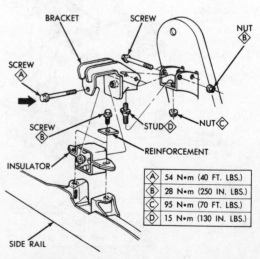

BRACKET
SCREW
NUT Ⓑ
SCREW Ⓐ
SCREW Ⓑ
STUD Ⓓ
NUT Ⓒ
REINFORCEMENT
INSULATOR
SIDE RAIL

Ⓐ	54 N•m (40 FT. LBS.)
Ⓑ	28 N•m (250 IN. LBS.)
Ⓒ	95 N•m (70 FT. LBS.)
Ⓓ	15 N•m (130 IN. LBS.)

2.2L right engine mount

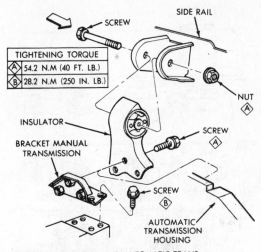

1.7L left engine mount

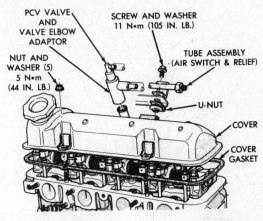

1.6L engine valve cover

13. Install the oil filter and refill the engine crankcase with the proper oil to the correct level.

14. If equipped with air conditioning, reinstall the A/C compressor.

15. Reinstall the air cleaner and hoses.

16. Install the radiator and hoses.

17. Fill the cooling system.

18. Install the hood.

19. Connect the battery.

20. Start the engine and run it to normal operating temperature.

21. Adjust the transmission linkage if necessary.

Rocker Arm/Camshaft Cover
REMOVAL AND INSTALLATION
1978-86 Models
1.6L ENGINE

1. Separate the crankcase ventilator hose from the valve cover.

2. Disconnect the diverter hose from the bracket.

3. Remove the six screws that retain the cover to the cylinder head and remove the cover.

4. To install, clean the cylinder head cover thoroughly, ensure that the cover rails are straight and then, install a new gasket.

5. Replace the six screws and tighten to 44 in. lbs.

6. Connect the diverter hose to the bracket and the crankcase ventilator hose to the valve cover.

1.7L ENGINE

1. Separate the crankcase ventilator hose from the valve cover.

2. Remove the eight screws that retain the cover to the cylinder head and remove the cover.

3. To install, clean the cylinder head cover thoroughly, ensure that the cover rails are straight, and then, install a new gasket.

4. Replace the eight screws and tighten to 48 in. lbs.

5. Connect the crankcase ventilator hose to the valve cover.

2.2L ENGINE

1. Separate the crankcase ventilator hose from the PCV module.

2. Depress the retaining clip on the PCV module, turn the module counterclockwise and remove it from the cylinder head cover taking care not to damage the module of the cylinder head cover during the removal.

3. Remove the ten screws that retain the cover to the cylinder head and remove the cover.

4. To install, clean the cylinder head cover and its mating surface on the cylinder head thoroughly.

5. Depress the retaining clip on the PCV module, turn the module clockwise and install the PCV module into the cylinder head cover,

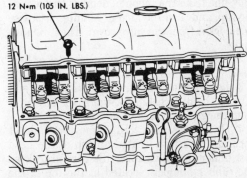

Camshaft cover—1981–86 with 2.2L engine

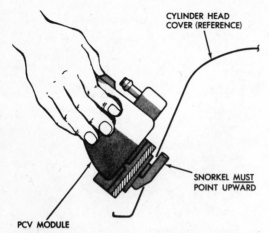

PCV module removal and installation—1981–86 with 2.2L engine

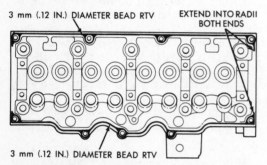

RTV application for camshaft cover—1981–87 with 2.2L engine

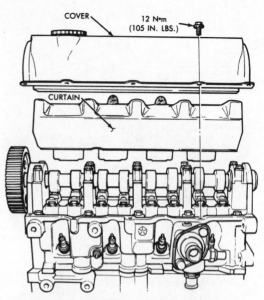

Cylinder head cover and curtain-TBI engines

check to see that the snorkle is positioned so that the open end is facing up. The snorkle should not be free to rotate.

6. Apply RTV gasket sealer in a continuous bead approximately ⅛″ in diameter as shown in the illustration.

7. Install the ten screws that retain the cover to the cylinder head and tighten to 105 in. lbs.

8. Connect the crankcase ventilator hose to the PCV module.

1987-89 Models

1. On carbureted engines, disconnect the PCV line from the module, depress the retaining clip, and turn the module counterclockwise to unlock it from the valve cover. Then, remove it.

2. Remove/disconnect any other lines or hoses that run across the cam cover.

3. Loosen the 10 cover installation bolts and remove them. Gently rock the cover to free it from the gasket or sealer and remove it.

4. On models with TBI, remove the air/oil separating curtain located on top of the head just under the valve cover. Be careful to keep the rubber bumpers located at the top of the curtain in place.

5. On 1987 covers, replace the two end seals, forcing the locating tabs into the matching holes in the cover.

6. To install, first, if the engine has the air/oil separating curtain, install it as described below (otherwise, proceed to the next step):

a. Position the curtain manifold side first with the upper surface contacting the cylinder head and the cutouts over the cam towers. The cutouts must face the manifold.

b. Press the distributor side of the curtain into position below the cylinder head rail.

c. Make sure both rubber bumpers are in place at the top.

7. On 1987 engines, form a gasket on the sealing surface of the head. It is necessary to use an RTV silicone aerobic gasket material (Chrysler Part No. 4318025 or equivalent).

8. On 1988-89 engines, install the gasket onto the cam cover (on normally aspirated engines with Throttle Body Injection, fasten the gasket in place by forcing the tabs through the holes in the cover).

9. On 1987 engines, install the reinforcements over both sides. Install the mounting bolts and torque them alternately and evenly to 105 in. lbs.

Rocker Arm Shaft

REMOVAL AND INSTALLATION

1.6L Engine

NOTE: *Allow the cylinder head to cool before performing this procedure.*

1. Remove the cylinder head cover as previously described in "Rocker Arm/Camshaft Cover" in this chapter.

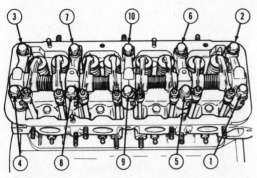

Remove the Rocker Arm/Cylinder Head bolts in numerical order.

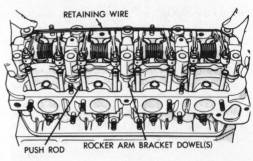

Install the push rods on the rocker arms and position the assembly in place.

Tie the rocker arm brackets together and then remove the entire assembly

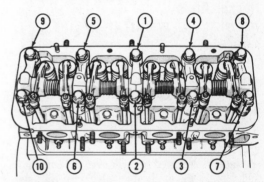

Head/Rocker Arm Assembly bolt tightening sequence

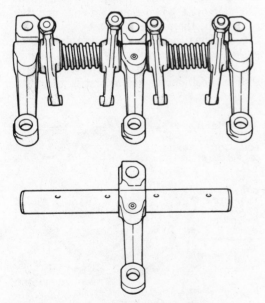

Rocker arm shaft assembly—1.6L engine

2. Loosen the cylinder head bolts evenly, beginning at the ends and working towards the center.

3. Tie the rocker arm assembly together with safety wire or equivalent.

4. Remove the bolts and lift the rocker arm assembly off the cylinder head.

NOTE: *Before disassembly of the rocker arm assemblies, mark the component positions so they be installed in their original order.*

5. To disassemble, remove the retaining wire from the assembly. Slide the rocker shaft end brackets, rockers, and springs from the rocker shafts.

6. Check the fit of the rockers on the shafts, also check to see that the oil holes in the shafts are clear. Replace any worn components. If replacing the rocker shafts, the roll pin that secures it to the center bracket (no. 2 or no. 4) must be driven out.

7. To assemble, position the closed end of each rocker shaft so that they are at the outer ends of the assembly. Insert the rocker shaft into its center bracket (no. 2 or no. 4) with the flat on the shaft aligned with the hole in the bracket, and the plugged end right or left as required. Drive the rollpins back into the brackets.

8. Lubricate the components and assemblies with engine oil.

9. Tie the end brackets with wire to retain them as one assembly.

10. Position each rocker arm assembly on its dowel.

11. Lubricate the head bolt threads with engine oil and install through the rocker shaft brackets. Screw the bolts down finger tight

while checking to see that each rocker adjusting screw engages its push rod. Remove the retaining wire.

12. Tighten the head bolts in progressive steps as shown in the illustration to 52 ft. lbs.

13. Start and run the engine to normal operating temperature, allow to cool down and retighten as described in step 12. Check valve clearance and adjust as necessary.

14. Replace the cylinder head cover as previously described in "Rocker Arm/Camshaft Cover" in this chapter.

Rocker Arms
REMOVAL AND INSTALLATION
2.2L Engines

The rocker arms may be removed very easily after camshaft removal. In case they are to be removed as a group for inspection or to proceed further with disassembly, mark each as to location for installation in the same position.

If the rockers are to be removed in order to gain access to a valve or lifter, you will need a special tool designed to hook over the camshaft and depress the applicable valve. Use Chrysler Tool No. 4682 or an equivalent tool purchased in the aftermarket. To remove a rocker:

1. Mark the rocker as to its location, unless you expect to remove only one, or one at a time.

2. Turn the engine over, using a wrench on the crankshaft pulley, until the cam that actuates the rocker you want to remove it pointing straight up.

3. Install the tool so that the jaws on its fulcrum fit on either side of the valve cap. Then, clip the hook at its forward end over the adjacent thin section of the camshaft (a part not incorporating either a cam or a bearing journal).

4. Lift the rocker gently at the lash adjuster end (the end opposite the tool). Pull downward gently on the outer end of the tool lever just un-

til the rocker can be disengaged from the lifter. Pull it out from between the valve and camshaft.

5. Install the new rocker or reinstall the old one in reverse. That is, depress the valve just far enough to slide the lever in between the top of the valve stem and the camshaft and still clear the lifter. When the rocker is located on the valve stem and lifter, gradually release the tension on the tool.

6. Repeat the procedure until all the necessary rockers have been replaced.

Thermostat
REMOVAL AND INSTALLATION

1. Drain the cooling system to a level below the thermostat.

CAUTION: *When draining the coolant, keep in mind that cats and dogs are attracted by the ethylene glycol antifreeze, and are quite likely to drink any that is left in an uncovered container or in puddles on the ground. This will prove fatal in sufficient quantity. Always drain the coolant into a sealable container. Coolant should be reused unless it is contaminated or several years old.*

2. Remove the hose clamp and then disconnect the hose from the thermostat housing.

3. Remove the two mounting bolts and then remove the thermostat housing.

4. Remove the thermostat and discard the gasket. Clean both gasket surfaces thoroughly.

5. Dip the new gasket in water and then install it. Position the thermostat in the water

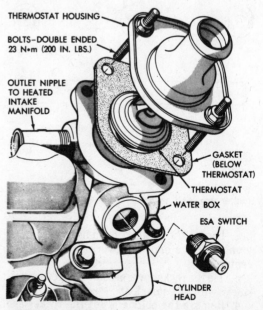

1.6L engine thermostat and water box

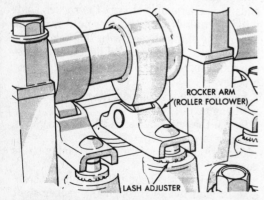

Rocker arm and lash adjuster

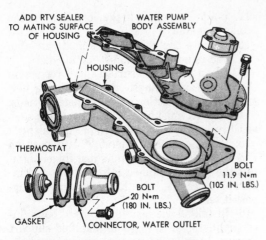

2.2L engine thermostat and water pump

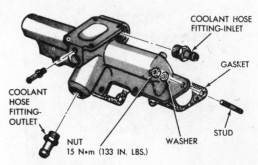

Intake manifold—1.6L engine

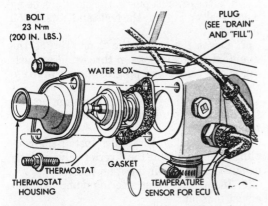

Thermostat housing and water box—2.2L engine

box, making sure it is properly seated by centering it in the water box, on top of the gasket. Install the housing and install the two bolts.

6. Reconnect the hose and install and tighten the hose clamp.

7. Refill the cooling system, start the engine, and check for leaks. After the engine has reached operating temperature, allow it to cool. Then, recheck coolant level in the radiator, refilling as necessary.

Intake Manifold

REMOVAL AND INSTALLATION

1.6L Engine

1. Disconnect the battery.

2. Remove the air cleaner and disconnect all vacuum lines, electrical connections and fuel line from the carburetor.

3. Drain the cooling system. Disconnect the inlet hose from the water box to the heated intake manifold and the outlet hose to the heater.

CAUTION: *When draining the coolant, keep in mind that cats and dogs are attracted by*

the ethylene glycol antifreeze, and are quite likely to drink any that is left in an uncovered container or in puddles on the ground. This will prove fatal in sufficient quantity. Always drain the coolant into a sealable container. Coolant should be reused unless it is contaminated or several years old.

4. Disconnect the EGR tube at the manifold.

5. Remove the eight mounting nuts and washers from the manifold and remove it from the engine.

6. Remove the carburetor from the manifold.

7. To install, clean all gasket surfaces, install new gaskets and torque the mounting nuts to 15 ft. lbs. The remaining procedures are reverse the removal.

1.7L Engine

1. Remove the air cleaner and hoses.

2. Remove all wiring and any hoses connected to the carburetor and manifold.

3. Disconnect the accelerator linkage.

4. Remove the intake-to-exhaust manifold bolts.

5. Remove the manifold-to-head bolts and lift out the intake manifold.

6. Clean all gasket surfaces and, using new gaskets, install the manifold.

7. Connect all hoses and wires, and install the air cleaner.

8. Connect the accelerator linkage.

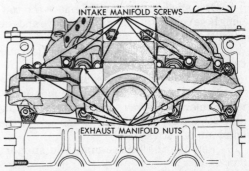

Intake and exhaust manifold mounting points—1.7L engine

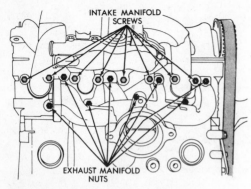

Intake and exhaust manifold mounting points—2.2L engine

Intake and Exhaust Manifold

2.2L Normally Aspirated Engines

NOTE: *These engines use a combined intake/exhaust manifold gasket. Therefore, the manifolds must always be removed and replaced together.*

1. Disconnect the negative battery cable. Drain the cooling system.

CAUTION: *When draining the coolant, keep in mind that cats and dogs are attracted by the ethylene glycol antifreeze, and are quite likely to drink any that is left in an uncovered container or in puddles on the ground. This will prove fatal in sufficient quantity. Always drain the coolant into a sealable container. Coolant should be reused unless it is contaminated or several years old.*

2. Remove the air cleaner and hoses.

3. If the engine is fuel injected, depressurize the fuel system, as described in Chapter 1. Remove all wiring and any hoses connected to the carburetor or injection throttle body and the manifold.

4. Disconnect the accelerator linkage.

5. Loosen the power steering pump mounting bolts and remove the belt. Disconnect the power brake vacuum hose at the manifold.

6. On Canadian cars only: Remove the coupling hose connecting the diverter valve and the exhaust manifold air injection tube.

7. Disconnect the water hose from the water crossover.

8. Raise the vehicle and support it securely. Disconnect the exhaust pipe at the manifold.

9. Remove the power steering pump, leaving lines connected, and hang it to one side so the hoses are not stressed.

10. Remove the intake manifold support bracket.

11. Remove the intake manifold-to-head bolts.

12. Lower the vehicle to the floor. Remove the intake manifold.

13. Remove the exhaust manifold retaining nuts and remove the exhaust manifold.

14. Clean all gasket surfaces and reposition the intake and exhaust manifolds using new gaskets. A composition gasket is installed as-is; a steel gasket must be coated with a sealer such as Chrysler Part No. 3419115 or equivalent.

15. Put the exhaust manifold into position and install the retaining nuts just finger-tight. Put the intake manifold into position and install all accessible bolts. Raise the car and support it securely.

16. Install all the manifold-to-head bolts finger-tight. Install the intake manifold support bracket. Install the power steering pump, bolting it into position with bolts just finger-tight. Connect the exhaust pipe at the manifold, using a new seal, and torque the bolts and nuts to 250 in. lbs.

17. Lower the car to the floor. Torque the manifold nuts and bolts in three stages, starting at the center and progressing outward, to the specified torque.

18. Connect the power brake vacuum hose to the manifold. Connect the water hose to the water crossover.

19. On Canadian cars only: Install the coupling hose connecting the diverter valve and the exhaust manifold air injection tube.

20. Install the power steering pump belt and adjust tension.

21. Connect the accelerator linkage. Install the air cleaner and hoses.

22. Install all wiring and any hoses disconnected from the carburetor or injection throttle body and the manifold. Refill the cooling system, reconnect the battery, start the engine and run it to check for leaks. Refill the cooling system after the engine has reached operating temperature (air has been bled out) and it has cooled off again.

Exhaust Manifold

REMOVAL AND INSTALLATION

1.6L Engine

1. Disconnect the battery.

2. Separate the carburetor air heater tube from the manifold stove.

3. Remove the oxygen sensor form the manifold.

4. Disconnect the air injection pipe from the manifold and separate the EGR assembly.

5. Raise the vehicle and support on jackstands, remove the exhaust pipe from the manifold.

6. Remove the exhaust manifold retaining nuts and remove the assembly.

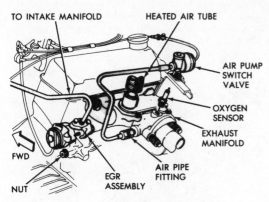

Exhaust manifold components—1.6L engine

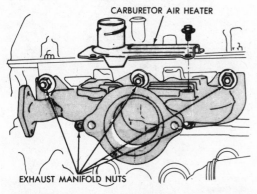

Exhaust manifold and carburetor heater—1.6L engine

7. Remove the carburetor air heater from the manifold.

8. To install, clean all gasket surfaces, install new gaskets and torque the mounting nuts to 15 ft. lbs. The remaining procedures are reverse the removal.

1.7L Engine

1. Follow the intake manifold removal procedures above.

2. Disconnect the exhaust pipe.

3. Unbolt and remove the exhaust manifold.

4. Clean the gasket surfaces, and using a new gasket, install the manifold.

Turbocharger

REMOVAL AND INSTALLATION

1. Disconnect the battery and drain coolant.
CAUTION: *When draining the coolant, keep in mind that cats and dogs are attracted by the ethylene glycol antifreeze, and are quite likely to drink any that is left in an uncovered container or in puddles on the ground. This will prove fatal in sufficient quantity. Always drain the coolant into a sealable container. Coolant should be reused unless it is contaminated or several years old.*

2. From under the car:

a. Disconnect the exhaust pipe at the articulated joint and disconnect the O_2 sensor electrical connections.

b. Remove the turbocharger-to-block support bracket.

c. Loosen the clamps for the oil drain-back tube and then move the tube downward onto the block fitting so it no longer connects with the turbocharger.

d. Disconnect the turbocharger coolant supply tube at the block outlet below the power steering pump bracket and at the tube support bracket.

3. Disconnect and remove the air cleaner complete with the throttle body adaptor, hose, and air cleaner box and support bracket.

4. Loosen the throttle body to turbocharger inlet hose clamps. Then, remove the three throttle body-to-intake manifold attaching screws and remove the throttle body.

5. Loosen the turbocharger discharge hose end clamps, leaving the center band in place to retain the de-swirler.

6. Pull the fuel rail out of the way after removing the hose retaining bracket screw, four bracket screws from the intake manifold, and two bracket-to-heat shield retaining clips. The rail, injectors, wiring harness, and fuel lines will be moved as an assembly.

7. Disconnect the oil feed line at the turbocharger bearing housing.

8. Remove the three screws attaching the heat shield to the intake manifold and remove the shield.

9. Disconnect the coolant return tube and hose assembly at the turbocharger and water box. Remove the tube support bracket from the cylinder head and remove the assembly.

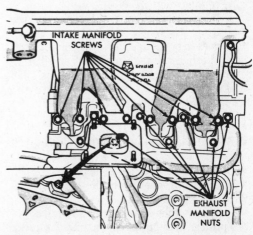

Intake and exhaust manifolds—turbocharged engines

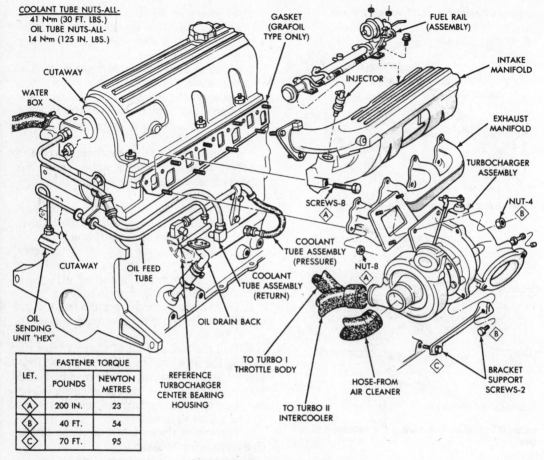

Turbocharged engine components

LET.	FASTENER TORQUE	
	POUNDS	NEWTON METRES
(A)	200 IN.	23
(B)	40 FT.	54
(C)	70 FT.	95

10. Remove the four nuts attaching the turbocharger to the exhaust manifold. Then, remove the turbocharger by lifting it off the exhaust manifold studs, tilting it downward toward the passenger side of the car, and then pulling it up and out of the car, and out of the engine compartment.

a. When repositioning the turbo on the mounting studs, make sure the discharge tube goes in position so it's properly connected to both the intake manifold and turbocharger. Apply an anti-seize compound such as Loctite® 771-64 or equivalent to the threads. Torque the nuts to 30 ft. lbs.

b. Observe the following torques:
- Oil feed line nuts: 125 in. lbs.
- Heat shield to intake manifold screws: 105 ft. lbs.
- Coolant tube nuts: 30 ft. lbs.
- Fuel rail bracket-to-intake manifold retaining screws: 250 in. lbs.
- Discharge tube hose clamp: 35 in. lbs.
- Throttle body-to-intake manifold screws: 250 in. lbs.
- Throttle body hose clamps: 35 in. lbs.
- Hose adapter-to-throttle body screws: 55 in. lbs.
- Air cleaner box support bracket screws: 40 ft. lbs.
- Coolant tube nut-to-block connector: 30 ft. lbs.

c. When installing the turbocharger-to-block support bracket, first install screws finger tight. Tighten the block screw first (to 40 ft. lbs.), and then tighten the screw going into the turbocharger housing (to 20 ft. lbs.). Tighten the articulated ball joint shoulder bolts to 250 in. lbs.

d. Make sure to fill the cooling system back up before starting the engine, recheck the level after the coolant begins circulating through the radiator, and check for leaks after you install the pressure cap. Check the turbocharger carefully for any oil leaks and correct if necessary.

Air Conditioner Compressor

WARNING: *If the compressor must be completely removed from the car for repairs, and the compressor refrigerant lines must be disconnected, refer to Chapter 1 for safe discharging procedures for the refrigerant. The system must be discharged before attempting to disconnect the lines. Also note that you will need caps or another positive method to tightly seal the refrigerant lines immediately after you open them.*

1. Disconnect the negative battery cable. Discharge the system as described in Chapter 1. Disconnect the clutch electrical connector.

2. Once the system has been discharged, unbolt the connections at the compressor and plug all four openings.

3. Loosen the A/C compressor belt idler pulley tensioning bracket mounting and pivot

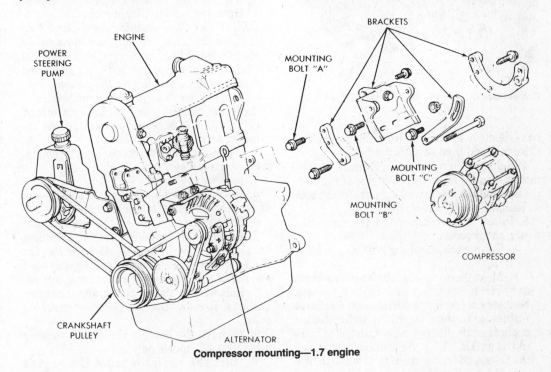

Compressor mounting—1.7 engine

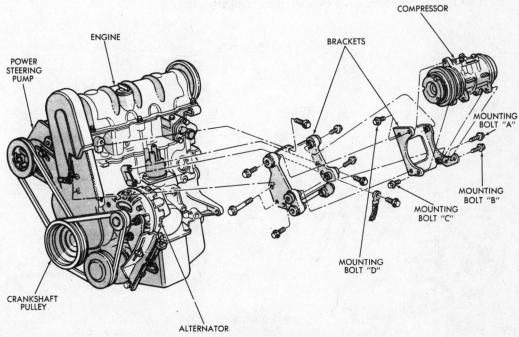

Compressor mounting—1981–86 with 2.2L engine

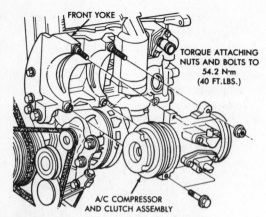

Compressor mounting—1987–89 with 2.2L engine

bolts. Remove the tension from the compressor drive belt and then remove the belt.

4. Support the compressor. Remove the two mounting bolts from the lower side of the compressor and the two mounting nuts from above it. Remove the compressor.

5. Install the compressor in reverse order, noting these points:

a. Torque the attaching nuts and bolts to 40 ft. lbs.

b. Make sure sealing surfaces are clean and free of scratches and replace gaskets. Gaskets are specific to suction and discharge fittings, so fit them according to the number of pilots on the fitting and/or number of holes in the gasket. Make the connections, install the bolts, and torque them to 170-230 in. lbs.

c. Have the system thoroughly evacuated

at a repair shop and then have it recharged, or recharge it according to the procedures given in Chapter 1.

Radiator

REMOVAL AND INSTALLATION

1. Move the temperature selector to full on.
2. Open the radiator drain cock.

CAUTION: *When draining the coolant, keep in mind that cats and dogs are attracted by the ethylene glycol antifreeze, and are quite likely to drink any that is left in an uncovered container or in puddles on the ground. This will prove fatal in sufficient quantity. Always drain the coolant into a sealable container. Coolant should be reused unless it is contaminated or several years old.*

3. When the coolant reserve tank is empty, remove the radiator cap.
4. Remove the hoses.
5. If equipped with automatic transmission, disconnect and plug the fluid cooler lines.
6. Disconnect the fan electrical connector.
7. Remove the fan shroud/motor attaching bolts. *Being careful not to damage the fan blades,* remove the shroud by pulling it upward and out of the attachment clips at the bottom.
8. Remove the upper and lower mounting brackets. Remove the top radiator attaching bolts.
9. Remove the bottom radiator attaching bolts 1981-85 models only).
10. Lift the radiator from the engine compartment.

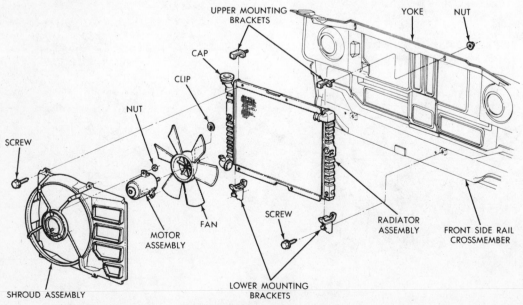

Radiator, fan and shroud—typical

11. Installation is the reverse of removal. On 1987-89 models without rubber grommets at the top, preload the upper mounting brackets with 10 lbs. force downward. Tighten all mounting bolts to 105 in. lbs. Make sure the hoses are fully installed onto the fittings and that clamps are properly tightened. Refill the cooling system with 50/50 water/antifreeze mix by filling the radiator to the top and the overflow tank to the fill line. If there is no overflow tank, recheck the coolant level after the system has reached operating temperature and has then cooled.

Air Conditioning Condenser

REMOVAL AND INSTALLATION

CAUTION: *The air conditioning system in filled with refrigerant under high pressure. The refrigerant must be discharged before you can safely work on any of the components.*

1. Have the air conditioning system discharged by a professional or discharge it yourself as described in Chapter 1. Remove the radiator as described above.

2. Remove the refrigerant line attaching nut and separate the lines at the condenser sealing plate. Immediately cap the ends with a plastic cap designed for this purpose or with plastic sheeting and tape.

3. Remove the two mounting bolts located near the top of the condenser. These attach the condenser to the radiator core support.

4. Lift the condenser out of the engine compartment, being careful not to damage fins or piping.

5. Install the condenser in reverse order. Replace all gaskets and O-rings. O-rings must be coated with refrigerant oil drawn from an unopened container prior to installation.

6. If the condenser used is a new one, make sure to have oil added to the system to replace that which was removed with the old compressor. This requires specialized service knowledge. A 500 SUS viscosity, wax-free oil must be used. The compressor holds 198-212 grams.

Water Pump

REMOVAL AND INSTALLATION

1.6L Engine

1. Remove the radiator cap and drain the cooling system.
CAUTION: *When draining the coolant, keep in mind that cats and dogs are attracted by the ethylene glycol antifreeze, and are quite likely to drink any that is left in an uncovered container or in puddles on the ground. This will prove fatal in sufficient quantity. Always drain the coolant into a sealable container.*

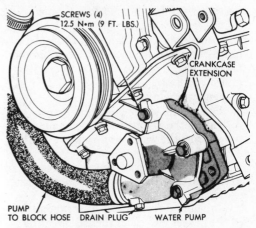

1.6L engine water pump

Coolant should be reused unless it is contaminated or several years old.
2. Remove the drive belts.
3. Disconnect the water pump to block coolant hose at the pump.
4. Remove the water pump pulley.
5. Remove the four water pump to crankcase extension bolts and remove the water pump assembly.
6. Installation is the reverse of removal. Be sure to use a new gasket.

1.7L Engine

1. Drain the cooling system.
CAUTION: *When draining the coolant, keep in mind that cats and dogs are attracted by the ethylene glycol antifreeze, and are quite*

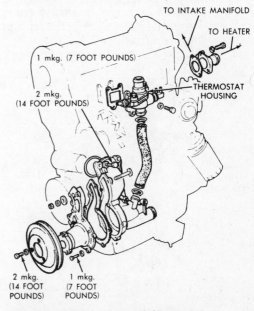

1.7L engine water pump and thermostat

likely to drink any that is left in an uncovered container or in puddles on the ground. This will prove fatal in sufficient quantity. Always drain the coolant into a sealable container. Coolant should be reused unless it is contaminated or several years old.

2. Remove the drive belts.

3. Remove the water pump pulley.

4. Unbolt the compressor and/or air pump brackets from the water pump and secure them out of the way.

5. Position the bypass hose lower clamp in the center of the hose and disconnect the heater hose.

6. Unbolt and remove the water pump. Discard the gasket and clean the gasket surfaces.

7. Installation is the reverse of removal. Torque the water pump bolts to 25 ft. lbs., the alternator adjusting bolt to 30-50 ft. lbs.; the pulley bolts to 85-125 in. lbs.

2.2L Engine

1. Disconnect the battery negative cable. Drain the cooling system.

CAUTION: *When draining the coolant, keep in mind that cats and dogs are attracted by the ethylene glycol antifreeze, and are quite likely to drink any that is left in an uncovered container or in puddles on the ground. This will prove fatal in sufficient quantity. Always drain the coolant into a sealable container. Coolant should be reused unless it is contaminated or several years old.*

2. Remove the upper radiator hose.

3. Remove the alternator.

WARNING: *Do not disconnect the air conditioner compressor lines in the next step. The compressor can be moved far enough out of the way to remove the water pump without disturbing the refrigerant filled lines.*

4. Unbolt the air conditioning compressor

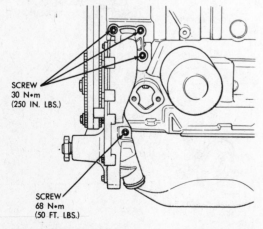

2.2L engine water pump

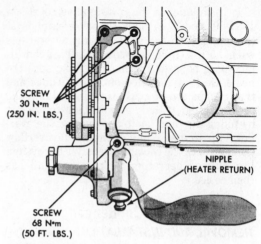

Water pump—2.2L engine

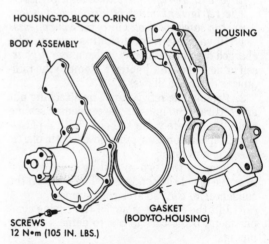

Water pump components—2.2L engine

brackets from the water pump and secure the compressor out of the way. Support the compressor so it will not put stress on the lines.

5. Disconnect the bypass hose, heater return hose, and lower radiator hose.

6. Unbolt and remove the water pump assembly. Disassemble the pump as follows:

   a. Remove the three bolts fastening the drive pulley to the water pump.

   b. Remove the 9 bolts fastening the water pump body to the housing. Then, use a chisel to gently break the bond between the pump and housing.

   c. Clean the gasket surfaces on the pump body and housing. Remove the O-ring gasket and discard it. Clean the O-ring groove.

   d. Apply RTV sealer to the sealing surface of the water pump body. The bead should be ⅛" in diameter and should encircle all bolt holes. Assemble the pump body to the housing, install the 9 bolts, and torque them to

105 in. lbs. Make sure the gasketing material has set (as per package instructions) before actually filling the system.

e. Position a new O-ring in the O-ring groove. Then, put the pulley on the pump, install the 3 attaching bolts, and torque them to 105 in. lbs.

7. Installation is the reverse of removal. Torque the top 3 water pump bolts to 250 in. lbs. and the lower bolt to 50 ft. lbs. Make sure to refill the system with 50/50 antifreeze/water mix.

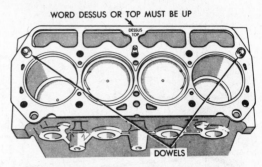
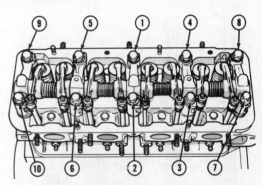

Cylinder head gasket mounting—1.6L engines

Cylinder head bolt tightening sequence—1.6L engine

Cylinder Head

REMOVAL AND INSTALLATION

1.6L Engine

WARNING: *The cylinder head must be cool before removing to avoid distortion.*

1. Disconnect the battery.
2. Drain the cooling system.

CAUTION: *When draining the coolant, keep in mind that cats and dogs are attracted by the ethylene glycol antifreeze, and are quite likely to drink any that is left in an uncovered container or in puddles on the ground. This will prove fatal in sufficient quantity. Always drain the coolant into a sealable container. Coolant should be reused unless it is contaminated or several years old.*

3. Remove the air cleaner assembly.
4. Disconnect all lines, hoses and wires from the head, manifold and carburetor.
5. Disconnect the accelerator linkage.
6. Remove the intake and exhaust manifolds.
7. If equipped with air conditioning, remove the compressor from the mounting brackets and support it out of the way. DO NOT remove the hoses from the compressor.
8. Remove the cylinder head cover as previously described in "Rocker Arm/Camshaft Cover" in this chapter.
9. Loosen the cylinder head bolts evenly, beginning at the ends and working towards the center.

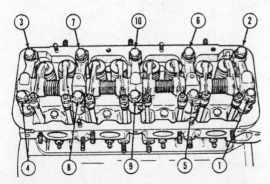

Cylinder head bolt removal sequence—1.6L engine

10. Tie the rocker arm assembly together with safety wire or equivalent.
11. Remove the bolts and lift the rocker arm assembly off the cylinder head.
12. Label all the push rods so they be reinstalled in their original locations and remove them from the cylinder head.
13. Lift off the cylinder head and discard the gasket.
14. Before installation, make certain the gasket surfaces are thoroughly cleaned and are free of nicks or scratches.

NOTE: *Always use a new head gasket and make certain the word "Dessus" or Top faces up when the gasket is laid on the engine block.*

15. Lubricate the head bolt threads with engine oil and install through the rocker shaft brackets.
16. Screw the bolts down finger tight while checking to see that each rocker adjusting screw engages its push rod.
17. Tighten the head bolts in progressive steps as shown in the illustration to 52 ft. lbs. Start and run the engine to normal operating temperature, allow to cool down and retorque as described above.
18. Check valve clearance and adjust as necessary.
19. Install the air conditioning compressor.

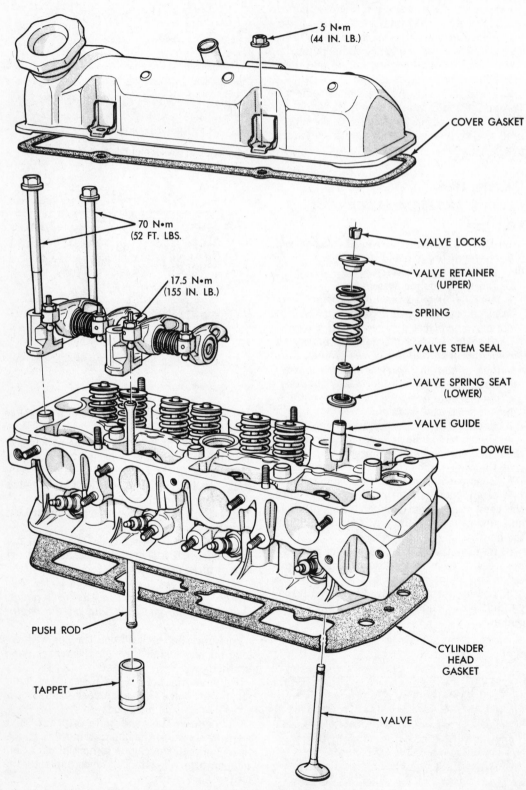

5 N•m
(44 IN. LB.)

COVER GASKET

70 N•m
(52 FT. LBS.)

17.5 N•m
(155 IN. LB.)

VALVE LOCKS

VALVE RETAINER
(UPPER)

SPRING

VALVE STEM SEAL

VALVE SPRING SEAT
(LOWER)

VALVE GUIDE

DOWEL

PUSH ROD

CYLINDER
HEAD
GASKET

TAPPET

VALVE

Cylinder head and valve assembly—1.6L engine

20. Install the intake and exhaust manifolds.
21. Connect the accelerator linkage.
22. Connect all lines, hoses and wires to the head, manifold and carburetor.
23. Install the air cleaner assembly.
24. Fill the cooling system.
25. Connect the battery.

1.7L Engines

The engine should be cold before the cylinder head is removed. The head is retained by 10 socket head bolts.

1. Disconnect the battery.
2. Drain the cooling system.

CAUTION: *When draining the coolant, keep in mind that cats and dogs are attracted by the ethylene glycol antifreeze, and are quite likely to drink any that is left in an uncovered container or in puddles on the ground. This will prove fatal in sufficient quantity. Always drain the coolant into a sealable container. Coolant should be reused unless it is contaminated or several years old.*

3. Remove the air cleaner assembly.
4. Disconnect all lines, hoses and wires from the head, manifold and carburetor.
5. Disconnect the accelerator linkage.
6. Remove the distributor cap.
7. Disconnect the exhaust pipe.
8. Remove the carburetor.
9. Remove the intake and exhaust manifolds.
10. Remove the upper portion of the front cover.
11. Turn the engine by hand until all gear timing marks are aligned.
12. Loosen the drive belt tensioner and slip the belt off the camshaft gear.

NOTE: *The camshaft timing mark is on the back of the gear and is properly positioned when it is in line with the left corner of the camshaft cover at the head.*

13. If equipped with air conditioning, remove the compressor from the mounting brackets and support it out of the way with wires. Remove the mounting brackets from the head.
14. Remove the valve cover, gaskets and seals.
15. Remove head bolts in reverse order of the tightening sequence.
16. Lift off the head and discard the gasket.
17. Before installation, Make certain all gasket surfaces are thoroughly cleaned and are free of deep nicks or scratches.

NOTE: *Always use new gaskets and seals. The word "OBEN" (Top) faces up. Never reuse a gasket or seal, even if it looks good.*

18. When positioning the head on the block, insert bolts 8 and 10 (see illustration) to align the head.
19. Tighten bolts in the order shown in the illustration. Bolts should be tightened to 30 ft.

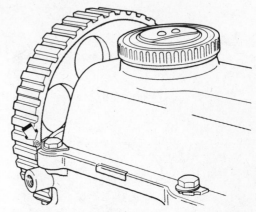

Aligning the 1.7L engine camshaft timing dot with the edge of the cylinder head

lbs. in rotation, then tightened to 60 ft. lbs. When all bolts are at 60 ft. lbs., tighten each ¼ turn more in sequence.

20. Install the valve cover, gaskets and seals.
21. Make sure all timing marks are aligned before installing the drive belt. The drive belt is correctly tensioned when it can be twisted 90° with the thumb and index finger midway between the camshaft and intermediate shaft.
22. If equipped with air conditioning, install the compressor.
23. Install the upper portion of the front cover.
24. Install the intake and exhaust manifolds.
25. Install the carburetor.
26. Connect the exhaust pipe.
27. Install the distributor cap.
28. Connect the accelerator linkage.
29. Connect all lines, hoses and wires to the head, manifold and carburetor.
30. Install the air cleaner assembly.
31. Fill the cooling system.
32. Connect the battery.

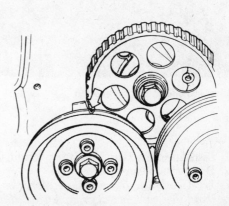

1.7L engine crankshaft-to-intermediate shaft timing mark alignment

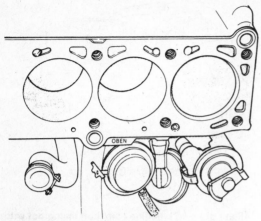

On the 1.7L engine, the head gasket is installed with the word OBEN facing up

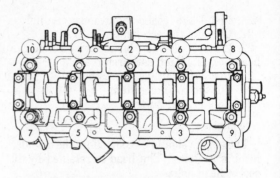

1.7L engine cylinder head torque sequence

1.7L engine timing belt installation

container or in puddles on the ground. This will prove fatal in sufficient quantity. Always drain the coolant into a sealable container. Coolant should be reused unless it is contaminated or several years old.

3. Remove the air cleaner assembly.

4. Disconnect all lines, hoses and wires from the head, manifold and carburetor.

5. Disconnect the accelerator linkage.

6. Remove the distributor cap.

7. Disconnect the exhaust pipe.

8. Remove the carburetor or throttle body.

NOTE: If equipped with fuel injection, release the fuel system pressure as outlined in Chapter 1.

9. Remove the intake and exhaust manifolds.

10. Remove the upper portion of the front cover.

11. Turn the engine by hand until all gear timing marks are aligned.

12. Loosen the drive belt tensioner and slip the belt off the camshaft gear.

13. If equipped with air conditioning, remove the compressor from the mounting brackets and support it out of the way with wires. Remove the mounting brackets from the head.

14. Remove the valve cover, gaskets and seals.

15. Remove head bolts in reverse order of tightening sequence.

16. Lift off the head and discard the gasket.

17. Before installation, make certain all gasket surfaces are thoroughly cleaned and are free of deep nicks or scratches. Always use new

2.2L Engine

1. Disconnect the negative battery terminal.

2. Drain the cooling system.

CAUTION: When draining the coolant, keep in mind that cats and dogs are attracted by the ethylene glycol antifreeze, and are quite likely to drink any that is left in an uncovered

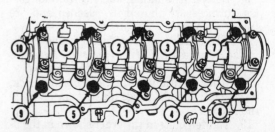

2.2L cylinder head bolt tightening sequence

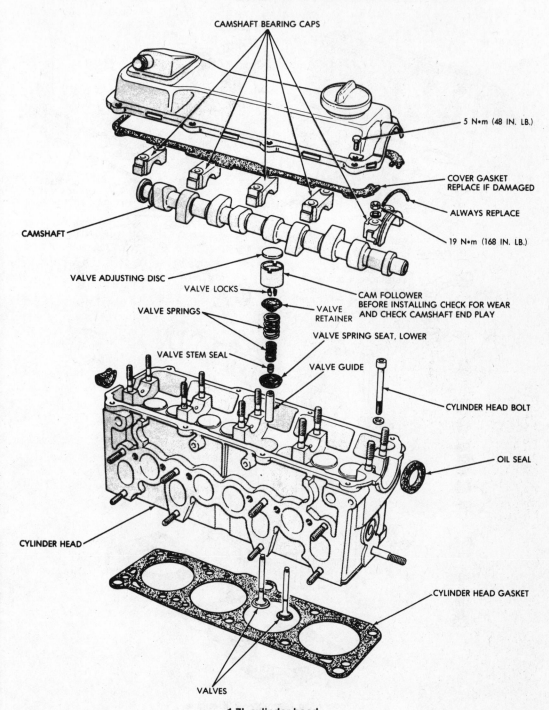

CAMSHAFT BEARING CAPS

5 N•m (48 IN. LB.)

COVER GASKET
REPLACE IF DAMAGED

ALWAYS REPLACE

19 N•m (168 IN. LB.)

CAMSHAFT

VALVE ADJUSTING DISC

VALVE LOCKS

CAM FOLLOWER
BEFORE INSTALLING CHECK FOR WEAR
AND CHECK CAMSHAFT END PLAY

VALVE SPRINGS

VALVE
RETAINER

VALVE SPRING SEAT, LOWER

VALVE STEM SEAL

VALVE GUIDE

CYLINDER HEAD BOLT

OIL SEAL

CYLINDER HEAD

CYLINDER HEAD GASKET

VALVES

1.7L cylinder head

gaskets and seals. Never reuse a gasket or seal, even if it looks good.

18. When positioning the head on the block, insert bolts 8 and 10 (see illustration) to align the head. Tighten bolts in the order shown to specifications.

19. On models through 1986 tighten to 45 ft. lbs. plus ¼ turn. On 1987-89 models tighten in a four step sequence. 1st step tighten all to 45 ft. lbs., 2nd step all to 65 ft. lbs., 3rd step all to 65 ft. lbs again and 4th step ¼ turn more.

20. Make sure all timing marks are aligned before installing the drive belt. The drive belt is correctly tensioned when it can be twisted 90° with the thumb and index finger midway between the camshaft and the intermediate shaft.

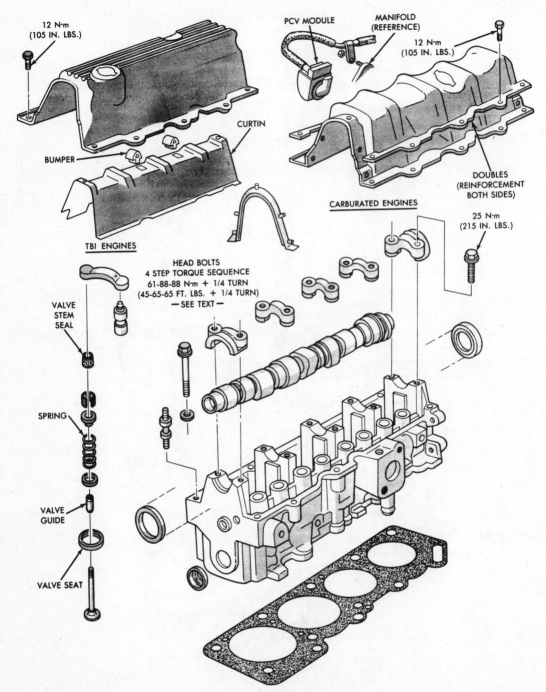

12 N·m
(105 IN. LBS.)

PCV MODULE

MANIFOLD
(REFERENCE)

12 N·m
(105 IN. LBS.)

CURTIN

BUMPER

DOUBLES
(REINFORCEMENT
BOTH SIDES)

TBI ENGINES

CARBURATED ENGINES

25 N·m
(215 IN. LBS.)

HEAD BOLTS
4 STEP TORQUE SEQUENCE
61-88-88 N·m + 1/4 TURN
(45-65-65 FT. LBS. + 1/4 TURN)
— SEE TEXT —

VALVE
STEM
SEAL

SPRING

VALVE
GUIDE

VALVE SEAT

Cylinder head assembly—2.2L engine

21. If equipped with air conditioning, install the compressor.

22. Install the upper portion of the front cover.

23. Install the intake and exhaust manifolds.

24. Install the carburetor or throttle body.

25. Connect the exhaust pipe.

26. Install the distributor cap.

27. Connect the accelerator linkage.

28. Connect all lines, hoses and wires to the head, manifold and carburetor.

29. Install the air cleaner assembly.

30. Fill the cooling system.

31. Connect the battery.

CLEANING AND INSPECTION

NOTE: *With the cylinder head removed from the engine, the rocker arm assemblies and*

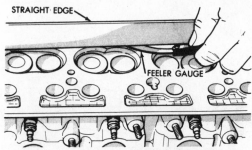

Checking the cylinder head flatness—typical

camshaft removed, the valves, valve springs and valve stem oil seals can now be serviced.

Since the machining of valve seats and valves, and the insertion of new valve guides or valve seats may tax the experience and equipment resources of the car owner, it is suggested that the cylinder head be taken to an automotive machine shop for rebuilding.

1. Remove the cylinder head from the car engine (see Cylinder Head Removal). Place the head on a workbench and remove any manifolds that are still connected. Remove all rocker arm assembly parts, if still installed and the camshaft (see Camshaft Removal).

2. Turn the cylinder head over so that the mounting surface is facing up and support evenly on wooden blocks.

3. Use a scraper and remove all of the gasket material and carbon stuck to the head mounting surface. Mount a wire carbon removal brush in an electric drill and clean away the carbon on the valve heads and head combustion chambers.

WARNING: *When scraping or decarbonizing the cylinder head, take care not to damage or nick the gasket mounting surface or combustion chamber.*

4. Number the valve heads with a permanent felt-tipped marker for cylinder location.

RESURFACING

If the cylinder head is warped resurfacing by an automotive machine shop, will be required. After cleaning the gasket surface, place a straightedge across the mounting surface of the head. Using feeler gauges, determine the clearance at the center and along the lengths of both diagonals. If warpage exceeds 0.08mm in a 152mm span, or 0.15mm over the total length, the cylinder head must be resurfaced.

Valves and Springs

VALVE ADJUSTMENT

NOTE: *For all valve adjustment procedures please refer to Chapter 2 under "Valve Adjustment."*

REMOVAL AND INSTALLATION

1.6L Engine

CYLINDER HEAD REMOVED

1. Follow the procedures under "Cylinder Head Removal" in this chapter and remove the head.

2. With the head removed from the engine block, compress the valve with a spring compressor tool.

3. Remove the valve retaining locks, spring retainer, spring, valve seals, and the spring seat.

4. Before removing the valves, remove any burrs from the valve stem lock grooves to prevent damage tot he valve guides. Mark all the valves so they may be installed in their original position.

5. To install, coat the valve stems with oil and insert in the cylinder head. Install the spring seat on each guide.

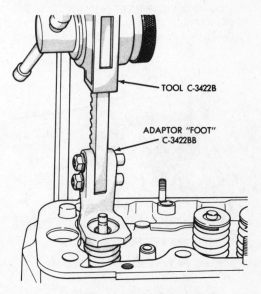

Removing the valve spring—1.6L engine

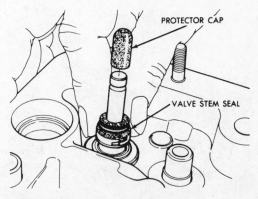

Installing valve stem seals—1.6L engine

6. Place a protective cap over the end of the valve, or wrap the lock grooves with tape to prevent the edges of the valve from damaging the oil seals.

7. Install the new valve stem seals on all of the valves. The seals should be pushed firmly and squarely over the valve guide and down until it bottoms out.

8. Install the valve springs and retainers. Compress the valve spring only enough to install the locks, being careful not to misalign the direction of compression.

9. The remaining procedures are reverse the removal.

1.7L Engine

CYLINDER HEAD NOT REMOVED

1. Remove the rocker arm cover.
2. Remove the camshaft as described later in this chapter.
3. Remove the spark plugs.
4. Turn the crankshaft until the piston of the cylinder being serviced is in the BDC, bottom dead center position.
5. With an airline adapter and an air hose in-

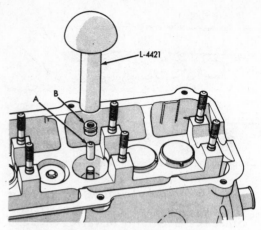

Installing valve stem seals—1.7L engine

stalled into the spark plug hole, apply 90-122 psi of air pressure.

6. Compress the valve spring with tool L-4419 or equivalent.

7. Remove the adjusting disc, valve keeper, spring retainer and valve spring.

8. Remove the seal by pulling side-to-side with a pair of long nose pliers or the C-4745 Seal Remover tool may be used.

9. Place a protective cap over the end of the valve, or wrap the lock grooves with tape to prevent the edges of the valve from damaging the oil seals.

10. Install the new valve stem seals on all of the valves. The seals should be pushed firmly and squarely over the valve guide with tool L-4421 or equivalent and down until it bottoms out.

11. The remainder of the installation is the reverse the removal procedures.

2.2L Engine

CYLINDER HEAD NOT REMOVED

1. Remove the rocker arm cover.
2. For each rocker arm, rotate the cam until the base circle is in contact with the rocker arm.
3. Depress the valve spring using tool 4682 or equivalent and slide the rocker arm out. Label all rocker arms so that they may be reassembled in their original order.
4. Remove the hydraulic lash adjusters.
5. Rotate the crankshaft so that the cylinder is at TDC with the intake and exhaust valves closed.
6. With an airline adapter and an air hose installed into the spark plug hole, apply 90-120 psi of air pressure.
7. Using tool 4682 or equivalent compress the valve spring and remove the valve locks.
8. Remove the valve spring.
9. Remove the seal by pulling side-to-side with a pair of long nose pliers.

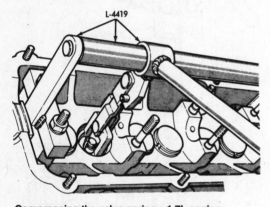

Compressing the valve spring—1.7L engine

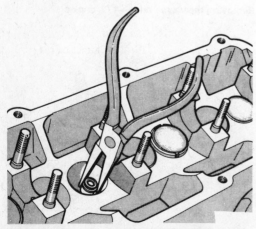

Removing the valve stem seal—1.7L engine

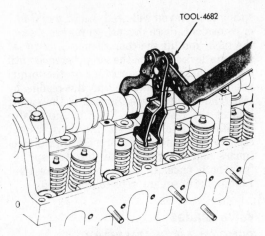

TOOL-4682

Removing the valve springs—2.2L engine

10. To install, install the spring seat on each guide.

11. Place a protective cap over the end of the valve, or wrap the lock grooves with tape to prevent the edges of the valve from damaging the oil seals.

12. Install the new valve stem seals on all of the valves. The seals should be pushed firmly and squarely over the valve guide and down until it bottoms out.

NOTE: *When using tool 4682 the valve locks can become dislocated. Check to be certain that both locks are in position after removing the tool.*

13. Install the valve springs and retainers. Compress the valve spring with tool 4682 or equivalent, only enough to install the locks being careful not to misalign the direction of compression.

14. Check the installed spring height of the springs. This measurement should be made from the lower edge of the spring to its upper edge, not including the spring seat.

15. Install the rocker arms and adjusters in their original locations. Check the clearance between the projecting ears of the rocker arm and the valve spring retainers. At least 0.5mm clearance must be present, if necessary, the rocker arm ears may have to be ground to obtain this clearance.

16. Check the dry lash. Dry lash is the amount of clearance that exists between the base circle of the installed camshaft and the rocker arm pad when the adjuster is completely collapsed. Dry lash should be 0.6-1.5mm. The adjusters must be drained to perform this check. Refill the adjusters before final assembly and allow 10 minutes for the adjusters to bleed down before rotating the cam.

17. Reinstall the rocker arm cover.

VALVE INSPECTION

1. Clean the valves thoroughly and discard burned, warped, or cracked valves.

2. If the valve face is only lightly pitted, the valve may be refaced to an angle of 45° by a qualified machine shop.

3. Measure the valve stem for wear at various points and check it against the specifications shown in the "Valve Specifications" chart.

VALVE REFACING

Using a valve grinder, resurface the valves according to the specifications given in the "Valve Specifications" chart.

NOTE: *The valve face angle is not always identical to the valve seat angle.*

A minimum margin of 0.8mm should remain after grinding the valve. The valve stem top should also be squared and resurfaced, by placing the stem in the V-block of the grinder, and turning it while pressing lightly against the grinding wheel.

CHECK SPRINGS

Whenever the valves have been removed for inspection, reconditioning or replacement, the valve springs should be tested. To test the

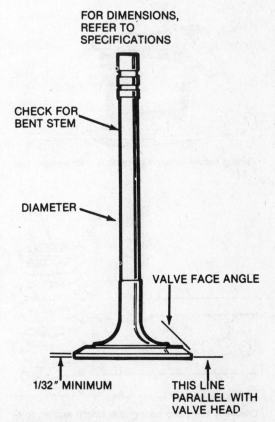

FOR DIMENSIONS, REFER TO SPECIFICATIONS

CHECK FOR BENT STEM

DIAMETER

VALVE FACE ANGLE

1/32" MINIMUM

THIS LINE PARALLEL WITH VALVE HEAD

Critical valve dimensions

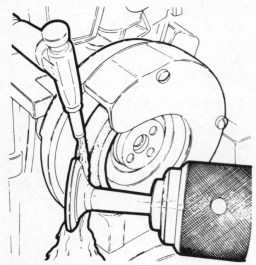

Valve grinding by machine

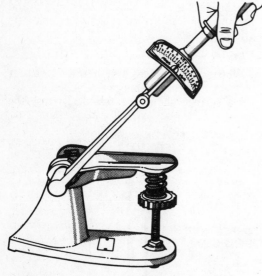

Testing the valve spring pressure with special tool C-647

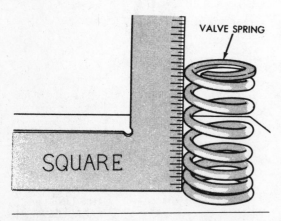

Checking the valve spring free height and squareness

spring tension you will need special tool C-647 or equivalent. Place the spring over the stud on the table and lift the compressing lever to set the tone device. Pull on the torque wrench until a ping is heard. Take a reading on the torque wrench at this instant. Multiply this reading by two. The resulting specification is the spring load at the test length. Refer to the "Valve Specifications" chart for specifications. Inspect each valve spring for squareness with a steel square and a surface plate, test the springs from both ends. If the spring is more than 1.5mm out of square, replace the spring.

Valve Guides

REMOVAL AND INSTALLATION

Valve guides are replaceable, but they should not be replaced in a cylinder head in which the valve seats cannot be refaced.

Worn guides should be pressed out from the

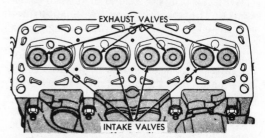

Valve identification

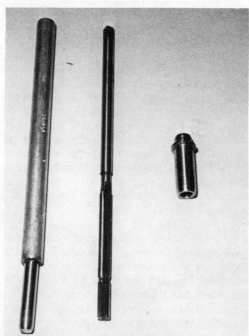

Valve guide tools

combustion chamber side and new guides pressed in as far as they will go.

WARNING: *Service valve guides have a shoulder. Once the guide is seated, do not use more than 1 ton pressure or the guide shoulder could break.*

Valve Seats
REMOVAL AND INSTALLATION

Valve seats can be refaced if they are worn or burned, but the correction angle and seat width must be maintained. If not, the cylinder head must be replaced.

Intake valve seats should be ground to a 45° angle and the valve margin should not be less than 0.5mm. Check the valve stem diameter.

Exhaust valves are sodium filled and should not be ground by machine. Use lapping compound and lap by hand. Valve margin should be at least 0.5mm. Check the stem diameter. The exhaust valve seat should be ground to a 45° angle.

Intake and exhaust valves are available with stems 0.5mm shorter than production valves. If the seats are cut too much during repairs, these shorter valves should be installed to allow the use of proper sized valve adjusting discs.

Oil Pan
REMOVAL AND INSTALLATION
1.6L and 1.7L Engines

1. Drain the oil pan.
CAUTION: *The EPA warns that prolonged contact with used engine oil may cause a number of skin disorders, including cancer! You should make every effort to minimize your exposure to used engine oil. Protective gloves should be worn when changing the oil. Wash your hands and any other exposed skin areas as soon as possible after exposure to used engine oil. Soap and water, or waterless hand cleaner should be used.*
2. Support the pan and remove the attaching bolts.
3. Lower the pan and discard the gaskets.
4. Clean all gasket surfaces thoroughly and install the pan using gasket sealer and a new gasket.
5. Torque the pan bolts to 7 ft. lbs.
6. Refill the pan, start the engine, and check for leaks.

2.2L Engine

1. Drain the engine oil.
CAUTION: *The EPA warns that prolonged contact with used engine oil may cause a number of skin disorders, including cancer! You should make every effort to minimize*

your exposure to used engine oil. Protective gloves should be worn when changing the oil. Wash your hands and any other exposed skin areas as soon as possible after exposure to used engine oil. Soap and water, or waterless hand cleaner should be used.*
2. Support the pan and remove the attaching bolts.
3. Lower the pan and remove the gasket, if it has one.
4. Clean all gasket surfaces thoroughly.
5. On all engines from 1981-87, use new end seals and apply a 1.2" bead of sealer to the rest of the pan. Make sure to apply sealer where the end seals meet the block. On 1988-89 engines, replace the end seals and the side gaskets. Apply RTV to the parting lines between end and side seals on these engines. If necessary, use grease or RTV to hold the side seals in place.
6. Torque the pan bolts to 200 in. lbs.
7. Refill the engine with oil, start the engine, and check for leaks.

Oil Pump
REMOVAL AND INSTALLATION
1.6L Engine

1. Drain the crankcase oil and remove the oil filter.
CAUTION: *The EPA warns that prolonged contact with used engine oil may cause a number of skin disorders, including cancer! You should make every effort to minimize your exposure to used engine oil. Protective gloves should be worn when changing the oil. Wash your hands and any other exposed skin areas as soon as possible after exposure to used engine oil. Soap and water, or waterless hand cleaner should be used.*
2. While holding the cover and housing together, remove the seven mounting bolts and pull the assembly from the engine block.
3. To install, seal all the oil pump attaching bolt threads with an oil resistant sealer.
4. Install new gaskets on the pump, housing to block and housing to cover.
5. Place the cover on the housing and insert two bolts to maintain alignment.
6. Install the housing into the block and rotate the assembly until the driving gear shaft engages the slot in the driveshaft.
7. Align the bolt pattern to the block, install the remaining five bolts and tighten to 9 ft. lbs.
8. Install the oil filter and refill the crankcase.

1.7L Engine

1. Remove the oil pan.
2. Remove the two pump mounting bolts.

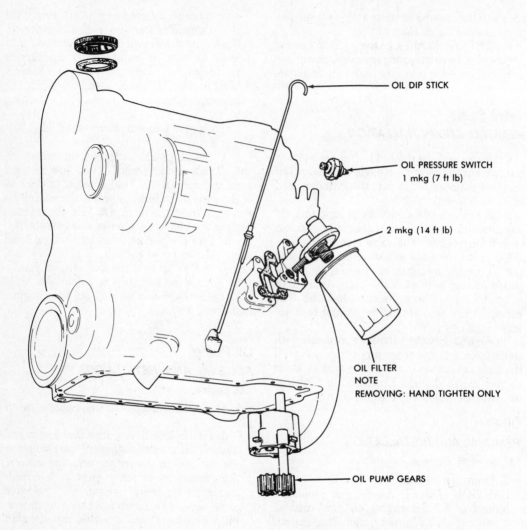

OIL DIP STICK

OIL PRESSURE SWITCH
1 mkg (7 ft lb)

2 mkg (14 ft lb)

OIL FILTER
NOTE
REMOVING: HAND TIGHTEN ONLY

OIL PUMP GEARS

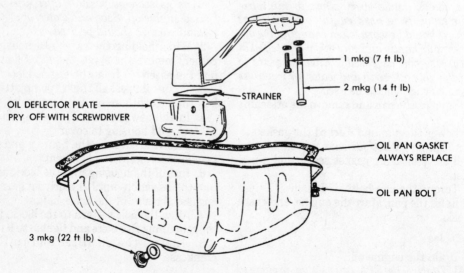

1 mkg (7 ft lb)

2 mkg (14 ft lb)

STRAINER

OIL DEFLECTOR PLATE
PRY OFF WITH SCREWDRIVER

OIL PAN GASKET
ALWAYS REPLACE

OIL PAN BOLT

3 mkg (22 ft lb)

1.7L engine lubricating system components

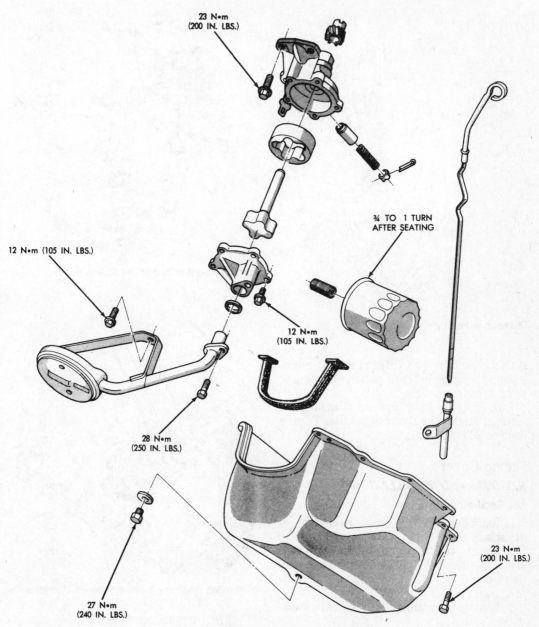

23 N•m
(200 IN. LBS.)

12 N•m (105 IN. LBS.)

¾ TO 1 TURN
AFTER SEATING

12 N•m
(105 IN. LBS.)

28 N•m
(250 IN. LBS.)

23 N•m
(200 IN. LBS.)

27 N•m
(240 IN. LBS.)

2.2L lubricating system components

3. Pull the oil pump down and out of the engine.

4. Installation is the reverse of removal. Torque pump mounting bolts to 14 ft. lbs. on the 1.7L and 9 ft. lbs. on the 2.2L.

1981-84 2.2L Engine

1. Remove the oil pan.
2. Remove the two pump mounting bolts.
3. Pull the pump down and out of the engine.
4. Installation is the reverse of removal. Make sure the pump body is *fully* seated in the block before installing the mounting bolts. Torque the pump mounting bolts to 200 in. lbs.

1985-89 2.2L Engines

1. Remove the oil pan as described above.
2. Remove the mounting bolts and remove the pump.
3. Apply a sealer such as Loctite 515® to the pump/block sealing surfaces.
4. Lubricate the pump rotor, shaft, and drive gear.
5. When installing the pump, rotate the

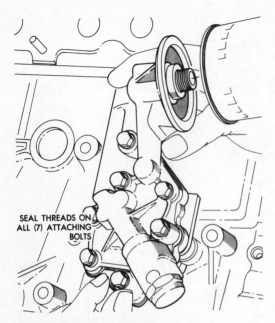

Oil pump assembly—1.6L engine

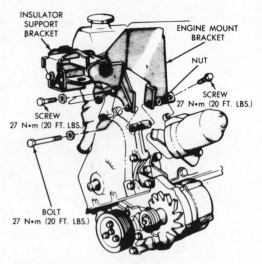

Engine mounting bracket—1.6L engine

shaft back and forth slightly so the drive mechanism will engage fully and permit the pump to sit squarely against the block.

6. *Holding the pump upward to ensure full seating*, install the mounting bolts. Torque them to 200 in. lbs.

Timing Cover

REMOVAL AND INSTALLATION

1.6L Engine

1. Raise the vehicle and remove the right inner splash shield.

2. Loosen the alternator adjusting screw. Move the alternator and remove the alternator/ water pump belt and the air pump belt (if so equipped).

3. Remove the crankshaft pulley bolt, washer, and pulley.

4. Drain the cooling system through the water pump drain plug and remove the water pump to timing cover hose.

CAUTION: *When draining the coolant, keep in mind that cats and dogs are attracted by the ethylene glycol antifreeze, and are quite likely to drink any that is left in an uncovered container or in puddles on the ground. This will prove fatal in sufficient quantity. Always drain the coolant into a sealable container. Coolant should be reused unless it is contaminated or several years old.*

5. Raise the timing cover end of the engine and carefully support.

6. Remove the bolts supporting the engine mount bracket to the timing cover and block.

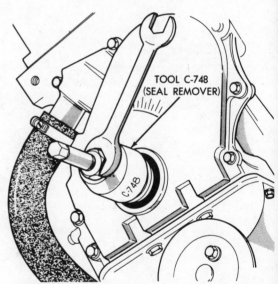

Removing the timing cover oil seal—1.6L engine

WARNING: *Two of the cover to block screws pass through the tubular locating dowels. Make sure the dowels DO NOT fall into the crankcase extension during the cover removal.*

7. Remove the crankcase extension to cover and the cover to block screws and remove the cover.

8. To remove the oil seal, install the seal removal tool C-748 or equivalent over the crankshaft nose and turn tightly into the seal. Tape the side of the thrust to loosen and remove the seal.

9. To install the oil seal, position tool C-4761 or equivalent on the seal and drive the seal into the timing cover until the tool stops against the cover.

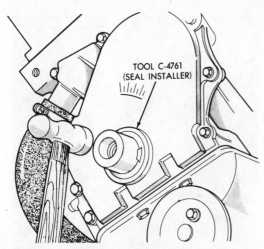

Installing the timing cover oil seal—1.6L engine

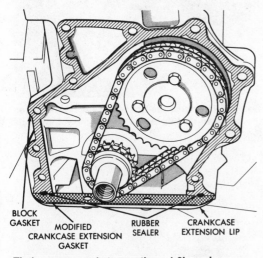

Timing cover gasket mounting—1.6L engine

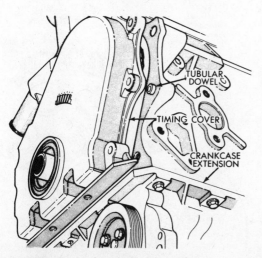

Installing the timing cover—1.6L engine

10. To install the timing cover, reverse the removal procedures.

1.7L Engines

1. Loosen the alternator mounting bolts, pivot the alternator and remove the drive belt.
2. Do the same thing with the air conditioning compressor.
3. Remove the cover retaining nuts, washers and spacers.
4. Remove the cover retaining nuts, washers and spacers.
5. Remove the cover.
6. Installation is the reverse of removal.

2.2L Engines

1. Loosen the alternator mounting bolts, pivot the alternator and remove the drive belt.
2. Do the same thing with the air conditioning compressor.
3. Remove the cover retaining nuts, washers and spacers.
4. Remove the cover.
5. Installation is the reverse of removal.

Timing Chain and Gears
REMOVAL AND INSTALLATION

1.6L Engine

1. Remove the timing cover as outlined earlier.
2. Remove the camshaft sprocket bolts and remove the sprocket and chain.
3. Remove the crankshaft gear with a pilot adapter tool C-4760 and gear puller C-3894-A or equivalent.
4. To install, align the crankshaft sprocket with the key and drive it onto the shaft.
5. Position the camshaft sprocket into place and turn it so that the timing marks on both sprockets are on a line passing through the sprocket centers as shown in the illustration.

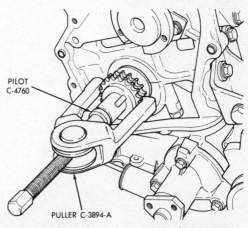

Removing the crankshaft sprocket—1.6L engine

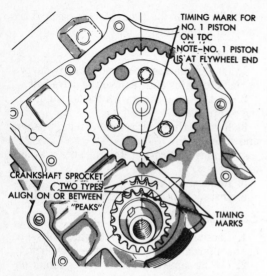

TIMING MARK FOR
NO. 1 PISTON
ON TDC
NOTE–NO. 1 PISTON
IS AT FLYWHEEL END

CRANKSHAFT SPROCKET
TWO TYPES
ALIGN ON OR BETWEEN
"PEAKS"

TIMING
MARKS

Alignment of the camshaft and crankshaft sprockets

6. Remove the camshaft sprocket without turning the camshaft, place the timing chain over it and reinstall the camshaft sprocket.

7. Recheck the timing marks. Install and torque the camshaft sprocket bolts to 113 in. lbs.

8. Install the timing cover.

On the 1.7L engine the belt tension is correct when the belt can be twisted 90° at the mid-point of its longest run

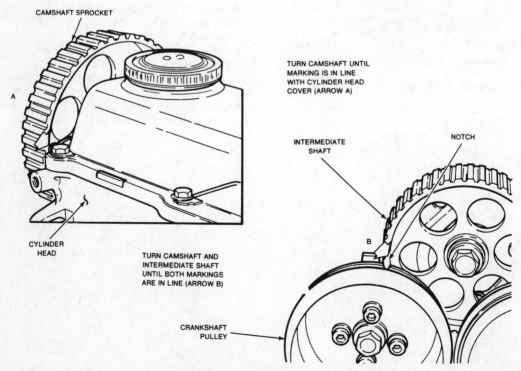

CAMSHAFT SPROCKET

A

CYLINDER
HEAD

TURN CAMSHAFT AND
INTERMEDIATE SHAFT
UNTIL BOTH MARKINGS
ARE IN LINE (ARROW B)

TURN CAMSHAFT UNTIL
MARKING IS IN LINE
WITH CYLINDER HEAD
COVER (ARROW A)

INTERMEDIATE
SHAFT

NOTCH

B

CRANKSHAFT
PULLEY

1.7L engine valve train timing marks

Timing Belt Wear

DESCRIPTION	FLAW CONDITIONS

1. Hardened back surface rubber

Back surface glossy. Non-elastic and so hard that even if a finger nail is forced into it, no mark is produced.

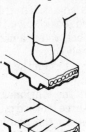

2. Cracked back surface rubber

3. Cracked or exfoliated canvas

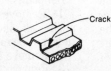

4. Badly worn teeth (initial stage)

Canvas on load side tooth flank worn (Fluffy canvas fibers, rubber gone and color changed to white, and unclear canvas texture)

Flank worn (On load side)

5. Badly worn teeth (last stage)

Canvas on load side tooth flank worn down and rubber exposed (tooth width reduced)

Rubber exposed

6. Cracked tooth bottom

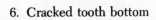

Crack

7. Missing tooth

Tooth missing and canvas fiber exposed

8. Side of belt badly worn

Rounded belt side

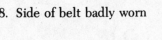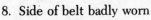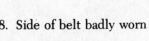

Abnormal wear (Fluffy canvas fiber)

NOTE: *Normal belt should have clear-cut sides as if cut by a sharp knife.*

9. Side of belt cracked

Timing Belt
REMOVAL AND INSTALLATION
1.7L Engines

The timing belt is designed to last a long time without requiring tension adjustments. If the belt is removed or replaced, basic valve timing must be checked and the belt retensioned.

1. Remove the timing belt cover.
2. While holding the large hex on the tension pulley, loosen the pulley nut.
3. Remove the belt from the tensioner.
4. Slide the belt off the three toothed pulleys.
5. Using the larger bolt on the crankshaft pulley, turn the engine until the #1 cylinder is at TDC of the compression stroke. At this point the valves for the #1 cylinder will be closed and the timing mark will be aligned with the pointer on the flywheel housing. Make sure that the timing mark on the rear face of the camshaft pulley is aligned with the lower left corner of the valve cover.
6. Check that the V-notch in the crankshaft pulley aligns with the dot mark on the intermediate shaft.

WARNING: *If the timing marks are not perfectly aligned, poor engine performance and probably engine damage will result!*

7. Install the belt on the pulleys.
8. Adjust the tension by turning the large tensioner hex to the right. Tension is correct when the belt can be twisted 90° with the thumb and forefinger, midway between the camshaft and intermediate pulleys.
9. Tighten the tensioner locknut to 32 ft. lbs.
10. Install the timing belt cover and check the ignition timing.

2.2L Engines

1. Remove the timing belt cover.
2. While holding the large hex on the tension pulley, loosen the pulley nut.
3. Remove the belt from the tensioner.
4. Slide the belt off the three toothed pulleys.
5. Using the larger bolt on the crankshaft pulley, turn the engine until the #1 cylinder is at TDC of the compression stroke. At this point the valves for the #1 cylinder will be closed and the timing mark will be aligned with the pointer on the flywheel housing. Make sure that the dots on the cam sprocket and cylinder head are aligned.
6. Check that the V-notch in the crankshaft pulley aligns with the dot mark on the intermediate shaft.

WARNING: *If the timing marks are not perfectly aligned, poor engine performance and probably engine damage will result!*

7. Install the belt on the pulleys.
8. Adjust the tensioner by turning the large

tensioner hex to the right. Tension is correct when the belt can be twisted 90° with the thumb and forefinger, midway between the camshaft and intermediate pulleys.
9. Tighten the tensioner locknut to 32 ft. lbs.
10. Install the timing belt cover and check the ignition timing.

Camshaft
REMOVAL AND INSTALLATION
1.6L Engine

NOTE: *The camshaft has an integral oil pump/distributor helical drive gear and an eccentric which drives the fuel pump. These items must be removed to enable camshaft removal.*

1. Remove the valve cover, rocker arms, push rods and tappets. Label these items so they may be installed in their original locations.
2. Remove the timing cover.
3. Remove the timing chain and sprockets.
4. Remove the oil pump and fuel pump.
5. Remove the distributor and drive housing, mark the crankcase in relation to the distributor drive slot.
6. With a magnet, remove the distributor drive from the driveshaft spindle.
7. Remove the oil pump shaft drive gear circlip.

NOTE: *Place a clean rag in the cavity around the gear to prevent the circlip from falling into the crankcase.*

8. Tap the driveshaft toward the oil pump side of the crankcase until the gear and thrust washer are free from the spline, and remove the gear and washer.
9. Pull the driveshaft out from the oil pump side of the crankcase.
10. Remove the camshaft thrust plate and carefully remove the camshaft.

WARNING: *Care should be exercised not to cock the camshaft during removal or damage*

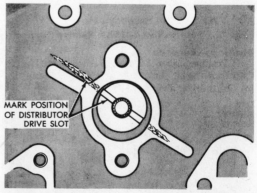

Marking the position of the distributor driveshaft— 1.6L engine

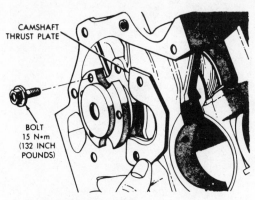

Camshaft thrust plate—1.6L engine

CAMSHAFT
THRUST PLATE

BOLT
15 N•m
(132 INCH
POUNDS)

to the camshaft or bearing thrust surfaces may result.

11. Installation is the reverse of the removal. Lubricate the camshaft, bearings, tappets, rockers and push rods. Lubricate the thrust plate and install with the open end up towards the cylinder head.

NOTE: *If a new camshaft or tappets have been installed, one pint of Chrysler oil conditioner 3419130 or an equivalent break in lubricant should be added to the crankcase.*

1.7L Engine

1. Remove the timing belt cover.
2. Remove the timing belt.
3. Remove the air cleaner assembly.
4. Remove the valve cover.
5. Remove the Nos. 1, 3, and 5 camshaft bearing caps.

6. Loosen caps 2 and 4 diagonally and in increments.
7. Lift the camshaft out.
8. Lubricate the camshaft journals and lobes with engine assembly lubricant and position it in the head.
9. Install a new oil seal.
10. Install the Nos. 1, 3, 5 bearing caps and torque the nuts to 14 ft. lbs.

NOTE: *All bearing caps are slightly offset. They should be installed so that the numbers on the cap read right side up from the driver's seat.*

11. Install the Nos. 2 and 4 caps and diagonally torque the nuts to 14 ft. lbs.

NOTE: *All bearing caps are slightly offset. They should be installed so that the numbers on the cap read right side up from the driver's seat.*

12. Position a dial indicator so that the feeler touches the front end of the camshaft. Check for end play. Play should not exceed 0.15mm.
13. Place a new seal on the #1 bearing cap. If necessary, replace the end plug in the head.
14. Follow the procedures under Timing Belt Removal and Installation for belt installation and timing.
15. Check the valve clearance and ignition.

2.2L Engine

1. Remove the timing belt.
2. Mark the rocker arms for installation identification.
3. Loosen the camshaft bearing capnuts several turns each.

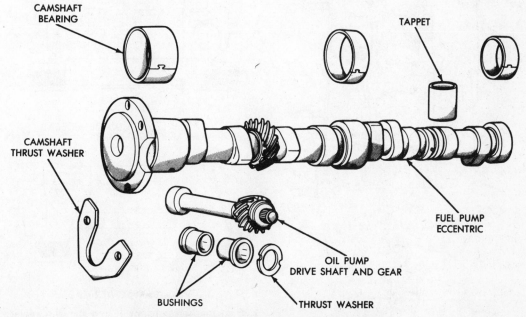

CAMSHAFT
BEARING

TAPPET

CAMSHAFT
THRUST WASHER

FUEL PUMP
ECCENTRIC

OIL PUMP
DRIVE SHAFT AND GEAR

BUSHINGS

THRUST WASHER

Camshaft and oil pump/distributor drive—1.6L engine

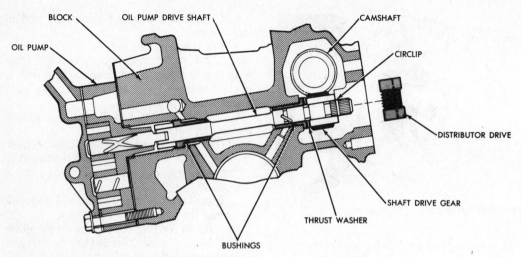

Oil pump/distributor driveshaft—1.6L engine

4. Using a wooden or rubber mallet, rap the rear of the camshaft a few times to break it loose.

5. Remove the capnuts and caps being very careful that the camshaft does not cock. Cocking the camshaft could cause irreparable damage to the bearings.

6. Check all oil holes for blockage.

7. Install the bearing caps with #1 at the timing belt end and #5 at the transmission end. Caps are numbered and have arrows facing forward. Cap nut torque is 14 ft. lbs.

8. Apply RTV silicone gasket material as per the accompanying picture.

9. Install the bearing caps before the seals are installed.

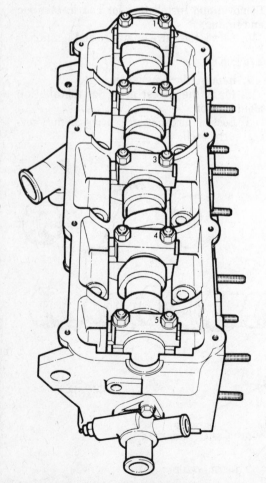

1.7L engine bearing cap installation

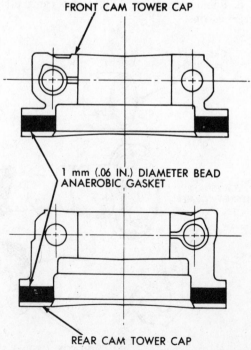

2.2L engine camshaft tower cap showing sealer location

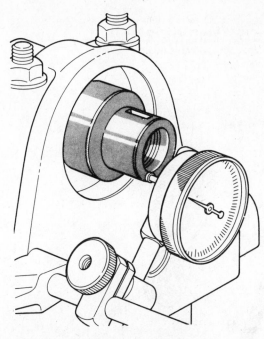

Measuring camshaft end-play—typical

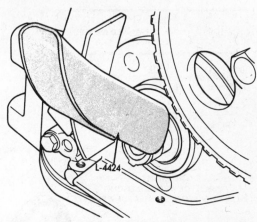

Removing 1.7L engine crankshaft front oil seal with tool L-4424

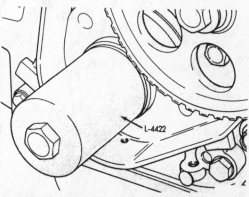

Installing 1.7L engine crankshaft front oil seal with tool L-4422

10. The rest of the procedure is the reverse of disassembly.

CAMSHAFT ENDPLAY CHECK

1. Move the camshaft as far forward as possible.

2. Install a dial indicator as per the accompanying picture.

3. Zero the indicator, push the camshaft backward, then forward as far as possible and record the play. Maximum play should be 0.15mm.

Timing Sprockets and Oil Seal

REMOVAL AND INSTALLATION

1.7L Engine

The camshaft, intermediate shaft, and crankshaft pulleys are located by keys on their respective shafts and each is retained by a bolt. To remove any or all of the pulleys, first remove the timing belt cover and belt and then use the following procedure.

NOTE: *When removing the crankshaft pulley, don't remove the four socket head bolts which retain the outer belt pulley to the timing belt pulley.*

1. Remove the center bolt.

2. Gently pry the pulley off the shaft.

3. If the pulley is stubborn in coming off, use a gear puller. Don't hammer on the pulley.

4. Remove the pulley and key. The oil seal may now be carefully pried out. Special tools are available for this purpose, but a screwdriver can be used.

5. Install the pulley in the reverse order of removal.

6. Install a new seal using a seal installation tool.

7. Tighten the center bolt to 58 ft. lbs.

8. Install the timing belt, check valve timing, tension belt, and install the cover.

2.2L

1. Raise and support the car on jackstands.

2. Remove the right inner splash shield.

3. Remove the crankshaft pulley.

4. Unbolt and remove both halves of the timing belt cover.

5. Take up the weight of the engine with a jack.

6. Remove the right engine mount bolt and raise the engine slightly.

7. Remove the timing belt tensioner and remove the belt.

8. Remove the crankshaft sprocket bolt, and with a puller, remove the sprocket.

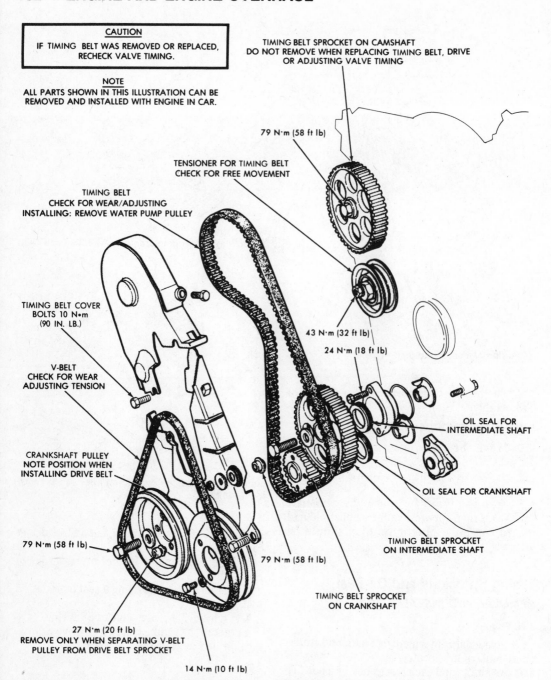

NOTE
ALL PARTS SHOWN IN THIS ILLUSTRATION CAN BE
REMOVED AND INSTALLED WITH ENGINE IN CAR.

TIMING BELT SPROCKET ON CAMSHAFT
DO NOT REMOVE WHEN REPLACING TIMING BELT, DRIVE
OR ADJUSTING VALVE TIMING

79 N·m (58 ft lb)

TENSIONER FOR TIMING BELT
CHECK FOR FREE MOVEMENT

TIMING BELT
CHECK FOR WEAR/ADJUSTING
INSTALLING: REMOVE WATER PUMP PULLEY

TIMING BELT COVER
BOLTS 10 N·m
(90 IN. LB.)

43 N·m (32 ft lb)

24 N·m (18 ft lb)

V-BELT
CHECK FOR WEAR
ADJUSTING TENSION

OIL SEAL FOR
INTERMEDIATE SHAFT

CRANKSHAFT PULLEY
NOTE POSITION WHEN
INSTALLING DRIVE BELT

OIL SEAL FOR CRANKSHAFT

79 N·m (58 ft lb)

TIMING BELT SPROCKET
ON INTERMEDIATE SHAFT

79 N·m (58 ft lb)

TIMING BELT SPROCKET
ON CRANKSHAFT

27 N·m (20 ft lb)
REMOVE ONLY WHEN SEPARATING V-BELT
PULLEY FROM DRIVE BELT SPROCKET

14 N·m (10 ft lb)

1.7L engine front cover, timing gears and belt

9. Using special Tool C-4679 or its equivalent, remove the crankshaft seal.

10. Unbolt and remove the camshaft and intermediate shaft sprockets.

11. To install the crankshaft seal, first polish the shaft with 400 grit emery paper. If the seal has a steel case, lightly coat the OD of the seal with Loctite Stud N' Bearing Mount or its equivalent. If the seal case is rubber coated, generously apply a soap and water solution to facilitate installation. Install the seal with a seal driver.

12. Install the sprockets making sure that the timing marks are aligned as illustrated. When installing the camshaft sprocket, make certain that the arrows on the sprocket are in line with the #1 camshaft bearing cap-to-cylinder head line.

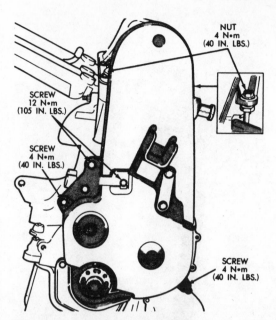

NUT
4 N•m
(40 IN. LBS.)

SCREW
12 N•m
(105 IN. LBS.)

SCREW
4 N•m
(40 IN. LBS.)

SCREW
4 N•m
(40 IN. LBS.)

2.2L engine front cover installation

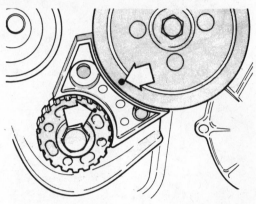

2.2L engine crankshaft and intermediate shaft timing mark alignment

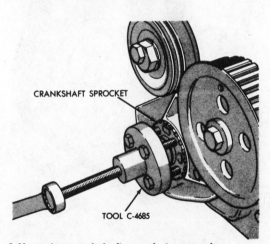

CRANKSHAFT SPROCKET

TOOL C-4685

2.2L engine crankshaft sprocket removal

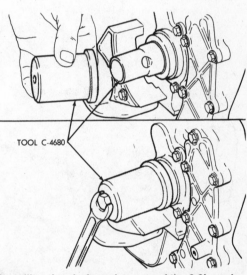

TOOL C-4680

Installing the shaft seal on any of the 2.2L engine shafts

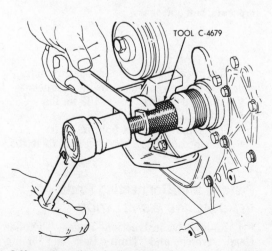

TOOL C-4679

2.2L engine oil seal remover tool

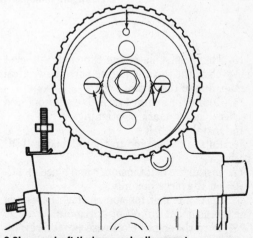

2.2L camshaft timing mark alignment

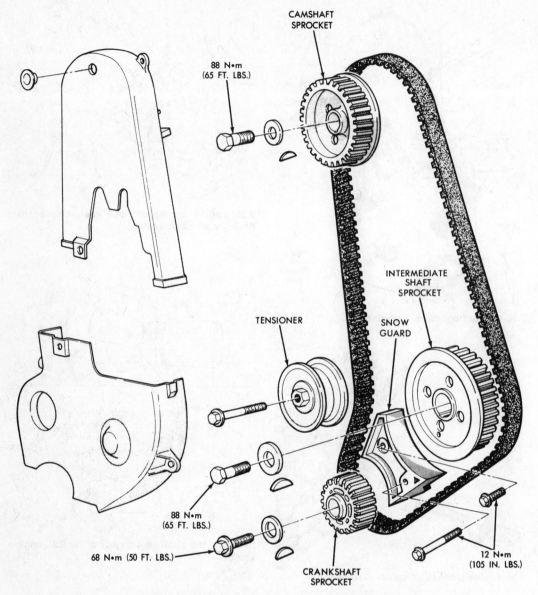

CAMSHAFT SPROCKET

88 N•m (65 FT. LBS.)

INTERMEDIATE SHAFT SPROCKET

TENSIONER

SNOW GUARD

88 N•m (65 FT. LBS.)

68 N•m (50 FT. LBS.)

12 N•m (105 IN. LBS.)

CRANKSHAFT SPROCKET

2.2L engine timing cover, sprockets, belt and seal

13. The small hole in the camshaft sprocket must be at the top and in line with the vertical center line of the engine.

14. Rotate the engine two full revolutions and recheck timing mark positioning.

15. Install the belt.

16. Rotate the engine to the #1 piston TDC position.

17. Install the belt tensioner and place tool C-4703 on the large hex nut.

18. Reset the belt tension so that the axis of the tool is about 15° off of horizontal.

19. Turn the engine clockwise two full revolutions to #1 TDC.

20. Tighten the tensioner locknut using a weighted wrench to the following torques:
- Timing belt cover bolts, 105 in. lbs.
- Camshaft sprocket bolt, 65 ft. lbs.
- Crankshaft sprocket bolt, 50 ft. lbs.
- Intermediate shaft sprocket bolt, 65 ft. lbs.

Pistons and Connecting Rods
REMOVAL AND INSTALLATION

1. Follow the instructions under "Cylinder Head" removal and "Timing Belt" or "Timing Chain" removal.

2. Remove the oil pan as described later in this chapter.

3. This procedure is much easier performed with the engine out of the car.

4. Pistons should be removed in the order: 1-3-4-2. Turn the crankshaft until the piston to be removed is at the bottom of its stroke.

5. Place a cloth on the head of the piston to be removed and, using a ridge reamer, remove the deposits from the upper end of the cylinder bore.

NOTE: *Never remove more than 0.8mm from the ring travel area when removing the ridges.*

6. Mark all connecting rod bearing caps so that they may be returned to their original locations in the engine. The connecting rod caps are marked with rectangular forge marks which must be mated during assembly and be installed on the intermediate shaft side of the engine. Mark all pistons so they can be returned to their original cylinders.

WARNING: *Don't score the cylinder walls or the crankshaft journal.*

7. Using an internal micrometer, measure the bores across the thrust faces of the cylinder and parallel to the axis of the crankshaft at a minimum of four equally spaced locations. The bore must not be out-of-round by more than 0.12mm and it must not taper more than 0.25mm. Taper is the difference in wear between two bore measurements in any cylinder. See the "Engine Rebuilding" section for complete details.

8. If the cylinder bore is in satisfactory condition, place each ring in the bore in turn and square it in the bore with the head of the piston. Measure the ring gap. If the ring gap is greater than the limit, get a new ring. If the ring gap is less than the limit, file the end of the ring to obtain the correct gap.

9. Check the ring side clearance by installing rings on the piston, and inserting a feeler gauge of the correct dimension between the ring and the lower land. The gauge should slide freely around the ring circumference without binding. Any wear will form a step on the lower land. Remove any pistons having high steps. Before checking the ring side clearance, be sure that the ring grooves are clean and free of carbon sludge, or grit.

10. Piston rings should be installed so that their ends are at three equal spacings. Avoid installing the rings with their ends in line with the piston pin bosses and the thrust direction.

11. Install the pistons in their original bores, if you are reusing the same pistons. Install short lengths of rubber hose over the connecting rod bolts to prevent damage to the cylinder walls or rod journal.

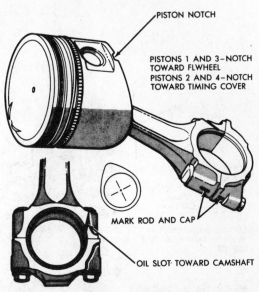

1.6L engine piston and connecting rod

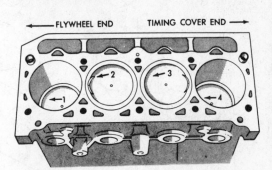

1.6L piston marking

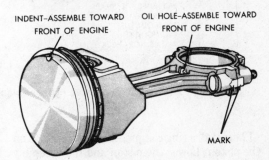

2.2L engine piston and connecting rod

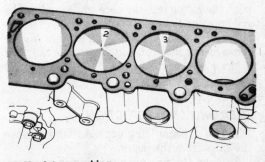

2.2L piston marking

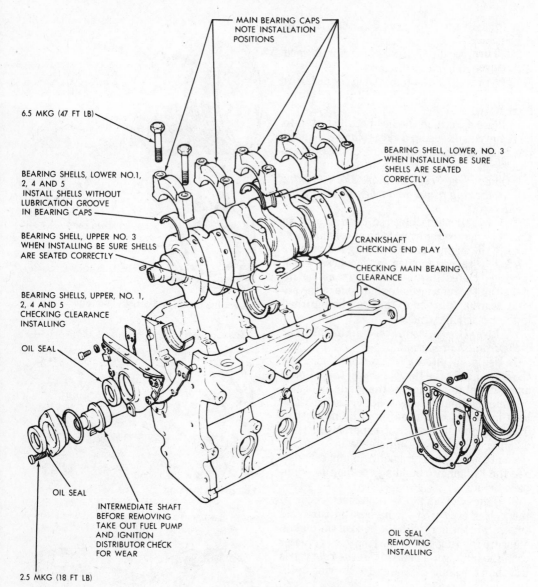

MAIN BEARING CAPS
NOTE INSTALLATION
POSITIONS

6.5 MKG (47 FT LB)

BEARING SHELL, LOWER, NO. 3
WHEN INSTALLING BE SURE
SHELLS ARE SEATED
CORRECTLY

BEARING SHELLS, LOWER NO.1,
2, 4 AND 5
INSTALL SHELLS WITHOUT
LUBRICATION GROOVE
IN BEARING CAPS

BEARING SHELL, UPPER NO. 3
WHEN INSTALLING BE SURE SHELLS
ARE SEATED CORRECTLY

CRANKSHAFT
CHECKING END PLAY

CHECKING MAIN BEARING
CLEARANCE

BEARING SHELLS, UPPER, NO. 1,
2, 4 AND 5
CHECKING CLEARANCE
INSTALLING

OIL SEAL

OIL SEAL

INTERMEDIATE SHAFT
BEFORE REMOVING
TAKE OUT FUEL PUMP
AND IGNITION
DISTRIBUTOR CHECK
FOR WEAR

OIL SEAL
REMOVING
INSTALLING

2.5 MKG (18 FT LB)

1.7L cylinder block and crankshaft

12. Install a ring compressor over the rings on the piston. Lower the piston and rod assembly into the bore until the ring compressor contacts the block. Using a wooden hammer handle, push the piston into the bore while guiding the rod onto the journal.

NOTE: *On the 1.7 and 2.2L engines the arrow on the piston should face toward the front (drive belt) of the engine.*

CLEANING AND INSPECTION

1. Use a piston ring expander and remove the rings from the piston.
2. Clean the ring grooves using an appropriate cleaning tool, exercise care to avoid cutting too deeply.
3. Clean all varnish and carbon from the piston with a safe solvent. Do not use a wire brush or caustic solution on the pistons.
4. Inspect the pistons for scuffing, scoring, cracks, pitting or excessive ring groove wear. If wear is evident, the piston must be replaced.
5. Have the piston and connecting rod assembly checked by a machine shop for correct alignment, piston pin wear and piston diameter. If the piston has "collapsed" it will have to be replaced or knurled to restore original diameter. Connecting rod bushing replacement, piston pin fitting and piston changing can be handled by the machine shop.

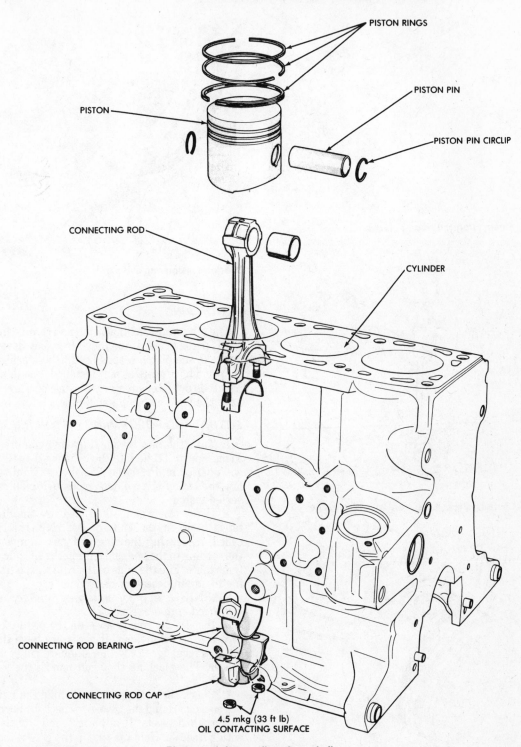

PISTON RINGS

PISTON PIN

PISTON

PISTON PIN CIRCLIP

CONNECTING ROD

CYLINDER

CONNECTING ROD BEARING

CONNECTING ROD CAP

4.5 mkg (33 ft lb)
OIL CONTACTING SURFACE

Piston and rings—all engines similar

CYLINDER BORE

Check the cylinder bore for wearing using a telescope gauge and a micrometer, measure the cylinder bore diameter perpendicular to the piston pin at a point 63.5mm below the top of the engine block. Measure the piston skirt perpendicular to the piston pin. The difference between the two measurements is the piston clearance. If the clearance is within specifications, finish honing or glaze breaking is all that

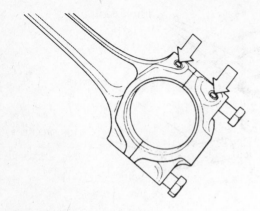

Connecting rod match marks

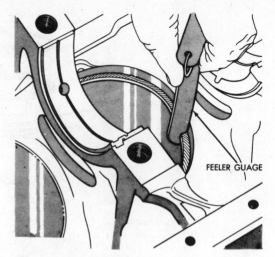

Checking piston ring end gap

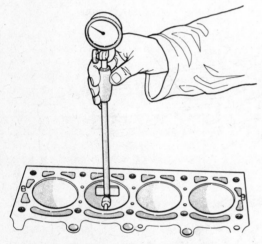

Checking the cylinder bore with bore gauge

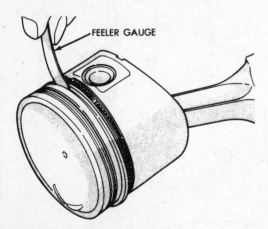

FEELER GAUGE

Checking piston ring side clearance

is required. If clearance is excessive a slightly oversize piston may be required. If greatly oversize, the engine will have to be bored and 0.25mm or larger oversized pistons installed.

PISTON PINS

The pin connecting the piston and connecting rod is press fitted. If too much free play develops take the piston assemblies to the machine shop and have oversize pins installed. Installing new rods or pistons requires the use of a press; have the machine shop handle the job for you.

FITTING AND POSITIONING PISTON RINGS

1. Take the new piston rings and compress them, one at a time into the cylinder that they will be used in. Press the ring about 25mm below the top of the cylinder block using an inverted piston.

2. Use a feeler gauge and measure the distance between the ends of the ring, this is called, measuring the ring end-gap. Compare the reading to the one called for in the specifications table. File the ends of the ring with a fine file to obtain necessary clearance.

WARNING: *If inadequate ring end-gap is utilized ring breakage will result.*

3. Inspect the ring grooves on the piston for excessive wear or taper. If necessary have the grooves recut for use with a standard ring and spacer. The machine shop can handle the job for you.

4. Check the ring groove by rolling the new piston ring around the groove to check for burrs or carbon deposits. If any are found, remove with a fine file. Hold the ring in the groove and measure side clearance with a feeler gauge. If clearance is excessive, spacer(s) will have to be added.

NOTE: *Always add spacers above the piston ring.*

5. Install the rings on the piston, lower ring first using a ring installing tool. Consult the instruction sheet that comes with the rings to be

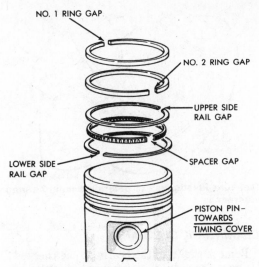

Piston ring positioning—1.6L engine

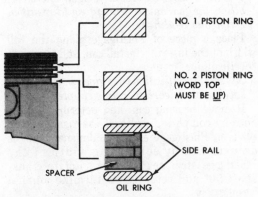

Piston ring installation—1.6L engine

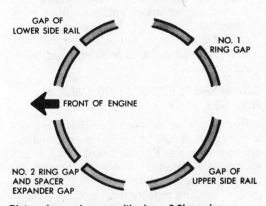

Piston ring end gap positioning—2.2L engine

sure they are installed with the correct side up. A mark on the ring usually faces upward.

6. When installing oil rings; first, install the ring in the groove. Hold the ends of the ring butted together (they must not overlap) and install the bottom rail (scraper) with the end

about 25mm away from the butted end of the control ring. Install the top rail about an 25mm away from the butted end of the control but on the opposite side from the lower rail.

7. Install the two compression rings.

8. Consult the illustration with piston ring set instruction sheet for ring positioning, arrange the rings as shown, install a ring compressor and insert the piston and rod assembly into the engine.

Crankshaft and Bearings

1. Rod bearings can be installed when the pistons have been removed for servicing (rings etc) or, in most cases, while the engine is still in the car. Rearing replacement, however, is far easier with the engine out of the car and disassembled.

2. For in car service, remove the oil pan, spark plugs and front cover if necessary. Turn the engine until the connecting rod to be serviced is at the bottom of its travel. Remove the bearing cap, place two pieces of rubber hose over the rod cap bolts and push the piston and rod assembly up the cylinder bore until enough room is gained for bearing insert removal. Take care not to push the rod assembly up too far or the top ring will engage the cylinder ridge or come out of the cylinder and require head removal for reinstallation.

3. Clean the rod journal, the connecting rod end and the bearing cap after removing the old bearing inserts. Install the new inserts in the rod and bearing cap, lubricate them with oil. Position the rod over the crankshaft journal and install the rod caps. Make sure the cap and rod numbers match, torque the rod nuts to specifications.

4. Main bearings may be replaced while the engine is still in the car by "rolling" them out and in.

5. Special roll-out pins are available from automotive parts houses or can be fabricated from a cotter pin. The roll out pin fits in the oil hole of the main bearing journal. When the crankshaft is rotated opposite the direction of the bearing lock tab, the pin engages the end of the bearing and "rolls" out the insert.

6. Remove main bearing cap and roll out upper bearing insert. Remove insert from main bearing cap. Clean the inside of the bearing cap and crankshaft journal.

7. Lubricate and roll upper insert into position, make sure the lock tab is anchored and the insert is not "cocked." Install the lower bearing insert into the cap; lubricate and install on the engine. Make sure the main bearing cap is installed facing in the correct direction and torque to specifications.

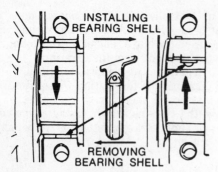

Remove or install the upper bearing insert using a roll-out pin

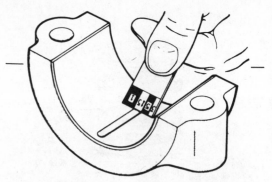

Measure Plastigage® to determine main bearing clearance

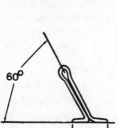

Home-made bearing roll-out pin

8. With the engine out of the car, remove the intake manifold, cylinder head, front cover, timing gears and/or chain, oil pan, oil pump and flywheel.

9. Remove the piston and rod assemblies. Remove the main bearing caps after marking them for position and direction.

10. Remove the crankshaft bearing inserts and rear main oil seal. Clean the engine block and cap bearing saddles. Clean the crankshaft and inspect for wear. Check the bearing journals with a micrometer for out-of-round condition and to determine what size rod and main bearing inserts to install.

11. Install the main bearing upper inserts and rear main oil seal half into the engine block.

12. Lubricate the bearing insets and the crankshaft journals. Slowly and carefully lower the crankshaft into position.

13. Install the bearing inserts and rear main seal into the bearing caps, install the caps working from the middle out. Torque cap bolts to specifications in stages, rotate the crankshaft after each torque stage.

14. Remove bearing caps, one at a time and check the oil clearance with Plastigage. Reinstall if clearance is within specifications. Check the crankshaft end-play, if within specifications, install connecting rod and piton assemblies with new rod bearing inserts. Check connecting rod bearing oil clearance and rod side play, if correct and assemble the rest of the engine.

BEARING OIL CLEARANCE

Remove cap from the bearing to be checked. Using a clean, dry rag, thoroughly clean all oil from crankshaft journal and bearing insert.

NOTE: *Plastigage is soluble in oil; therefore, oil on the journal or bearing could result in erroneous readings.*

Place a piece of Plastigage along the full width of the insert, reinstall cap, and torque to specifications.

NOTE: *Specifications are given in the engine specifications earlier in this chapter.*

Remove bearing cap, and determine clearance by comparing width of Plastigage to the scale on Plastigage envelope. Journal taper is determined by comparing width of the Plastigage strip near its ends. Rotate crankshaft 90° and retest, to determine journal eccentricity.

NOTE: *Do not rotate crankshaft with Plastigage installed. If bearing insert and journal appear intact, and are within tolerances, no further main bearing service is required. If bearing or journal appear defective, cause of failure should be determined before replacement.*

CRANKSHAFT END-PLAY/CONNECTING ROD SIDE PLAY

Place a pry bar between a main bearing cap and crankshaft casting taking care not to damage any journals. Pry backward and forward measure the distance between the thrust bearing (center main 3) and crankshaft with a feeler gauge. Compare reading with specifications. If too great a clearance is determined, a larger thrust bearing or crank machining may be required. Check with an automotive machine shop for their advice.

Connecting rod clearance between the rod and crankthrow casting can be checked with a feeler gauge. Pry the rod carefully to one side as far as possible and measure the distance on the other side of the rod.

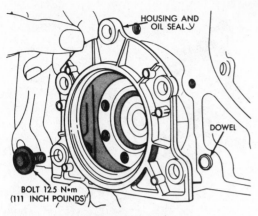

Rear main oil seal housing—1.6L engine

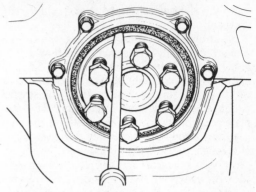

2.2L rear oil seal removal

CRANKSHAFT REPAIRS

If a journal is damaged on the crankshaft, repair is possible by having the crankshaft machined, after removal from engine to a standard undersize. Consult the machine shop for their advice.

Rear Main Seal

REMOVAL AND INSTALLATION

The rear main seal is located in a housing on the rear of the block. To replace the seal it is necessary to remove the engine.

1. Remove the transmission and flywheel.
NOTE: *Before removing the transmission, align the dimple on the flywheel with the pointer on the flywheel housing. The transmission will not mate with the engine during installation unless this alignment is observed.*

2. Very carefully, pry the old seal out of the support ring with a suitable tool.

3. Coat the new seal with clean engine oil and press it into place with a flat piece of metal. Take great care not to scratch the seal or crankshaft.

4. Install the flywheel and transmission.

Flywheel and Ring Gear

REMOVAL AND INSTALLATION

The flywheel on manual transmission cars serves as the forward clutch engagement surface. It also serves as the ring gear with which the starter pinion engages to crank the engine. The most common reason to replace the flywheel is broken teeth on the starter ring gear. To remove it, remove the transmission as described in Chapter 7. Then, unbolt and remove the clutch and pressure plate. Finally, *support the flywheel in a secure manner* and then re-

2.2L rear main oil seal installation

Prying the 1.7L engine rear main seal housing

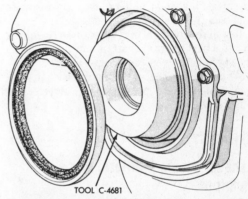

On the 1.7L engine, a rear main seal protector is needed when installing the new seal

move the eight attaching bolts and remove the flywheel.

On automatic transmission cars, the torque converter actually forms part of the flywheel. It is bolted to a thin flexplate which, in turn, is bolted to the crankshaft. The flex plate also serves as the ring gear with which the starter pinion engages in engine cranking. The flex plate occasionally cracks; the teeth on the ring gear may also break, especially if the starter is often engaged while the pinion is still spinning. The torque converter and flex plate are separated so the converter and transmission can be removed together. Remove the automatic transaxle as described in Chapter 7. Then, remove the attaching bolts and remove the flexplate from the flywheel.

Install the flywheel in reverse order, torquing the flywheel-to-crankshaft mounting bolts to the specifications in the Torque Chart.

When the flywheel or flexplate is back in position, reinstall the transmission as described in Chapter 7.

EXHAUST SYSTEM

Exhaust Pipes, Mufflers, and Tailpipes

For a number of different reasons, exhaust system work can be the most dangerous type of work you can do on your car. *Always observe the following precautions:*

1. Support the car extra securely. Not only will you often be working directly under it, but you'll frequently be using a lot of force—say, heavy hammer blows, to dislodge rusted parts. This can cause a car that's improperly supported to shift and possibly fall.

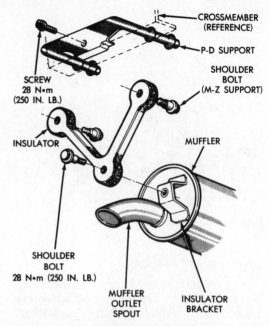

Tail pipe and muffler support insulator

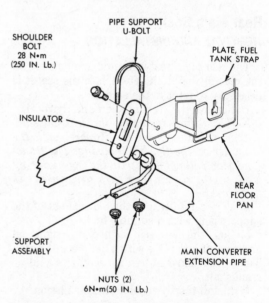

Underfloor converter extension pipe support

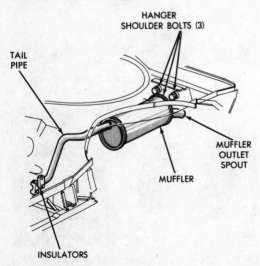

Tail pipe with muffler, typical

2. Wear goggles. Exhaust system parts are always rusty. Metal chips can be dislodged, even when you're only turning rusted bolts. Attempting to pry pipes apart with a chisel makes chips fly even more frequently.

3. If you're using a cutting torch, keep it at a great distance from either the fuel tank or lines. Stop what you're doing and feel the temperature of fuel bearing pipes or the tank frequently. Even slight heat can expand or vaporize the fuel, resulting in accumulated vapor or even a liquid leak near your torch.

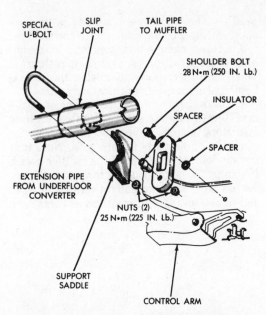

Exhaust pipe extension assembly-to-tail pipe

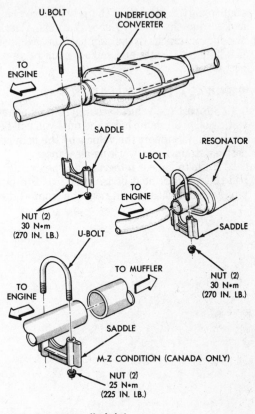

Mid-connection slip joint

4. Watch where your hammer blows fall. You could easily tap a brake or fuel line when you hit an exhaust system part with a galncing blow. Inspect all lines and hoses in the area where you've been working before driving the car.

Special Tools

A number of special exhaust system tools can be rented from auto supply houses or local stores that rent special equipment. A common one is a tail pipe expander, designed to enable you to join pipes of identical diameter.

It may also be quite helpful to use solvents designed to loosen rusted bolts or flanges. Soaking rusted parts the night before you do the job can speed the work of freeing rusted parts considerably. Remember that these solvents are often flammable. Apply them only after the parts are cool.

Note that a special flexible coupling is used to connect the exhaust pipe to the exhaust manifold. If this important coupling should develop a leak, be sure to replace the seal ring with a

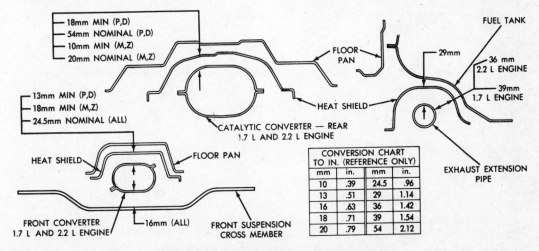

Proper exhaust system component clearances

CONVERSION CHART TO IN. (REFERENCE ONLY)			
mm	in.	mm	in.
10	.39	24.5	.96
13	.51	29	1.14
16	.63	36	1.42
18	.71	39	1.54
20	.79	54	2.12

quality part, install it in the proper direction, and torque the bolts to specifications. Check also for any cracks in the exhaust pipe, exhaust manifold, or flanges and replace such parts as necessary.

REMOVAL AND INSTALLATION

1. Support the vehicle securely. Apply penetrating oil to all clamp bolts and nuts you will be working on. Support the vehicle by the body, if possible, to increase working clearances.

2. If the tailpipe is integral with the muffler, and the muffler must be replaced, cut the tail pipe with a hacksaw right near the front of the muffler. The replacement muffler is then installed using a clamp to attach to the tailpipe.

3. Loosen clamps and supports to permit alignment of all parts, and then retighten. Make sure there is adequate clearance so exhaust parts stay clear of underbody parts.

4. Clean the mating surfaces of pipes or the muffler to ensure a tight seal. Use new insulators, clamps, and supports unless the condition of old parts is very good. Note that the slip joint at the front of the muffler uses a U-clamp. The bolts should be torqued to 270 in. lbs. on cars with normally aspirated engines and to 360 in. lbs. on turbocharged cars.

Emission Controls

EMISSION CONTROLS

Several different systems are used on each car. Most require no service and those which may require service also require sophisticated equipment for testing purposes. Following is a brief description of each system.

Catalytic Converter

Two catalysts are used in a small one located just after the exhaust manifold and a larger one located under the car body. Catalysts promote complete oxidation of exhaust gases through the effect of a platinum coated mass in the catalyst shell. Two things act to destroy the catalyst, functionally: excessive heat and leaded gas. Excessive heat during misfiring and prolonged testing with the ignition system in any way altered is the most common occurrence. Test procedures should be accomplished as quickly as possible, and the car should not be driven when misfiring is noted.

WARNING: *Operation of any type including idling should be avoided if engine misfiring occurs. Alteration or deterioration of the ignition system or fuel system must be avoided to prevent overheating the catalytic converter.*

All converter equipped cars are equipped with a special fuel filler neck that prevents the use of any filler nozzle except those designed for unleaded fuel. As a reminder to the operator, a decal "UNLEADED GASOLINE" is located near the fuller neck, and on the dash.

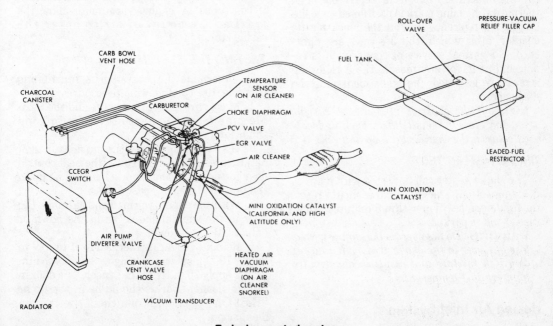

Emission control system

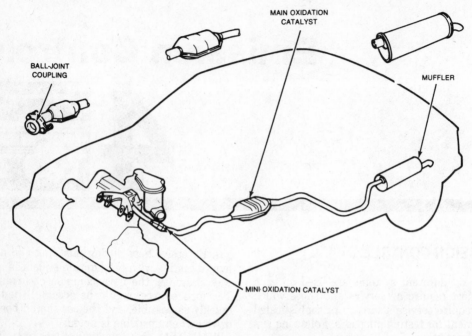

Exhaust system with catalytic converter

Electric Choke System

An electric heater and switch are sealed within the choke system, with electricity supplied from the oil pressure sending unit. A minimum of 4 psi oil pressure is required to close the contacts and send current to the choke control switch.

The electric choke unit is located on the side of the carburetor. The initial setting is made by the manufacturer, but it is adjustable. The thermostat housing mark is positioned opposite a specified reference line on the black plastic adapter, after which, the 3 screws are tightened. No normal service of this system is required, but if, for any reason, the 3 retaining screws are loosened, the adjustment must be made again.

NOTE: *If the choke is removed, be careful you don't lose the small plastic bushing located between the thermostat loop and pin.*

CHOKE HEATER TEST

The choke heater can be tested with a direct B+ connection. The choke valve should reach the fully open position within 5 minutes, when the vehicle is parked.

WARNING: *Do not operate the engine with a loss of power to the choke. This will cause a very rich mixture and result in abnormally high exhaust temperatures.*

Heated Air Inlet System

All engines are equipped with a vacuum device located in the carburetor air cleaner intake.

A small door is operated by a vacuum diaphragm and a thermostatic spring. When the air temperature outside is 40°F (4°C) or lower, the door will block off air entering from outside and allow air channelled from the exhaust manifold area to enter the intake. The air is heated by the hot manifold At 65°F (18°C) or above, the door fully blocks off the heated air. At temperatures in between, the door is operated in intermediate positions. During acceleration the door is controlled by engine vacuum to allow the maximum amount of air to enter the carburetor.

TESTING THE SYSTEM

To determine if the system is functioning properly, use the following procedures.

1. Make sure all vacuum hoses and the flexible pipe from the heat stove are in good condition.

2. On a cold engine and the outside air temperature less than 50°F (10°C), the heat control door in the air cleaner snorkel should be up in the up or "Heat On" position.

3. With the engine warmed and running, the door in the snorkel should be in the down or "Heat Off" position.

4. Remove the air cleaner. Allow it to cool to 50°F (10°C), or less. Using a hand vacuum pump, apply 20 in.Hg to the sensor. The door in the air cleaner snorkel should be in the up or "Heat On" position. If not, check the vacuum diaphragm.

5. To test the diaphragm, use a hand vacuum pump to apply about 20 in.Hg to the dia-

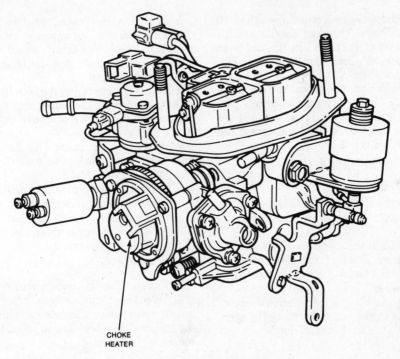

CHOKE
HEATER

Choke heater on carburetor

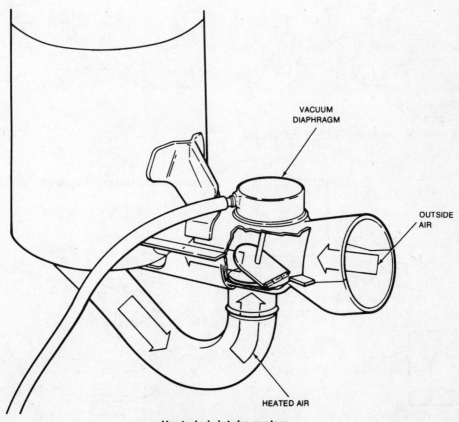

VACUUM
DIAPHRAGM

OUTSIDE
AIR

HEATED AIR

Heated air intake system

phragm. It should not leak down more than 10 in.Hg in 3 minutes. The door should not lift from the snorkel at less than 2 in.Hg, and be in the full up position with no more than 4 in.Hg.

6. If these conditions in Step 6 are not met, replace the diaphragm and repeat the checks in Steps 2 and 3. If the vacuum diaphragm performs properly, but proper temperature is not maintained, replace the sensor and repeat the checks in Steps 2 and 3.

REMOVAL AND INSTALLATION

Vacuum Diaphragm

1. Remove the air cleaner housing.
2. Disconnect the vacuum hose from the diaphragm.
3. Drill through the metal (welded) tab and tip the diaphragm slightly forward to disengage the lock. Rotate the diaphragm counterclockwise.
4. When the diaphragm is free, slide the complete assembly to one side and remove the operating rod from the heat control door.

5. With the diaphragm removed, check the door for freedom of operation. When the door is raised, it should fall freely when released. If not, check the snorkel walls for interference, or check the hinge pin.

6. Insert the operating rod into the heat control door. Position the diaphragm tangs in the openings in the snorkel and turn clockwise until the lock is engaged.

7. Apply 9 in.Hg vacuum to the diaphragm hose nipple and check to be sure the heat control door operates freely.

WARNING: *Manually operating the heat control door could cock the operating rod and restrict proper operation of the system.*

8. Assemble the air cleaner and install it on the car. Test the operation.

Sensor

1. Remove the air cleaner housing.
2. Disconnect the vacuum hoses from the sensor and remove the retainer clips. Discard the old clips; new ones are supplied with a new sensor.

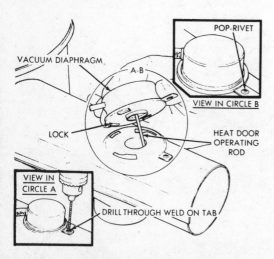
Testing vacuum diaphragm with hand vacuum pump

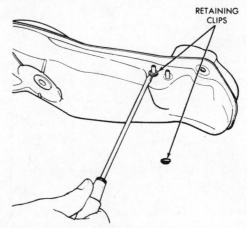
Remove the sensor retaining clip

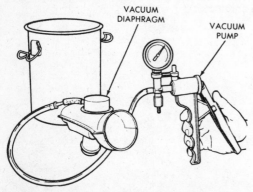
Removing or installing the vacuum diaphragm

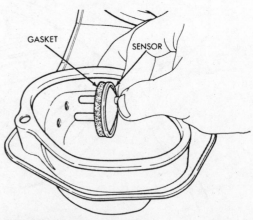
Install the gasket and sensor

3. Remove the sensor and gasket.

4. Install a new gasket and sensor. Hold the sensor in place and install new retainer clips. Be sure the gasket forms a tight air seal. Do not attempt to adjust the sensor.

Exhaust Gas Recirculation System

This system reduces the amount of oxides of nitrogen in the exhaust by allowing a predetermined amount of hot exhaust gases to recirculate and dilute the incoming fuel/air mixture. The principal components of the system are the EGR valve and the Coolant Control Exhaust Gas Recirculation Valve (CCEGR). The former is located in the intake manifold and directly regulates the flow of exhaust gases into the intake. The latter is located in the thermostat housing and overrides the EGR valve when coolant temperature is below 125°F (52°C).

Ported vacuum uses a slot in the carburetor throttle body which is exposed to an increasing percentage of manifold vacuum as the throttle opens. The throttle bore port is connected to the EGR valve. The flow rate of recirculation is dependent on manifold vacuum, throttle position and exhaust gas back pressure. Recycling at wide open throttle is eliminated, by calibrating the valve opening point above the manifold vacuum available at wide open throttle, which provides maximum performance.

TESTING THE SYSTEM

EGR Valve

1. Inspect all hose connections between the carburetor, intake manifold and EGR valve.

2. Check the valve with the engine warmed and running.

3. Allow the engine to idle in Neutral for 70 seconds, with the throttle closed. Abruptly ac-

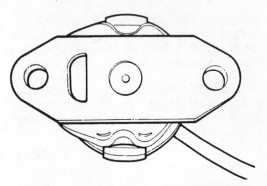

Bottom view (poppet seat area) of EGR valve

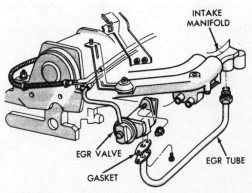

EGR system—carbureted engine, 1984–87 shown

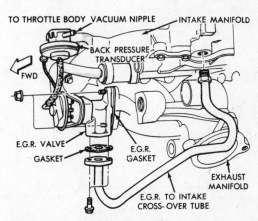

EGR system—fuel injected engine

celerate the engine to about 2000 rpm, but not more than 3000 rpm.

4. Visible movement of the EGR valve stem should occur during this operation. Movement can be seen by the position of the groove on the EGR valve stem. You may have to repeat the operation several times to definitely ascertain movement.

Inspect the EGR valve for deposits, particularly around the poppet and seat area. If deposits amount to more than a thin film, the valve should be cleaned. Apply a liberal amount of

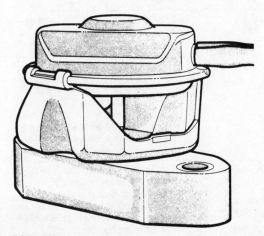

EGR valve

manifold heat control valve solvent to the poppet and seat area and allow the deposits to soften. Open the valve with an external vacuum source and remove the deposits, with a suitable sharp tool.

WARNING: *During the cleaning operation, do not spill solvent on the valve diaphragm or it will cause failure of the diaphragm. Do not*

push on the diaphragm to operate the valve; use an external vacuum source.

An alternate procedure to this messy operation is to simply replace the valve if it is extremely clogged.

NOTE: *A new EGR valve was used on models built after February 20, 1978. Vehicles built prior to the change can increase fuel*

EGR Diagnosis

NOTE: *All tests must be made with fully warm engine running continuously for at least two minutes*

Condition	Possible Cause	Correction
EGR valve stem does not move on system test.	(a) Check, leaking, disconnected or plugged hoses.	(a) Verify correct hose connections and leak check and confirm that all hoses are open. If defective hoses are found, replace hose harness.
	(b) Defective EGR valve.	(b) Disconnect hose harness from EGR valve. Connect external vacuum source, 10 in./Hg or greater, to valve diaphragm while checking valve movement. If no valve movement occurs, replace valve. If valve opens, approx. ⅛″ travel, clamp off supply hose to check for diaphragm leakage. Valve should remain open 30 seconds or longer. If leakage occurs, replace valve. If valve is satisfactory, evaluate control system.
EGR valve stem does not move on system test, operates normally on external vacuum source.	(a) Defective thermal control valve.	(a) Disconnect CCEGR valve and bypass the valve with a short length of 3/16″ tubing. If normal movement of the EGR valve is restored, replace the thermal valve.
	(b) Defective control system— Plugged passages.	(b) Ported Vacuum Control System: Remove carburetor and inspect port (slot type) in throttle bore and associated vacuum passages in carburetor throttle body including limiting orifice at hose end of passages. Use suitable solvent to remove deposits and check for flow with light air pressure. Normal operation should be restored to ported vacuum control EGR system.
Engine will not idle, dies out on return to idle or idle is very rough or slow. EGR valve open at idle.	(a) Control system defective.	(a) Disconnect hose from EGR valve and plug hose. If idle is unsatisfactory, replace EGR valve. If idle is still unsatisfactory, install a vacuum guage on ported signal tap and observe gauge for vacuum reading. If vacuum signal is greater than 1 inch/Hg, check idle set (refer to Carburetor, Engine Idle Check and Set Procedure). If vacuum is ok, remove carburetor, Group 14, Fuel System, and check linkage and throttle blades for binding.
Engine will not idle, dies out on return to idle or idle is rough or slow. EGR valve closed at idle.	(a) High EGR valve leakage in closed position.	(a) If removal of vacuum hose from EGR valve does not correct rough idle, remove EGR valve and inspect to insure that poppet is seated. Clean deposits if necessary or replace EGR valve if found defective.

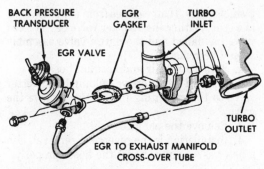

EGR system—turbo engine

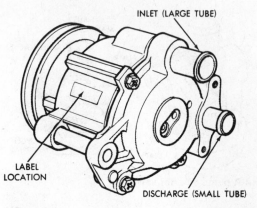

AIR pump

economy slightly by using the new EGR valve (part no. 4131219) and gasket (part no. 3671425).

CCEGR Valve

This valve is mounted in the thermostat housing and is color coded yellow for its calibrated temperature of 120-130°F (49-54°C). During warm-up, when engine coolant temperature exceeds 125°F (52°C), the valve opens, allowing vacuum to reach the EGR valve, causing recirculation of exhaust gasses.

1. Remove the valve from the housing.
2. Place it in an ice bath below 40°F (4°C) so that the threaded portion of the valve is covered.
3. Connect a hand vacuum pump to the valve nipple corresponding to the yellow stripe hose. Apply 10 in.Hg vacuum. There should be no more than 1 in.Hg drop in vacuum in 1 minute. If the vacuum reading falls off, the valve should be replaced.

Air Injection System

This system's job is to reduce carbon monoxide and hydrocarbons to required levels. The system adds a controlled amount of air to exhaust gases, via an air pump and induction

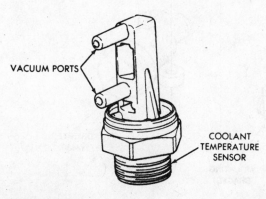

CCEGR valve

tubes, causing oxidation of the gases. The California and other American cars, introduces air through the head at the exhaust port. The system is composed of an air pump, a combination diverter/pressure-relief valve, hoses, a check valve to protect the hoses from exhaust gas, and an injection tube.

NOTE: *The system is not noiseless. A certain squeal is present in pump operation.*

SERVICING THE SYSTEM

For proper operation of the system, the drive belt should be in good condition and properly tensioned. The air pump is not a serviceable item; if necessary, it should be replaced.

WARNING: *Do not attempt to disassemble the pump or clamp it in a vise.*

Complaints of road surge at about 40-60 mph on 1978 Federal models equipped with manual transmission and AIR pump can be corrected, in most cases, by installing a kit (Part No. 4131207).

The kit consists of a vacuum bleed, an idle air bleed, a carburetor ID tag, main metering jet, air horn gasket and hose routing label.

1. Remove the carburetor air horn.
2. Replace the primary main metering jet with the one supplied in the kit.
3. Install the new carburetor air horn gasket.
4. Install the air horn.
5. Install the idle air bleed in the opening next to the primary choke housing. It should be installed flush with the surface. Use a driver (brass drift) larger than the diameter of the bleed fitting.
6. Install the vacuum bleed between the EGR ported vacuum nipple of the carburetor and install the CCEGR valve hose in place of the existing plastic reducer. The large end of the vacuum bleed should be toward the carburetor.
7. Install the new hose routing label over the old one.

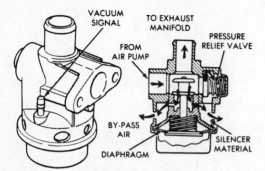

AIR pump diverter valve

8. Install the new carburetor ID tag under the air horn screw in place of the old one.

REMOVAL AND INSTALLATION

Air Pump

1. Disconnect and tag the hoses from the pump.
2. Loosen the air pump idler pivot and adjusting bolts. Remove the drive belt.
3. Remove the air pump pulley and attaching bolts.
4. Remove the air pump.
5. Installation is the reverse of removal. Tension the drive belt, see Chapter 1.

Diverter Valve

Servicing the diverter valve is limited to replacement. If the valve fails it will become ex-

tremely noisy. If air escapes from the silencer at idle speed, either the diverter valve or the relief valve has failed and the entire valve assembly should be replaced.

1. Remove the air and vacuum hoses.
2. Remove the 2 screws holding the diverter valve to the mounting flange and remove the valve.
3. Remove the old gasket.
4. Installation is the reverse of removal. Use a new gasket and connect the hoses properly.

Check Valve

The check valve is not repairable; if necessary to service it, replace it with a new one. The valve can be tested by removing the hose from the valve inlet tube. If exhaust gasses escape from the inlet tube the valve has failed. On California cars, if the tube nut joint is leaking, retorque the nut to 25-35 ft. lbs. If the adapter to the exhaust manifold joint is leaking, retorque the connection to a maximum of 40 ft. lbs. On Canadian cars, if the air injection tube to the head joint is leaking, retorque the hollow bolts to 20 ft. lbs.

CALIFORNIA CARS

1. Release the clamp and disconnect the air hose from the check valve.
2. Remove the tube nut holding the injection tube to the exhaust manifold.

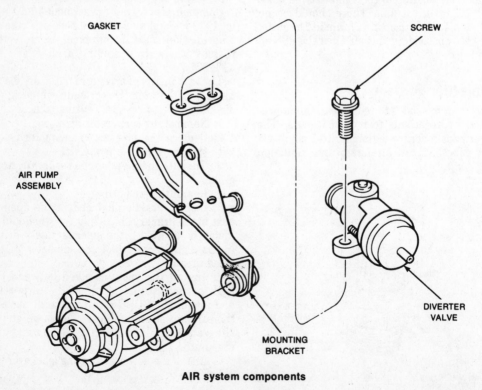

AIR system components

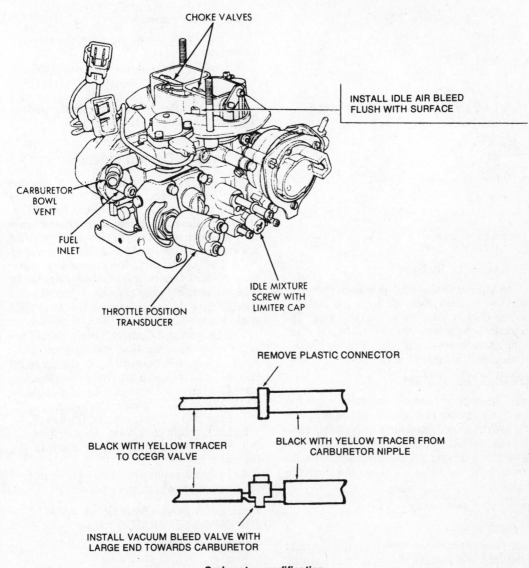

Carburetor modification

3. Remove the injection tube from the engine.

4. Installation is the reverse of removal.

CANADIAN CARS

1. Release the clamp and remove the air hose from the check valve inlet.

2. On air conditioned cars, remove the air conditioning compressor from the mount.

CAUTION: *Do not disconnect any air conditioning system hoses.*

Remove the 4 isolated rubber compressor mounting bracket bolts and the compressor-to-cylinder head bolt. Set the compressor aside and keep it upright.

3. Drain the cooling system to a level below the thermostat housing.

4. Remove the housing from the bypass hose.

5. Remove the 4 hollow bolts holding the injection tube assembly to the cylinder head.

6. Install the injection tube assembly on the cylinder head. The 4 copper washers must be used between the tube assembly and the cylinder head.

7. Install the 4 hollow bolts with copper washers between each bolt and the injection tube assembly. The washers must be used. Torque the bolts to 20 ft. lbs.

8. Install the thermostat housing and connect the bypass hose.

9. On engines with air conditioning, reinstall the compressor. Adjust the drive belt. See Chapter 1.

10. Reconnect the air hose to the check valve inlet.

11. Refill the cooling system. See Chapter 1.

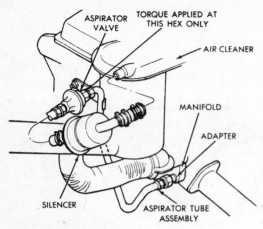

AIR aspirator system

Air Aspirator System

The aspirator valve utilizes exhaust pressure pulsation to draw clean air from the inside of the air cleaner into the exhaust system. The function is to reduce HC (hydrocarbon) emissions. It is located in a tube between the exhaust manifold and the air cleaner.

TESTING THE SYSTEM

To determine if the air aspirator valve has failed, disconnect the hose from the aspirator inlet. With the engine idling in Neutral, vacuum exhaust pulses can be felt at the aspirator inlet. If hot exhaust gas is escaping from the aspirator inlet, the valve has failed and should be replaced.

REMOVAL AND INSTALLATION

Aspirator Valve

1. Disconnect the air hose from the aspirator valve inlet and unscrew the valve from the aspirator tube assembly.
2. Installation is the reverse of removal. Replace the hose if it has hardened.

Aspirator Tube Assembly

1. Disconnect the air hose fro the aspirator valve inlet.
2. Remove the nut securing the aspirator tube assembly to the engine.
3. Remove the aspirator tube.
4. Installation is the reverse of removal. Tighten the tube nut to 25-35 ft. lbs.

Evaporation Control System

This system prevents the release of gasoline vapors from the fuel tank and the carburetor into the atmosphere. The system is vacuum operated and draws the fumes into a charcoal canister where they are temporarily held until they are drawn into the intake manifold for burning. For proper operation of the system and to prevent gas tank failure, the lines should never be plugged, and no other cap other than the one specified should be used on the fuel tank filler neck.

The Evaporation Control System should not require service other than replacement of the charcoal canister filter. All hoses should be inspected and replaced if cracked or leaking. Any loss of fuel or vapor from the filler cap would indicate one of the following conditions:

1. Poor seal between cap and filler neck,
2. Malfunction of fuel cap release valve,
3. Plugged vent line roll-over valve in the fuel tank, or
4. Plugged vapor vent lines between fuel tank and charcoal canister.

FUEL TANK ROLL-OVER VALVE AND LIQUID VAPOR SEPARATOR VALVE

Removal and Installation

1. Remove the fuel tank.
2. Wedge the blade of a suitable pry bar between the rubber grommet and the support rib on the fuel tank.

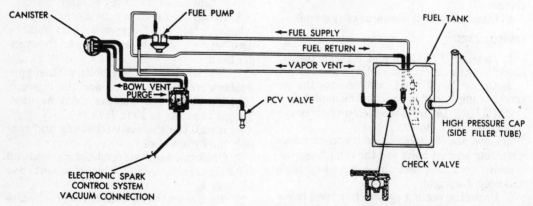

Fuel evaporation control system schematic

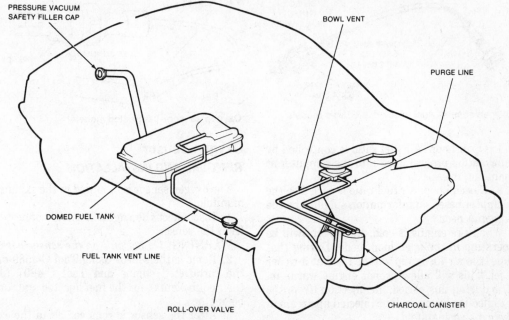

Components of Fuel Evaporation system

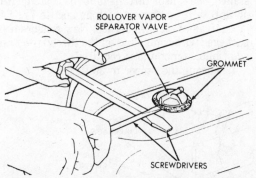

Removing rollover/vapor separation valve from fuel tank

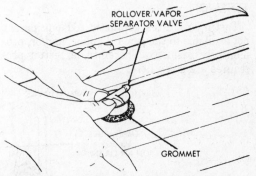

Installing the rollover/vapor separator valve

CAUTION: *Chrysler recommends the use of 2 screwdrivers for this operation. Before performing this operation with screwdrivers, read the Safety Notice on the acknowledgements page of this book and read the section in Chapter 1 concerning Safety.*

3. Use a second screwdriver as a support and pry the valve and grommet from the tank.

WARNING: *Do not pry between the valve and grommet.*

4. To remove the grommet from the valve, place the valve upright on a flat surface and push down on the grommet.

5. Install the rubber grommet in the fuel tank and work it around the curled lip.

6. Lubricate the grommet with engine oil and twist the valve down into the grommet.

7. Install the fuel tank.

Electronic Feedback Carburetor (EFC) System
GENERAL INFORMATION

The EFC system is essentially an emissions control system which utilizes an electronic signal, generated by an exhaust gas oxygen sensor, to precisely control the air-fuel mixture ratio in the carburetor. This allows the engine to produce exhaust gases of the proper composition to permit the use of a three-way catalyst. The three-way catalyst is designed to convert the three pollutants (1) Hydrocarbons (HC), (2) Carbon Monoxide (CO), and (3) Oxides of Nitrogen (NOx) into harmless substances.

There are two operating modes in the EFC system:

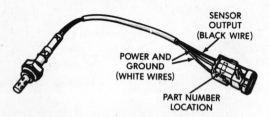

Oxygen sensor—fuel injected and turbo models

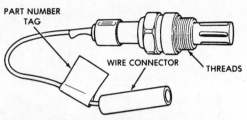

Oxygen sensor—carbureted models

1. Open Loop: Air fuel ratio is controlled by information programmed into the computer at manufacture.

2. Closed Loop: Air fuel ratio is varied by the computer based on information supplied by the oxygen sensor.

When the engine is cold, the system will be operating in the open loop mode. During that time, the air fuel ratio will be fixed at a richer level. This will allow proper engine warm-up. Also during this period, air injection (from the air injection pump) will be injected upstream in the exhaust manifold.

TESTING

Testing requires sophisticated equipment not available to the general public, and/or, prohibitively expensive. Therefore, no testing procedures are given here.

Oxygen Sensor
REMOVAL AND INSTALLATION

The oxygen sensor is mounted in the exhaust manifold.

1. Disconnect the engine harness connector from the sensor.

WARNING: *Do not pull on the sensor wire.*

2. Remove the sensor using Tool C-4589 on the carbureted engine and Tool C-4907 (or their equivalents), for the fuel injected and turbo engines.

3. After the sensor is removed clean the exhaust manifold threads with an 18mm × 1.5mm × 6E tap. If the old sensor is to be reinstalled, the sensor threads must be coated with an anti seize compound such as Loctite 771-64 or equivalent on the threads. New sensors are packeged with compound on the threads and no additional compound is required.

4. Torque the sensor to 20 ft. lbs.

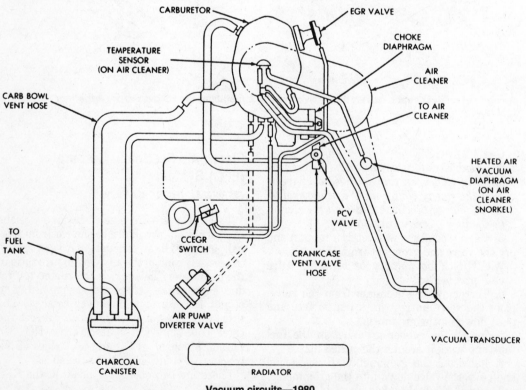

Vacuum circuits—1980

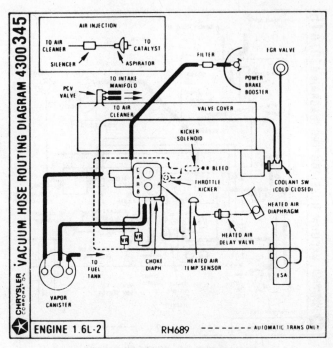

Vacuum circuits—1983 1.6L Federal/California

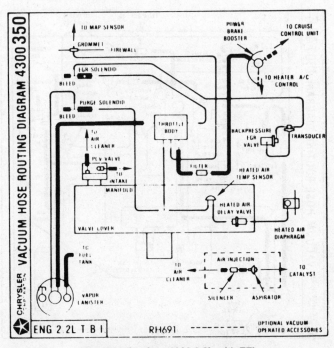

Vacuum circuits—1983 2.2L with EFI

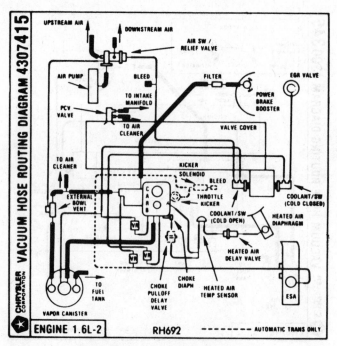

Vacuum circuits—1983 1.6L Canada

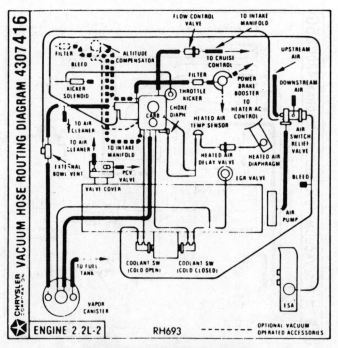

Vacuum circuits—1983 2.2L Federal

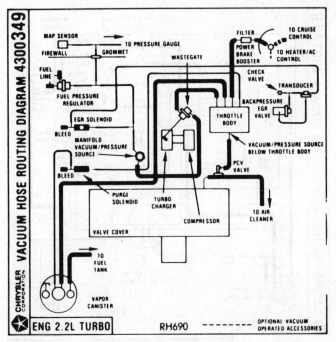

Vacuum circuits—1983 2.2LTurbo

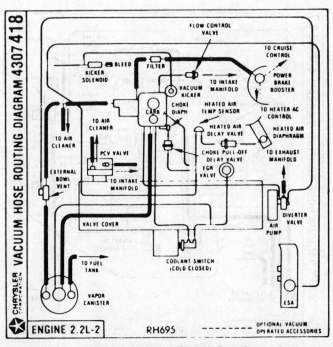

Vacuum circuits—1983 2.2L Canada

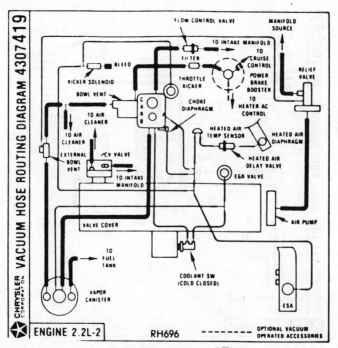

Vacuum circuits—1983 2.2L California

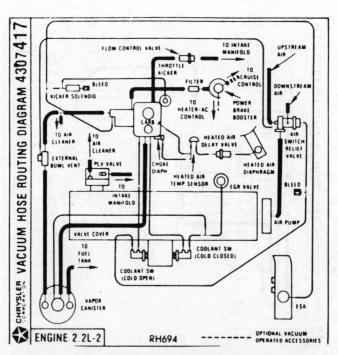

Vacuum circuits—1983 2.2L High Altitude

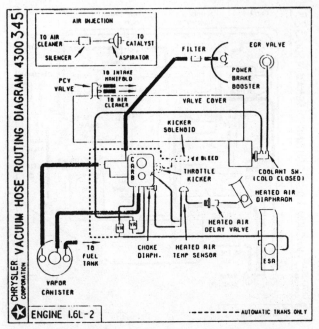

Vacuum circuits—1984 1.6L Automatic transmission

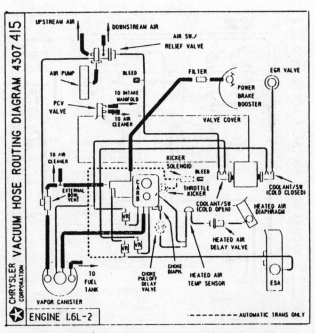

Vacuum circuits—1984 1.6L Automatic transmission

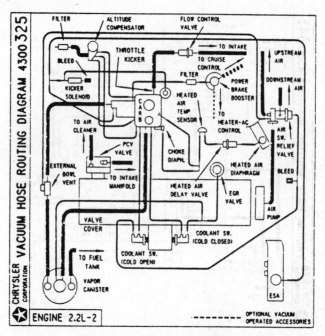

Vacuum circuits—1984 2.2L

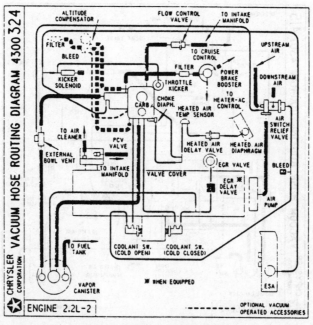

Vacuum circuits—1984 2.2L

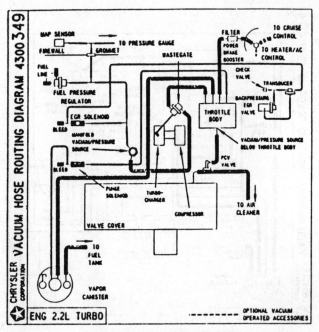

Vacuum circuits—1984 2.2L Turbo

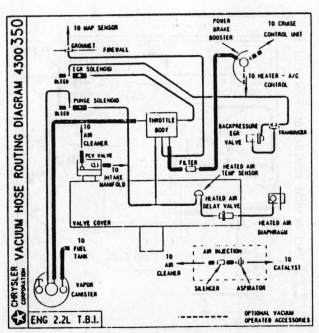

Vacuum circuits—1984 2.2L TBI

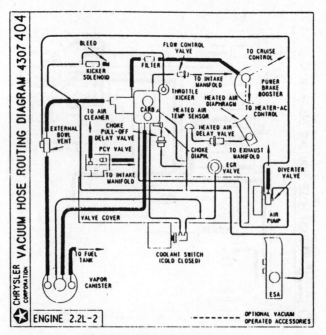

Vacuum circuits—1984 2.2L Canada

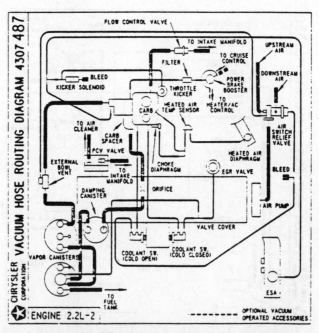

Vacuum circuits—1984 2.2L E.S.A., 2 bbl., Canada

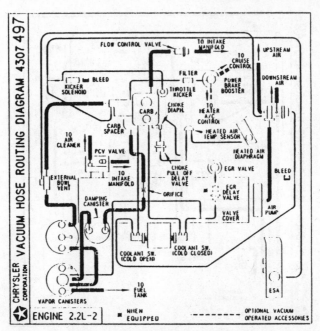

Vacuum circuits—1984 2.2L California

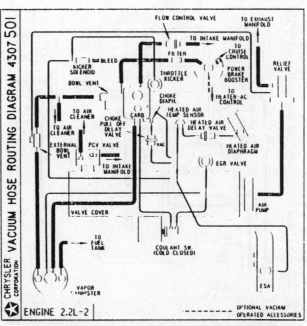

Vacuum circuits—1984 2.2L Federal & High Altitude

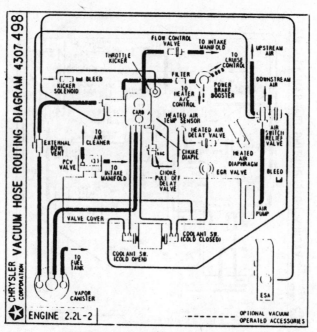

Vacuum circuits—1984 2.2L California

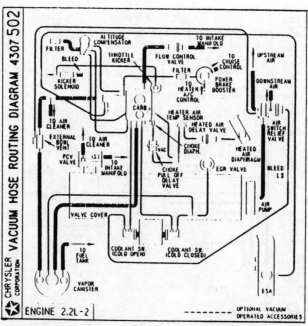

Vacuum circuits—1984 2.2L E.S.A., 2 bbl., Federal

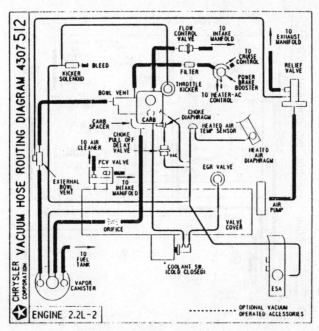

Vacuum circuits—1984 2.2L E.S.A., 2 bbl., Canada

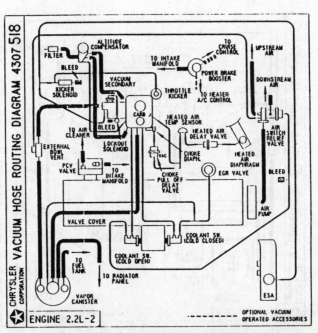

Vacuum circuits—1984 2.2L Federal & High Altitude

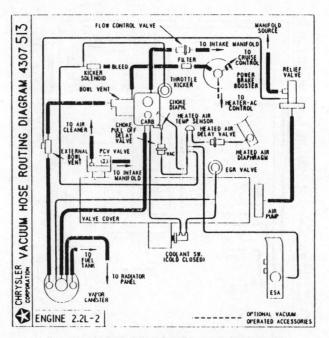

Vacuum circuits—1984 2.2L E.S.A., 2 bbl., Federal

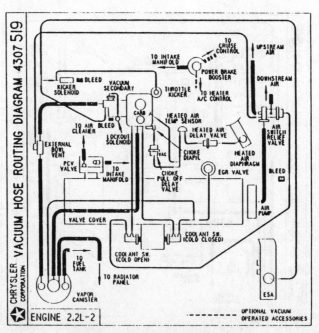

Vacuum circuits—1984 2.2L California

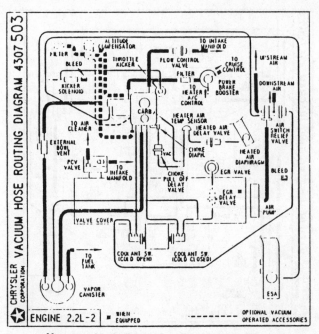

Vacuum circuits—1984 2.2L Federal & High Altitude

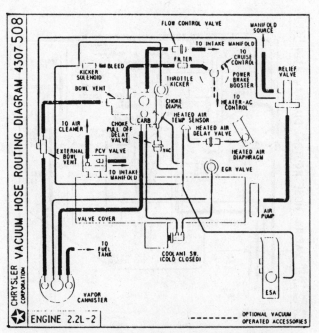

Vacuum circuits—1984 2.2L E.S.A., 2 bbl., Federal

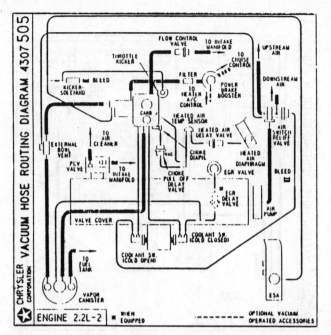

Vacuum circuits—1984 2.2L California

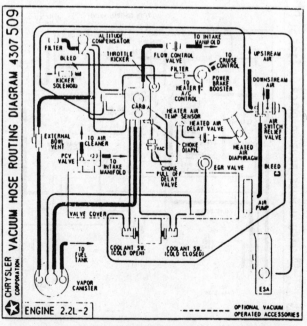

Vacuum circuits—1984 2.2L Federal & High Altitude

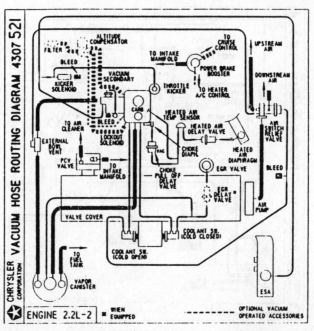

Vacuum circuits—1984 2.2L E.S.A., Manual trans., Federal & High Altitude

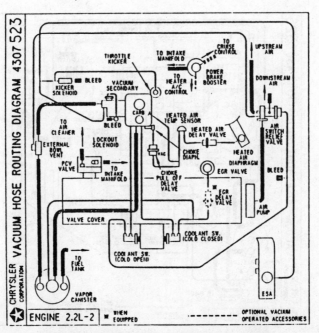

Vacuum circuits—1984 2.2L E.S.A., 2 bbl., Federal

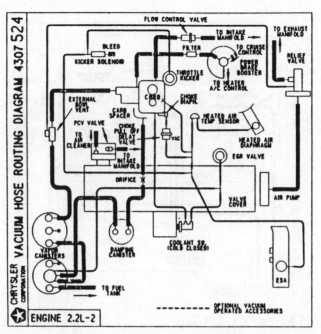

Vacuum circuits—1984 2.2L California

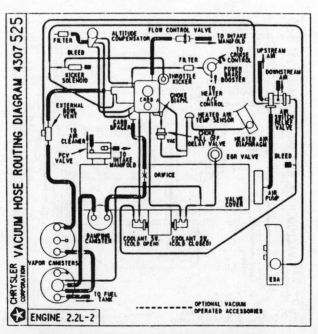

Vacuum circuits—1984 2.2L Federal & High Altitude

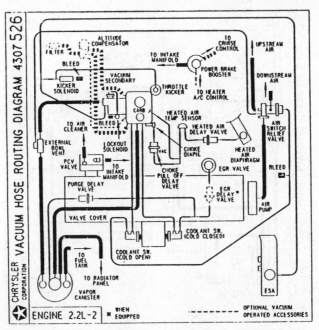

Vacuum circuits—1984 2.2L E.S.A., Federal & High Altitude

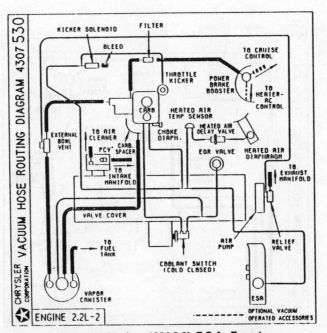

Vacuum circuits—1984 2.2L E.S.A., Export

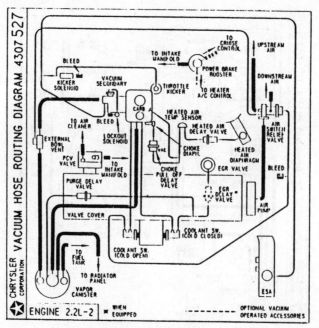

Vacuum circuits—1984 2.2L E.S.A., California

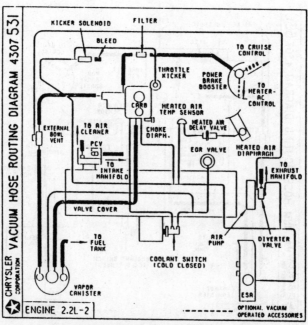

Vacuum circuits—1984 2.2L E.S.A., Export

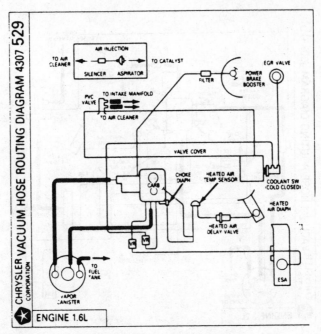

Vacuum circuits—1985 1.6L Canada

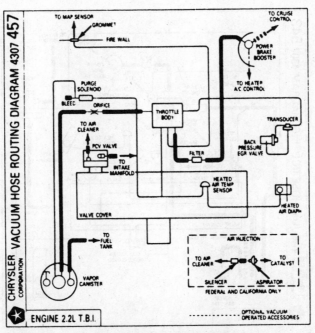

Vacuum circuits—1985 2.2L EFI

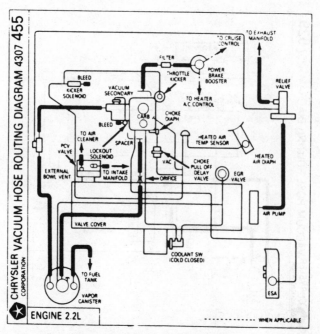

Vacuum circuits—1985 2.2L Canada

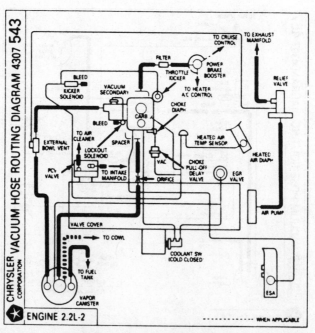

Vacuum circuits—1985 2.2L Canada

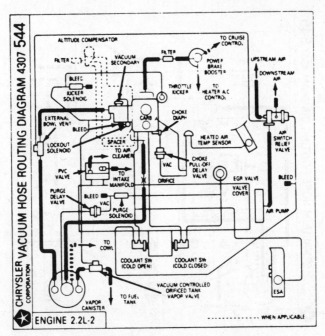

Vacuum circuits—1985 2.2L Federal

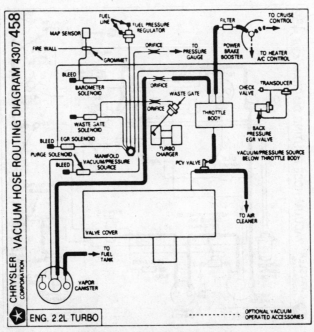

Vacuum circuits—1985 2.2L Turbo

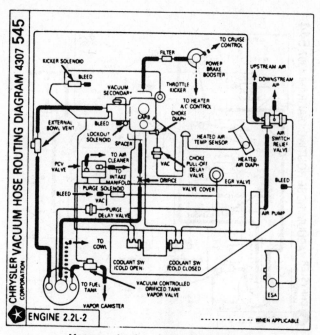

Vacuum circuits—1985 2.2L California

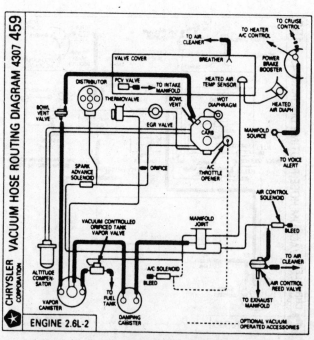

Vacuum circuits—1985 2.2L California & Canada

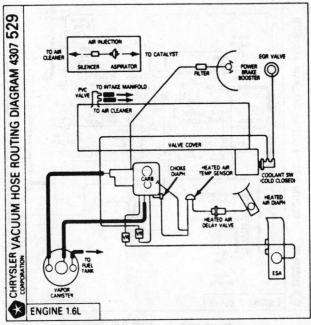

Vacuum circuits—1986 1.6L Canada

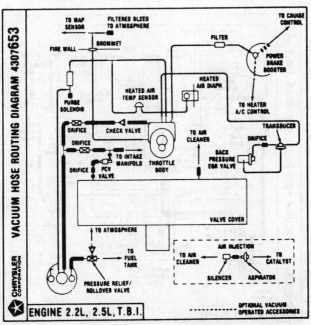

Vacuum circuits—1986 2.2L EFI

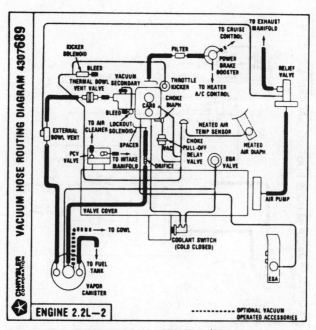

Vacuum circuits—1986 2.2L Canada

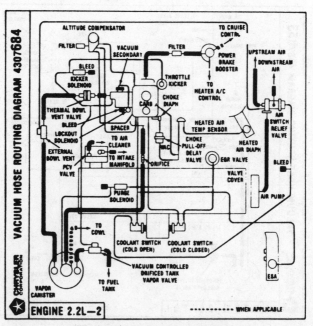

Vacuum circuits—1986 2.2L Federal

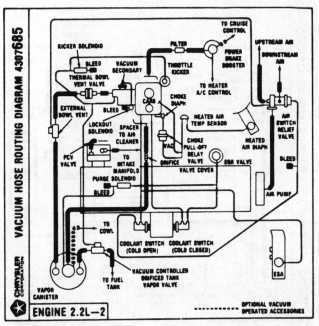

Vacuum circuits—1986 2.2L California

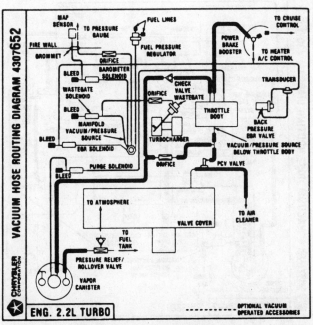

Vacuum circuits—1986 2.2L Turbo

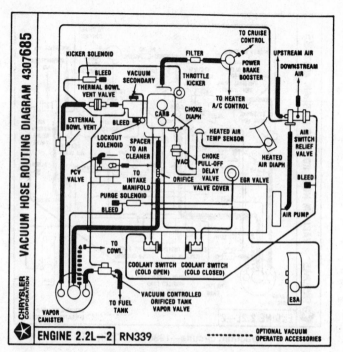

Vacuum circuits—1987 2.2L California & Canada

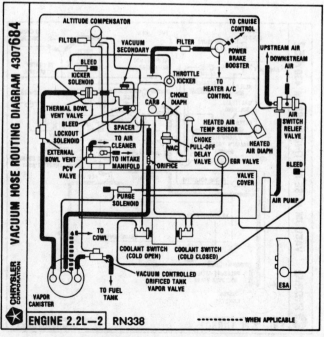

Vacuum circuits—1987 2.2L Federal

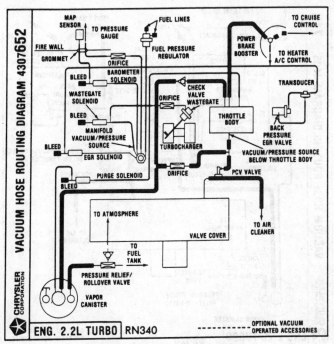

Vacuum circuits—1987 2.2L Turbo

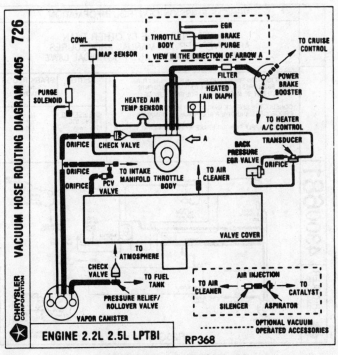

Vacuum circuits—1987 2.2L EFI

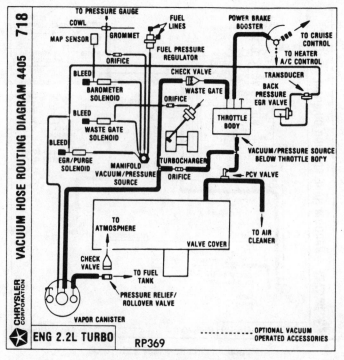

Vacuum circuits—1987 2.2L Turbo

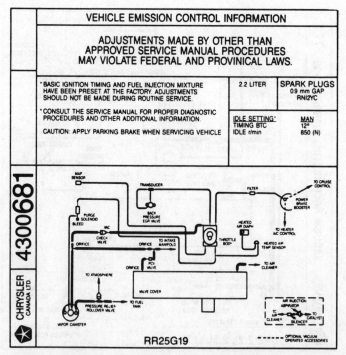

Vacuum circuits—1988 2.2L Canada & Federal, Altitude with EFI

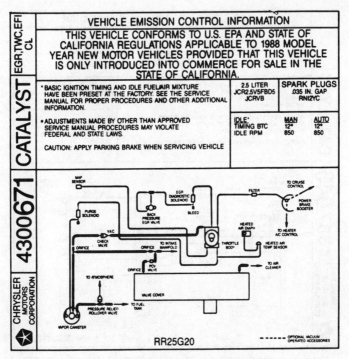

Vacuum circuits—1988 2.2L California with EFI

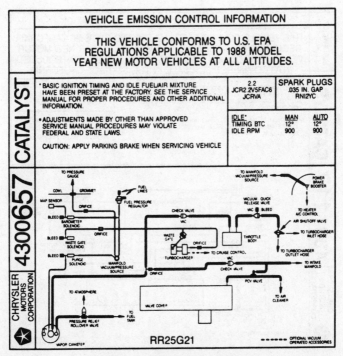

Vacuum circuits—1988 2.2L Turbo

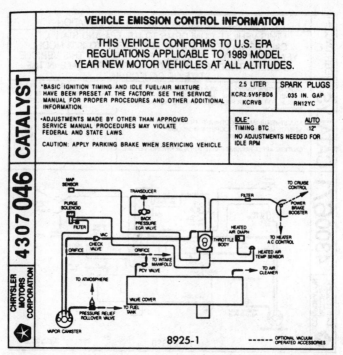

Vacuum circuits—1989 2.2L Canada & Federal, Altitude with EFI

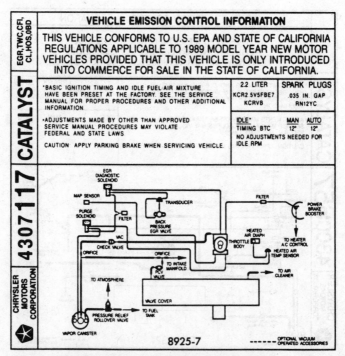

Vacuum circuits—1989 2.2L California with EFI

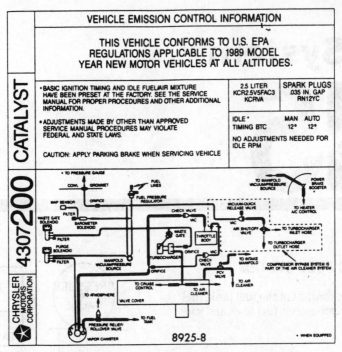

Vacuum circuits—1989 2.2L Turbo except California

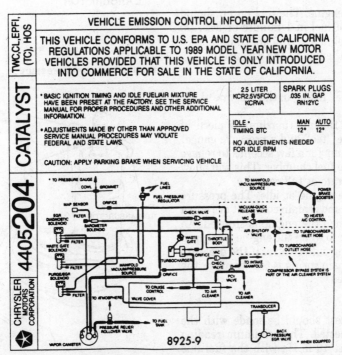

Vacuum circuits—1989 2.2L Turbo California

Fuel System

CARBURETED FUEL SYSTEM

The fuel system consists of the fuel tank, fuel pump, fuel filter, carburetor, fuel lines and vacuum lines.

Fuel Pump

TESTING

The fuel pump can be tested in a variety of ways, depending on the equipment available.

Volume Test

1. Disconnect the fuel supply line from the carburetor (leave it connected to the fuel pump).
2. Crank the engine. The fuel pump should supply 1 quart of fuel in 1 minute or less. Do not catch the fuel in a styrofoam container.
3. Reconnect the line to the carburetor.

Pressure Test

1. Insert a "tee" fitting in the fuel line at the carburetor.
2. Connect a 152mm (maximum) piece of hose between the "tee" and a pressure gauge.
3. Vent the pump for a few seconds to relieve air trapped in the fuel chamber. This will allow the pump to operate at full capacity.
4. Operate the engine at idle. The pressure should be 4-6 psi and remain constant or return slowly to zero when the engine is stopped. An instant drop to zero when the engine is stopped indicates a leaking outlet valve. If the pressure is too high, the main spring is too strong or the air vent is plugged.

Vacuum Test

The vacuum test should be made with the fuel line disconnected. The minimum reading should be at least 10 in.Hg with the fuel line disconnected at the carburetor.

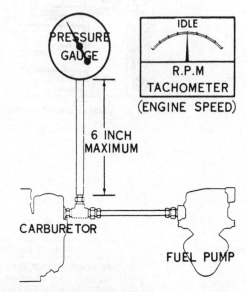

Testing fuel pump pressure

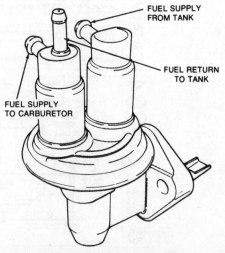

1.7L engine fuel pump through 1980

CHILTON'S
FUEL ECONOMY
& TUNE-UP TIPS

Tune-up • Spark Plug Diagnosis • Emission Controls

Fuel System • Cooling System • Tires and Wheels

General Maintenance

55 WAYS TO IMPROVE FUEL ECONOMY

CHILTON'S FUEL ECONOMY & TUNE-UP TIPS

Fuel economy is important to everyone, no matter what kind of vehicle you drive. The maintenance-minded motorist can save both money and fuel using these tips and the periodic maintenance and tune-up procedures in this Repair and Tune-Up Guide.

There are more than 130,000,000 cars and trucks registered for private use in the United States. Each travels an average of 10-12,000 miles per year, and, and in total they consume close to 70 billion gallons of fuel each year. This represents nearly ⅔ of the oil imported by the United States each year. The Federal government's goal is to reduce consumption 10% by 1985. A variety of methods are either already in use or under serious consideration, and they all affect you driving and the cars you will drive. In addition to "down-sizing", the auto industry is using or investigating the use of electronic fuel delivery, electronic engine controls and alternative engines for use in smaller and lighter vehicles, among other alternatives to meet the federally mandated Corporate Average Fuel Economy (CAFE) of 27.5 mpg by 1985. The government, for its part, is considering rationing, mandatory driving curtailments and tax increases on motor vehicle fuel in an effort to reduce consumption. The government's goal of a 10% reduction could be realized — and further government regulation avoided — if every private vehicle could use just 1 less gallon of fuel per week.

How Much Can You Save?

Tests have proven that almost anyone can make at least a 10% reduction in fuel consumption through regular maintenance and tune-ups. When a major manufacturer of spark plugs sur-

TUNE-UP

1. Check the cylinder compression to be sure the engine will really benefit from a tune-up and that it is capable of producing good fuel economy. A tune-up will be wasted on an engine in poor mechanical condition.

2. Replace spark plugs regularly. New spark plugs alone can increase fuel economy 3%.

3. Be sure the spark plugs are the correct type (heat range) for your vehicle. See the Tune-Up Specifications.

Heat range refers to the spark plug's ability to conduct heat away from the firing end. It must conduct the heat away in an even pattern to avoid becoming a source of pre-ignition, yet it must also operate hot enough to burn off conductive deposits that could cause misfiring.

The heat range is usually indicated by a number on the spark plug, part of the manufacturer's designation for each individual spark plug. The numbers in bold-face indicate the heat range in each manufacturer's identification system.

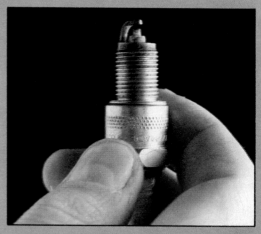

Periodically, check the spark plugs to be sure they are firing efficiently. They are excellent indicators of the internal condition of your engine.

Manufacturer	Typical Designation
AC	R **45** TS
Bosch (old)	WA **145** T30
Bosch (new)	HR **8** Y
Champion	RBL **15** Y
Fram/Autolite	**415**
Mopar	P-**62** PR
Motorcraft	BRF-**42**
NGK	BP **5** ES-15
Nippondenso	W **16** EP
Prestolite	14GR **5** 2A

On AC, Bosch (new), Champion, Fram/Autolite, Mopar, Motorcraft and Prestolite, a higher number indicates a hotter plug. On Bosch (old), NGK and Nippondenso, a higher number indicates a colder plug.

4. Make sure the spark plugs are properly gapped. See the Tune-Up Specifications in this book.

5. Be sure the spark plugs are firing efficiently. The illustrations on the next 2 pages show you how to "read" the firing end of the spark plug.

6. Check the ignition timing and set it to specifications. Tests show that almost all cars have incorrect ignition timing by more than 2°.

veyed over 6,000 cars nationwide, they found that a tune-up, on cars that needed one, increased fuel economy over 11%. Replacing worn plugs alone, accounted for a 3% increase. The same test also revealed that 8 out of every 10 vehicles will have some maintenance deficiency that will directly affect fuel economy, emissions or performance. Most of this mileage-robbing neglect could be prevented with regular maintenance.

Modern engines require that all of the functioning systems operate properly for maximum efficiency. A malfunction anywhere wastes fuel. You can keep your vehicle running as efficiently and economically as possible, by being aware of your vehicle's operating and performance characteristics. If your vehicle suddenly develops performance or fuel economy problems it could be due to one or more of the following:

PROBLEM	POSSIBLE CAUSE
Engine Idles Rough	Ignition timing, idle mixture, vacuum leak or something amiss in the emission control system.
Hesitates on Acceleration	Dirty carburetor or fuel filter, improper accelerator pump setting, ignition timing or fouled spark plugs.
Starts Hard or Fails to Start	Worn spark plugs, improperly set automatic choke, ice (or water) in fuel system.
Stalls Frequently	Automatic choke improperly adjusted and possible dirty air filter or fuel filter.
Performs Sluggishly	Worn spark plugs, dirty fuel or air filter, ignition timing or automatic choke out of adjustment.

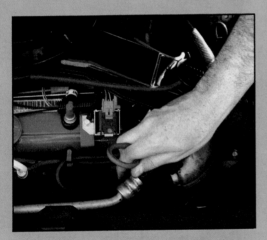

Check spark plug wires on conventional point type ignition for cracks by bending them in a loop around your finger.

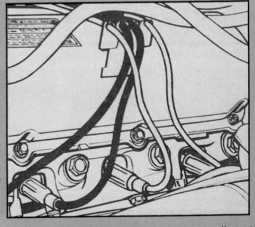

Be sure that spark plug wires leading to adjacent cylinders do not run too close together. (Photo courtesy Champion Spark Plug Co.)

7. If your vehicle does not have electronic ignition, check the points, rotor and cap as specified.

8. Check the spark plug wires (used with conventional point-type ignitions) for cracks and burned or broken insulation by bending them in a loop around your finger. Cracked wires decrease fuel efficiency by failing to deliver full voltage to the spark plugs. One misfiring spark plug can cost you as much as 2 mpg.

9. Check the routing of the plug wires. Misfiring can be the result of spark plug leads to adjacent cylinders running parallel to each other and too close together. One wire tends to pick up voltage from the other causing it to fire "out of time".

10. Check all electrical and ignition circuits for voltage drop and resistance.

11. Check the distributor mechanical and/or vacuum advance mechanisms for proper functioning. The vacuum advance can be checked by twisting the distributor plate in the opposite direction of rotation. It should spring back when released.

12. Check and adjust the valve clearance on engines with mechanical lifters. The clearance should be slightly loose rather than too tight.

SPARK PLUG DIAGNOSIS

Normal

APPEARANCE: This plug is typical of one operating normally. The insulator nose varies from a light tan to grayish color with slight electrode wear. The presence of slight deposits is normal on used plugs and will have no adverse effect on engine performance. The spark plug heat range is correct for the engine and the engine is running normally.

CAUSE: Properly running engine.

RECOMMENDATION: Before reinstalling this plug, the electrodes should be cleaned and filed square. Set the gap to specifications. If the plug has been in service for more than 10-12,000 miles, the entire set should probably be replaced with a fresh set of the same heat range.

Oil Deposits

APPEARANCE: The firing end of the plug is covered with a wet, oily coating.

CAUSE: The problem is poor oil control. On high mileage engines, oil is leaking past the rings or valve guides into the combustion chamber. A common cause is also a plugged PCV valve, and a ruptured fuel pump diaphragm can also cause this condition. Oil fouled plugs such as these are often found in new or recently overhauled engines, before normal oil control is achieved, and can be cleaned and reinstalled.

RECOMMENDATION: A hotter spark plug may temporarily relieve the problem, but the engine is probably in need of work.

Incorrect Heat Range

APPEARANCE: The effects of high temperature on a spark plug are indicated by clean white, often blistered insulator. This can also be accompanied by excessive wear of the electrode, and the absence of deposits.

CAUSE: Check for the correct spark plug heat range. A plug which is too hot for the engine can result in overheating. A car operated mostly at high speeds can require a colder plug. Also check ignition timing, cooling system level, fuel mixture and leaking intake manifold.

RECOMMENDATION: If all ignition and engine adjustments are known to be correct, and no other malfunction exists, install spark plugs one heat range colder.

Carbon Deposits

APPEARANCE: Carbon fouling is easily identified by the presence of dry, soft, black, sooty deposits.

CAUSE: Changing the heat range can often lead to carbon fouling, as can prolonged slow, stop-and-start driving. If the heat range is correct, carbon fouling can be attributed to a rich fuel mixture, sticking choke, clogged air cleaner, worn breaker points, retarded timing or low compression. If only one or two plugs are carbon fouled, check for corroded or cracked wires on the affected plugs. Also look for cracks in the distributor cap between the towers of affected cylinders.

RECOMMENDATION: After the problem is corrected, these plugs can be cleaned and reinstalled if not worn severely.

MMT Fouled

APPEARANCE: Spark plugs fouled by MMT (Methycyclopentadienyl Maganese Tricarbonyl) have reddish, rusty appearance on the insulator and side electrode.

CAUSE: MMT is an anti-knock additive in gasoline used to replace lead. During the combustion process, the MMT leaves a reddish deposit on the insulator and side electrode.

RECOMMENDATION: No engine malfunction is indicated and the deposits will not affect plug performance any more than lead deposits (see Ash Deposits). MMT fouled plugs can be cleaned, regapped and reinstalled.

High Speed Glazing

APPEARANCE: Glazing appears as shiny coating on the plug, either yellow or tan in color.

CAUSE: During hard, fast acceleration, plug temperatures rise suddenly. Deposits from normal combustion have no chance to fluff-off; instead, they melt on the insulator forming an electrically conductive coating which causes misfiring.

RECOMMENDATION: Glazed plugs are not easily cleaned. They should be replaced with a fresh set of plugs of the correct heat range. If the condition recurs, using plugs with a heat range one step colder may cure the problem.

Ash (Lead) Deposits

APPEARANCE: Ash deposits are characterized by light brown or white colored deposits crusted on the side or center electrodes. In some cases it may give the plug a rusty appearance.

CAUSE: Ash deposits are normally derived from oil or fuel additives burned during normal combustion. Normally they are harmless, though excessive amounts can cause misfiring. If deposits are excessive in short mileage, the valve guides may be worn.

RECOMMENDATION: Ash-fouled plugs can be cleaned, gapped and reinstalled.

Detonation

APPEARANCE: Detonation is usually characterized by a broken plug insulator.

CAUSE: A portion of the fuel charge will begin to burn spontaneously, from the increased heat following ignition. The explosion that results applies extreme pressure to engine components, frequently damaging spark plugs and pistons.

Detonation can result by over-advanced ignition timing, inferior gasoline (low octane) lean air/fuel mixture, poor carburetion, engine lugging or an increase in compression ratio due to combustion chamber deposits or engine modification.

RECOMMENDATION: Replace the plugs after correcting the problem.

EMISSION CONTROLS

13. Be aware of the general condition of the emission control system. It contributes to reduced pollution and should be serviced regularly to maintain efficient engine operation.

14. Check all vacuum lines for dried, cracked or brittle conditions. Something as simple as a leaking vacuum hose can cause poor performance and loss of economy.

15. Avoid tampering with the emission control system. Attempting to improve fuel econ-

FUEL SYSTEM

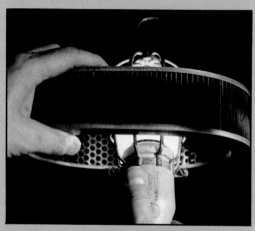

Check the air filter with a light behind it. If you can see light through the filter it can be reused.

Extremely clogged filters should be discarded and replaced with a new one.

18. Replace the air filter regularly. A dirty air filter richens the air/fuel mixture and can increase fuel consumption as much as 10%. Tests show that ⅓ of all vehicles have air filters in need of replacement.

19. Replace the fuel filter at least as often as recommended.

20. Set the idle speed and carburetor mixture to specifications.

21. Check the automatic choke. A sticking or malfunctioning choke wastes gas.

22. During the summer months, adjust the automatic choke for a leaner mixture which will produce faster engine warm-ups.

COOLING SYSTEM

29. Be sure all accessory drive belts are in good condition. Check for cracks or wear.

30. Adjust all accessory drive belts to proper tension.

31. Check all hoses for swollen areas, worn spots, or loose clamps.

32. Check coolant level in the radiator or expansion tank.

33. Be sure the thermostat is operating properly. A stuck thermostat delays engine warm-up and a cold engine uses nearly twice as much fuel as a warm engine.

34. Drain and replace the engine coolant at least as often as recommended. Rust and scale

TIRES & WHEELS

38. Check the tire pressure often with a pencil type gauge. Tests by a major tire manufacturer show that 90% of all vehicles have at least 1 tire improperly inflated. Better mileage can be achieved by over-inflating tires, but never exceed the maximum inflation pressure on the side of the tire.

39. If possible, install radial tires. Radial tires deliver as much as ½ mpg more than bias belted tires.

40. Avoid installing super-wide tires. They only create extra rolling resistance and decrease fuel mileage. Stick to the manufacturer's recommendations.

41. Have the wheels properly balanced.

omy by tampering with emission controls is more likely to worsen fuel economy than improve it. Emission control changes on modern engines are not readily reversible.

16. Clean (or replace) the EGR valve and lines as recommended.

17. Be sure that all vacuum lines and hoses are reconnected properly after working under the hood. An unconnected or misrouted vacuum line can wreak havoc with engine performance.

23. Check for fuel leaks at the carburetor, fuel pump, fuel lines and fuel tank. Be sure all lines and connections are tight.

24. Periodically check the tightness of the carburetor and intake manifold attaching nuts and bolts. These are a common place for vacuum leaks to occur.

25. Clean the carburetor periodically and lubricate the linkage.

26. The condition of the tailpipe can be an excellent indicator of proper engine combustion. After a long drive at highway speeds, the inside of the tailpipe should be a light grey in color. Black or soot on the insides indicates an overly rich mixture.

27. Check the fuel pump pressure. The fuel pump may be supplying more fuel than the engine needs.

28. Use the proper grade of gasoline for your engine. Don't try to compensate for knocking or "pinging" by advancing the ignition timing. This practice will only increase plug temperature and the chances of detonation or pre-ignition with relatively little performance gain.

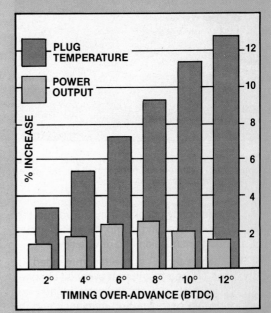

Increasing ignition timing past the specified setting results in a drastic increase in spark plug temperature with increased chance of detonation or preignition. Performance increase is considerably less. (Photo courtesy Champion Spark Plug Co.)

that form in the engine should be flushed out to allow the engine to operate at peak efficiency.

35. Clean the radiator of debris that can decrease cooling efficiency.

36. Install a flex-type or electric cooling fan, if you don't have a clutch type fan. Flex fans use curved plastic blades to push more air at low speeds when more cooling is needed; at high speeds the blades flatten out for less resistance. Electric fans only run when the engine temperature reaches a predetermined level.

37. Check the radiator cap for a worn or cracked gasket. If the cap does not seal properly, the cooling system will not function properly.

42. Be sure the front end is correctly aligned. A misaligned front end actually has wheels going in differed directions. The increased drag can reduce fuel economy by .3 mpg.

43. Correctly adjust the wheel bearings. Wheel bearings that are adjusted too tight increase rolling resistance.

Check tire pressures regularly with a reliable pocket type gauge. Be sure to check the pressure on a cold tire.

GENERAL MAINTENANCE

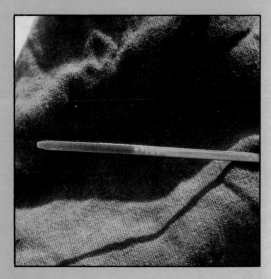

Check the fluid levels (particularly engine oil) on a regular basis. Be sure to check the oil for grit, water or other contamination.

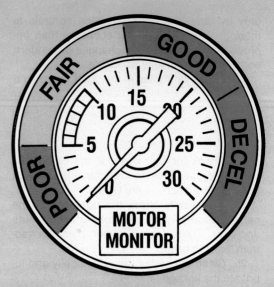

A vacuum gauge is another excellent indicator of internal engine condition and can also be installed in the dash as a mileage indicator.

44. Periodically check the fluid levels in the engine, power steering pump, master cylinder, automatic transmission and drive axle.

45. Change the oil at the recommended interval and change the filter at every oil change. Dirty oil is thick and causes extra friction between moving parts, cutting efficiency and increasing wear. A worn engine requires more frequent tune-ups and gets progressively worse fuel economy. In general, use the lightest viscosity oil for the driving conditions you will encounter.

46. Use the recommended viscosity fluids in the transmission and axle.

47. Be sure the battery is fully charged for fast starts. A slow starting engine wastes fuel.

48. Be sure battery terminals are clean and tight.

49. Check the battery electrolyte level and add distilled water if necessary.

50. Check the exhaust system for crushed pipes, blockages and leaks.

51. Adjust the brakes. Dragging brakes or brakes that are not releasing create increased drag on the engine.

52. Install a vacuum gauge or miles-per-gallon gauge. These gauges visually indicate engine vacuum in the intake manifold. High vacuum = good mileage and low vacuum = poorer mileage. The gauge can also be an excellent indicator of internal engine conditions.

53. Be sure the clutch is properly adjusted. A slipping clutch wastes fuel.

54. Check and periodically lubricate the heat control valve in the exhaust manifold. A sticking or inoperative valve prevents engine warm-up and wastes gas.

55. Keep accurate records to check fuel economy over a period of time. A sudden drop in fuel economy may signal a need for tune-up or other maintenance.

Inlet Valve Test

A vacuum gauge is needed to test the inlet valve.

1. Disconnect the fuel inlet line at the fuel pump.
2. Connect a vacuum gauge to the inlet fitting of the fuel pump.
3. Crank the engine.
4. There should be a noticeable vacuum present, not alternated by blowback.
5. If blowback is present, the inlet valve is not seating properly and the pump should be replaced.

6. Remove the vacuum gauge and reconnect the fuel line.

REMOVAL AND INSTALLATION

A mechanical fuel pump is located on the left side of the engine. To remove the pump, disconnect the fuel and vapor lines and remove the attaching bolts. Installation is the reverse of removal. Always use a new gasket when installing the pump and make certain the gasket surfaces are clean.

Troubleshooting Basic Fuel System Problems

Problem	Cause	Solution
Engine cranks, but won't start (or is hard to start) when cold	• Empty fuel tank • Incorrect starting procedure • Defective fuel pump • No fuel in carburetor • Clogged fuel filter • Engine flooded • Defective choke	• Check for fuel in tank • Follow correct procedure • Check pump output • Check for fuel in the carburetor • Replace fuel filter • Wait 15 minutes; try again • Check choke plate
Engine cranks, but is hard to start (or does not start) when hot— (presence of fuel is assumed)	• Defective choke	• Check choke plate
Rough idle or engine runs rough	• Dirt or moisture in fuel • Clogged air filter • Faulty fuel pump	• Replace fuel filter • Replace air filter • Check fuel pump output
Engine stalls or hesitates on acceleration	• Dirt or moisture in the fuel • Dirty carburetor • Defective fuel pump • Incorrect float level, defective accelerator pump	• Replace fuel filter • Clean the carburetor • Check fuel pump output • Check carburetor
Poor gas mileage	• Clogged air filter • Dirty carburetor • Defective choke, faulty carburetor adjustment	• Replace air filter • Clean carburetor • Check carburetor
Engine is flooded (won't start accompanied by smell of raw fuel)	• Improperly adjusted choke or carburetor	• Wait 15 minutes and try again, without pumping gas pedal • If it won't start, check carburetor

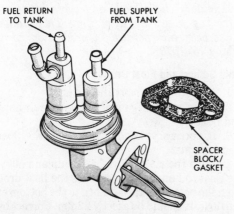

1981–83 1.7L engine fuel pump

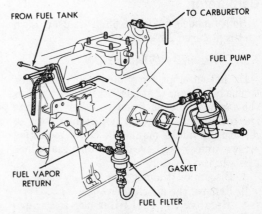

1.6L fuel line routing

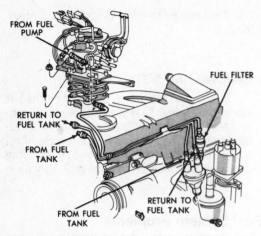

1.7L fuel line routing

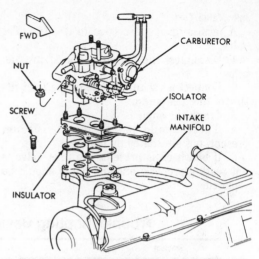

Carburetor removal and installation—typical

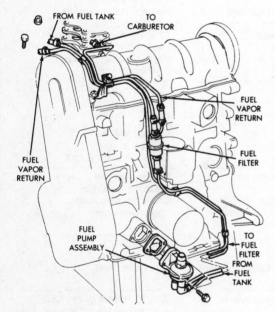

2.2L fuel line routing

Carburetor

Holley models 5220 and 6520 are used. Each unit is a staged 2-barrel unit.

REMOVAL AND INSTALLATION

Do not attempt to remove the carburetor from a hot engine that has just been run. Allow the engine to cool sufficiently. When removing the carburetor, it should not be necessary to disturb the intake manifold isolator mounting screws, unless you have determined that a leak exists in the isolator.

1. Disconnect the negative battery cable.
2. Remove the air cleaner.
3. Remove the fuel filler cap to relieve pressure.

4. Disconnect the fuel inlet fitting and catch any excess fuel that may flow out.
5. Disconnect all electrical connections. Tag these for installation.
6. Disconnect the throttle linkage.
7. Disconnect and tag all hoses.
8. Remove the carburetor mounting nuts and remove the carburetor. Hold the carburetor level to avoid spilling fuel on a hot engine.
9. Installation is the reverse of removal. Be careful when installing the mounting nut nearest the fast idle lever. It is very easy to bend the lever. Tighten the mounting nuts evenly to prevent vacuum leaks.

Check to be sure the choke plate opens and closes fully and that full throttle travel is obtained.

ADJUSTMENTS

NOTE: *Before attempting any adjustments, complaints of fuel loading on a cold engine on all 1978 models (except those with Federal emission package and aspirator and manual transmission) can be cured by removing the secondary choke blade and choke blade attaching screws and discarding. This change has been incorporated in production as of May 15, 1978.*

Float Setting and Float Drop

1. Remove and invert the air horn.
2. Insert a 12mm gauge between the air horn and float.
3. If necessary, bend the tang on the float arm to adjust.
4. Turn the air horn right side up and allow the float to hang freely. Measure the float drop from the bottom of the air horn to the bottom of the float. It should be exactly 22mm. Correct by bending the float tang.

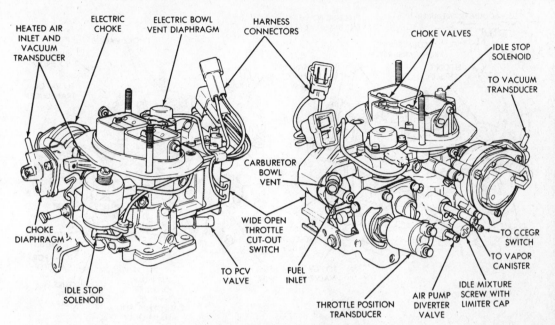

1978 Holley 5220 Carburetor (with A/C)

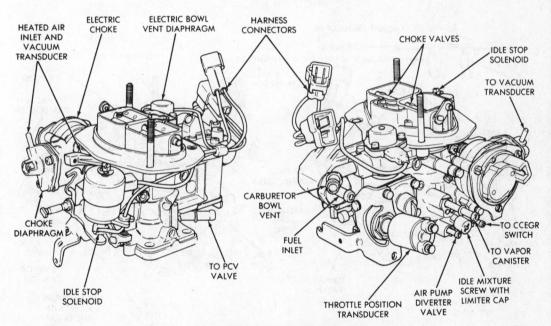

1978 Holley 5220 Carburetor (w/o A/C)

Vacuum Kick

1. Open the throttle, close the choke, then close the throttle to trap the fast idle system at the closed choke position.

2. Disconnect the vacuum hose to the carburetor and connect it to an auxiliary vacuum source.

3. Apply at least 15 in.Hg vacuum to the unit.

4. Apply sufficient force to close the choke valve without distorting the linkage.

5. Insert a gauge (see Specification Chart) between the top of the choke plate and the air horn wall.

6. Adjust by rotating the Allen screw in the center diaphragm housing.

7. Replace the vacuum hose.

Throttle Position Transducer

1978 ONLY

1. Disconnect the wire from the transducer.

2. Loosen the locknut.

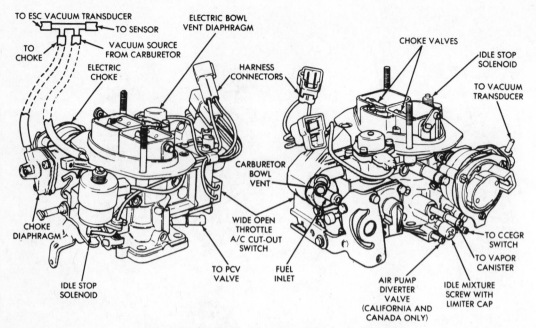

1979–80 Holley 5220 carburetor with air conditioning

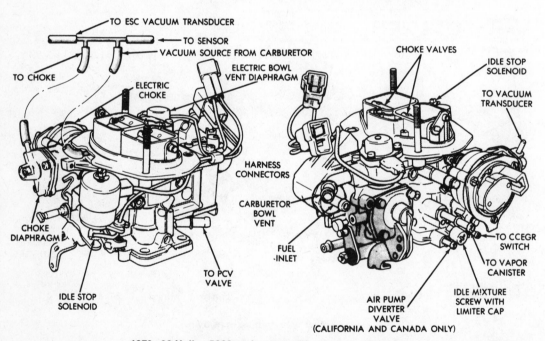

1979–80 Holley 5220 carburetor without air conditioning

3. Place a 17mm gauge between the outer portion of the transducer and the mounting bracket.

4. To adjust the gap, turn the transducer.

5. Tighten the locknut.

Fast Idle

1. Remove the top of the air cleaner.

2. Disconnect and plug the EGR vacuum line. On 2.2L engines, disconnect the 2-way electrical connector at the carburetor (red and tan wires).

3. Plug any open vacuum lines, which were connected to the air cleaner.

4. Do not disconnect the vacuum line to the spark control computer. Instead, use a jumper wire to ground the idle stop switch. The air conditioning should be off.

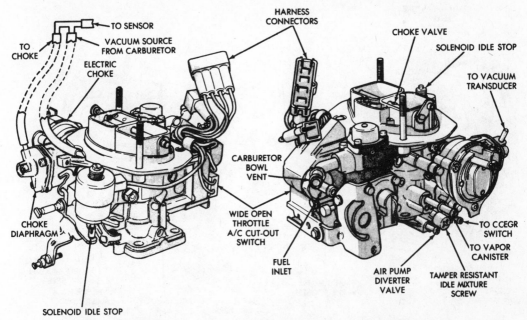

1981–82 Holley 5220 carburetor with manual transaxle and air conditioning

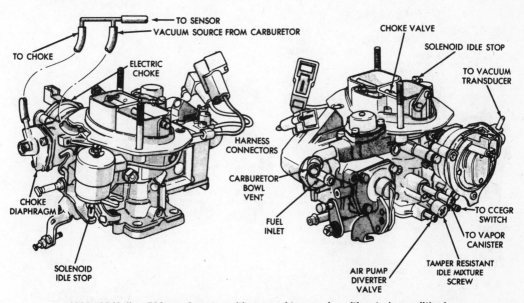

1981–82 Holley 5220 carburetor with manual transaxle, without air conditioning

5. Disconnect the engine cooling fan at the radiator and complete the circuit at the plug with a jumper wire to energize the fan.

6. Set the brake, place the transmission in Neutral and position the first step of the fast idle cam under the adjusting screw.

7. Connect a tachometer according to the manufacturer's specifications.

8. Start the engine and observe the idle speed. With the choke fully open, the speed should remain steady. If it gradually increases, the idle stop switch is not properly grounded.

9. Turn the adjusting screw to give the specified rpm. Do not adjust with the screw contacting the plastic cam.

10. Operate the throttle linkage a few times and return the screw to the first cam step to recheck rpm.

Throttle Stop Speed Adjustment (w/o Air Conditioning)

1. The engine should be fully warmed.

2. Put the transmission in Neutral and set the parking brake.

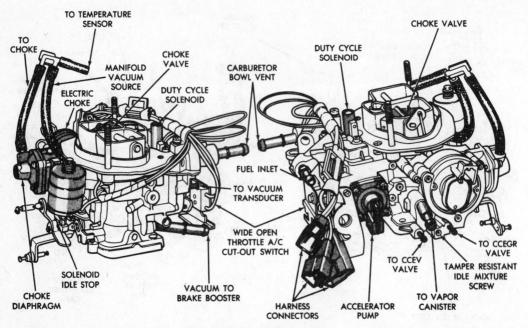

1981–82 Holley 6520 carburetor

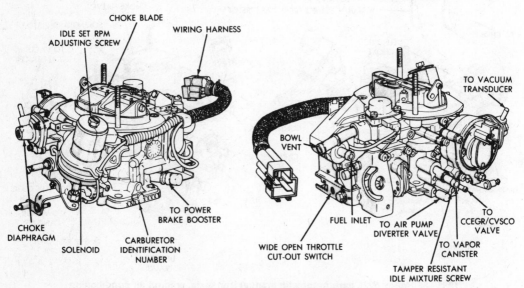

1983 and later Holley 5220 carburetor

3. Turn the headlights off.

4. Using a jumper wire, ground the idle stop carburetor switch.

5. Disconnect the idle stop solenoid wire at the connector.

6. Adjust the throttle stop speed screw to 700 rpm.

7. Reconnect the idle stop solenoid wire.

8. Disconnect the jumper wire from the carburetor switch.

OVERHAUL

Efficient carburetion depends greatly on careful cleaning and inspection during overhaul, since dirt, gum, varnish, water in or on the carburetor parts are mainly responsible for poor performance.

Carburetor overhaul should be performed in a clean, dust-free area. Carefully disassemble the carburetor, keeping look-alike parts segregated. Note all jet sizes.

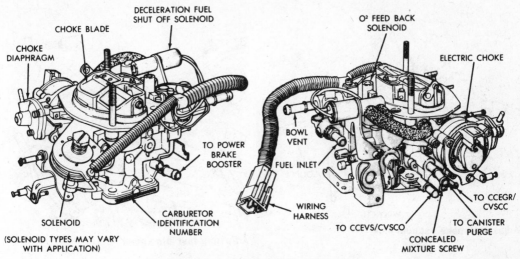

1983 and later Holley 6520 carburetor

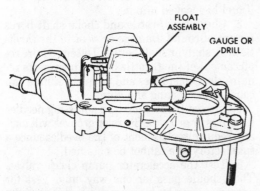

Checking float level

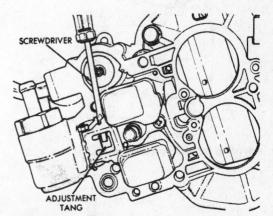

Adjusting float level

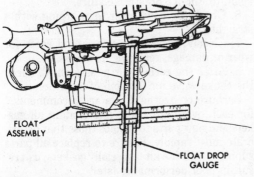

Checking float drop

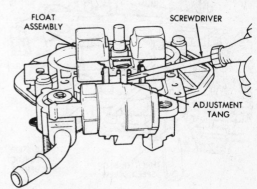

Adjusting float drop

Once the carburetor is disassembled, wash all parts (except diaphragms, electric choke units, pump plunger and any other plastic, leather or fiber parts) in clean carburetor solvent. Do not leave the parts in solvent any longer than necessary to sufficiently loosen the deposits. Excessive cleaning may remove the special finish from the float bowl and choke valve bodies, leaving them unfit for service. Rinse all parts in clean solvent and blow dry with compressed air. Wipe all plastic, leather or fiber parts with a clean, lint-free cloth.

Blow out all passages and jets with compressed air and be sure there are no restrictions or blockages. Never use wire to clean jets, fuel passages or air bleeds.

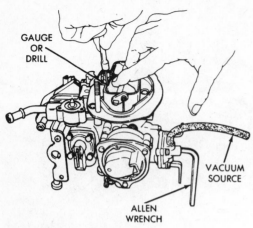

Adjusting choke vacuum kick

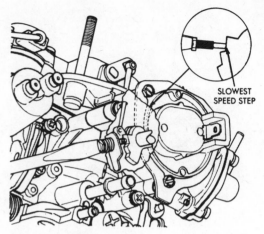

Adjusting fast idle speed

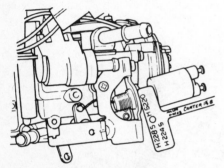

Adjusting throttle position transducer

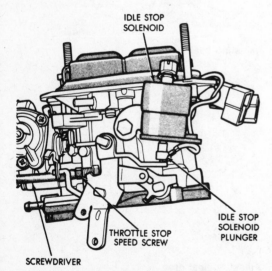

Adjusting throttle stop speed (w/o A/C)

Check all parts for wear or damage. If wear or damage is found, replace the complete assembly. Especially check the following.

1. Check the float and needle seat for wear. If any is found, replace the assembly.

2. Check the float hinge pin for wear and the floats for distortion or dents. Replace the float if fuel has leaked into it.

3. Check the throttle and choke shaft bores for out-of-round. Damage or wear to the throttle arm, shaft or shaft bore will often require replacement of the throttle body. These parts require close tolerances and an air leak here can cause poor starting and idling.

4. Inspect the idle mixture adjusting needles for burrs or grooves. Burrs or grooves will usually require replacement of the needles since a satisfactory idle cannot be obtained.

5. Test the accelerator pump check valves. They should pass air one way only. Test for proper seating by blowing and sucking on the valve. If the valve is satisfactory, wash the valve again to remove breath moisture.

6. Check the bowl cover for warping with a straightedge.

7. Closely inspect the valves and seats for wear or damage, replacing as necessary.

8. After the carburetor is assembled, check the choke valve for freedom of operation.

Carburetor overhaul kits are recommended for each overhaul. These kits contain all gaskets and new parts to replace those that deteriorate most rapidly. Failure to replace all parts supplied with the kit (especially gaskets) can result in poor performance later.

Some carburetor manufacturers supply overhaul kits of three types: minor repair, major repair and gasket kits. They basically consist of:

Minor Repair Kits:
- All gaskets
- Float needle valve
- Volume control screw
- All diaphragms
- Pump diaphragm spring

Major Repair Kits:
- All jets and gaskets
- All diaphragms

Carburetor Specifications
Holley 5220

Year	Carb Part No.	Accelerator Pump	Dry Float Level (in.)	Vacuum Kick (in.)	Fast Idle RPM (w/fan)	Throttle Position Transducer (in.)	Throttle Stop Speed RPM	Choke
1978	R-8376A, 8378A, 8384A, 8439A, 8441A, 8505A, 8507A	#2 hole	.480	.070	1100	.547	700	2 Rich
1979	R-8524A, 8526A, 8532A, 8534A, 8528A, 8530A	#2 hole	.480	.040	1700	—	700	2 Rich
	R8525A, 8541A, 8531A, 8533A, 8527A, 8529A	#2 hole	.480	.070	1400	—	700	2 Rich
1980	R8838A R8839A R9110A R9111A	—	.480	.040	1700		700	—
	R8726A R8727A R9108A	—	.480	.070	1400		700	—
	R9109A	—	.480	.100	1400	—	700	—
1981	R9058A R9059A	—	.480	.040	1400	—	850	—
	R9056A R9057A	—	.480	.070	1400	—	850	—
	R9064A R9065A				1300			
	R9684A R9685A	—	.480	.060	1300	—	850	—
1982	R9582A R9583A R9584A	—	.480	.060	1200	—	—	—
	R9585A				1500			
	R9820A	—	.480	.080	1200	—	—	—
	R9513A R9514A	—	.480	.120	1400	—	—	—
	R9499A R9511A R9512A	—	.480	.130	1200	—	—	—
1983	R40020A	#3 hole	.480	.055	1300	—	—	—
	R40022A	#3 hole	.480	.055	1500	—	—	—
	R40023A R40024 R40025A R40026A	#2 hole	.480	.070	1400	—	700	—
1984	R400601A	#2 hole	.480	.055	1200	—	—	—
	R400851A	#2 hole	.480	.040	1500	—	—	—
	R40170A	#3 hole	.480	.060	1650	—	—	—
	R40171A	#3 hole	.480	.060	1700	—	—	—
	R400671A	#3 hole	.480	.070	1500	—	—	—
	R400681A	#3 hole	.480	.070	1700	—	—	—

Carburetor Specifications
Holley 6520

Year	Carb. Part No.	Dry Float Setting (in.)	Solenoid Idle Stop (rpm)	Fast Idle Speed (rpm)	Vacuum Kick (in.)
1981	R9060A R9061A	.480	850	1100	.030
	R9125A R9126A	.480	850	1200	.030
	R9052A R9053A	.480	850	1400	.070
	R9054A R9055A	.480	850	1400	.040
	R9602A R9603A	.480	850	1500	.065
	R9604A R9605A	.480	850	1600	.065
1982	R9824A	.480	900	1400	.065
	R9503A R9504A R9750A R9751A	.480	850	1300	.085
	R9822A R9823A	.480	850	1400	.080
	R9505A R9506A R9752A R9753A	.480	900	1600	.100
1983	R40080A R40081A	.480	850	1400	.045
	R40003A R40007A	.480	775	1400	.070
	R40010A R40004A	.480	900	1500	.080
	R40012A R4008A	.480	900	1600	.070
	R40014A R40006A	.480	850	1275	.080
1984	R400581A	.480	850	1400	.070
	R401071A	.480	1000	1600	.055
	R400641A R400811A	.480	800	1500	.080
	R400651A R400821A	.480	900	1600	.080
	R40071A R40122A	.480	850	1500	.080

- Float needle valve
- Volume control screw
- Pump ball valve
- Main jet carrier
- Float
- Complete intermediate rod

- Intermediate pump lever
- Complete injector tube
- Assorted screws and washers

Gasket Kits:
- All gaskets

After cleaning and checking all components,

Carburetor Specifications
Holley 5220/6520

Year/ Part No.	Dry Float Setting	Solenoid Idle Stop	Fast Idle Speed (rpm)	Vacuum Kick (in.)
1985				
R40058A	.480	①	①	.070
R40060A	.480	①	①	.055
R40116A	.480	①	①	.095
R40117A	.480	①	①	.095
R40134A	.480	①	①	.075
R40135A	.480	①	①	.075
R40138A	.480	①	①	.075
R40139A	.480	①	①	.075
1986				
R400581A	.480	①	①	.070
R400602A	.480	①	①	.055
R401341A	.480	①	①	.075
R401351A	.480	①	①	.075
R401381A	.480	①	①	.075
R401391A	.480	①	①	.075
R401161A	.480	①	①	.095
R401171A	.480	①	①	.095
1987				
R40295A	.480	①	①	.075
R40296A	.480	①	①	.075

① Refer to specification on VECI label under the hood.

reassemble the carburetor using new parts, using the exploded views in the car sections, if necessary. Make sure that all screws and jets are tight in their seats, but do not overtighten or the tips will be distorted. Do not tighten needle valves into their seats or uneven jetting will result. Always use new gaskets and adjust the float.

THROTTLE BODY FUEL INJECTION SYSTEM

NOTE: *This book contains only basic testing and service procedures for your car's fuel injection system. More comprehensive testing and diagnosis procedures may be found in CHILTON'S GUIDE TO TO FUEL INJECTION AND FEEDBACK CARBURETORS, book part number 7288, available at your local retailer. Note also that whenever replacing any fuel lines, it is necessary to use hoses* marked *"EFI/EFM" or an equivalent product from the aftermarket. Whenever replacing hose clamps, use clamps incorporating a rolled edge to prevent hose damage, rather than standard aviation type clamps. This will prevent damage to the hoses that could produce dangerous leaks.*

General Information

This electronic fuel injection system is a computer regulated single point fuel injection system that provides precise air/fuel ratio for all driving conditions. At the center of this system is a digital pre-programmed computer known as a logic module that regulates ignition timing, air-fuel ratio, emission control devices and idle speed. This component has the ability to update and revise its programming to meet changing operating conditions.

Various sensors provide the input necessary for the logic module to correctly regulate the fuel flow at the fuel injector. These include the manifold absolute pressure, throttle position, oxygen feedback, coolant temperature, charge temperature and vehicle speed sensors. In addition to the sensors, various switches also provide important information. These include the neutral-safety, heated rear window, air conditioning, air conditioning clutch switches, and an electronic idle switch.

All inputs to the logic module are converted into signals sent to the power module. These signals cause the power module to change either the fuel flow at the injector or ignition timing or both.

The logic module tests many of its own input and output circuits. If a fault is found in a major system this information is stored in the logic module. Information on this fault can be displayed to a technician by means of a flashing light emitting diode (LED) or by connecting a diagnostic read out and reading a numbered display code which directly relates to a specific fault.

NOTE: *Experience has shown that many complaints that may occur with EFI can be traced to poor wiring or hose connections. A visual check will help spot these most common faults and save unnecessary test and diagnosis time.*

Electric Fuel Pump
REMOVAL AND INSTALLATION

An electric fuel pump is used with fuel injection systems in order to provide higher and more uniform fuel pressures. It is located in the tank. To remove it, disconnect the battery, and then remove the fuel tank, as described at the

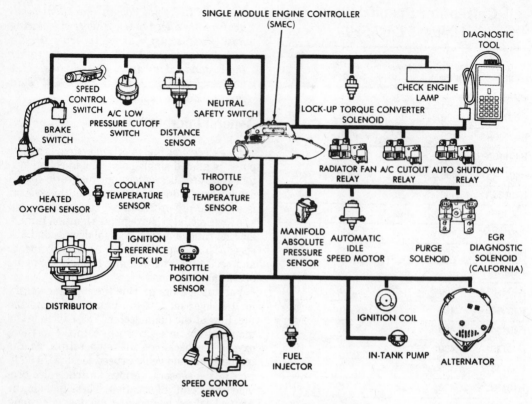

Throttle body injection sensors and switches

end of this chapter. Then, with a hammer and non-metallic punch, tap the fuel pump lock ring counterclockwise to release the pump.

To install the pump, first wipe the seal area of the tank clean and install a new O-ring seal. Replace the filter on the end of the pump if it appears to be damaged. Then position the pump in the tank and install the locking ring. Tighten the ring in the same general way in which you loosened it. Do not overtighten it, as this can cause leakage. Install the tank as described at the end of this chapter.

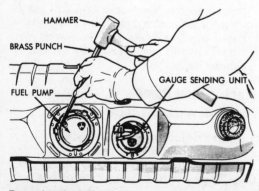

Removing the fuel pump

TESTING

NOTE: *To perform this procedure, you will need a gauge capable of reading 10-20 psi and the extra length of hose, clamps and fittings necessary to Tee the gauge into a $\frac{5}{16}$" fuel line. Have a metal container handy to collect any fuel that may spill.*

1. Release the fuel system pressure. Disconnect the fuel supply line at the throttle body. Tee in the gauge between the fuel supply line and the fuel supply nipple on the throttle body, connecting the inlet side of the tee to the fuel supply line and the throttle body side of the Tee to the throttle body with a rubber hose and clamps.

WARNING: *At the beginning of the next step, watch carefully for fuel leaks. Shut the engine off immediately at any sign of leakage.*

2. Start the engine and run it at idle. Read the fuel pressure gauge. Pressure should be 14.5 psi. If pressure is correct, the pump is okay and you should depressurize the system, remove the gauge, and restore the normal fuel line connections. If the pressure is low, proceed with the next step to test for filter clogging. If the pressure is too high, proceed with Step 4.

3. Stop the engine and then depressurize the system as described under the procedure for

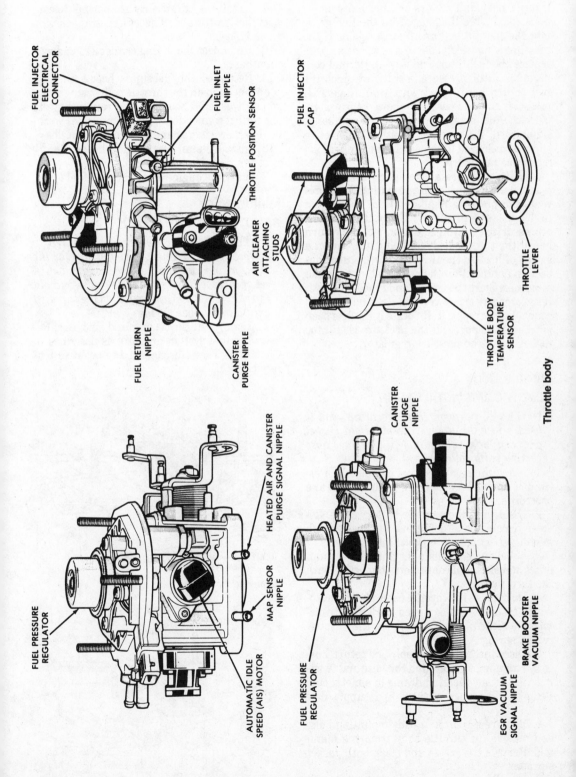

FUEL INJECTOR ELECTRICAL CONNECTOR

FUEL INLET NIPPLE

THROTTLE POSITION SENSOR

AIR CLEANER ATTACHING STUDS

FUEL RETURN NIPPLE

CANISTER PURGE NIPPLE

FUEL INJECTOR CAP

THROTTLE LEVER

THROTTLE BODY TEMPERATURE SENSOR

FUEL PRESSURE REGULATOR

HEATED AIR AND CANISTER PURGE SIGNAL NIPPLE

MAP SENSOR NIPPLE

AUTOMATIC IDLE SPEED (AIS) MOTOR

CANISTER PURGE NIPPLE

FUEL PRESSURE REGULATOR

EGR VACUUM SIGNAL NIPPLE

BRAKE BOOSTER VACUUM NIPPLE

Throttle body

changing the fuel filter in Chapter 1. Remove the gauge Tee from the line going into the throttle body and restore the normal connections. Then, Tee the gauge into the line going into the fuel filter. Run the test again. If the pressure is now okay, depressurize the system, replace the fuel filter, and restore normal connections. If the pressure is still low, pinch the fuel return hose closed with your fingers. If pressure now increases to above 14.5 psi, replace the fuel pressure regulator. If no change is observed, the problem is either a defective pump or a clogged filter sock in the tank. Make repairs as necessary.

4. With pressure above specification, you must check for a clogged return line that prevents the pressure regulator from controlling fuel pressure properly. Stop the engine, depressurize the system, disconnect the return line at the throttle body and plug it. Connect a length of hose to the throttle body return connection and position the open end into a clean container. Start the engine and repeat the test. If the pressure is now correct, clean out the fuel return line or repair it. Relocate it if it has been pinched or damaged. If the pressure is still too high, replace the pressure regulator.

Throttle Body

REMOVAL AND INSTALLATION

NOTE: *To perform this operation, you'll need a new throttle body-to-manifold gasket and new original equipment-type fuel hose clamps (with rolled edges).*

1. Allow the engine to cool completely. Perform the fuel system pressure release procedure.

2. Disconnect the negative battery cable. Remove the air cleaner and those air hoses which might restrict access to the throttle body.

3. Label and then disconnect all the vacuum hoses and electrical connectors connecting with the throttle body.

4. Disconnect the throttle cable and, on automatic transmission-equipped cars the transmission kickdown cable. Remove the throttle return spring.

5. Disconnect the fuel supply and return hoses by wrapping a rag around the hose and twisting. Collect any fuel that drains in a metal cup. Remove the copper washers and supply new ones.

6. Remove the throttle body mounting bolts and remove the throttle body from the manifold. Remove the gasket and clean both gasket surfaces.

7. Install the new gasket and carefully put the throttle body into position with the bolt holes in it and the manifold lined up.

8. Install the mounting bolts and torque them alternately and evenly to 200 in. lbs.

9. Install the throttle return spring. Reconnect the throttle and, if necessary, transmission cable linkages.

10. Reconnect the wiring connectors and vacuum hoses.

11. Reconnect the fuel supply hose to the supply connection on the throttle body, using a new copper washer. Reconnect the return hose to the return connection with a new copper washer. Use new clamps and torque to 10 in. lbs.

12. Install the air cleaner and hoses. Reconnect the negative battery cable.

13. Start the engine and check for fuel leaks.

Fuel Injector

REMOVAL AND INSTALLATION

NOTE: *A Torx® screwdriver is required to perform this operation. New O-rings for the injector and cap should also be supplied. A set of three will be required to re-use and old injector, while a new injector will be supplied with a new upper O-ring.*

1. Remove the air cleaner and air hoses. Release the fuel system pressure as described in Chapter 1. Then, disconnect the negative battery cable.

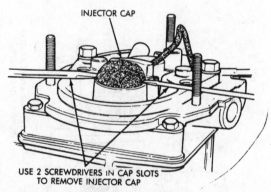

USE 2 SCREWDRIVERS IN CAP SLOTS TO REMOVE INJECTOR CAP

Removing the injector cap

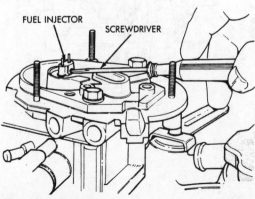

Removing the injector

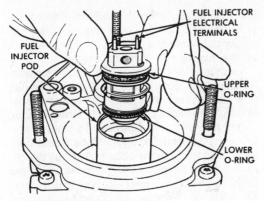

Removing the injector

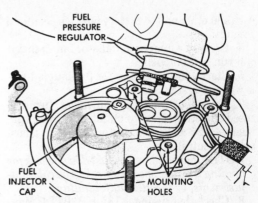

Removing the pressure regulator

2. Remove the Torx® head screw with the right screwdriver. With two appropriate, blunt prying instruments located in the screwdriver slot on either side, gently and evenly pry upward to remove the injector cap.

3. Then, place an appropriate, blunt prying instrument into the screwdriver slot on either side of the electrical connector and gently and evenly pry the injector upward and out of the throttle body unit. Once the injector is removed, check that the lower O-ring has been removed from the throttle body unit.

4. Remove the two O-rings from the injector body and the single O-ring from the cap and replace them. If the injector is being replaced, a new upper O-ring will already be installed.

5. Carefully assemble the injector and cap together with the keyway and key aligned. Then, align the cap and injector so the cap's hole aligns with the bolt hole in the throttle body. Start the injector/cap assembly into the throttle body without applying downward pressure.

6. With the assembly almost seated, rotate the cap as necessary to ensure perfect alignment of the cap and throttle body. Then apply gentle, downward pressure on both sides to seat the injector and cap.

7. Install the Torx® screw and torque it to 30-35 in. lbs.

8. Connect the battery. Start the engine and check for leaks with the air cleaner off. Then, replace the air cleaner and hoses.

Pressure Regulator

REMOVAL AND INSTALLATION

NOTE: *Make sure to have a towel or rag on hand to absorb fuel. Supply a new O-ring and gasket for the pressure regulator.*

1. Remove the air cleaner and air hoses. Release the fuel system pressure as described in Chapter 1. Then, disconnect the negative battery cable.

2. Remove the three screws which attach the

pressure regulator to the throttle body. Then, *quickly* place a rag over the fuel inlet chamber to absorb any fuel that remains in the system. When fuel is absorbed, dispose of the rag safely.

3. Pull the pressure regulator from the throttle body. Carefully remove the O-ring and gasket.

4. Carefully install the new O-ring and gasket onto the regulator.

5. Position the pressure regulator onto the throttle body. Press it into place squarely so as to seal the O-ring and gasket.

6. Install the three attaching screws and torque to 40 in. lbs.

7. Connect the battery. Start the engine and check for leaks with the air cleaner off. Then, replace the air cleaner and hoses.

Idle Speed Adjustment

NOTE: *This procedure applies to vehicles built through 1986. Later models require a "Throttle Body Minimum Airflow Check Procedure". This cannot be performed without utilizing an expensive electronic test system. If airflow is incorrect on these models, the throttle body must be replaced.*

1. Before adjusting the idle on an electronic fuel injected vehicle the following items must be checked.

   a. AIS motor has been checked for operation.

   b. Engine has been checked for vacuum or EGR leaks.

   c. Engine timing has been checked and set to specifications.

   d. Coolant temperature sensor has been checked for operation.

2. Connect a tachometer and timing light to engine.

3. Disconnect throttle body 6-way connector. Remove brown with white trace AIS wire from connector and reconnect the connector.

4. Connect one end of a jumper wire to AIS

wire and other end to battery positive post for 5 seconds.

5. Connect a jumper to radiator fan so that it will run continuously.

6. Start and run engine for 3 minutes to allow speed to stabilize.

7. Using tool C-4804 or equivalent, turn idle speed adjusting screw to obtain 800 ± 10 rpm Manual; 725 ± 10 rpm (Automatic) with transaxle in neutral.

NOTE: *If idle will not adjust down, check for binding linkage, speed control servo cable adjustments, or throttle shaft binding.*

8. Check that timing is 18° ± 2° BTDC Manual; 12° ± 2° BTDC Automatic.

9. If timing is not to above specifications turn idle speed adjusting screw until correct idle speed and ignition timing are obtained.

10. Turn off engine, disconnect tachometer and timing light, reinstall AIS wire and remove jumper wire.

MULTI-PORT ELECTRONIC FUEL INJECTION

General Information

The turbocharged multi-port Electronic Fuel Injection system combines an electronic fuel and spark advance control system with a turbocharged intake system. At the center of this system is a digital, pre-programmed computer known as a Logic Module that regulates igni-tion timing, air-fuel ratio, emission control devices and idle speed. This component has the ability to update and revise its programming to meet changing operating conditions.

Various sensors provide the input necessary for the Logic Module to correctly regulate fuel flow at the fuel injectors. These include the Manifold Absolute Pressure, Throttle Position, Oxygen Feedback, Coolant Temperature, Charge Temperature, and Vehicle Speed Sensors. In addition to the sensors, various switches also provide important information. These include the Transmission Neutral-Safety, Heated Rear Window, Air Conditioning, and the Air Conditioning Clutch Switches.

Inputs to the Logic Module are converted into signals sent to the Power Module. These signals cause the Power Module to change either the fuel flow at the injector or ignition timing or both. The Logic Module tests many of its own input and output circuits. if a fault is found in a major circuit, this information is stored in the Logic Module. Information on this fault can be displayed to a technician by means of the instrument panel power loss lamp or by connecting a diagnostic readout and observing a numbered display code which directly relates to a general fault.

NOTE: *Most complaints that may occur with turbocharged muti-point Electronic Fuel Injection can be traced to poor wiring or hose connections. A visual check will help stop these faults and save unnecessary test and diagnosis time.*

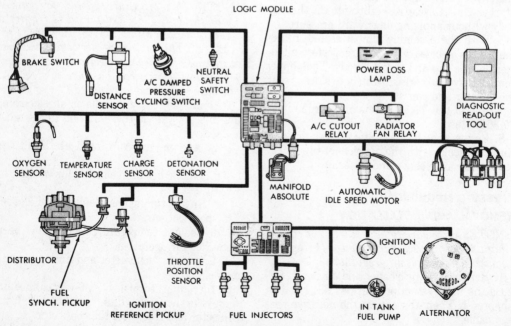

Electronic fuel injection sensors

Electric Fuel Pump

REMOVAL AND INSTALLATION

An electric fuel pump is used with fuel injection systems in order to provide higher and more uniform fuel pressures. It is located in the tank. To remove it, disconnect the battery, and then remove the fuel tank, as described at the end of this chapter. Then, with a hammer and non-metallic punch, tap the fuel pump lock ring counterclockwise to release the pump.

To install the pump, first wipe the seal area of the tank clean and install a new O-ring seal. Replace the filter on the end of the pump if it appears to be damaged. Then position the pump in the tank and install the locking ring. Tighten the ring in the same general way in which you loosened it. Do not overtighten it, as this can cause leakage. Install the tank as described at the end of this chapter.

TESTING

NOTE: *To perform this test, you will need a pressure gauge capable of reading pressures above 55 psi. The gauge must have a connection that will fit the fuel rail service valve. The gauge will be compatible with Chrysler part No. C-3292 and the connector fitting compatible with C-4805. You may also need a Tee and fittings necessary to Tee the gauge into the fuel supply line at the tank, and a 2 gallon container suitable for collecting fuel.*

1. Release the fuel system pressure as described in Chapter 1. Remove the protective cover from the service valve on the fuel rail.

2. Connect the gauge to the pressure tap on the fuel rail. Hold the gauge and have someone start the engine. Run the engine at idle speed in Neutral (manual transmissions) or Park (automatic transmissions).

3. Read the pressure. It should be 53-57 psi. If it is outside the range, take note of it. Stop the engine, depressurize the system, disconnect the gauge and replace the protective cover. If the pressure is correct, the test is complete. If the pressure is below the range, proceed with the steps following; if it is too high, proceed with Step 7.

WARNING: *In the next step, note that fuel may drain from the lines as you disconnect them. Make sure all surrounding exhaust system parts are cool and that all sources of ignition are removed from the area. Collect fuel and dispose of it safely.*

4. Connect the gauge into the fuel supply line running between the tank and the filter which is located at the rear of the vehicle.

WARNING *Make sure all connections are secure.*

5. Have someone start the engine. Read the pressure gauge. If the pressure has risen more than 5 psi, replace the filter. If the pressure is now within range: allow the engine to cool; remove all sources of ignition; depressurize the system; disconnect the gauge from the lines; replace the fuel filter; and restore connections.

6. If the pressure is still too low, gently and gradually pinch the fuel return line closed as you watch the gauge. If the pressure increases, the fuel pressure regulator is at fault. If there is no change, the problem is either clogging of the filter sock mounted on the pump itself or a defective pump.

7. If the pressure is too high, shut off the engine, allow it to cool, depressurize the system and then disconnect the fuel return hose at the chassis, near the fuel tank. Connect a 3 foot length of hose to the open end of the line running along the chassis. Position the open end of the line into a container suitable for collecting fuel. Have a helper start the engine and check the pressure. If it is now correct, check the in-tank fuel return hose for kinking. If the hose is okay, and the system still exhibits excessive pressure with the tank half full or more, the fuel pump reservoir check valve or aspirator jet may be obstructed and the assembly must be replaced.

8. If the pressure is still too high, shut off the engine, and allow it to cool. Depressurize the system and then reconnect the fuel lines at the rear. Disconnect the fuel return hose at the pressure regulator. Collect all fuel that drains. Then, run the open connection into a large metal container. Connect the fuel gauge back into the fuel rail. Start the engine and repeat the test. If the fuel pressure is now correct, clean a clogged return line or replace pinched or kinked sections of the return line. If no such problems exist, replace the fuel pressure regulator.

Idle Speed Adjustment

NOTE: *This procedure applies to vehicles built through 1986. Later models require a "Throttle Body Minimum Airflow Check Procedure". This cannot be performed without utilizing an expensive electronic test system. If airflow is incorrect on these models, the throttle body must be replaced.*

Before adjusting the idle on an electronic fuel injected vehicle the following items must be checked:

    a. AIS motor has been checked for operation.

    b. Engine has been checked for vacuum or EGR leaks.

    c. Engine timing has been checked and set to specifications.

    d. Coolant temperature sensor has been checked for operation.

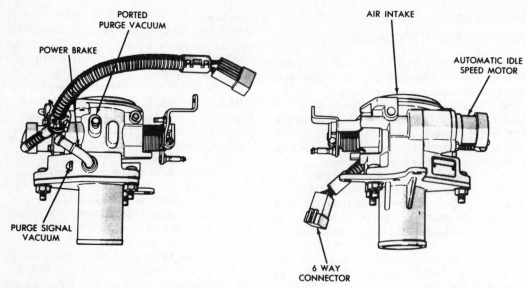

Throttle body (Turbo)

Once these checks have been made and you know these components are performing satisfactorily:

1. Install a tachometer.

2. Warm up engine to normal operating temperature (accessories off).

3. Shut engine off and disconnect radiator fan.

4. Disconnect Throttle Body 6-way connector. Remove the brown with white tracer AIS wire from the connector and reconnect connector.

5. Start engine with transaxle selector in park or neutral.

6. Apply 12 volts to AIS brown with white tracer wire. This will drive the AIS fully closed and the idle should drop.

7. Disconnect then reconnect coolant temperature sensor.

8. With transaxle in neutral, idle speed should be 775 ± 25 rpm (700 ± 25 rpm green engine).

9. If idle is not to specifications adjust idle air bypass screw.

10. If idle will not adjust down, check for vacuum leaks, AIS motor damage, throttle body damage, or speed control cable adjustment.

Throttle Body

REMOVAL AND INSTALLATION

1. Disconnect the negative battery cable. Remove the nuts attaching the air cleaner adaptor to the throttle body, loosen the hose clamps, and remove the air cleaner adaptor.

2. Remove the three control cables—accelerator, accelerator and, if so-equipped, automatic transmission kickdown and speed control ca-

bles. Then remove the throttle cable bracket from the throttle body.

3. Note locations and then disconnect the electrical connectors.

4. Note their locations or, if necessary, label them and then disconnect the vacuum hoses from the throttle body.

5. Remove the throttle body-to-adaptor attaching nuts. Then, remove the throttle body and its gasket.

6. Clean gasket surfaces and install a new gasket. Instal the throttle body-to-adaptor attaching nuts and tighten them alternately and evenly.

7. Reconnect the vacuum hoses, checking the routing and making certain the connections are secure. Reconnect each electrical connector to its connection on the throttle body.

8. Install the throttle and, as necessary, transmission kickdown and speed control cables. Install the air cleaner adaptor. Reconnect the battery.

Fuel Rail and Injectors

REMOVAL AND INSTALLATION

NOTE: *You should have a set of four injector nozzle protective caps and a set of new O-rings before removing the injectors.*

1. Release fuel system pressure as described in Chapter 1. Disconnect the negative battery cable.

2. Loosen the hose clamp on the fuel supply hose at the fuel rail inlet and disconnect it. Collect any fuel that may drain out into a metal cup and dispose of it safely.

3. Disconnect the fuel pressure regulator

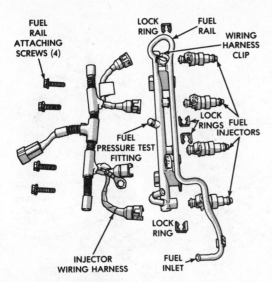

Fuel rail and injectors

vacuum hose at the intake manifold vacuum tree.

4. Remove the 2 fuel pressure regulator-to-intake manifold bracket screws.

5. Loosen the clamp at the rail end of the fuel rail-to-pressure regulator hose and then remove the regulator and hose. Collect any fuel that may drain out into a metal cup and dispose of it safely.

6. Remove the bolt from the fuel rail-to-valve cover bracket.

7. Remove the fuel injector head shield clips. Then, remove the four intake manifold-to-rail mounting bolts. Note that one bolt retains a ground strap.

8. Pull the rail away from the manifold in such a way as to pull the injectors straight out of their mounting holes. Pull the injectors out straight so as to avoid damaging their O-rings.

9. To remove individual injectors from the rail, first position the rail on a bench or other surfaces so that the injectors are easily reached. Perform the following for each injector to be removed:

   a. Disconnect the wiring connector.

   b. Remove the lock ring from the rail and injector.

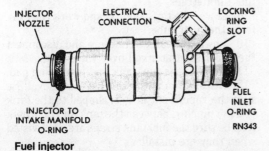

Fuel injector

c. Pull the injector straight out of the injector receiver cup in the fuel rail.

d. Inspect the injector O-rings for damage. Replace it if necessary. If the injector will be re-used and will be off the rail while other work is performed, install a protective cap over the nozzle.

e. Lubricate the O-ring that seals the upper end with a drop of clean engine oil. Then, install the inlet end carefully into the fuel rail receiver cup. Proceed slowly and insert the injector straight in to avoid damaging the O-ring.

f. Slide the open end of the injector lock ring down over the injector, and onto the ridge in the receiver cup. The lock ring must lock into the slot on the top of the injector.

10. Remove all protective covers installed over the injector tips. Make sure the bores of the injector mounting holes are clean.

11. Put a drop of clean engine oil on the O-ring at the nozzle end of each injector. Then position the rail with the injectors headed squarely into their mounting holes and gently and evenly slide all four injectors into place.

12. Install the four rail mounting bolts and torque them to 250 in. lbs. Make sure to reconnect the ground strap removed earlier.

13. Connect each plug to its corresponding injector. Install each wiring harness into its clips. Connect the injector wiring harness to the main harness.

14. Install the heat shield clips. Install the bolt fastening the rail mounting bracket to the valve cover.

15. Connect the vacuum line for the fuel pressure regulator to the vacuum tree on the manifold. Then, connect the fuel return hose to the fuel pressure regulator and position and tighten the clamp. Install the bolts fastening the regulator bracket to the intake manifold.

16. Attach the fuel supply hose to the fuel rail and position and tighten the clamp.

17. Recheck all wiring and hose connections for routing and tightness. Then, connect the battery, start the engine, and check for leaks.

FUEL TANK

REMOVAL AND INSTALLATION

1. Raise and support the car.

2. Disconnect the negative battery cable.

3. Remove the fuel filler cap.

4. Disconnect the fuel supply line at the right front shock tower. Connect a drain or siphon line and empty the tank into another container.

WARNING: *Do not begin the siphoning process by sucking on the line.*

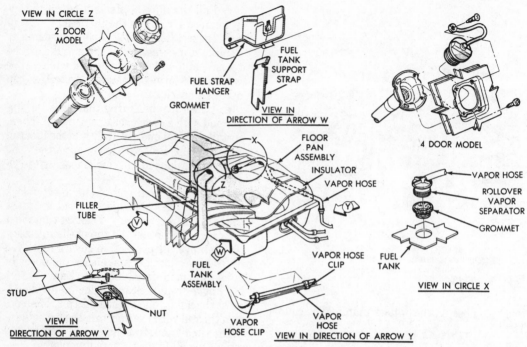

Fuel tank assembly

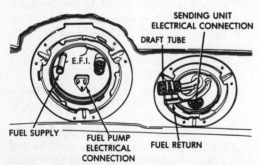

Siphon hose connection location—fuel injection models

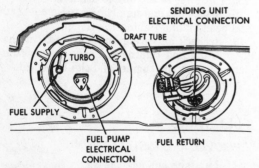

Siphon hose connection location—Turbo except Shelby

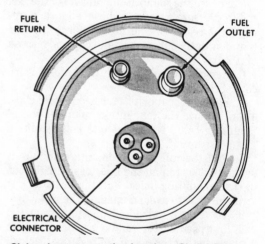

Siphon hose connection location—Shelby Turbo

7. Remove the exhaust pipe shield. Allow the shield to rest on the exhaust pipe.

8. Support the fuel tank and disconnect the fuel tank straps.

9. Lower the tank slightly and work the tank from the filler tube.

10. Lower the tank some more and disconnect the vapor separator roll-over valve hose.

11. Remove the fuel tank and insulating pad.

12. Installation is the reverse of removal. Be sure the vapor vent hose is clipped to the tank and not pinched between the tank and floorpan. Also be sure the fuel tank straps are not twisted when they are installed.

5. Remove the screws holding the filler tube to the inner and outer quarter panel.

6. Disconnect and tag the wiring and lines from the tank.

Chassis Electrical

6

UNDERSTANDING AND TROUBLESHOOTING ELECTRICAL SYSTEMS

With the rate at which both import and domestic manufacturers are incorporating electronic control systems into their production lines, it won't be long before every new vehicle is equipped with one or more on-board computer, like the EEC-IV unit installed on the truck. These electronic components (with no moving parts) should theoretically last the life of the vehicle, provided nothing external happens to damage the circuits or memory chips.

While it is true that electronic components should never wear out, in the real world malfunctions do occur. It is also true that any computer-based system is extremely sensitive to electrical voltages and cannot tolerate careless or haphazard testing or service procedures. An inexperienced individual can literally do major damage looking for a minor problem by using the wrong kind of test equipment or connecting test leads or connectors with the ignition switch ON. When selecting test equipment, make sure the manufacturers instructions state that the tester is compatible with whatever type of electronic control system is being serviced. Read all instructions carefully and double check all test points before installing probes or making any test connections.

The following section outlines basic diagnosis techniques for dealing with computerized automotive control systems. Along with a general explanation of the various types of test equipment available to aid in servicing modern electronic automotive systems, basic repair techniques for wiring harnesses and connectors is given. Read the basic information before attempting any repairs or testing on any computerized system, to provide the background of information necessary to avoid the most common

and obvious mistakes that can cost both time and money. Although the replacement and testing procedures are simple in themselves, the systems are not, and unless one has a thorough understanding of all components and their function within a particular computerized control system, the logical test sequence these systems demand cannot be followed. Minor malfunctions can make a big difference, so it is important to know how each component affects the operation of the overall electronic system to find the ultimate cause of a problem without replacing good components unnecessarily. It is not enough to use the correct test equipment; the test equipment must be used correctly.

Safety Precautions

CAUTION: *Whenever working on or around any computer based microprocessor control system, always observe these general precautions to prevent the possibility of personal injury or damage to electronic components.*

• Never install or remove battery cables with the key ON or the engine running. Jumper cables should be connected with the key OFF to avoid power surges that can damage electronic control units. Engines equipped with computer controlled systems should avoid both giving and getting jump starts due to the possibility of serious damage to components from arcing in the engine compartment when connections are made with the ignition ON.

• Always remove the battery cables before charging the battery. Never use a high output charger on an installed battery or attempt to use any type of "hot shot" (24 volt) starting aid.

• Exercise care when inserting test probes into connectors to insure good connections without damaging the connector or spreading the pins. Always probe connectors from the rear (wire) side, NOT the pin side, to avoid accidental shorting of terminals during test procedures.

● Never remove or attach wiring harness connectors with the ignition switch ON, especially to an electronic control unit.

● Do not drop any components during service procedures and never apply 12 volts directly to any component (like a solenoid or relay) unless instructed specifically to do so. Some component electrical windings are designed to safely handle only 4 or 5 volts and can be destroyed in seconds if 12 volts are applied directly to the connector.

● Remove the electronic control unit if the vehicle is to be placed in an environment where temperatures exceed approximately 176°F (80°C), such as a paint spray booth or when arc or gas welding near the control unit location in the car.

ORGANIZED TROUBLESHOOTING

When diagnosing a specific problem, organized troubleshooting is a must. The complexity of a modern automobile demands that you approach any problem in a logical, organized manner. There are certain troubleshooting techniques that are standard:

1. Establish when the problem occurs. Does the problem appear only under certain conditions? Were there any noises, odors, or other unusual symptoms?

2. Isolate the problem area. To do this, make some simple tests and observations; then eliminate the systems that are working properly. Check for obvious problems such as broken wires, dirty connections or split or disconnected vacuum hoses. Always check the obvious before assuming something complicated is the cause.

3. Test for problems systematically to determine the cause once the problem area is isolated. Are all the components functioning properly? Is there power going to electrical switches and motors? Is there vacuum at vacuum switches and/or actuators? Is there a mechanical problem such as bent linkage or loose mounting screws? Doing careful, systematic checks will often turn up most causes on the first inspection without wasting time checking components that have little or no relationship to the problem.

4. Test all repairs after the work is done to make sure that the problem is fixed. Some causes can be traced to more than one component, so a careful verification of repair work is important to pick up additional malfunctions that may cause a problem to reappear or a different problem to arise. A blown fuse, for example, is a simple problem that may require more than another fuse to repair. If you don't look

for a problem that caused a fuse to blow, for example, a shorted wire may go undetected.

Experience has shown that most problems tend to be the result of a fairly simple and obvious cause, such as loose or corroded connectors or air leaks in the intake system; making careful inspection of components during testing essential to quick and accurate troubleshooting. Special, hand held computerized testers designed specifically for diagnosing the EEC-IV system are available from a variety of aftermarket sources, as well as from the vehicle manufacturer, but care should be taken that any test equipment being used is designed to diagnose that particular computer controlled system accurately without damaging the control unit (ECU) or components being tested.

NOTE: *Pinpointing the exact cause of trouble in an electrical system can sometimes only be accomplished by the use of special test equipment. The following describes commonly used test equipment and explains how to put it to best use in diagnosis. In addition to the information covered below, the manufacturer's instructions booklet provided with the tester should be read and clearly understood before attempting any test procedures.*

TEST EQUIPMENT

Jumper Wires

Jumper wires are simple, yet extremely valuable, pieces of test equipment. Jumper wires are merely wires that are used to bypass sections of a circuit. The simplest type of jumper wire is merely a length of multistrand wire with an alligator clip at each end. Jumper wires are usually fabricated from lengths of standard automotive wire and whatever type of connector (alligator clip, spade connector or pin connector) that is required for the particular vehicle being tested. The well equipped tool box will have several different styles of jumper wires in several different lengths. Some jumper wires are made with three or more terminals coming from a common splice for special purpose testing. In cramped, hard-to-reach areas it is advisable to have insulated boots over the jumper wire terminals in order to prevent accidental grounding, sparks, and possible fire, especially when testing fuel system components.

Jumper wires are used primarily to locate open electrical circuits, on either the ground (-) side of the circuit or on the hot (+) side. If an electrical component fails to operate, connect the jumper wire between the component and a good ground. If the component operates only with the jumper installed, the ground circuit is open. If the ground circuit is good, but the component does not operate, the circuit between the power feed and component is open. You can sometimes connect the jumper wire directly from the battery to the hot terminal of the component, but first make sure the component uses 12 volts in operation. Some electrical components, such as fuel injectors, are designed to operate on about 4 volts and running 12 volts directly to the injector terminals can burn out the wiring. By inserting an inline fuseholder between a set of test leads, a fused jumper wire can be used for bypassing open circuits. Use a 5 amp fuse to provide protection against voltage spikes. When in doubt, use a voltmeter to check the voltage input to the component and measure how much voltage is being applied normally. By moving the jumper wire successively back from the lamp toward the power source, you can isolate the area of the circuit where the open is located. When the component stops functioning, or the power is cut off, the open is in the segment of wire between the jumper and the point previously tested.

CAUTION: *Never use jumpers made from wire that is of lighter gauge than used in the circuit under test. If the jumper wire is of too small gauge, it may overheat and possibly melt. Never use jumpers to bypass high resistance loads (such as motors) in a circuit. Bypassing resistances, in effect, creates a short circuit which may, in turn, cause damage and fire. Never use a jumper for anything other than temporary bypassing of components in a circuit.*

12 Volt Test Light

The 12 volt test light is used to check circuits and components while electrical current is flowing through them. It is used for voltage and ground tests. Twelve volt test lights come in different styles but all have three main parts; a ground clip, a probe, and a light. The most commonly used 12 volt test lights have pick-type probes. To use a 12 volt test light, connect the ground clip to a good ground and probe wherever necessary with the pick. The pick should be sharp so that it can penetrate wire insulation to make contact with the wire, without making a large hole in the insulation. The wrap-around light is handy in hard to reach areas or where it is difficult to support a wire to push a probe pick into it. To use the wrap around light, hook the wire to probed with the hook and pull the trigger. A small pick will be forced through the wire insulation into the wire core.

CAUTION: *Do not use a test light to probe electronic ignition spark plug or coil wires. Never use a pick-type test light to probe wir-*

ing on computer controlled systems unless specifically instructed to do so. Any wire insulation that is pierced by the test light probe should be taped and sealed with silicone after testing.

Like the jumper wire, the 12 volt test light is used to isolate opens in circuits. But, whereas the jumper wire is used to bypass the open to operate the load, the 12 volt test light is used to locate the presence of voltage in a circuit. If the test light glows, you know that there is power up to that point; if the 12 volt test light does not glow when its probe is inserted into the wire or connector, you know that there is an open circuit (no power). Move the test light in successive steps back toward the power source until the light in the handle does glow. When it does glow, the open is between the probe and point previously probed.

NOTE: *The test light does not detect that 12 volts (or any particular amount of voltage) is present; it only detects that some voltage is present. It is advisable before using the test light to touch its terminals across the battery posts to make sure the light is operating properly.*

Self-Powered Test Light

The self-powered test light usually contains a 1.5 volt penlight battery. One type of self-powered test light is similar in design to the 12 volt test light. This type has both the battery and the light in the handle and pick-type probe tip. The second type has the light toward the open tip, so that the light illuminates the contact point. The self-powered test light is dual purpose piece of test equipment. It can be used to test for either open or short circuits when power is isolated from the circuit (continuity test). A powered test light should not be used on any computer controlled system or component unless specifically instructed to do so. Many engine sensors can be destroyed by even this small amount of voltage applied directly to the terminals.

Open Circuit Testing

To use the self-powered test light to check for open circuits, first isolate the circuit from the vehicle's 12 volt power source by disconnecting the battery or wiring harness connector. Connect the test light ground clip to a good ground and probe sections of the circuit sequentially with the test light. (start from either end of the circuit). If the light is out, the open is between the probe and the circuit ground. If the light is on, the open is between the probe and end of the circuit toward the power source.

Short Circuit Testing

By isolating the circuit both from power and from ground, and using a self-powered test light, you can check for shorts to ground in the circuit. Isolate the circuit from power and ground. Connect the test light ground clip to a good ground and probe any easy-to-reach test point in the circuit. If the light comes on, there is a short somewhere in the circuit. To isolate the short, probe a test point at either end of the isolated circuit (the light should be on). Leave the test light probe connected and open connectors, switches, remove parts, etc., sequentially, until the light goes out. When the light goes out, the short is between the last circuit component opened and the previous circuit opened.

NOTE: *The 1.5 volt battery in the test light does not provide much current. A weak battery may not provide enough power to illuminate the test light even when a complete circuit is made (especially if there are high resistances in the circuit). Always make sure that the test battery is strong. To check the battery, briefly touch the ground clip to the probe; if the light glows brightly the battery is strong enough for testing. Never use a self-powered test light to perform checks for opens or shorts when power is applied to the electrical system under test. The 12 volt vehicle power will quickly burn out the 1.5 volt light bulb in the test light.*

Voltmeter

A voltmeter is used to measure voltage at any point in a circuit, or to measure the voltage drop across any part of a circuit. It can also be used to check continuity in a wire or circuit by indicating current flow from one end to the other. Voltmeters usually have various scales on the meter dial and a selector switch to allow the selection of different voltages. The voltmeter has a positive and a negative lead. To avoid damage to the meter, always connect the negative lead to the negative (-) side of circuit (to ground or nearest the ground side of the circuit) and connect the positive lead to the positive (+) side of the circuit (to the power source or the nearest power source). Note that the negative voltmeter lead will always be black and that the positive voltmeter will always be some color other than black (usually red). Depending on how the voltmeter is connected into the circuit, it has several uses.

A voltmeter can be connected either in parallel or in series with a circuit and it has a very high resistance to current flow. When connected in parallel, only a small amount of current will flow through the voltmeter current path; the rest will flow through the normal circuit current path and the circuit will work normally. When the voltmeter is connected in series with a circuit, only a small amount of current can flow through the circuit. The circuit will not work properly, but the voltmeter reading will show if the circuit is complete or not.

Available Voltage Measurement

Set the voltmeter selector switch to the 20V position and connect the meter negative lead to the negative post of the battery. Connect the positive meter lead to the positive post of the battery and turn the ignition switch ON to provide a load. Read the voltage on the meter or digital display. A well charged battery should register over 12 volts. If the meter reads below 11.5 volts, the battery power may be insufficient to operate the electrical system properly. This test determines voltage available from the battery and should be the first step in any electrical trouble diagnosis procedure. Many electrical problems, especially on computer controlled systems, can be caused by a low state of charge in the battery. Excessive corrosion at the battery cable terminals can cause a poor contact that will prevent proper charging and full battery current flow.

Normal battery voltage is 12 volts when fully charged. When the battery is supplying current to one or more circuits it is said to be "under load". When everything is off the electrical system is under a "no-load" condition. A fully charged battery may show about 12.5 volts at no load; will drop to 12 volts under medium load; and will drop even lower under heavy load. If the battery is partially discharged the voltage decrease under heavy load may be excessive, even though the battery shows 12 volts or more at no load. When allowed to discharge further, the battery's available voltage under load will decrease more severely. For this reason, it is important that the battery be fully charged during all testing procedures to avoid errors in diagnosis and incorrect test results.

Voltage Drop

When current flows through a resistance, the voltage beyond the resistance is reduced (the larger the current, the greater the reduction in voltage). When no current is flowing, there is no voltage drop because there is no current flow. All points in the circuit which are connected to the power source are at the same voltage as the power source. The total voltage drop always equals the total source voltage. In a long circuit with many connectors, a series of small, unwanted voltage drops due to corrosion at the connectors can add up to a total loss of voltage which impairs the operation of the normal loads in the circuit.

INDIRECT COMPUTATION OF VOLTAGE DROPS

1. Set the voltmeter selector switch to the 20 volt position.
2. Connect the meter negative lead to a good ground.
3. Probe all resistances in the circuit with the positive meter lead.
4. Operate the circuit in all modes and observe the voltage readings.

DIRECT MEASUREMENT OF VOLTAGE DROPS

1. Set the voltmeter switch to the 20 volt position.
2. Connect the voltmeter negative lead to the ground side of the resistance load to be measured.
3. Connect the positive lead to the positive side of the resistance or load to be measured.
4. Read the voltage drop directly on the 20 volt scale.

Too high a voltage indicates too high a resistance. If, for example, a blower motor runs too slowly, you can determine if there is too high a resistance in the resistor pack. By taking voltage drop readings in all parts of the circuit, you can isolate the problem. Too low a voltage drop indicates too low a resistance. If, for example, a blower motor runs too fast in the MED and/or LOW position, the problem can be isolated in the resistor pack by taking voltage drop readings in all parts of the circuit to locate a possibly shorted resistor. The maximum allowable voltage drop under load is critical, especially if there is more than one high resistance problem in a circuit because all voltage drops are cumulative. A small drop is normal due to the resistance of the conductors.

HIGH RESISTANCE TESTING

1. Set the voltmeter selector switch to the 4 volt position.
2. Connect the voltmeter positive lead to the positive post of the battery.
3. Turn on the headlights and heater blower to provide a load.
4. Probe various points in the circuit with the negative voltmeter lead.
5. Read the voltage drop on the 4 volt scale. Some average maximum allowable voltage drops are:

FUSE PANEL – 7 volts
IGNITION SWITCH – 5volts
HEADLIGHT SWITCH – 7 volts
IGNITION COIL (+) – 5 volts
ANY OTHER LOAD – 1.3 volts

NOTE: *Voltage drops are all measured while a load is operating; without current flow, there will be no voltage drop.*

Ohmmeter

The ohmmeter is designed to read resistance (ohms) in a circuit or component. Although there are several different styles of ohmmeters, all will usually have a selector switch which permits the measurement of different ranges of resistance (usually the selector switch allows the multiplication of the meter reading by 10, 100, 1000, and 10,000). A calibration knob allows the meter to be set at zero for accurate measurement. Since all ohmmeters are powered by an internal battery (usually 9 volts), the ohmmeter can be used as a self-powered test light. When the ohmmeter is connected, current from the ohmmeter flows through the circuit or component being tested. Since the ohmmeter's internal resistance and voltage are known values, the amount of current flow through the meter depends on the resistance of the circuit or component being tested.

The ohmmeter can be used to perform continuity test for opens or shorts (either by observation of the meter needle or as a self-powered test light), and to read actual resistance in a circuit. It should be noted that the ohmmeter is used to check the resistance of a component or wire while there is no voltage applied to the circuit. Current flow from an outside voltage source (such as the vehicle battery) can damage the ohmmeter, so the circuit or component should be isolated from the vehicle electrical system before any testing is done. Since the ohmmeter uses its own voltage source, either lead can be connected to any test point.

NOTE: *When checking diodes or other solid state components, the ohmmeter leads can only be connected one way in order to measure current flow in a single direction. Make sure the positive (+) and negative (-) terminal connections are as described in the test procedures to verify the one-way diode operation.*

In using the meter for making continuity checks, do not be concerned with the actual resistance readings. Zero resistance, or any resistance readings, indicate continuity in the circuit. Infinite resistance indicates an open in the circuit. A high resistance reading where there should be none indicates a problem in the circuit. Checks for short circuits are made in the same manner as checks for open circuits except that the circuit must be isolated from both power and normal ground. Infinite resistance indicates no continuity to ground, while zero resistance indicates a dead short to ground.

RESISTANCE MEASUREMENT

The batteries in an ohmmeter will weaken with age and temperature, so the ohmmeter must be calibrated or "zeroed" before taking measurements. To zero the meter, place the selector switch in its lowest range and touch the two ohmmeter leads together. Turn the calibration knob until the meter needle is exactly on zero.

NOTE: *All analog (needle) type ohmmeters must be zeroed before use, but some digital ohmmeter models are automatically calibrated when the switch is turned on. Self-calibrating digital ohmmeters do not have an adjusting knob, but its a good idea to check for a zero readout before use by touching the leads together. All computer controlled systems require the use of a digital ohmmeter with at least 10 meagohms impedance for testing. Before any test procedures are attempted, make sure the ohmmeter used is compatible with the electrical system or damage to the onboard computer could result.*

To measure resistance, first isolate the circuit from the vehicle power source by disconnecting the battery cables or the harness connector. Make sure the key is OFF when disconnecting any components or the battery. Where necessary, also isolate at least one side of the circuit to be checked to avoid reading parallel resistances. Parallel circuit resistances will always give a lower reading than the actual resistance of either of the branches. When measuring the resistance of parallel circuits, the total resistance will always be lower than the smallest resistance in the circuit. Connect the meter leads to both sides of the circuit (wire or component) and read the actual measured ohms on the meter scale. Make sure the selector switch is set to the proper ohm scale for the circuit being tested to avoid misreading the ohmmeter test value.

CAUTION: *Never use an ohmmeter with power applied to the circuit. Like the self-powered test light, the ohmmeter is designed to operate on its own power supply. The normal 12 volt automotive electrical system current could damage the meter.*

Ammeters

An ammeter measures the amount of current flowing through a circuit in units called amperes or amps. Amperes are units of electron flow which indicate how fast the electrons are flowing through the circuit. Since Ohms Law dictates that current flow in a circuit is equal to the circuit voltage divided by the total circuit resistance, increasing voltage also increases the current level (amps). Likewise, any decrease in resistance will increase the amount of amps in a circuit. At normal operating voltage, most circuits have a characteristic amount of amperes, called "current draw" which can be measured using an ammeter. By referring to a specified current draw rating, measuring the amperes, and comparing the two values, one can determine what is happening within the circuit to aid in diagnosis. An open circuit, for example, will not allow any current to flow so the ammeter reading will be zero. More current flows through a heavily loaded circuit or when the charging system is operating.

An ammeter is always connected in series with the circuit being tested. All of the current that normally flows through the circuit must also flow through the ammeter; if there is any other path for the current to follow, the ammeter reading will not be accurate. The ammeter itself has very little resistance to current flow and therefore will not affect the circuit, but it will measure current draw only when the circuit is closed and electricity is flowing. Excessive current draw can blow fuses and drain the battery, while a reduced current draw can cause motors to run slowly, lights to dim and other components to not operate properly. The ammeter can help diagnose these conditions by locating the cause of the high or low reading.

Multimeters

Different combinations of test meters can be built into a single unit designed for specific tests. Some of the more common combination test devices are known as Volt/Amp testers, Tach/Dwell meters, or Digital Multimeters. The Volt/Amp tester is used for charging system, starting system or battery tests and consists of a voltmeter, an ammeter and a variable resistance carbon pile. The voltmeter will usually have at least two ranges for use with 6, 12 and 24 volt systems. The ammeter also has more than one range for testing various levels of battery loads and starter current draw and the carbon pile can be adjusted to offer different amounts of resistance. The Volt/Amp tester has heavy leads to carry large amounts of current and many later models have an inductive ammeter pickup that clamps around the wire to simplify test connections. On some models, the ammeter also has a zero-center scale to allow testing of charging and starting systems without switching leads or polarity. A digital multimeter is a voltmeter, ammeter and ohmmeter combined in an instrument which gives a digital readout. These are often used when testing solid state circuits because of their high input impedance (usually 10 megohms or more).

The tach/dwell meter combines a tachometer and a dwell (cam angle) meter and is a specialized kind of voltmeter. The tachometer scale is marked to show engine speed in rpm and the dwell scale is marked to show degrees of distributor shaft rotation. In most electronic ignition systems, dwell is determined by the control unit, but the dwell meter can also be used to check the duty cycle (operation) of some electronic engine control systems. Some tach/dwell meters are powered by an internal battery, while others take their power from the car battery in use. The battery powered testers usually require calibration much like an ohmmeter before testing.

Special Test Equipment

A variety of diagnostic tools are available to help troubleshoot and repair computerized engine control systems. The most sophisticated of these devices are the console type engine analyzers that usually occupy a garage service bay, but there are several types of aftermarket electronic testers available that will allow quick circuit tests of the engine control system by plugging directly into a special connector located in the engine compartment or under the dashboard. Several tool and equipment manufacturers offer simple, hand held testers that measure various circuit voltage levels on command to check all system components for proper operation. Although these testers usually cost about $300-$500, consider that the average computer control unit (or ECM) can cost just as much and the money saved by not replacing perfectly good sensors or components in an attempt to correct a problem could justify the purchase price of a special diagnostic tester the first time it's used.

These computerized testers can allow quick and easy test measurements while the engine is operating or while the car is being driven. In addition, the on-board computer memory can be read to access any stored trouble codes; in effect allowing the computer to tell you where it hurts and aid trouble diagnosis by pinpointing exactly which circuit or component is malfunctioning. In the same manner, repairs can be tested to make sure the problem has been corrected. The biggest advantage these special testers have is their relatively easy hookups that minimize or eliminate the chances of making the wrong connections and getting false voltage readings or damaging the computer accidentally.

NOTE: *It should be remembered that these testers check voltage levels in circuits; they don't detect mechanical problems or failed components if the circuit voltage falls within the preprogrammed limits stored in the tester PROM unit. Also, most of the hand held testes are designed to work only on one or two systems made by a specific manufacturer.*

A variety of aftermarket testers are available to help diagnose different computerized control systems. Owatonna Tool Company (OTC), for example, markets a device called the OTC Monitor which plugs directly into the assembly line diagnostic link (ALDL). The OTC tester makes diagnosis a simple matter of pressing the correct buttons and, by changing the internal PROM or inserting a different diagnosis cartridge, it will work on any model from full size to subcompact, over a wide range of years. An adapter is supplied with the tester to allow connection to all types of ALDL links, regardless of the number of pin terminals used. By inserting an updated PROM into the OTC tester, it can be easily updated to diagnose any new modifications of computerized control systems.

Wiring Harnesses

The average automobile contains about ½ mile of wiring, with hundreds of individual connections. To protect the many wires from damage and to keep them from becoming a confusing tangle, they are organized into bundles, enclosed in plastic or taped together and called wire harnesses. Different wiring harnesses serve different parts of the vehicle. Individual wires are color coded to help trace them through a harness where sections are hidden from view.

A loose or corroded connection or a replacement wire that is too small for the circuit will add extra resistance and an additional voltage drop to the circuit. A ten percent voltage drop can result in slow or erratic motor operation, for example, even though the circuit is complete. Automotive wiring or circuit conductors can be in any one of three forms:

1. Single strand wire
2. Multistrand wire
3. Printed circuitry

Single strand wire has a solid metal core and is usually used inside such components as alternators, motors, relays and other devices. Multistrand wire has a core made of many small strands of wire twisted together into a single conductor. Most of the wiring in an automotive electrical system is made up of multistrand wire, either as a single conductor or grouped together in a harness. All wiring is color coded on the insulator, either as a solid color or as a colored wire with an identification stripe. A printed circuit is a thin film of copper or other conductor that is printed on an insulator backing. Occasionally, a printed circuit is sandwiched between two sheets of plastic for more protection and flexibility. A complete printed circuit, consisting of conductors, insulating material and connectors for lamps or other components is called a printed circuit board. Printed circuitry is used in place of individual wires or harnesses in places where space is limited, such as behind instrument panels.

Wire Gauge

Since computer controlled automotive electrical systems are very sensitive to changes in resistance, the selection of properly sized wires is critical when systems are repaired. The wire gauge number is an expression of the cross section area of the conductor. The most common system for expressing wire size is the American Wire Gauge (AWG) system.

Wire cross section area is measured in circular mils. A mil is $\frac{1}{1000}''$ (0.001''); a circular mil is the area of a circle one mil in diameter. For example, a conductor ¼'' in diameter is 0.250 in. or 250 mils. The circular mil cross section area of the wire is 250 squared (250^2)or 62,500 circular mils. Imported car models usually use metric wire gauge designations, which is simply the cross section area of the conductor in square millimeters (mm^2).

Gauge numbers are assigned to conductors of various cross section areas. As gauge number increases, area decreases and the conductor becomes smaller. A 5 gauge conductor is smaller than a 1 gauge conductor and a 10 gauge is smaller than a 5 gauge. As the cross section area of a conductor decreases, resistance increases and so does the gauge number. A conductor with a higher gauge number will carry less current than a conductor with a lower gauge number.

NOTE: *Gauge wire size refers to the size of the conductor, not the size of the complete wire. It is possible to have two wires of the same gauge with different diameters because one may have thicker insulation than the other.*

12 volt automotive electrical systems generally use 10, 12, 14, 16 and 18 gauge wire. Main power distribution circuits and larger accessories usually use 10 and 12 gauge wire. Battery cables are usually 4 or 6 gauge, although 1 and 2 gauge wires are occasionally used. Wire length must also be considered when making repairs to a circuit. As conductor length increases, so does resistance. An 18 gauge wire, for example, can carry a 10 amp load for 10 feet without excessive voltage drop; however if a 15 foot wire is required for the same 10 amp load, it must be a 16 gauge wire.

An electrical schematic shows the electrical current paths when a circuit is operating properly. It is essential to understand how a circuit works before trying to figure out why it doesn't. Schematics break the entire electrical system down into individual circuits and show only one particular circuit. In a schematic, no attempt is made to represent wiring and components as they physically appear on the vehicle; switches and other components are shown as simply as

possible. Face views of harness connectors show the cavity or terminal locations in all multi-pin connectors to help locate test points.

If you need to backprobe a connector while it is on the component, the order of the terminals must be mentally reversed. The wire color code can help in this situation, as well as a keyway, lock tab or other reference mark.

NOTE: *Wiring diagrams are not included in this book. As trucks have become more complex and available with longer option lists, wiring diagrams have grown in size and complexity. It has become almost impossible to provide a readable reproduction of a wiring diagram in a book this size. Information on ordering wiring diagrams from the vehicle manufacturer can be found in the owner's manual.*

WIRING REPAIR

Soldering is a quick, efficient method of joining metals permanently. Everyone who has the occasion to make wiring repairs should know how to solder. Electrical connections that are soldered are far less likely to come apart and will conduct electricity much better than connections that are only "pig-tailed" together. The most popular (and preferred) method of soldering is with an electrical soldering gun. Soldering irons are available in many sizes and wattage ratings. Irons with higher wattage ratings deliver higher temperatures and recover lost heat faster. A small soldering iron rated for no more than 50 watts is recommended, especially on electrical systems where excess heat can damage the components being soldered.

There are three ingredients necessary for successful soldering; proper flux, good solder and sufficient heat. A soldering flux is necessary to clean the metal of tarnish, prepare it for soldering and to enable the solder to spread into tiny crevices. When soldering, always use a resin flux or resin core solder which is non-corrosive and will not attract moisture once the job is finished. Other types of flux (acid core) will leave a residue that will attract moisture and cause the wires to corrode. Tin is a unique metal with a low melting point. In a molten state, it dissolves and alloys easily with many metals. Solder is made by mixing tin with lead. The most common proportions are 40/60, 50/50 and 60/40, with the percentage of tin listed first. Low priced solders usually contain less tin, making them very difficult for a beginner to use because more heat is required to melt the solder. A common solder is 40/60 which is well suited for all-around general use, but 60/40 melts easier, has more tin for a better joint and is preferred for electrical work.

Soldering Techniques

Successful soldering requires that the metals to be joined be heated to a temperature that will melt the solder—usually 360-460°F (182-238°C). Contrary to popular belief, the purpose of the soldering iron is not to melt the solder itself, but to heat the parts being soldered to a temperature high enough to melt the solder when it is touched to the work. Melting flux-cored solder on the soldering iron will usually destroy the effectiveness of the flux.

NOTE: *Soldering tips are made of copper for good heat conductivity, but must be "tinned" regularly for quick transference of heat to the project and to prevent the solder from sticking to the iron. To "tin" the iron, simply heat it and touch the flux-cored solder to the tip; the solder will flow over the hot tip. Wipe the excess off with a clean rag, but be careful as the iron will be hot.*

After some use, the tip may become pitted. If so, simply dress the tip smooth with a smooth file and "tin" the tip again. An old saying holds that "metals well cleaned are half soldered." Flux-cored solder will remove oxides but rust, bits of insulation and oil or grease must be removed with a wire brush or emery cloth. For maximum strength in soldered parts, the joint must start off clean and tight. Weak joints will result in gaps too wide for the solder to bridge.

If a separate soldering flux is used, it should be brushed or swabbed on only those areas that are to be soldered. Most solders contain a core of flux and separate fluxing is unnecessary. Hold the work to be soldered firmly. It is best to solder on a wooden board, because a metal vise will only rob the piece to be soldered of heat and make it difficult to melt the solder. Hold the soldering tip with the broadest face against the work to be soldered. Apply solder under the tip close to the work, using enough solder to give a heavy film between the iron and the piece being soldered, while moving slowly and making sure the solder melts properly. Keep the work level or the solder will run to the lowest part and favor the thicker parts, because these require more heat to melt the solder. If the soldering tip overheats (the solder coating on the face of the tip burns up), it should be retinned. Once the soldering is completed, let the soldered joint stand until cool. Tape and seal all soldered wire splices after the repair has cooled.

Wire Harness and Connectors

The on-board computer (ECM) wire harness electrically connects the control unit to the various solenoids, switches and sensors used by the control system. Most connectors in the engine compartment or otherwise exposed to the elements are protected against moisture and dirt which could create oxidation and deposits on the terminals. This protection is important because of the very low voltage and current levels used by the computer and sensors. All connectors have a lock which secures the male and female terminals together, with a secondary lock holding the seal and terminal into the connector. Both terminal locks must be released when disconnecting ECM connectors.

These special connectors are weather-proof and all repairs require the use of a special terminal and the tool required to service it. This tool is used to remove the pin and sleeve terminals. If removal is attempted with an ordinary pick, there is a good chance that the terminal will be bent or deformed. Unlike standard blade type terminals, these terminals cannot be straightened once they are bent. Make certain that the connectors are properly seated and all of the sealing rings in place when connecting leads. On some models, a hinge-type flap provides a backup or secondary locking feature for the terminals. Most secondary locks are used to improve the connector reliability by retaining the terminals if the small terminal lock tangs are not positioned properly.

Molded-on connectors require complete replacement of the connection. This means splicing a new connector assembly into the harness. All splices in on-board computer systems should be soldered to insure proper contact. Use care when probing the connections or replacing terminals in them as it is possible to short between opposite terminals. If this happens to the wrong terminal pair, it is possible to damage certain components. Always use jumper wires between connectors for circuit checking and never probe through weather-proof seals.

Open circuits are often difficult to locate by sight because corrosion or terminal misalignment are hidden by the connectors. Merely wiggling a connector on a sensor or in the wiring harness may correct the open circuit condition. This should always be considered when an open circuit or a failed sensor is indicated. Intermittent problems may also be caused by oxidized or loose connections. When using a circuit tester for diagnosis, always probe connections from the wire side. Be careful not to damage sealed connectors with test probes.

All wiring harnesses should be replaced with identical parts, using the same gauge wire and connectors. When signal wires are spliced into a harness, use wire with high temperature insulation only. With the low voltage and current levels found in the system, it is important that the best possible connection at all wire splices be made by soldering the splices together. It is seldom necessary to replace a complete harness. If replacement is necessary, pay close attention to insure proper harness routing. Secure the harness with suitable plastic wire clamps to prevent vibrations from causing the harness to wear in spots or contact any hot components.

NOTE: *Weatherproof connectors cannot be replaced with standard connectors. Instructions are provided with replacement connector and terminal packages. Some wire harnesses have mounting indicators (usually pieces of colored tape) to mark where the harness is to be secured.*

In making wiring repairs, it's important that you always replace damaged wires with wires that are the same gauge as the wire being replaced. The heavier the wire, the smaller the gauge number. Wires are color-coded to aid in identification and whenever possible the same color coded wire should be used for replacement. A wire stripping and crimping tool is necessary to install solderless terminal connectors. Test all crimps by pulling on the wires; it should not be possible to pull the wires out of a good crimp.

Wires which are open, exposed or otherwise damaged are repaired by simple splicing. Where possible, if the wiring harness is accessible and the damaged place in the wire can be located, it is best to open the harness and check for all possible damage. In an inaccessible harness, the wire must be bypassed with a new insert, usually taped to the outside of the old harness.

When replacing fusible links, be sure to use fusible link wire, NOT ordinary automotive wire. Make sure the fusible segment is of the same gauge and construction as the one being replaced and double the stripped end when crimping the terminal connector for a good contact. The melted (open) fusible link segment of the wiring harness should be cut off as close to the harness as possible, then a new segment spliced in as described. In the case of a damaged fusible link that feeds two harness wires, the harness connections should be replaced with two fusible link wires so that each circuit will have its own separate protection.

NOTE: *Most of the problems caused in the wiring harness are due to bad ground connections. Always check all vehicle ground connections for corrosion or looseness before performing any power feed checks to eliminate the chance of a bad ground affecting the circuit.*

Repairing Hard Shell Connectors

Unlike molded connectors, the terminal contacts in hard shell connectors can be replaced. Weatherproof hard-shell connectors with the leads molded into the shell have non-replaceable terminal ends. Replacement usually involves the use of a special terminal removal tool that depress the locking tangs (barbs) on the connector terminal and allow the connector to be removed from the rear of the shell. The connector shell should be replaced if it shows any evidence of burning, melting, cracks, or breaks. Replace individual terminals that are burnt, corroded, distorted or loose.

NOTE: *The insulation crimp must be tight to prevent the insulation from sliding back on the wire when the wire is pulled. The insulation must be visibly compressed under the crimp tabs, and the ends of the crimp should be turned in for a firm grip on the insulation.*

The wire crimp must be made with all wire strands inside the crimp. The terminal must be fully compressed on the wire strands with the ends of the crimp tabs turned in to make a firm grip on the wire. Check all connections with an ohmmeter to insure a good contact. There should be no measurable resistance between the wire and the terminal when connected.

Mechanical Test Equipment

Vacuum Gauge

Most gauges are graduated in inches of mercury (in.Hg), although a device called a manometer reads vacuum in inches of water (in. H_2O). The normal vacuum reading usually varies between 18 and 22 in.Hg at sea level. To test engine vacuum, the vacuum gauge must be connected to a source of manifold vacuum. Many engines have a plug in the intake manifold which can be removed and replaced with an adapter fitting. Connect the vacuum gauge to the fitting with a suitable rubber hose or, if no manifold plug is available, connect the vacuum gauge to any device using manifold vacuum, such as EGR valves, etc. The vacuum gauge can be used to determine if enough vacuum is reaching a component to allow its actuation.

Hand Vacuum Pump

Small, hand-held vacuum pumps come in a variety of designs. Most have a built-in vacuum gauge and allow the component to be tested without removing it from the vehicle. Operate the pump lever or plunger to apply the correct amount of vacuum required for the test specified in the diagnosis routines. The level of vacuum in inches of Mercury (in.Hg) is indicated on the pump gauge. For some testing, an additional vacuum gauge may be necessary.

Intake manifold vacuum is used to operate various systems and devices on late model vehicles. To correctly diagnose and solve problems in vacuum control systems, a vacuum source is necessary for testing. In some cases, vacuum can be taken from the intake manifold when the engine is running, but vacuum is normally provided by a hand vacuum pump. These hand vacuum pumps have a built-in vacuum gauge that allow testing while the device is still attached to the component. For some tests, an additional vacuum gauge may be necessary.

HEATING AND AIR CONDITIONING

Heater Case Assembly

REMOVAL AND INSTALLATION WITHOUT AIR CONDITIONING

1978-79

1. Disconnect the battery and drain the cooling system.

CAUTION: *When draining the coolant, keep in mind that cats and dogs are attracted by the ethylene glycol antifreeze, and are quite likely to drink any that is left in an uncovered container or in puddles on the ground. This will prove fatal in sufficient quantity. Always drain the coolant into a sealable container. Coolant should be reused unless it is contaminated or several years old.*

2. Remove the center outside air floor vent housing.

3. Remove the ash tray.

4. Remove the two defroster duct adapter screws. The left one is reached through the ash tray opening.

5. Remove the defrost duct adapter and push the flexible hose up out of the way.

6. Disconnect the temperature control cable.

7. Disconnect the blower motor wiring connector.

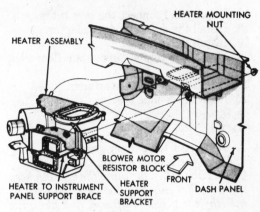

Removing or installing the heater

8. Disconnect the hoses from the heater core and plug the core openings.

9. Remove the two nuts retaining the heater unit to the firewall.

10. Remove the glove compartment and door.

11. Remove the screw attaching the heater brace bracket to the instrument panel.

12. Remove the heater assembly support strap nut. Disconnect the strap from the plenum stud and lower the heater from the instrument panel.

13. Disconnect the control cable and remove the unit from the car.

14. Connect the control cable and raise the unit into position so that the core tubes and mounting studs fit through their holes in the firewall.

15. Install the support strap and hand tighten the nut.

16. Install and tighten the two heater-to-firewall nuts.

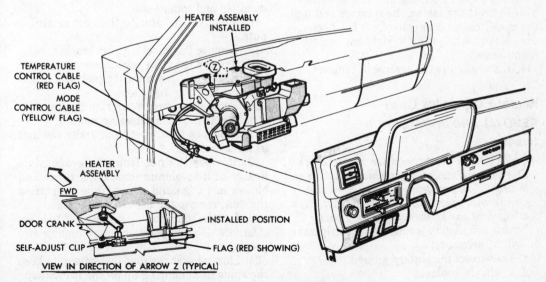

Heater control holders and attachment

17. Unplug and connect the core tubes.
18. Install the defroster duct adaptor.
19. Install the ash tray.
20. Install the center outside air floor vent housing.
21. Install the glove compartment.
22. Refill the cooling system.

1980-89

1. Disconnect the battery ground.
2. Drain the cooling system.
CAUTION: *When draining the coolant, keep in mind that cats and dogs are attracted by the ethylene glycol antifreeze, and are quite likely to drink any that is left in an uncovered container or in puddles on the ground. This will prove fatal in sufficient quantity. Always drain the coolant into a sealable container. Coolant should be reused unless it is contaminated or several years old.*
3. Disconnect the blower motor wiring connector.
4. Remove the ash tray.
5. Depress the retaining tab and pull the temperature control cable out of the receptacle on the heater.
6. Remove the glove compartment and door.
7. Disconnect the heater hoses at the core tubes, and cover the tube openings to prevent spillage.
8. Remove the two nuts holding the heater case to the firewall.
9. Remove the wire connector from the blower motor resistor block.
10. Remove the bolt holding the heater support brace to the instrument panel.
11. Remove the heater support bracket nut. Disconnect the strap from the plenum stud and lower the heater from the instrument panel.
12. Depress the tab on the retainer and pull the mode control door cable from the heater.
13. Move the heater to the right and remove it from the car.
14. Installation is the reverse of removal.

Heater/Evaporator Case
REMOVAL AND INSTALLATION
1978-79

CAUTION: *This procedure requires the discharge, evacuation, recharge and leak testing of the system. This is a relatively dangerous operation, since contact with refrigerant can cause injury. See Chapter 1.*
During installation, a small can of refrigerant oil will be necessary.
1. Disconnect the battery ground.
2. Drain the coolant.
CAUTION: *When draining the coolant, keep*

in mind that cats and dogs are attracted by the ethylene glycol antifreeze, and are quite likely to drink any that is left in an uncovered container or in puddles on the ground. This will prove fatal in sufficient quantity. Always drain the coolant into a sealable container. Coolant should be reused unless it is contaminated or several years old.
3. Disconnect the temperature door cable from the heater-evaporator unit.
4. Disconnect the temperature door cable from the retaining clips.
5. Remove the glovebox.
6. Disconnect the vacuum harness from the control head.
7. Disconnect the blower motor lead and anti-diesel relay wire.
8. Remove the seven screws fastening the right trim bezel to the instrument panel. Starting at the right side, swing the bezel clear and remove it.
9. Remove the three screws on the bottom of the center distribution duct cover and slide the cover rearward and remove it.
10. Remove the center distribution duct.
11. Remove the defroster duct adaptor.
12. Remove the H-type expansion valve, located on the right side of the firewall:
   a. remove the $5/16''$ bolt in the center of the plumbing sealing plate.
   b. carefully pull the refrigerant lines toward the front of the car, taking care to avoid scratching the valve sealing surfaces.
   c. remove the two 1/4-20 Allen head cap screws and remove the valve.
13. Cap the pipe openings at once. Wrap the valve in a plastic bag.
14. Disconnect the hoses from the core tubes.
15. Disconnect the vacuum lines at the intake manifold and water valve.
16. Remove the unit-to-firewall retaining nuts.
17. Remove the panel support bracket.
18. Remove the right cowl lower panel.
19. Remove the instrument panel pivot bracket screw from the right side.
20. Remove the screws securing the lower instrument panel at the steering column.
21. Pull back the carpet from under the unit as far as possible.
22. Remove the nut from the evaporator-heater unit-to-plenum mounting brace and blower motor ground cable. While supporting the unit, remove the brace from its stud.
23. Lift the unit, pulling it rearward to allow clearance. These operations may require two people.
24. Slowly lower the unit taking care to keep the studs from hanging-up on the insulation.
25. When the unit reaches the floor, slide it

rearward until it is out from under the instrument panel.

26. Remove the unit from the car.

WARNING: *When installing the unit in the car, care must be taken that the vacuum lines to the engine compartment do not hang-up on the accelerator or become trapped between the unit and the firewall. If this happens, kinked lines will result and the unit will have to be removed to free them. Proper routing of these lines will require two people. The portion of the vacuum harness which is routed through the steering column support MUST be positioned BEFORE the distribution housing is installed. The harness MUST be routed ABOVE the temperature control cable.*

27. Place the unit on the floor as far under the panel as possible.

28. Raise the unit carefully, at the same time pull the lower instrument panel rearward as far as possible.

29. Position the unit in place and attach the brace to the stud.

30. Install the lower ground cable and attach the nut.

31. Install and tighten the unit-to-firewall nuts.

32. Reposition the carpet and install, but do not tighten the right instrument panel pivot bracket screw.

33. Place a piece of sheet metal or thin cardboard against the evaporator-heater assembly to center the assembly duct seal.

34. Position the center distributor duct in place making sure that the upper left tab comes in through the left center air conditioning outlet opening and that each air take-off is properly inserted in its respective outlet.

NOTE: *Make sure that the radio wiring connector does not interfere with the duct.*

35. Install and tighten the screw securing the upper left tab of the center air distribution duct to the instrument panel.

36. Remove the sheet metal or cardboard from between the unit and the duct.

NOTE: *Make sure that the unit seal is properly aligned with the duct opening.*

37. Install and tighten the two lower screws fastening the center distribution duct to the instrument panel.

38. Install and tighten the screws securing the lower instrument panel at the steering column.

39. Install and tighten the nut securing the instrument panel to the support bracket.

40. Make sure that the seal on the unit is properly aligned and seated against the distribution duct assembly.

41. Tighten the instrument panel pivot bracket screw and install the right cowl lower trim.

42. Slide the distributor duct cover assembly onto the center distribution duct so that the notches lock into the tabs and the tabs slide over the rear and side ledges of the center duct assembly.

43. Install the three screws securing the ducting.

44. Install the right trim bezel.

45. Connect the vacuum harness to the control head.

46. Connect the blower lead and the anti-diesel wire.

47. Install the glove box.

48. Connect the temperature door cable.

49. Install new O-rings on the evaporator plate and the plumbing plate. Coat the new O-rings with clean refrigerant oil.

50. Place the H-valve against the evaporator sealing plate surface and install the two ½-20NC throughbolts. Torque to 6-10 ft. lbs.

51. Carefully hold the refrigerant line connector against the valve and install the $5/16$-18NC bolt. Torque to 14-20 ft. lbs.

52. Install the heater hoses at the core tubes.

53. Connect the vacuum lines at the manifold and water valve.

54. Install the condensate drain tube.

55. Have the system evacuated, charged and leak tested by a trained technician.

1980 and Later

CAUTION: *This procedure requires the discharge, evacuation, recharge and leak testing of the system. This is a relatively dangerous operation, since, contact with refrigerant can cause injury. See Chapter 1.*

1. Discharge the system.

2. Drain the cooling system.

CAUTION: *When draining the coolant, keep in mind that cats and dogs are attracted by the ethylene glycol antifreeze, and are quite likely to drink any that is left in an uncovered container or in puddles on the ground. This will prove fatal in sufficient quantity. Always drain the coolant into a sealable container. Coolant should be reused unless it is contaminated or several years old.*

3. Disconnect the battery.

4. Disconnect the heater hoses at the core tubes. Cap the tube openings to prevent spillage.

5. Disconnect the vacuum lines at the intake manifold and the water valve. Tag the lines for installation.

6. Remove the "H" valve:

　a. Disconnect the wire from the low pressure cut-off switch.

　b. Remove the bolt in the center of the plumbing sealing plate.

　c. Pull the refrigerant line assembly toward the front of the car. Take care to avoid scratching the valve sealing surfaces with the tube pilots.

    d. Hold the "H" valve, remove the two allen head screws and lift out the valve.

7. Unclamp and remove the condensation drain.

8. Remove the nuts holding the heater/evaporator case to the firewall.

9. Depress the tab and unhook the cable retainer from the case.

10. Remove the glove compartment.

11. Disconnect the vacuum harness from the air conditioning control head.

12. Disconnect the blower feed wire and the anti-diesel solenoid wires.

13. Remove the seven screws retaining the right trim bezel to the instrument panel. Starting at the right side, swing the trim bezel clear of the panel and remove it.

14. Remove the three screws securing the center distribution duct to the instrument panel and remove it.

15. Remove the defroster duct adapter.

16. Remove the instrument panel support bracket.

17. Remove the instrument panel pivot bracket screw from the right side.

18. Remove the screws securing the instrument panel to the steering column.

19. Pull the carpet away from the case.

20. Remove the nut securing the case to the plenum and ground cable.

21. Support the case and remove the plenum bracket.

22. Lift the case and pull it rearward as far as possible to clear the panel. The lower panel may have to be pulled rearward to aid in case removal.

NOTE: *Two people will make this job a lot easier.*

23. When the case clears the panel, lower it slowly so that the studs don't hang up in the panel liner.

24. Lower the case to the floor and remove it from the car.

WARNING: *When installing the unit, make sure that none of the vacuum lines is kinked. Kinked lines would require removal of the unit again.*

25. Place the case on the floor as far forward as possible.

26. Lift the unit being careful of the studs. Manipulate the panel to aid installation of the case.

27. Attach the brace to the stud. Install the ground wire and tighten the nut.

28. Install and tighten the case-to-firewall nuts.

29. Install the drain tube.

30. Install the heater hoses.

31. Install the vacuum lines.

32. Install the "H" valve.

33. Reposition the carpet.

34. Install, but don't tighten the right side instrument panel pivot bracket screw.

35. Install the defroster duct adapter, making certain that the opening is properly aligned.

36. Place a piece of thin cardboard against the evaporator/heater assembly-to-center distribution duct seal.

37. Position the center distribution duct in place. Make sure that the upper left tab comes out through the left center duct. Each end air outlet must be properly aligned with its respective spot cooler.

NOTE: *Be certain that the radio wiring connecter does not interfere with the center duct.*

38. Install and tighten the screw retaining the upper left tab of the center duct.

39. Remove the cardboard. Make sure that the evaporator/heater seal is properly aligned with the top of the center duct opening.

40. Install and tighten the two lower center duct-to-panel screws.

41. Installation of all remaining parts is the reverse of the removal sequence. Fill the cooling system; evacuate, charge and leak test the air conditioning system.

Blower Motor

REMOVAL AND INSTALLATION

Without Air Conditioning

The blower motor is located under the instrument panel on the left side of the heater assembly.

1. Disconnect the motor wiring.

2. Remove the left outlet duct.

3. Remove the motor retaining screws and remove the motor.

4. Installation is the reverse of removal.

Air Conditioned Cars

1. Disconnect the battery ground.

2. Remove the three screws securing the glovebox to the instrument panel.

3. Disconnect the wiring from the blower and case.

4. Remove the blower vent tube from the case.

5. Loosen the recirculating door from the bracket and remove the actuator from the housing. Leave the vacuum lines attached.

6. Remove the seven screws attaching the recirculating housing to the air conditioning unit and remove the housing.

7. Remove the three mounting flange nuts and washers.

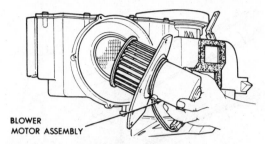

Removing or installing the blower motor

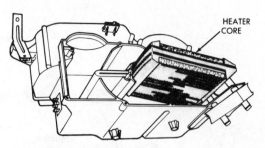

Removing the heater core

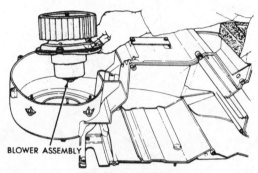

Removing the blower motor (with A/C)

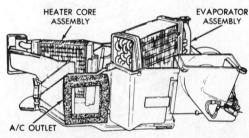

Removing the heater core and evaporator coil

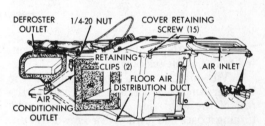

Heater/evaporator unit positioned for disassembly

8. Remove the blower motor from the unit.

9. Installation is the reverse of removal. Replace any damaged sealer.

Heater Core

REMOVAL AND INSTALLATION

Without Air Conditioning

1. Remove the heater assembly as described earlier.
2. Remove the left outlet duct.
3. Remove the blower motor.
4. Remove the defroster duct adapter.
5. Remove the outside air and defroster door cover.
6. Remove the defroster door.
7. Remove the defroster door control rod.
8. Remove the core cover.
9. Lift the core from the unit.
10. Installation is the reverse of removal.

Heater/Evaporator Core

REMOVAL AND INSTALLATION

NOTE: *Core removal requires removal of the entire heater assembly.*

1. Remove the heater/evaporator assembly.
2. Place the unit on a workbench. On the inside-the-car side, remove the ¼-20 nut from the mode door actuator on the top cover and the two retaining clips from the front edge of the cover. To remove the mode door actuator, remove the two screws securing it to the cover.

3. Remove the fifteen screws attaching the cover to the assembly and lift off the cover. Lift the mode door out of the unit.
4. Remove the screw from the core retaining bracket and lift out the core.
5. Place the core in the unit and install the bracket.
6. Install the actuator arm.

RADIO

AM, AM/FM monoaural, or AM/FM stereo multiplex units are available. All radios are trimmed at the factory and should require no further adjustment. However, after a repair or if the antenna trim is to be verified, proceed as follows:

ANTENNA TRIMMING

1. Turn radio on.
2. Manually tune the radio to a weak station between 1400 and 1600 KHz on AM.

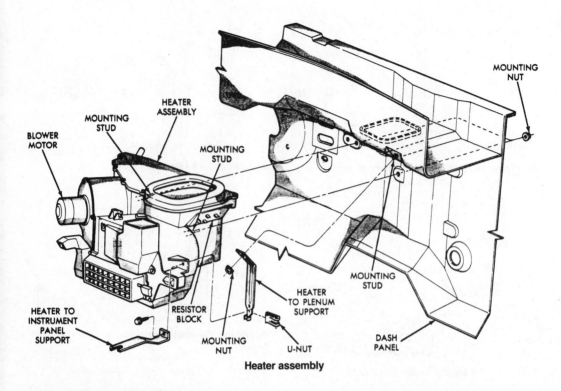

Heater assembly

3. Increase the volume and set the tone control to full treble (clockwise).

4. Viewing the radio from the front, the trimmer control is a slot-head located at the rear of the right side. Adjust it carefully by turning it back and forth with a screwdriver until maximum loudness is achieved.

NOTE: *Some 1978 and early production 1979 cars exhibit an ignition noise interfering with radio reception. This can be corrected by installing the following items:*

a. Ground strap (engine-mount-to-frame) (Chrysler Part No. 5211212)

b. Ground strap (engine-to-cowl) (Chrysler Part No. 5211211)

c. Ground strap (air conditioning evaporator-to-cowl) (Chrysler Part No. 5211210)

Ground straps can also be obtained in kit form from local radio or CB shops.

REMOVAL AND INSTALLATION

1. Remove the bezel attaching screws and open the glove compartment.

2. Remove the bezel, guiding the right end around the glove compartment and away from the panel.

3. Disconnect the radio ground strap and remove the two radio mounting screws.

4. Pull the radio from the panel and disconnect the wiring and antenna lead.

5. Installation is the reverse of removal.

WINDSHIELD WIPERS

Wiper Blade

REPLACEMENT

1. Lift the wiper arm away from the glass.

2. Depress the release lever on the bridge and remove the blade assembly from the arm.

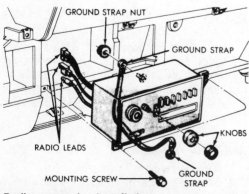

Radio removed or installation

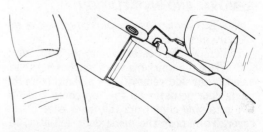

Removing front wiper arm

3. Lift the tab and pinch the end bridge to release it from the center bridge.

4. Slide the end bridge from the blade element and the element from the opposite end bridge.

5. Assembly is the reverse of removal. Make sure that the element locking tabs are securely locked in position.

Front Wiper Motor
REMOVAL AND INSTALLATION

1. Disconnect the linkage from the motor crank arm.

2. Remove the wiper motor plastic cover.

3. Disconnect the wiring harness from the motor.

4. Remove the three mounting bolts from the motor bracket and remove the motor.

5. Installation is the reverse of removal.

Rear Wipers
Blade and Arm
REMOVAL AND INSTALLATION

1. Turn the wipers ON and position the blade at a convenient place on the glass by turning the ignition OFF.

2. Lift the wiper arm off the glass.

3. Depress the release lever on the center bridge and remove the center bridge.

4. Depress the release button on the end bridge to release it from the center bridge.

5. Remove the wiper element from the end bridge.

6. To remove the arm, pull out the latch knob and remove the arm from the pivot.

7. Installation is the reverse of removal. Be sure the element is engaged in all 4 bridge claws.

Rear Wiper Motor

A new wiper motor was used beginning with mid-February 1978 production. The new motor is Part No. 5211024 with date code 0378 imprinted in red ink. Early motors have the date code in black ink (same part no.) If failure of the early motor occurs, replace it with the new motor.

REMOVAL AND INSTALLATION

1. Open the liftgate.

2. Remove the wiper motor plastic cover.

3. Remove the blade and arm assembly.

4. Remove the chrome nut from the pivot shaft and the chrome ring from the pivot shaft.

5. From inside the tailgate, remove the motor mounting screws.

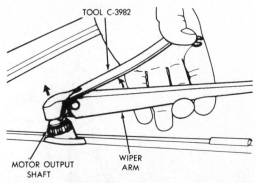

Removing liftgate wiper arm with tool available locally

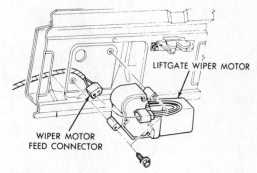

Liftgate wiper motor

6. Disconnect the main liftgate wiring harness from the motor pigtail wire.

7. Remove the motor.

8. Installation is the reverse of removal.

Windshield Washer Reservoir and Pump
REMOVAL AND INSTALLATION
Front

1. Open the hood and disconnect the wiring harness from the pump.

2. Remove the sheet metal screws holding the reservoir to the inner fender shield.

3. Disconnect the washer hose and remove the reservoir. Keep your thumb over the liquid outlet to avoid spilling the washer solvent on painted surfaces.

4. Drain the reservoir to remove the pump. Insert a $19/32''$ socket and extension through the filler opening and remove the pump filter and nut.

5. Disconnect the outside portion of the pump and remove the inner and outer portions of the pump.

6. Installation is the reverse of removal. Be sure the rubber grommet is in place when installing the pump.

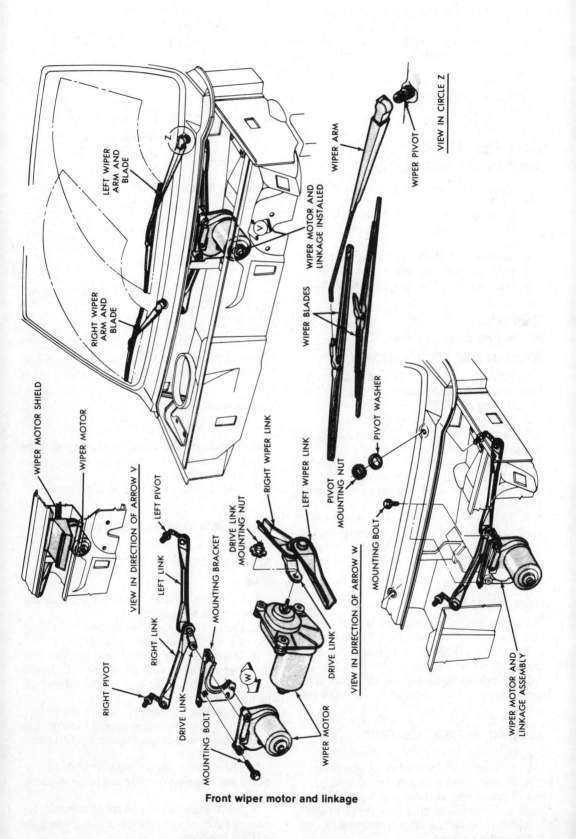

Front wiper motor and linkage

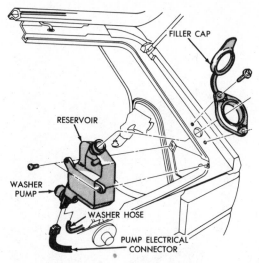

RESERVOIR

FILLER CAP

WASHER PUMP

WASHER HOSE

PUMP ELECTRICAL CONNECTOR

Rear windshield washer system

Rear

1. Open the liftgate.
2. Remove the plastic cap and mounting retainer from the reservoir filler on the right side of the liftgate. Reach through the side drain and remove the sheet metal screws.
3. Disconnect the wiring from the pump.
4. Remove the 2 side panel reservoir mounting screws.
5. Disconnect the washer hose from the reservoir.

6. Remove the reservoir and pump from the side panel through the aperture panel access hole. Try not to spill windshield washer solvent on the paint.
7. Drain the reservoir to remove the pump. Insert a $^{19}/_{32}$" socket and extension through the filler opening and remove the pump filter and nut.
8. Disconnect the outside portion of the pump and remove the inner and outer parts of the pump.
9. Installation is the reverse of removal. Be sure the rubber grommet is in place when installing the pump.

INSTRUMENT AND SWITCHES

The fuel, temperature and oil pressure gauges work on the constant voltage principle through a common voltage limiter which pulses to provide intermittent current to the gauge system.

Cluster Assembly

REMOVAL AND INSTALLATION

1978-83

1. Remove the two lens assembly lower attaching retaining springs by pulling rearward with a pliers.

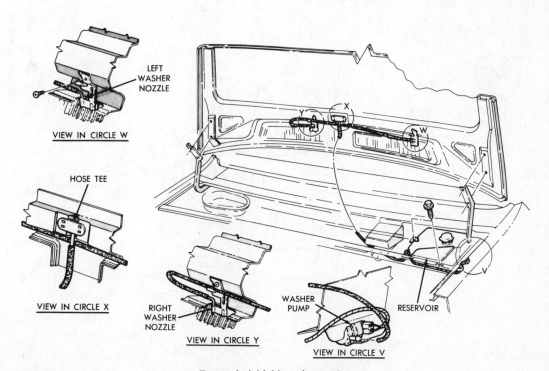

LEFT WASHER NOZZLE

VIEW IN CIRCLE W

HOSE TEE

VIEW IN CIRCLE X

RIGHT WASHER NOZZLE

VIEW IN CIRCLE Y

WASHER PUMP

RESERVOIR

VIEW IN CIRCLE V

Front windshield washer system

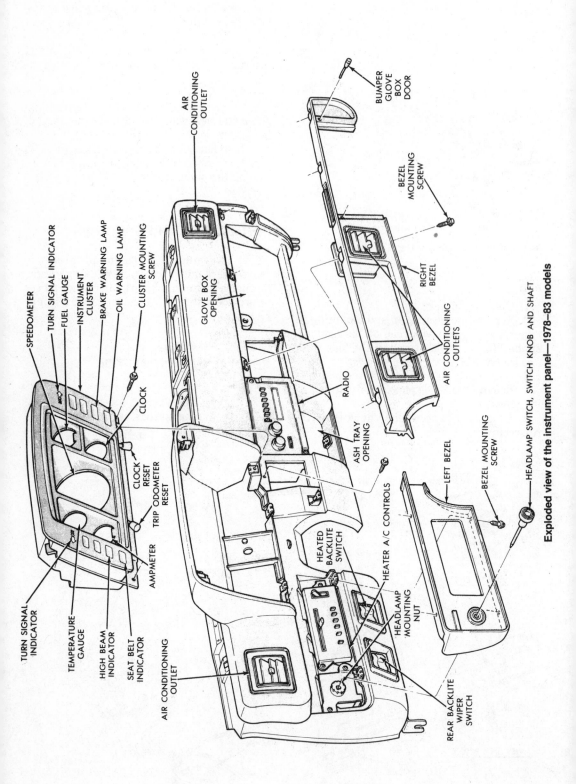

Exploded view of the instrument panel—1978-83 models

TURN SIGNAL INDICATOR

TEMPERATURE GAUGE

HIGH BEAM INDICATOR

SEAT BELT INDICATOR

AIR CONDITIONING OUTLET

AMPMETER

TRIP ODOMETER RESET

CLOCK RESET

CLOCK

CLUSTER MOUNTING SCREW

OIL WARNING LAMP

BRAKE WARNING LAMP

INSTRUMENT CLUSTER

FUEL GAUGE

TURN SIGNAL INDICATOR

SPEEDOMETER

AIR CONDITIONING OUTLET

GLOVE BOX OPENING

RADIO

ASH TRAY OPENING

HEATED BACKLITE SWITCH

HEATER A/C CONTROLS

REAR BACKLITE WIPER SWITCH

HEADLAMP MOUNTING NUT

LEFT BEZEL

BEZEL MOUNTING SCREW

HEADLAMP SWITCH, SWITCH KNOB AND SHAFT

AIR CONDITIONING OUTLETS

RIGHT BEZEL

BEZEL MOUNTING SCREW

BUMPER GLOVE BOX DOOR

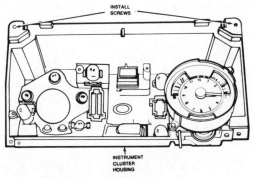

Instrument cluster modification

2. Allow the lens assembly to drop as it is pulled rearward.

3. Remove the speedometer assembly (two screws).

4. Remove the two wiring harness connectors.

5. Remove the two (1978-79), or four (1980-83) cluster attaching screws.

6. (1978-79 only) Pull the two upper spring retainers away from the panel.

7. If equipped with a clock, reach behind the panel and disconnect the wires.

8. Remove the cluster assembly.

9. Installation is the reverse of removal.

Rattles in a 1978 or 1979 instrument cluster may be caused by loose or missing upper cluster mounting clips. To correct rattles, a screw (Chrysler Part No 9414172) in the screw holes provided in the upper part of the cluster.

1984 and later

1. Remove the two lower cluster bezel retaining screws.

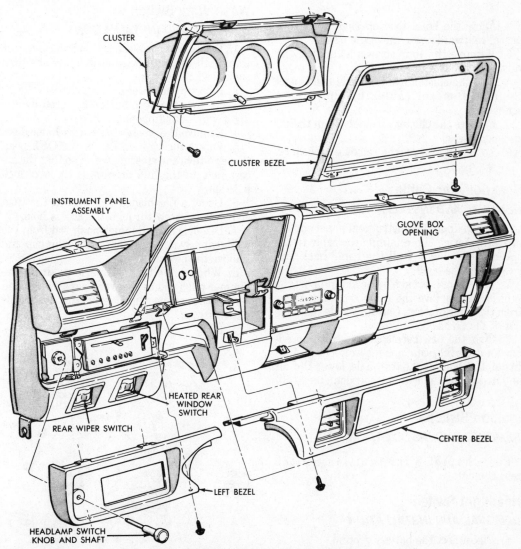

Typical instrument panel—1984 and later

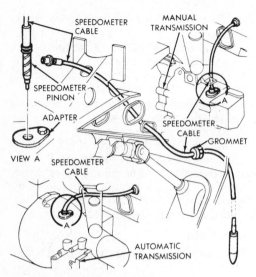

Speedometer cable mounting

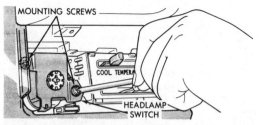

Headlamp switch mounting screws

2. Allow the bezel to drop slightly as it is moved rearward and remove the bezel.

3. Remove the four screws attaching the cluster to the base panel.

4. Pull the cluster rearward and disconnect the speedometer cable and the wiring connector.

5. Remove the cluster assembly from the instrument panel.

6. To install, reverse the removal procedure.

Speedometer Cable

REMOVAL AND INSTALLATION

1. Reach under the instrument panel and depress the spring clip retaining the cable to the speedometer head. Pull the cable back and away from the head.

2. If the core is broken, raise and support the vehicle and remove the cable retaining screw from the cable bracket. Carefully slide the cable out of the transaxle.

3. Coat the new core sparingly with speedometer cable lubricant and insert it in the cable. Install the cable at the transaxle, lower the car and install the cable at the speedometer head.

Ignition Switch

REMOVAL AND INSTALLATION

See Chapter 8 for Ignition Switch replacement.

Headlight Switch

REMOVAL AND INSTALLATION

1. Disconnect the battery ground.

2. Remove the left bezel.

3. Remove the headlamp switch mounting screws.

4. Remove the switch from the panel and disconnect the wiring harness connector.

5. Separate the switch and bracket by removing the bracket retainer.

6. Install in the reverse of removal.

Wash/Wipe Switch

REMOVAL AND INSTALLATION

1. Disconnect the electrical switch connector from both the wash/wipe switch and the turn signal switch.

2. Remove the lower column cover.

3. Remove the horn button by carefully lifting it with your fingers.

4. Remove the wash/wipe switch hider disc.

5. Rotate the ignition key to the **OFF** position and turn the steering wheel so that the access hole in the hub area is at the 9 o'clock position.

6. Using a flat bladed tool, loosen the turn signal lever screw through the access hole.

7. Disengage the dimmer push rod from the wash/wipe switch, unsnap the wiring clip and remove the switch.

8. When installing, properly position the dimmer push rod in the wash/wipe switch and secure the wiring clip. Install the wash/wipe hider disc.

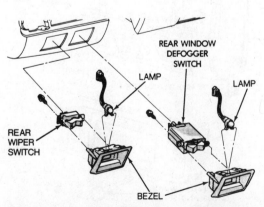

Rear wiper and rear window defogger switches

Headlight retaining ring screws

Rear Wiper, Hatch Release and Rear Window Defogger Switch

REMOVAL AND INSTALLATION

1. With the aid of a thin bladed tool, depress the two spring clips on top of the bezel.
2. Tip the bezel rearward and remove the assembly.
3. Disconnect the wiring and remove the switch.
4. To install, reconnect the wiring and snap the switch into position.

Clock

REMOVAL AND INSTALLATION

On earlier models the clock is in the instrument cluster and part of the fuel and alternator gauge assembly. On later models the electronic digital clock is built into the radio. Remove the cluster mounted clock as follows:

1. Remove the two mask/lens assembly lower attachment retaining spring pins by pulling rearward with pliers.
2. Allow the mask/lens assembly to drop slightly as it is moved rearward. Remove it from the cluster area.
3. Remove the clock/gauge assembly retaining screws then remove the clock from the gauge.
4. Installation is the reverse of removal.

LIGHTING

Headlights

REMOVAL AND INSTALLATION

1. Be sure the light switch is OFF.
2. Remove the 4 screws that hold the headlight bezel in place.
3. Remove the headlight bezel. Pull the bezel away and disconnect the parking/turn signal light. Twist to remove the light and socket.
4. Set the bezel aside.
5. Remove the 4 screws securing the headlight retainer and remove the retainer.
6. Pull the headlight out and disconnect the socket.

Headlight bezel mounting screws—typical

Headlight socket

7. Install a new headlight in the reverse order of removal. Check the operation of the lights before completing the assembly.

Front Park, Turn Signal and Side Marker Lamps

REMOVAL AND INSTALLATION

1. Remove the four headlamp bezel attaching screws and remove the bezel.
2. Twist out the socket from the rear.
3. To remove the lens, extend a wooden dowel through the housing socket holes and push against the lens with a steady force until the lens is free from the housing, making sure to release the locking tabs.
4. To install, clean the housing gasket track and apply butyl tape adhesive to all corners and at the bottom overlap the tape ends approximately ½".
5. Press the lens into position until the housing tabs snap over the lens.
6. Twist in the lamp socket.
7. Position the bezel and lamp assembly and install the four headlamp bezel attaching screws.

Tail, Stop, Turn Signal and Back-Up Lamps

REMOVAL AND INSTALLATION

1. Snap or twist out the sockets.
2. Remove the housing by depressing the four snap tabs and push against the housing with a steady force until the housing is free from the body.
3. With a small screwdriver release the lens locking tabs taking care not to damage the lens retaining tabs on the housing and remove the lens.
4. To install, clean both housing gasket tracks and apply butyl tape adhesive to all cor-

ners and overlap the tape ends approximately ½".
5. Press the lens into position until the housing tabs snap over the lens.
6. Press the lamp assembly into the body until the four housing retainers snap into the body.
7. Twist in the lamp socket.

Center High Mounted Stop Lamp

REMOVAL AND INSTALLATION

1. Remove the two lens attaching screws and pull the lens from the lamp assembly.
2. The bulbs may be removed by pulling straight out.
3. To remove the lamp assembly, from under the deck lid remove the two attaching nuts and lift the lamp from the mounting.
4. Installation is the reverse of removal.

CIRCUIT PROTECTION

Fusible Links

Fusible links are used to prevent major wire harness damage in the event of a short circuit or an overload condition in the electrical circuits. Each fusible link is of a fixed value for a specific electrical load. Should a link fail, the cause of a failure must be determined and repaired prior to installing a new link of the same value.

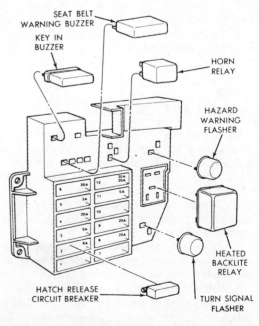

Fuse block—1978–79 models

Circuit Breakers

Circuit breakers are used along with fusible links to protect electrical system components such as headlamps, windshield wipers, electric windows, tailgate front and rear switches. The circuit breakers are located either in the switch or mounted on or near the lower lip of the instrument panel, to the right or left side of the steering column.

Fuse Panels

The fuse panel is used to house the fuses that protect the individual or combined electrical circuits within the vehicle. The turn signal flasher, the hazzard warning flasher and the seat belt warning buzzer/timer are located on the fuse panel for quick identification and replacement. The fuses are usually identified by abbreviated circuit names or number, with the number of the rated fuse needed to protect the circuit printed below the fuse holder.

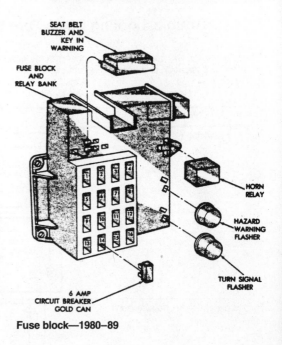

Fuse block—1980–89

Troubleshooting Basic Windshield Wiper Problems

Problem	Cause	Solution
Electric Wipers		
Wipers do not operate—Wiper motor heats up or hums	• Internal motor defect • Bent or damaged linkage • Arms improperly installed on linking pivots	• Replace motor • Repair or replace linkage • Position linkage in park and reinstall wiper arms
Wipers do not operate—No current to motor	• Fuse or circuit breaker blown • Loose, open or broken wiring • Defective switch • Defective or corroded terminals • No ground circuit for motor or switch	• Replace fuse or circuit breaker • Repair wiring and connections • Replace switch • Replace or clean terminals • Repair ground circuits
Wipers do not operate—Motor runs	• Linkage disconnected or broken	• Connect wiper linkage or replace broken linkage
Vacuum Wipers		
Wipers do not operate	• Control switch or cable inoperative • Loss of engine vacuum to wiper motor (broken hoses, low engine vacuum, defective vacuum/fuel pump) • Linkage broken or disconnected • Defective wiper motor	• Repair or replace switch or cable • Check vacuum lines, engine vacuum and fuel pump • Repair linkage • Replace wiper motor
Wipers stop on engine acceleration	• Leaking vacuum hoses • Dry windshield • Oversize wiper blades • Defective vacuum/fuel pump	• Repair or replace hoses • Wet windshield with washers • Replace with proper size wiper blades • Replace pump

Troubleshooting Basic Turn Signal and Flasher Problems

Most problems in the turn signals or flasher system, can be reduced to defective flashers or bulbs, which are easily replaced. Occasionally, problems in the turn signals are traced to the switch in the steering column, which will require professional service.

F = Front   R = Rear   ● = Lights off   ○ = Lights on

Problem		Solution
Turn signals light, but do not flash		· Replace the flasher
No turn signals light on either side		· Check the fuse. Replace if defective. · Check the flasher by substitution · Check for open circuit, short circuit or poor ground
Both turn signals on one side don't work		· Check for bad bulbs · Check for bad ground in both housings
One turn signal light on one side doesn't work		· Check and/or replace bulb · Check for corrosion in socket. Clean contacts. · Check for poor ground at socket
Turn signal flashes too fast or too slow		· Check any bulb on the side flashing too fast. A heavy-duty bulb is probably installed in place of a regular bulb. · Check the bulb flashing too slow. A standard bulb was probably installed in place of a heavy-duty bulb. · Check for loose connections or corrosion at the bulb socket
Indicator lights don't work in either direction		· Check if the turn signals are working · Check the dash indicator lights · Check the flasher by substitution

One indicator light doesn't light		· On systems with 1 dash indicator: See if the lights work on the same side. Often the filaments have been reversed in systems combining stoplights with taillights and turn signals.
		   Check the flasher by substitution
		· On systems with 2 indicators: Check the bulbs on the same side
		   Check the indicator light bulb
		   Check the flasher by substitution

Troubleshooting Basic Lighting Problems

Problem	Cause	Solution
Lights		
One or more lights don't work, but others do	· Defective bulb(s) · Blown fuse(s) · Dirty fuse clips or light sockets · Poor ground circuit	· Replace bulb(s) · Replace fuse(s) · Clean connections · Run ground wire from light socket housing to car frame
Lights burn out quickly	· Incorrect voltage regulator setting or defective regulator · Poor battery/alternator connections	· Replace voltage regulator · Check battery/alternator connections
Lights go dim	· Low/discharged battery · Alternator not charging · Corroded sockets or connections · Low voltage output	· Check battery · Check drive belt tension; repair or replace alternator · Clean bulb and socket contacts and connections · Replace voltage regulator
Lights flicker	· Loose connection · Poor ground · Circuit breaker operating (short circuit)	· Tighten all connections · Run ground wire from light housing to car frame · Check connections and look for bare wires
Lights "flare"—Some flare is normal on acceleration—if excessive, see "Lights Burn Out Quickly"	· High voltage setting	· Replace voltage regulator
Lights glare—approaching drivers are blinded	· Lights adjusted too high · Rear springs or shocks sagging · Rear tires soft	· Have headlights aimed · Check rear springs/shocks · Check/correct rear tire pressure
Turn Signals		
Turn signals don't work in either direction	· Blown fuse · Defective flasher · Loose connection	· Replace fuse · Replace flasher · Check/tighten all connections
Right (or left) turn signal only won't work	· Bulb burned out · Right (or left) indicator bulb burned out · Short circuit	· Replace bulb · Check/replace indicator bulb · Check/repair wiring
Flasher rate too slow or too fast	· Incorrect wattage bulb · Incorrect flasher	· Flasher bulb · Replace flasher (use a variable load flasher if you pull a trailer)
Indicator lights do not flash (burn steadily)	· Burned out bulb · Defective flasher	· Replace bulb · Replace flasher
Indicator lights do not light at all	· Burned out indicator bulb · Defective flasher	· Replace indicator bulb · Replace flasher

Troubleshooting Basic Dash Gauge Problems

Problem	Cause	Solution
Coolant Temperature Gauge		
Gauge reads erratically or not at all	• Loose or dirty connections • Defective sending unit • Defective gauge	• Clean/tighten connections • Bi-metal gauge: remove the wire from the sending unit. Ground the wire for an instant. If the gauge registers, replace the sending unit. • Magnetic gauge: disconnect the wire at the sending unit. With ignition ON gauge should register COLD. Ground the wire; gauge should register HOT.
Ammeter Gauge—Turn Headlights ON (do not start engine). Note reaction		
Ammeter shows charge Ammeter shows discharge Ammeter does not move	• Connections reversed on gauge • Ammeter is OK • Loose connections or faulty wiring • Defective gauge	• Reinstall connections • Nothing • Check/correct wiring • Replace gauge
Oil Pressure Gauge		
Gauge does not register or is inaccurate	• On mechanical gauge, Bourdon tube may be bent or kinked • Low oil pressure • Defective gauge • Defective wiring • Defective sending unit	• Check tube for kinks or bends preventing oil from reaching the gauge • Remove sending unit. Idle the engine briefly. If no oil flows from sending unit hole, problem is in engine. • Remove the wire from the sending unit and ground it for an instant with the ignition ON. A good gauge will go to the top of the scale. • Check the wiring to the gauge. If it's OK and the gauge doesn't register when grounded, replace the gauge. • If the wiring is OK and the gauge functions when grounded, replace the sending unit
All Gauges		
All gauges do not operate All gauges read low or erratically All gauges pegged	• Blown fuse • Defective instrument regulator • Defective or dirty instrument voltage regulator • Loss of ground between instrument voltage regulator and car • Defective instrument regulator	• Replace fuse • Replace instrument voltage regulator • Clean contacts or replace • Check ground • Replace regulator
Warning Lights		
Light(s) do not come on when ignition is ON, but engine is not started Light comes on with engine running	• Defective bulb • Defective wire • Defective sending unit • Problem in individual system • Defective sending unit	• Replace bulb • Check wire from light to sending unit • Disconnect the wire from the sending unit and ground it. Replace the sending unit if the light comes on with the ignition ON. • Check system • Check sending unit (see above)

Troubleshooting the Heater

Problem	Cause	Solution
Blower motor will not turn at any speed	• Blown fuse • Loose connection • Defective ground • Faulty switch • Faulty motor • Faulty resistor	• Replace fuse • Inspect and tighten • Clean and tighten • Replace switch • Replace motor • Replace resistor
Blower motor turns at one speed only	• Faulty switch • Faulty resistor	• Replace switch • Replace resistor
Blower motor turns but does not circulate air	• Intake blocked • Fan not secured to the motor shaft	• Clean intake • Tighten security
Heater will not heat	• Coolant does not reach proper temperature • Heater core blocked internally • Heater core air-bound • Blend-air door not in proper position	• Check and replace thermostat if necessary • Flush or replace core if necessary • Purge air from core • Adjust cable
Heater will not defrost	• Control cable adjustment incorrect • Defroster hose damaged	• Adjust control cable • Replace defroster hose

Drive Train

7

MANUAL TRANSAXLE

The Omni and Horizon models use four types of manual transaxles: the A412 Volkswagen designed 4-spd.; the Chrysler designed A460 4-spd.; the A465 5-spd.; and the A525 close ratio 5-spd. used in the high performance models.

A pad, located on top of the clutch housing contains the transaxle and VIN identification numbers. See Chapter 1 for further identification information.

Understanding the Manual Transaxle and Clutch

Because of the way an internal combustion engine breathes, it can produce torque, or twisting force, only within a narrow speed range. Most modern engines must turn at about 2,500 rpm to produce their peak torque. By 4,500 rpm they are producing so little torque that continued increases in engine speed produce no power increases.

The transmission and clutch are employed to vary the relationship between engine speed and the speed of the wheels so that adequate engine power can be produced under all circumstances. The clutch allows engine torque to be applied to the transaxle input shaft gradually, due to mechanical slippage. The vehicle can, consequently, be started smoothly from a full stop.

The transmission changes the ratio between the rotating speeds of the engine and the wheels by the use of gears. The lower gears allow full engine power to be applied to the rear wheels during acceleration at low speeds.

The clutch drive plate is a thin disc, the center of which is splined to the transaxle input shaft. Both sides of the disc are covered with a layer of material which is similar to brake lining and which is capable of allowing slippage without roughness or excessive noise.

The clutch cover is bolted to the engine flywheel and incorporates a diaphragm spring which provides the pressure to engage the clutch. The cover also houses the pressure plate. The driven disc is sandwiched between the pressure plate and the smooth surface of the flywheel when the clutch pedal is released, thus forcing it to turn at the same speed as the engine crankshaft.

The transaxle contains a main shaft which passes all the way through the transaxle, from the clutch to the driveshaft. This shaft is separated at one point, so that front and rear portions can turn at different speeds.

Power is transmitted by a countershaft in the lower gears and reverse. The gears of the countershaft mesh with gears on the main shaft, allowing power to be carried from one to the other. All the countershaft gears are integral with that shaft, while several of the main shaft gears can either rotate independently of the shaft or be locked to it. Shifting from one gear to the next causes one of the gears to be freed from rotating with the shaft and locks another to it. Gears are locked and unlocked by internal dog clutches which slide between the center of the gear and the shaft. The forward gears usually employ synchronizers, friction members which smoothly bring gear and shaft to the same speed before the toothed dog clutches are engaged.

SHIFT LINKAGE ADJUSTMENT
A-412

1. Place the transmission in neutral at the 3-4 position.

2. Loosen the shift tube clamp. Align the hole in the blocker bracket with the tab in the slider.

3. Place a ⅝" spacer between the shift tube flange and the yoke at the shift base.

4. Tighten the shift tube clamp and remove the spacer.

Troubleshooting the Manual Transmission

Problem	Cause	Solution
Transmission shifts hard	• Clutch adjustment incorrect • Clutch linkage or cable binding • Shift rail binding	• Adjust clutch • Lubricate or repair as necessary • Check for mispositioned selector arm roll pin, loose cover bolts, worn shift rail bores, worn shift rail, distorted oil seal, or extension housing not aligned with case. Repair as necessary.
	• Internal bind in transmission caused by shift forks, selector plates, or synchronizer assemblies • Clutch housing misalignment • Incorrect lubricant • Block rings and/or cone seats worn	• Remove, dissemble and inspect transmission. Replace worn or damaged components as necessary. • Check runout at rear face of clutch housing • Drain and refill transmission • Blocking ring to gear clutch tooth face clearance must be 0.030 inch or greater. If clearance is correct it may still be necessary to inspect blocking rings and cone seats for excessive wear. Repair as necessary.
Gear clash when shifting from one gear to another	• Clutch adjustment incorrect • Clutch linkage or cable binding • Clutch housing misalignment • Lubricant level low or incorrect lubricant • Gearshift components, or synchronizer assemblies worn or damaged	• Adjust clutch • Lubricate or repair as necessary • Check runout at rear of clutch housing • Drain and refill transmission and check for lubricant leaks if level was low. Repair as necessary. • Remove, disassemble and inspect transmission. Replace worn or damaged components as necessary.
Transmission noisy	• Lubricant level low or incorrect lubricant • Clutch housing-to-engine, or transmission-to-clutch housing bolts loose • Dirt, chips, foreign material in transmission • Gearshift mechanism, transmission gears, or bearing components worn or damaged • Clutch housing misalignment	• Drain and refill transmission. If lubricant level was low, check for leaks and repair as necessary. • Check and correct bolt torque as necessary • Drain, flush, and refill transmission • Remove, disassemble and inspect transmission. Replace worn or damaged components as necessary. • Check runout at rear face of clutch housing
Jumps out of gear	• Clutch housing misalignment • Gearshift lever loose • Offset lever nylon insert worn or lever attaching nut loose • Gearshift mechanism, shift forks, selector plates, interlock plate, selector arm, shift rail, detent plugs, springs or shift cover worn or damaged • Clutch shaft or roller bearings worn or damaged	• Check runout at rear face of clutch housing • Check lever for worn fork. Tighten loose attaching bolts. • Remove gearshift lever and check for loose offset lever nut or worn insert. Repair or replace as necessary. • Remove, disassemble and inspect transmission cover assembly. Replace worn or damaged components as necessary. • Replace clutch shaft or roller bearings as necessary

Troubleshooting the Manual Transmission (cont.)

Problem	Cause	Solution
Jumps out of gear (cont.)	• Gear teeth worn or tapered, synchronizer assemblies worn or damaged, excessive end play caused by worn thrust washers or output shaft gears • Pilot bushing worn	• Remove, disassemble, and inspect transmission. Replace worn or damaged components as necessary. • Replace pilot bushing
Will not shift into one gear	• Gearshift selector plates, interlock plate, or selector arm, worn, damaged, or incorrectly assembled • Shift rail detent plunger worn, spring broken, or plug loose • Gearshift lever worn or damaged • Synchronizer sleeves or hubs, damaged or worn	• Remove, disassemble, and inspect transmission cover assembly. Repair or replace components as necessary. • Tighten plug or replace worn or damaged components as necessary • Replace gearshift lever • Remove, disassemble and inspect transmission. Replace worn or damaged components.
Locked in one gear—cannot be shifted out	• Shift rail(s) worn or broken, shifter fork bent, setscrew loose, center detent plug missing or worn • Broken gear teeth on countershaft gear, clutch shaft, or reverse idler gear Gearshift lever broken or worn, shift mechanism in cover incorrectly assembled or broken, worn damaged gear train components	• Inspect and replace worn or damaged parts • Inspect and replace damaged part • Disassemble transmission. Replace damaged parts or assemble correctly.
Noisy in—or jumps out of four wheel drive low range	• Transfer case not completely engaged in 4L position • Shift linkage loose or binding • Shift fork cracked, inserts worn, or fork is binding on shift rail	• Stop vehicle, shift transfer case in Neutral, then shift back into 4L position • Tighten, lubricate, or repair linkage as necessary • Disassemble unit and repair as necessary
Lubricant leaking from output shaft seals or from vent	• Transfer case overfilled • Vent closed or restricted • Output shaft seals damaged or installed incorrectly	• Drain to correct level • Clear or replace vent if necessary • Replace seals. Be sure seal lip faces interior of case when installed. Also be sure yoke seal surfaces are not scored or nicked. Remove scores, nicks with fine sandpaper or replace yoke(s) if necessary.
Abnormal tire wear	• Extended operation on dry hard surface (paved) roads in 4H range	• Operate in 2H on hard surface (paved) roads

NOTE: *It is possible for the manual transaxle to become locked in two gears at once. This will occur if the interlock blocker on the gearshift selector lever has spread apart. The result of operating like this will be clutch failure at the least, and driveline failure at the worst. To correctly diagnose the problem, the interlock should be checked using the following procedure:*

1. Disconnect the shift linkage operating lever from the transaxle selector shaft.

2. Remove the transaxle detent spring assembly and selector shaft boot.

3. Remove the aluminum selector shaft plug.

4. Place the transaxle in neutral and pull the selector shaft assembly out of the case.

5. Measure the interlock blocker gap **A**, in the accompanying picture. If gap **A** exceeds 8mm replace the gearshift selector shaft assembly.

6. Apply a thick coating of chassis grease to the selector shaft shoulder at the threaded end

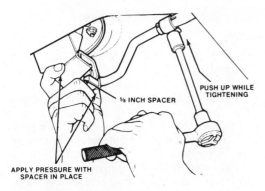

A-412 shift linkage adjustment

and carefully insert the shaft through the selector shaft oil seal. Reverse steps 1-4 to install.

7. Adjust the shift linkage.

A-460

1. From the left side of the car, remove the lockpin from the transaxle selector shaft housing.

2. Reverse the lockpin and insert it in the same threaded hole while pushing the selector shaft into the selector housing. A hole in the selector shaft will align with the lockpin, allowing the lockpin to be screwed into the housing. This will lock the selector shaft in the 1-2 neutral position.

3. Raise and support the vehicle on jackstands.

4. Loosen the clamp bolt that secures the gearshift tube to the gearshift connector.

5. Make sure that the gearshift connector slides and turns freely in the gearshift tube.

6. Position the shifter mechanism connector assembly so that the isolator is contacting the standing flange and the rib on the isolator is aligned front and back with the hole in the block-out bracket. Hold the connector in this position while tightening the clamp bolt on the gearshift tube to 14 ft. lbs.

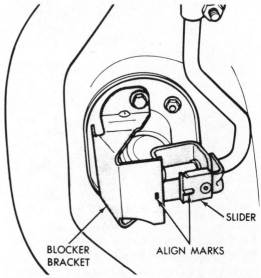

On the A-412, align the marks on the blocker and slides

7. Lower the car.

8. Remove the lockpin from the selector shaft housing and install it the original way in the housing.

9. Tighten the lockpin to 105 in. lbs.

10. Check shifter action.

A465 and A525

1. From the left side of the car, remove the lockpin from the transaxle selector shaft housing.

2. Reverse the lockpin and insert it in the same threaded hole while pushing the selector shaft into the selector housing. A hole in the selector shaft will align with the lockpin, allowing the lockpin to be screwed into the housing. This will lock the selector shaft in the 1-2 neutral position.

3. Remove the gearshift knob, the retaining nut and the pull-up ring.

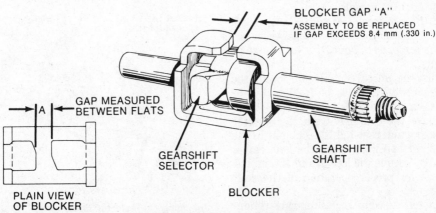

Checking the A-412 interlock blocker

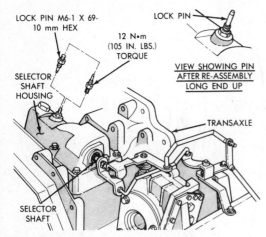

A-460, 465, and 525 transaxles pinned in the 1st to 2nd neutral position for linkage adjustment

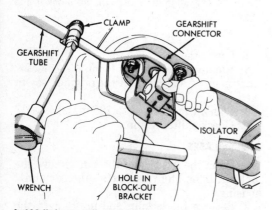

A-460 linkage adjustment

4. Remove the console attaching screws and remove the console.

5. Make two cable adjusting pins as shown in the illustration.

6. Adjust the selector cable and torque the adjusting screw to 60 in. lbs. on 1983 models, or 55 in. lbs. on 1984 models.

NOTE: *Proper torque of the selector cable and the crossover cable adjusting screw is important for proper operation of the shift linkage.*

7. Adjust the crossover cable and torque the adjusting screw to 60 in. lbs. on 1983 models, or 55 in. lbs. on 1984 models.

8. Remove the lock pin from the selector shaft housing and reinstall the lock pin in the selector shaft housing so that the long end is pointing up. Torque the lock pin to 105 in. lbs.

9. Check for proper operation of the shift cables.

10. Reinstall the console, pull-up ring, retaining nut and the gearshift knob.

REMOVAL AND INSTALLATION

A-412

NOTE: *Any time the differential cover is removed, a new gasket should be formed from RTV sealant. See Chapter 1.*

1. Remove the engine timing mark access plug.

2. Rotate the engine to align the drilled mark on the flywheel with the pointer on the engine.

3. Disconnect the battery ground.

4. Disconnect the shift linkage rods.

5. Disconnect the starter and ground wires.

6. Disconnect the backup light switch wire.

7. Remove the starter.

8. Disconnect the clutch cable.

9. Disconnect the speedometer cable.

10. Support the weight of the engine from above, preferably with a shop hoist or the fabricated holding fixture.

11. Raise and support the vehicle.

12. Disconnect the driveshafts and support them out of the way.

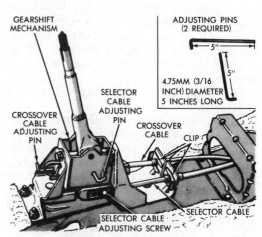

Make two cable adjusting pins—A-465, A-525 transaxles

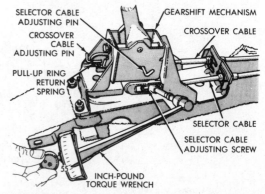

Adjusting the selector cable—A-465, A-525 transaxles

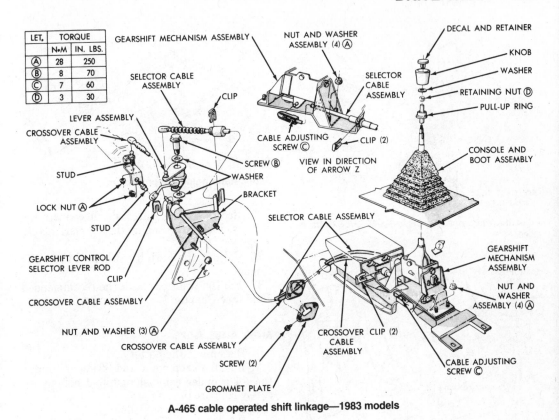

LET.	TORQUE	
	N•M	IN. LBS.
Ⓐ	28	250
Ⓑ	8	70
Ⓒ	7	60
Ⓓ	3	30

GEARSHIFT MECHANISM ASSEMBLY

NUT AND WASHER ASSEMBLY (4) Ⓐ

DECAL AND RETAINER

KNOB

WASHER

RETAINING NUT Ⓓ

PULL-UP RING

SELECTOR CABLE ASSEMBLY

SELECTOR CABLE ASSEMBLY

CLIP

CABLE ADJUSTING SCREW Ⓒ

CLIP (2)

VIEW IN DIRECTION OF ARROW Z

CONSOLE AND BOOT ASSEMBLY

LEVER ASSEMBLY

CROSSOVER CABLE ASSEMBLY

STUD

LOCK NUT Ⓐ

STUD

GEARSHIFT CONTROL SELECTOR LEVER ROD

CLIP

SCREW Ⓑ

WASHER

BRACKET

SELECTOR CABLE ASSEMBLY

GEARSHIFT MECHANISM ASSEMBLY

NUT AND WASHER ASSEMBLY (4) Ⓐ

CROSSOVER CABLE ASSEMBLY

NUT AND WASHER (3) Ⓐ

CROSSOVER CABLE ASSEMBLY

SCREW (2)

GROMMET PLATE

CROSSOVER CABLE ASSEMBLY

CLIP (2)

CABLE ADJUSTING SCREW Ⓒ

A-465 cable operated shift linkage—1983 models

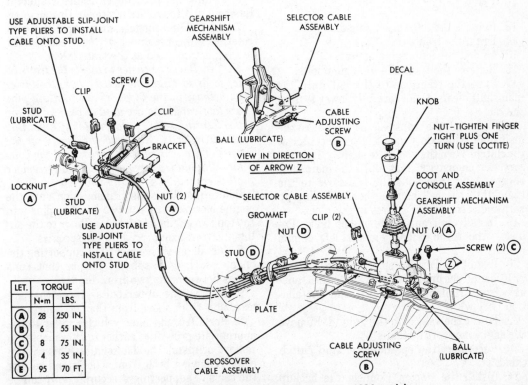

USE ADJUSTABLE SLIP-JOINT TYPE PLIERS TO INSTALL CABLE ONTO STUD.

GEARSHIFT MECHANISM ASSEMBLY

SELECTOR CABLE ASSEMBLY

DECAL

KNOB

CLIP

SCREW Ⓔ

CLIP

STUD (LUBRICATE)

BRACKET

CABLE ADJUSTING SCREW Ⓑ

BALL (LUBRICATE)

VIEW IN DIRECTION OF ARROW Z

NUT–TIGHTEN FINGER TIGHT PLUS ONE TURN (USE LOCTITE)

LOCKNUT Ⓐ

STUD (LUBRICATE)

NUT (2) Ⓐ

USE ADJUSTABLE SLIP-JOINT TYPE PLIERS TO INSTALL CABLE ONTO STUD

SELECTOR CABLE ASSEMBLY

GROMMET

NUT Ⓓ

STUD Ⓓ

CLIP (2)

PLATE

BOOT AND CONSOLE ASSEMBLY

GEARSHIFT MECHANISM ASSEMBLY

NUT (4) Ⓐ

SCREW (2) Ⓒ

CROSSOVER CABLE ASSEMBLY

CABLE ADJUSTING SCREW Ⓑ

BALL (LUBRICATE)

LET.	TORQUE	
	N•m	LBS.
Ⓐ	28	250 IN.
Ⓑ	6	55 IN.
Ⓒ	8	75 IN.
Ⓓ	4	35 IN.
Ⓔ	95	70 FT.

A-465 and A-525 cable operated shift linkage—1984 models

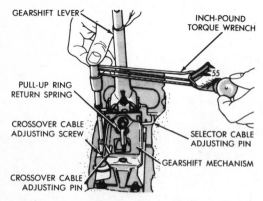

Adjusting the crossover cable—A-465, A-525 transaxles

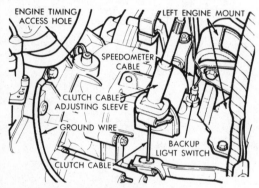

A-412 transmission mountings

13. Remove the left splash shield.
14. Drain the transaxle.
15. Unbolt the left engine mount.
16. Remove the transaxle-to-engine bolts.
17. Slide the transaxle to the left until the mainshaft clears, then, carefully lower it from the car.
18. To install the transaxle, position it so the mainshaft will slide straight into the center of the clutch. Turn the transaxle slightly, if necessary, and change the angle until the mainshaft engages, and then slide the transaxle to the right until the bell housing boltholes line up with the corresponding bores in the block.
19. Install the transaxle-to-engine bolts. Reinstall the through bolt for the left engine mount.
20. Install the left side splash shield.
21. Install the driveshafts back into the transaxle (see "Halfshafts Removal and Installation" below).
22. Lower the vehicle to the ground. Remove the engine support system.
23. Reconnect the speedometer and clutch cables.
24. Install the starter. Connect the backup light switch wire.

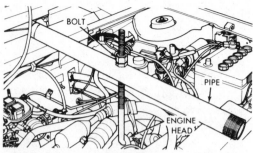

Fabricated engine support fixture

25. Reconnect the shift rods. Reconnect the battery. Install the engine timing mark access plug.
26. Adjust the clutch cable and the shift linkage.
27. Fill the transaxle with the recommended fluid (See Chapter 1).

A-460, A-465, A-525

1. Disconnect the battery.
2. Install a shop crane and lifting eye under the #4 cylinder exhaust manifold bolt to securely support the engine.
3. Disconnect the shift linkage.
4. Remove both front wheels.
5. Remove the left front splash shield, and left engine mount.
6. Follow the procedures under Halfshaft Removal and Installation later in this chapter.
7. On 1987-89 models, disconnect the anti-rotation link or damper *at the crossmember*, leaving it connected at the transaxle.
NOTE: *It will be easier to locate the transaxle, so as to align the bell housing boltholes with those in the block, if two locating pins are fabricated and are used in place of the top two locating bolts. To fabricate the pins: Buy two extra bolts. Hacksaw the heads off the bolts. Then, cut slots in the ends of the bolts for a flat-bladed screwdriver. Finally, remove all burrs with a grinding wheel.*
Before installing the transmission onto the engine block, install the two locating pins into the top two engine block holes. Refer to the automatic transaxle procedure for specifics.
8. Install a positive means of supporting the engine, such as a support fixture that runs across between the two front fenders.
9. Remove the upper bolts—those that are accessible from above from the bell housing.
10. For 1986 and later vehicles, refer to the appropriate procedure earlier in this chapter to remove or install the driveshafts. This will include removing both front wheels and raising the car and supporting it securely so it can be worked on from underneath. On 1985 and ear-

lier vehicles, remove the driveshafts as follows:

　a. Remove the left splash shield. Drain the differential and remove the cover.

　b. Remove the speedometer adapter, cable and gear.

　c. Remove the sway bar.

　d. Remove both lower ball joint-to-steering knuckle bolts.

　e. Pry the lower ball joint from the steering knuckle.

　f. Remove the driveshaft from the hub.

　g. Rotate both driveshafts to expose the circlip ends. Note the flat surface on the inner ends of both axle tripod shafts. Pry the circlip out.

　h. Remove both driveshafts.

11. On 1986 and later vehicles, remove the left side splash shield.

12. Disconnect the plug for the neutral safety/backup light switch.

13. Remove the engine mount bracket from the front crossmember.

14. Support the transmission from underneath.

15. Remove the front mount insulator through-bolts.

16. Remove the long through-bolt from the left hand engine mount.

17. Remove the starter. Then, remove any bell housing bolts that are still in position.

18. Slide the transaxle directly away from the engine so the transmission input shaft will slide smoothly out of the bearing in the flywheel and the clutch disc. Lower the transaxle and remove it from the engine compartment.

19. To install the transaxle, first support the unit securely and raise it into precise alignment with the engine block. Then, move it toward the block, inserting the transmission input shaft into the clutch disc. Turn the input shaft slightly, if necessary, to get the splines to engage.

20. Install the lower bell housing bolts and the starter. Bell housing bolts are torqued to 70 ft. lbs.

21. Install the long through-bolt into the left hand engine mount.

22. Install the front mount insulator through-bolts.

23. Remove the jack supporting the transmission. Then, install the engine mount bracket onto the front crossmember.

24. Reconnect the electrical connector for the backup light/neutral safety switch.

25. Install the driveshafts by reversing the removal procedure. Install the left side splash shield.

26. With the wheels remounted and the car back on the floor, install the remaining bell housing bolts and torque them to 105 in. lbs.

27. Remove the engine support fixture.

28. Connect the anti-rotation strut. Torque the bolts to 70 ft. lbs.

29. Connect the shift linkage. Always use new self-locking nuts on the shift linkage. Observe the following torques:

- Shift housing-to-case: 21 ft.lb.
- Strut-to-case: 70 ft.lb.
- Flywheel-to-crankshaft: 65 ft.lb.

A-412 Overhaul

TRANSAXLE CASE DISASSEMBLY

NOTE: *Final mainshaft adjustment requires a measurement made with a special tool. Check Step 16 of the assembly procedure before disassembly.*

1. Remove the clutch pushrod, being careful not to bend it.

2. Unscrew the selector shaft plug from the case. Remove the detent spring assembly and rubber boot, then tap out the selector shaft and pry out the oil seal.

3. Using a small pry bar, pry out the two mainshaft bearing retaining nut rubber plugs.

4. Remove the four bolts and the clutch release bearing end cover. Hold the clutch release lever upwards while removing the cover to avoid loading or damage to the case threads. Take out the release bearing and plastic sleeve.

5. Using two small pry bars, push the circlip off the clutch torque shaft. Pull the torque shaft out of the case, then remove the pedal return spring and release lever. Pry out the torque shaft oil seal.

6. Remove the three mainshaft bearing retainer nuts; two were under the rubber covers removed earlier and the 3rd is inside the clutch release housing. The three studs and clips will drop into the case. Remove the Reverse idler set screw (bolt) and the backup light switch.

7. Remove the ten case bolts and the four stud nuts, then the transmission case.

NOTE: *The factory uses a special tool to do this; it pushes against the end of the mainshaft. Make sure to tag the shims for reuse.*

8. Remove the two bolts, the Reverse shift fork and the supports.

9. Remove the snapring from the end of the pinion shaft.

10. Pull off the bearing and the 4th gear from the end of the mainshaft. Remove the 4th gear needle bearing needle bearing.

11. Using a small pry bar, pry off the shift rail E-clips, then remove the shift forks assembly.

12. Remove the mainshaft assembly; it can be disassembled by removing the snaprings and the components. The clutch pushrod seal and bushing assembly can be driven out of the shaft

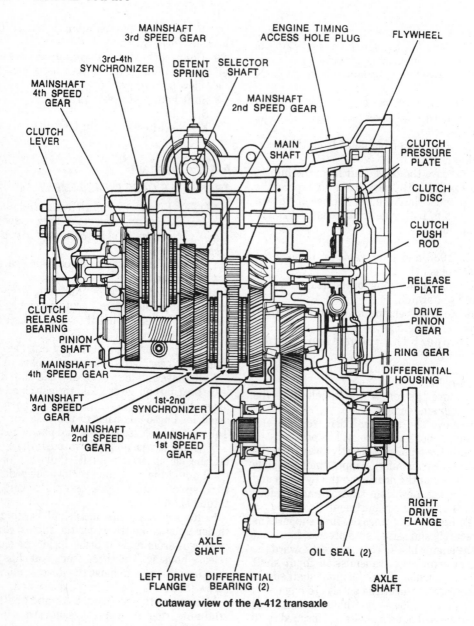

MAINSHAFT
3rd SPEED GEAR

3rd-4th
SYNCHRONIZER

MAINSHAFT
4th SPEED
GEAR

CLUTCH
LEVER

ENGINE TIMING
ACCESS HOLE PLUG

FLYWHEEL

DETENT
SPRING

SELECTOR
SHAFT

MAINSHAFT
2nd SPEED GEAR

MAIN
SHAFT

CLUTCH
PRESSURE
PLATE

CLUTCH
DISC

CLUTCH
PUSH
ROD

RELEASE
PLATE

CLUTCH
RELEASE
BEARING

PINION
SHAFT

MAINSHAFT
4th SPEED GEAR

MAINSHAFT
3rd SPEED
GEAR

MAINSHAFT
2nd SPEED
GEAR

1st-2nd
SYNCHRONIZER

MAINSHAFT
1st SPEED
GEAR

DRIVE
PINION
GEAR

RING GEAR

DIFFERENTIAL
HOUSING

RIGHT
DRIVE
FLANGE

AXLE
SHAFT

LEFT DRIVE
FLANGE

DIFFERENTIAL
BEARING (2)

OIL SEAL (2)

AXLE
SHAFT

Cutaway view of the A-412 transaxle

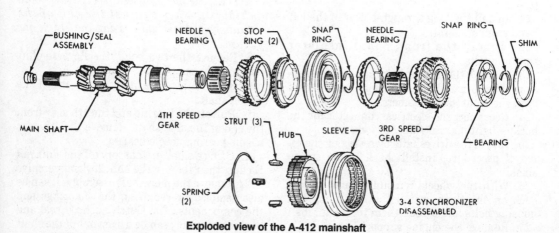

BUSHING/SEAL
ASSEMBLY

NEEDLE
BEARING

STOP
RING (2)

SNAP
RING

NEEDLE
BEARING

SNAP RING

SHIM

MAIN SHAFT

4TH SPEED
GEAR

STRUT (3)

HUB

SLEEVE

3RD SPEED
GEAR

BEARING

SPRING
(2)

3-4 SYNCHRONIZER
DISASSEMBLED

Exploded view of the A-412 mainshaft

with a ⅜″ diameter brass rod. Replace it by driving it with a plastic hammer.

13. Remove the pinion shaft snapring and the 3rd gear, then the 2nd gear and its needle bearing.

14. Pry or pull out the Reverse idler gear shaft.

15. Using a puller, remove the 1st gear and the 1st-2nd synchronizer assembly from the pinion shaft.

NOTE: *The inner sleeve for the 2nd and the 1st gear are removed together.*

16. Remove the 1st gear needle bearing and scribe a mark across the 1st-2nd synchronizer for reassembly.

17. Remove the pinion shaft bolts, the retainer, the thrust washer (the flat side goes up) and the pinion shaft.

TRANSAXLE CASE ASSEMBLY

1. Place a 0.65mm shim in the bearing housing and press the small bearing cup into the clutch housing, then move the pinion up and down, measuring the end play with a dial indicator.

NOTE: *Do not rotate the shaft while moving it up and down.*

2. The correct preload is determined by adding 0.20mm to the reading obtained from the dial indicator in Step 1, along with the shim thickness, 0.65mm. For example: if the measurement is 0.30mm, the correct shim to use is 1.15mm (0.65 + 0.03 + 0.20 = 1.15). Remove the pinion shaft ball bearing retainer and the pinion shaft. Remove the small bearing cup and the 0.65mm shim and install the correct shim.

3. If new bearings are installed on the pinion shaft, lubricate them with transmission oil, install the shaft and check the shaft turning torque with a torque wrench; it should be 4-13 in. lbs., if not, reset the preload.

4. Install the pinion shaft and place the 1st gear thrust washer over the shaft, with the flat side up facing the gear. Install the pinion shaft retainer and torque the bolts to 29 ft. lbs.

5. Install the needle bearing, the 1st gear and the 1st gear synchronizer stop ring over the shaft.

NOTE: *The wear limit for spacing between the synchronzier teeth on the 1st gear and those on the stop ring is 0.5mm. There is one tooth missing from the 1st gear stop ring on early models. The 1st gear will grind, if this ring isn't used. Later models have three teeth missing in three places, 120° apart.*

6. Align the marks on the 1st-2nd synchronizer hub and the sleeve, made on disassembly. Install the synchronizer, driving it into place.

7. Drive the 2nd gear needle bearing inner race into place over the shaft.

8. Drive the Reverse idler gear shaft into place.

NOTE: *Make sure that the threaded hole in the top of the shaft is centered, pointing out between the two nearest case edge bolt holes.*

9. Place the 2nd gear needle bearing over the pinion shaft, then the 2nd gear stop ring, the 2nd gear and the 3rd gear onto the shaft; make sure that the 3rd gear has the thrust face down.

10. Install the 3rd gear sanp ring. Measure the end play between 3rd gear and the snapring with a feeler gauge; it should be 0-0.1mm. The snaprings are available in thicknesses from 2.5-3.0mm for adjustment. Replace the snapring with the one selected.

11. Install the mainshaft assembly.

12. Install the shift fork assemblies and the E-clips.

13. Install the 4th gear needle bearing over the mainshaft and place the 4th gear synchronizer stop ring in place. Install the 4th gear and the snapring.

14. Install the Reverse shift fork and the support brackets, then torque the bolts to 105 in. lbs.

15. Using a feeler gauge, measure the clearance between the top of the pinion shaft 2nd gear and the bottom of the mainshaft 3rd gear.

NOTE: *The ideal clearance is adjusted by forcing the mainshaft up or down in relation to the clutch case. The factory has a special tool to do this from the clutch end.*

16. The next step is to determine the thickness of the shim or shims to be placed between the mainshaft roller bearing and the transmission case. The factory does this by inserting a special tool of the same thickness as the bearing in the case, installing the case, then measuring the up and down movement of the special tool with a dial indicator. Shims are available in 0.3-0.6mm sizes.

17. After the selected shim is installed behind the bearing, torque the bearing retainer clamp bolts to 13 ft. lbs. Install the transmission case-to-clutch housing bolts, using the guide pin for alignment, and torque the nuts and bolts to 20 ft. lbs.

A-460 Overhaul
TRANSAXLE CASE DISASSEMBLY

The Chrysler designed and built A-460 (4-speed) fully synchronized manual transaxle combines gear reduction, ratio selection and differential functions in one unit housed in a die cast aluminum case.

1. With the transaxle removed from the vehicle, remove the differential cover bolts and the stud nuts, then remove the cover.

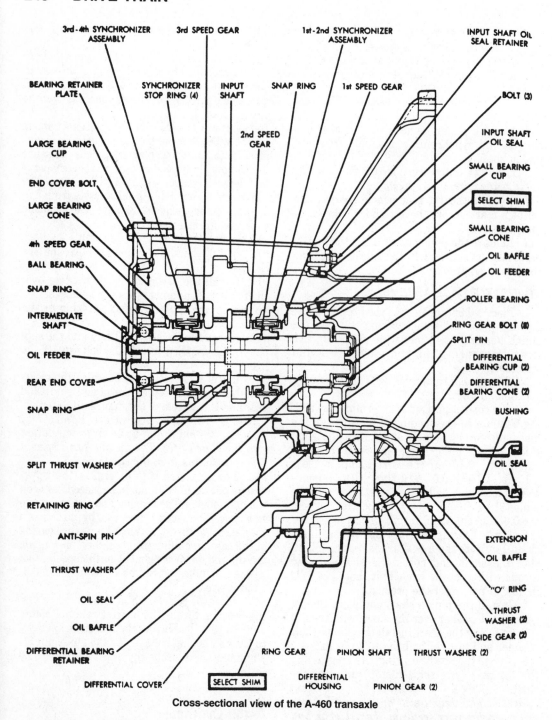

3rd-4th SYNCHRONIZER ASSEMBLY

3rd SPEED GEAR

1st-2nd SYNCHRONIZER ASSEMBLY

INPUT SHAFT OIL SEAL RETAINER

BEARING RETAINER PLATE

SYNCHRONIZER STOP RING (4)

INPUT SHAFT

SNAP RING

1st SPEED GEAR

BOLT (3)

INPUT SHAFT OIL SEAL

2nd SPEED GEAR

SMALL BEARING CUP

LARGE BEARING CUP

SELECT SHIM

END COVER BOLT

SMALL BEARING CONE

LARGE BEARING CONE

OIL BAFFLE

4th SPEED GEAR

OIL FEEDER

BALL BEARING

ROLLER BEARING

SNAP RING

RING GEAR BOLT (10)

INTERMEDIATE SHAFT

SPLIT PIN

DIFFERENTIAL BEARING CUP (2)

OIL FEEDER

DIFFERENTIAL BEARING CONE (2)

REAR END COVER

BUSHING

SNAP RING

OIL SEAL

SPLIT THRUST WASHER

RETAINING RING

ANTI-SPIN PIN

EXTENSION

THRUST WASHER

OIL BAFFLE

OIL SEAL

"O" RING

OIL BAFFLE

THRUST WASHER (2)

DIFFERENTIAL BEARING RETAINER

SIDE GEAR (2)

DIFFERENTIAL COVER

SELECT SHIM

RING GEAR

DIFFERENTIAL HOUSING

PINION SHAFT

PINION GEAR (2)

THRUST WASHER (2)

Cross-sectional view of the A-460 transaxle

2. Remove the differential bearing retainer bolts.

3. Using tool No. L-4435, rotate the differential bearing retainer to remove it.

4. Remove the extension housing bolts, then the differential assembly and extension housing.

5. Remove the selector shaft housing bolts, then the selector shaft housing.

6. Remove the stud nuts and the bolts from the rear end cover, then using a small pry bar, pry off the rear end cover.

7. Using snapring pliers, remove the large snapring from the intermediate shaft rear ball bearing.

8. Remove the bearing retainer plate by tapping it with a plastic hammer.

9. Remove the 3rd-4th shift fork rail.

10. Remove the Reverse idler gear shaft and gear.

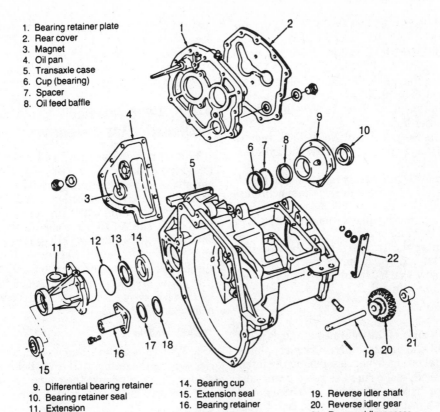

1. Bearing retainer plate
2. Rear cover
3. Magnet
4. Oil pan
5. Transaxle case
6. Cup (bearing)
7. Spacer
8. Oil feed baffle

9. Differential bearing retainer	14. Bearing cup	19. Reverse idler shaft
10. Bearing retainer seal	15. Extension seal	20. Reverse idler gear
11. Extension	16. Bearing retainer	21. Reverse idler spacer
12. Extension O-ring	17. Input shaft seal	22. Reverse gearshift lever
13. Retainer	18. Input shaft spacer	

A-460 transaxle case

11. Remove the input shaft gear assembly and the intermediate shaft gear assembly.

12. To remove the clutch release bearing, remove the E-clips from the clutch release shaft, then disassemble the clutch shaft components.

13. Remove the three input shaft seal retainer bolts, the seal, the retainer assembly and the select shim.

14. Using tools No. C-4171, C-4656 and an arbor press, press the input shaft front bearing cup from the transaxle case.

15. Using tool No. C-4660, remove the two bearing retainer strap bolts, then the intermediate shaft front bearing.

TRANSAXLE CASE ASSEMBLY

The assembly of the transaxle is the reverse of disassembly; however, please note the following:

1. Using tools No. C-4657, C4171 and an arbor press, press the front bearing onto the intermediate shaft; the input shaft front bearing cup is installed with the same tools used for removal.

2. Determine the shim thickness for the correct bearing end play only if any of the following parts are replaced:

a. The transaxle case.
b. The input shaft seal retainer.
c. The bearing retainer plate.
d. The rear end cover.
e. The input shaft or bearings.

3. To determine proper shim thickness, refer to the Input Shaft Bearing End Play Adjustment at the end of this section.

4. Using tool No. C-4674 and a plastic hammer, install the input shaft oil seal.

5. Using a 3mm bead of RTV sealant, place it around the edge of the input shaft seal retainer and making sure the drain hole of the retainer is facing downward.

6. The differential bearing retainer is installed with the same special tool used for removal.

NOTE: *The rear end cover, the selector shaft housing and the differential cover are sealed with RTV sealant.*

Intermediate Shaft

DISASSEMBLY

NOTE: *The 1st-2nd, the 3rd-4th shift forks and the synchronizer stop rings are interchangeable. However, if parts are to be reused, reassemble them in their original position.*

1. Remove the intermediate shaft rear bearing snapring.

2. Using the puller tool No. C-4693, remove the intermediate shaft rear bearing.

3. Using snapring pliers, remove the 3rd-4th synchronizer hub snapring.

4. Using the puller tool No. L-4534, remove the 3rd-4th synchronizer hub and the 3rd speed gear.

5. Remove the retaining ring, the split thrust washer, the 2nd speed gear and the synchronizer stop ring.

6. Using snapring pliers, remove the 1st-2nd synchronizer hub snapring.

7. Remove the 1st speed gear, the stop ring and the 1st-2nd synchronizer assembly.

8. Remove the 1st speed gear thrust washer and the anti-spin pin.

ASSEMBLY

The assembly of the intermediate shaft is the reverse of the disassembly; however, please note the following: When assembling the intermediate shaft, make sure the speed gears turn freely and have a minimum of 0.08mm end play. When installing the 1st speed gear thrust washer make sure the chamfered edge is facing the pinion gear. When installing the 1st-2nd synchronizer make sure the relief faces the 2nd speed gear. Use an arbor press to install the intermediate shaft rear bearing, the 3rd-4th synchronizer hub and the 3rd speed gear.

Input Shaft Bearing End Play
ADJUSTMENT

1. Using special tool No. L-4656 with handle C-4171, press the input shaft front bearing cup slightly forward in the case. Then, using tool No. L-4655 with handle C-4171, press the bearing cup back into the case, from the front, to the properly position the bearing cup before checking the input shaft endplay.

NOTE: *This step is not necessary if the special tool No. L-4655 was previously used to install the input shaft front bearing cup in the case and no input shaft select shim has been installed since pressing the cup into the case.*

2. Select a gauging shim which will give 0.025-0.50mm end play.

NOTE: *Measure the original shim from the input shaft seal retainer and select a shim 0.25mm thinner than the original for the gauging shim.*

3. Install the gauging shim on the bearing cup and the input shaft seal retainer.

4. Alternately tighten the input shaft seal retainer bolts until the retainer is bottomed against the case, then torque the bolts to 21 ft. lbs.

NOTE: *The input shaft seal retainer is used to draw the input shaft front bearing cup the proper distance into the case bore.*

A-465, A-525 Overhaul
TRANSAXLE CASE DISASSEMBLY

The Chrysler designed and built A-465 (1983-84) and the A-525 (1985-88) fully synchronized 5-speed manual transaxles combine gear reduction, ratio selection and differential functions in one unit housed in a die cast aluminum case. The A-525 has a close ratio gearset with different 2nd, 3rd and 4th gear ratios than the A-465, to provide better performance through the gears, while the 1st and the 5th gear ratios are the same as the A-465 to maintain the same launch and top gear characteristics.

1984-85 Models

1. With the transaxle removed from the vehicle, remove the differential cover bolts and the stud nuts, then remove the cover.

2. Remove the differential bearing retainer bolts.

3. Using tool No. L-4435, rotate the differential bearing retainer to remove it.

4. Remove the extension housing bolts, then the differential assembly and extension housing.

5. Remove the selector shaft housing bolts, then the selector shaft housing.

6. Remove the stud nuts and the bolts from the rear end cover, then using a small pry bar, pry off the rear end cover.

7. On 5-speeds, remove the 5th speed synchronizer strut retainer snapring, strut retainer plate, 5th speed synchronizer, shift fork with rail, intermediate shaft 5th speed gear, input shaft 5th gear snapring and 5th gear. Then, use a puller such as C-4693 with legs C-4621-1 to remove the 5th speed synchronizer hub. On 4-speeds, remove the large snapring from the intermediate shaft rear ball bearing.

8. Remove the bearing retainer plate by tapping it with a plastic hammer.

9. Remove the 3rd-4th shift fork rail.

10. Remove the Reverse idler gear shaft and gear.

11. Remove the input shaft gear assembly and the intermediate shaft gear assembly.

12. To remove the clutch release bearing, remove the E-clips from the clutch release shaft, then disassemble the clutch shaft components.

13. Remove the three input shaft seal retainer bolts, the seal, the retainer assembly and the select shim.

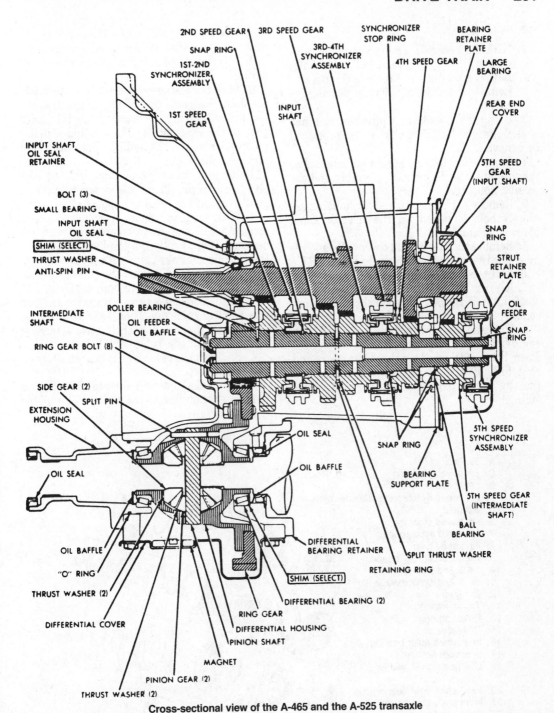

Cross-sectional view of the A-465 and the A-525 transaxle

14. Using tools No. C-4171, C-4656 and an arbor press, press the input shaft front bearing cup from the transaxle case.

15. Using tool No. C-4660, remove the two bearing retainer strap bolts, then the intermediate shaft front bearing.

16. Remove the 5th speed shifter pin, the 5th speed detent ball and the spring.

17. Remove the 5th speed synchronizer strut retainer plate snapring and the 5th speed synchronizer strut retainer plate.

18. Remove the 5th speed synchronizer assembly and shift fork with shift rail.

19. Remove the intermediate shaft 5th speed gear, the input shaft 5th speed gear snapring and the 5th speed gear.

20. Remove the bearing support plate bolts and pry off the bearing support plate.

1986-89 Models

1. With the transaxle removed from the vehicle, remove the eight differential cover bolts and the two stud nuts and remove the cover.

2. Remove the eight differential bearing retainer bolts.

3. Using the L-4435 or equivalent spanner wrench, rotate the differential bearing retainer to remove it.

4. Remove the four extension housing bolts, then remove the differential assembly and extension housing.

5. Remove the six selector shaft housing assembly bolts and remove the selector shaft housing assembly.

6. Remove the 10 rear end cover bolts and remove the rear end cover. Clean the bead of RTV sealer off the rear end cover.

7. Using snapring pliers, remove the snapring from the 5th speed synchronizer strut retainer plate.

8. Using an Allen wrench, unscrew and then remove the 5th speed shift fork set screw. Then, lift the 5th speed synchronizer sleeve and shift fork off the synchronizer hub. Retrieve the (3) winged struts and top synchronizer spring.

9. Use a puller such as C-4693 with legs C-4621-1 to remove the 5th speed synchronizer hub. Retrieve the remaining synchronizer spring.

10. Slide the 5th speed gear off the intermediate shaft. With snapring pliers, remove the copper colored snapring retaining the 5th speed gear to the input shaft. Then, using a pulley puller such as C-4333, pull the 5th speed gear off the input shaft.

11. Remove the two remaining bearing support plate bolts. Then, use a screwdriver to gently pry off the bearing support plate.

12. With snapring pliers, remove the large snapring from the intermediate shaft rear ball bearing. Then, gently tap the lower surface of the bearing retainer plate with a plastic hammer to free it and lift it off the transaxle case. Clean the RTV sealer from both surfaces.

13. With a socket wrench, unscrew the 5th speed shifter guide pin. Then, remove it. Do the same with the 1st-2nd shift fork setscrew. Then, slide out the 1-2, 3-4 shift fork rail.

14. Slide out the reverse idler gear shaft, gear, and plastic stop.

15. Rotate the 3-4 shift fork to the left, and the 5th gear shifter to the right. Pull out the

1. 5th gear
2. 5th speed stop ring
3. 5th speed synchronizer
4. 5th speed synchronizer retainer plate
5. 3rd gear
6. 4th speed stop ring
7. 3rd & 4th synchronizer
8. 4th speed gear
9. Interm. shaft rear bearing
10. 1st & 2nd stop ring
11. 1st & 2nd synchronizer
12. 2nd gear
13. Thrust washer
14. Retaining ring
15. Oil feeder
16. Inter. shaft roller bearing
17. Intermediate shaft
18. Low gear thrust washer
19. 1st gear
20. Input shaft front bearing cup
21. Input shaft front bearing
22. Input shaft
23. Input shaft rear bearing
24. Input shaft rear bearing cup
25. 5th gear input shaft

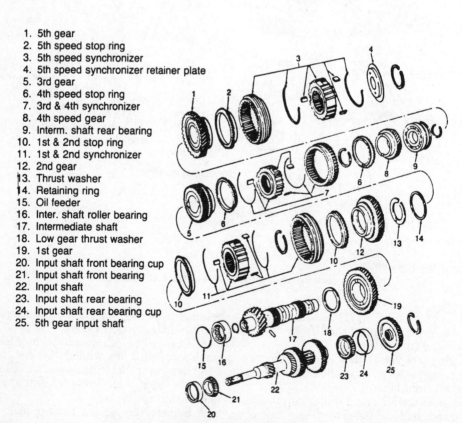

A-465 and the A-525 gear train

5th speed shift rail. Then, pull out the input shaft assembly. Finally, pull out the intermediate shaft assembly.

16. Now, remove the 1-2, 3-4, and 5th speed shift forks.

17. Proceed with Steps 12-20 of the procedure for 1984-85 models, which are identical with this transaxle for the remaining steps.

TRANSAXLE CASE ASSEMBLY

The assembly of the transaxle is the reverse of disassembly; however, please note the following:

1. Using tools No. C-4657, C4171 and an arbor press, press the front bearing onto the intermediate shaft; the input shaft front bearing cup is installed with the same tools used for removal.

2. Determine the shim thickness for the correct bearing end play only if any of the following parts are replaced:

    a. The transaxle case.

    b. The input shaft seal retainer.

    c. The bearing retainer plate.

    d. The rear end cover.

    e. The input shaft or bearings.

3. To determine proper shim thickness, refer to the Input Shaft Bearing End Play Adjustment at the end of this section.

4. Using tool No. C-4674 and a plastic hammer, install the input shaft oil seal.

5. Using a 3mm bead of RTV sealant, place it around the edge of the input shaft seal retainer and making sure the drain hole of the retainer is facing downward.

6. The differential bearing retainer is installed with the same special tool used for removal.

NOTE: *The rear end cover, the selector shaft housing and the differential cover are sealed with RTV sealant.*

Intermediate Shaft

DISASSEMBLY

NOTE: *The 1st-2nd, the 3rd-4th shift forks and the synchronizer stop rings are interchangeable. However, if parts are to be reused reassemble in the original position.*

1. Remove the intermediate shaft rear bearing snapring.

2. Using the puller tool No. C-4693, remove the intermediate shaft rear bearing.

3. Using snapring pliers, remove the 3rd-4th synchronizer hub snapring.

4. Using the puller tool No. L-4534, remove the 3rd-4th synchronizer hub and the 3rd speed gear.

5. Remove the retaining ring, the split thrust washer, the 2nd speed gear and the synchronizer stop ring.

6. Using snapring pliers, remove the 1st-2nd synchronizer hub snapring.

7. Remove the 1st speed gear, the stop ring and the 1st-2nd synchronizer assembly.

8. Remove the 1st speed gear thrust washer and the anti-spin pin.

ASSEMBLY

The assembly of the intermediate shaft is the Reverse of the disassembly; however, please note the following: When assembling the intermediate shaft, make sure the speed gears turn freely and have a minimum of 0.08mm end play. When installing the 1st speed gear thrust washer make sure the chamfered edge is facing the pinion gear. When installing the 1st-2nd synchronizer make sure the relief faces the 2nd speed gear. Use an arbor press to install the intermediate shaft rear bearing, the 3rd-4th synchronizer hub and the 3rd speed gear.

Input Shaft Bearing End Play

ADJUSTMENT

1. Using special tool No. L-4656 with handle C-4171, press the input shaft front bearing cup slightly forward in the case. Then, using tool No. L-4655 with handle C-4171, press the bearing cup back into the case, from the front, to the properly position the bearing cup before checking the input shaft endplay.

NOTE: *This step is not necessary if the special tool No. L-4655 was previously used to install the input shaft front bearing cup in the case and no input shaft select shim has been installed since pressing the cup into the case.*

2. Select a gauging shim which will give 0.025-0.50mm end play.

NOTE: *Measure the original shim from the input shaft seal retainer and select a shim 0.25mm thinner than the original for the gauging shim.*

3. Install the gauging shim on the bearing cup and the input shaft seal retainer.

4. Alternately tighten the input shaft seal retainer bolts until the retainer is bottomed against the case, then torque the bolts to 21 ft. lbs.

NOTE: *The input shaft seal retainer is used to draw the input shaft front bearing cup the proper distance into the case bore.*

Halfshaft

REMOVAL AND INSTALLATION

A-412 Models

NOTE: *Any time the differential cover is removed, a new gasket should be formed from RTV sealant. See Chapter 1.*

1. With the vehicle on the floor and the brakes applied, loosen the hub nut.

NOTE: *The hub and driveshafts are splined together and retained by the hub nut which is torqued to at least 180 ft. lbs.*

2. Raise and support the vehicle and remove the hub nut and washer.

NOTE: *Always support both ends of the driveshaft during removal to prevent damage to the boots.*

3. Disconnect the lower control arm ball joint stud nut from the steering knuckle.

4. Remove the Allenhead screws which secure the CV joint to the transmission flange.

5. Holding the CV housing, push the outer joint and knuckle assembly outward while disengaging the inner housing from the flange face.

NOTE: *The outer joint and shaft must be supported during disengagement of the inner joint.*

Quickly turn the open end of the joint upward to retain as much lubricant as possible, then carefully pull the outer joint spline out of the hub. Cover the joint with a clean towel to prevent dirt contamination.

6. Before installation, make sure that any lost lubricant is replaced. The only lubricant specified is Chrysler part number 4131389. No other lubricant of any type is to be used, as premature failure of the joint will result.

7. Clean the joint body and mating flange face.

8. Install the outer joint splined shaft into the hub. Do not secure with the nut and washer.

9. Early production vehicles were built with a cover plate between the hub and flange face. This cover is not necessary and should be discarded.

10. Position the inner joint in the transmission drive flange and secure it with new screws. Torque the screws to 37-40 ft. lbs.

11. Connect the lower control arm to the knuckle.

12. Install the outer joint and secure it with a new nut and washer. Torque the nut with the car on the ground and the brake set. Torque is:
- 200 ft. lbs.: 1978
- 180 ft. lbs.: 1979 and later

13. On 1978 models, stake the new nut to the joint spindle using a tool having a radiused end of 1.6mm and approximately 11mm wide. A sharp chisel should not be used since the collar will probably be split.

NOTE: *1979 and later models use a cotter pin and nut-lock to retain the nut. Staking is unnecessary.*

14. After attaching the driveshaft, if the inboard boot appears to be collapsed or deformed, vent the inner boot by inserting a round-tipped, small diameter rod between the boot and the

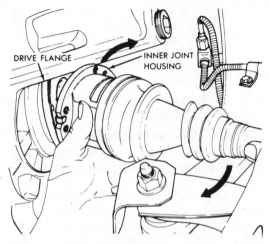

When removing the driveshaft, separate and tilt the joint housing to prevent leakage

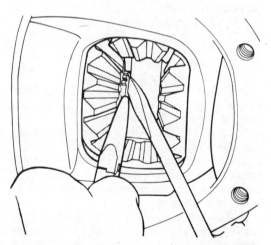

Compress the circlip tongs and push the shaft toward the side gear

shaft. As venting occurs, boot will return to its original shape.

A-460, A-465, A-525 and Automatic Transmission Models

The inboard CV joints are retained by circlips in the differential side gears. The circlip tangs are located on a machined surface on the inner end of the stub shaft.

1. With the car on the ground, loosen the hub nut, which has been torqued to 200 ft. lbs.

2. Drain the transaxle differential and remove the cover.

NOTE: *Any time the transaxle differential cover is removed, a new gasket should be formed from RTV sealant. See Chapter 1.*

3. To remove the right hand driveshaft, disconnect the speedometer cable and remove the cable and gear before removing the driveshaft.

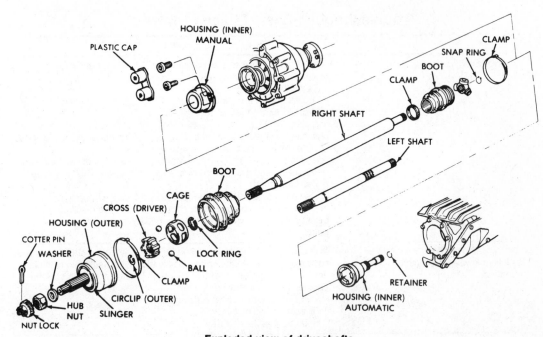

Exploded view of driveshafts

4. Rotate the driveshaft to expose the circlip tangs.

5. Compress the circlip with needle nose pliers and push the shaft into the side gear cavity.

6. Remove the clamp bolt from the ball stud and steering knuckle.

7. Separate the ball joint stud from the steering knuckle, by prying against the knuckle leg and control arm.

8. Separate the outer CV joint splined shaft from the hub by holding the CV housing and moving the hub away. Do not pry on the slinger or outer CV joint.

9. Support the shaft at the CV joints and remove the shaft. Do not pull on the shaft.

NOTE: *Removal of the left shaft may be made easier by inserting the blade of a thin prybar between the differential pinion shaft and prying against the end face of the shaft.*

10. Installation is the reverse of removal. Be sure the circlip tangs are positioned against the flattened end of the shaft before installing the shaft. A quick thrust will lock the circlip in the groove. Tighten the hub nut with the wheels on the ground to 180 ft. lbs.

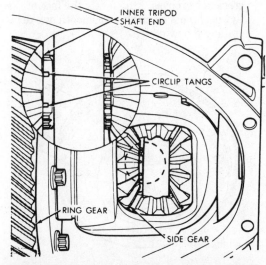

Rotate the driveshaft to expose the circlip retainer

CLUTCH

The clutch is a single dry disc unit, with no adjustment for wear provided in the clutch itself. Adjustment is made through an adjustable sleeve in the pedal linkage.

Clutch Disc

REMOVAL AND INSTALLATION

1. Remove the transmission as described earlier.

NOTE: Chrysler recommends the use of special tool L-4533 for disc alignment on the A-412 and tool C-4676 for the A-460, A-465 and A-525 transaxles.

2. Loosen the flywheel-to-pressure plate bolts diagonally, one or two turns at a time to avoid warpage.

Troubleshooting Basic Clutch Problems

Problem	Cause
Excessive clutch noise	Throwout bearing noises are more audible at the lower end of pedal travel. The usual causes are: • Riding the clutch • Too little pedal free-play • Lack of bearing lubrication A bad clutch shaft pilot bearing will make a high pitched squeal, when the clutch is disengaged and the transmission is in gear or within the first 2″ of pedal travel. The bearing must be replaced. Noise from the clutch linkage is a clicking or snapping that can be heard or felt as the pedal is moved completely up or down. This usually requires lubrication. Transmitted engine noises are amplified by the clutch housing and heard in the passenger compartment. They are usually the result of insufficient pedal free-play and can be changed by manipulating the clutch pedal.
Clutch slips (the car does not move as it should when the clutch is engaged)	This is usually most noticeable when pulling away from a standing start. A severe test is to start the engine, apply the brakes, shift into high gear and SLOWLY release the clutch pedal. A healthy clutch will stall the engine. If it slips it may be due to: • A worn pressure plate or clutch plate • Oil soaked clutch plate • Insufficient pedal free-play
Clutch drags or fails to release	The clutch disc and some transmission gears spin briefly after clutch disengagement. Under normal conditions in average temperatures, 3 seconds is maximum spin-time. Failure to release properly can be caused by: • Too light transmission lubricant or low lubricant level • Improperly adjusted clutch linkage
Low clutch life	Low clutch life is usually a result of poor driving habits or heavy duty use. Riding the clutch, pulling heavy loads, holding the car on a grade with the clutch instead of the brakes and rapid clutch engagement all contribute to low clutch life.

3. Remove the flywheel and clutch disc from the pressure plate.

4. Remove the retaining ring and release plate.

5. Diagonally loosen the pressure plate-to-crankshaft bolts. Mark all parts for reassembly.

6. Remove the bolts, spacer and pressure plate.

7. The flywheel and pressure plate surfaces should be cleaned thoroughly with fine sandpaper.

8. It is a false economy to replace either the clutch disc or pressure plate separately, since this will only lead to premature failure of the other component. In order to reuse any of the components, the following conditions should be met:

a. There should be no oil leakage through the rear main oil seal or transmission front oil seal.

b. The friction surface of the pressure plate should have a uniform appearance over the entire surface contact area. The pressure plate may be improperly mounted or sprung if a heavy wear pattern occurs directly opposite a light wear pattern.

c. The friction face of the flywheel should be free from discoloration, burned areas, cracks or grooves. Frequently the face of the flywheel must be machined smooth before installing a new clutch.

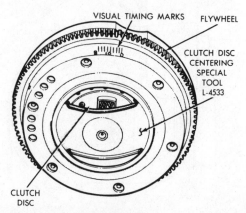

Centering the A-412 clutch disc

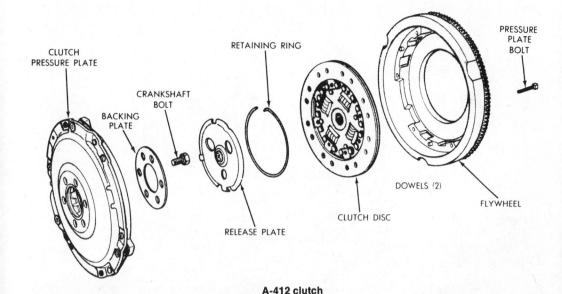

CLUTCH
PRESSURE PLATE

BACKING
PLATE

CRANKSHAFT
BOLT

RETAINING RING

PRESSURE
PLATE
BOLT

RELEASE PLATE

CLUTCH DISC

DOWELS (2)

FLYWHEEL

A-412 clutch

A-412 clutch dowel pin hole

A-412 clutch dowel pin

d. The disc should be free of oil or grease. If it is worn to within less than 0.4mm of the rivet heads, replace the disc.

e. Check the pressure plate for flatness. It should be flat within 0.5mm across the friction area, and be free from cracks, burns, grooves or ridges.

f. Inspect the cover outer mounting flange for flatness, burrs, nicks, or dents.

g. The 2 dowels in the flywheel should be tight and undamaged.

h. Inspect the center of the release plate for cracks or heavy wear. Wear up to 0.25mm is acceptable.

If the clutch assembly does not meet these conditions, it should be replaced.

9. Align marks and install the pressure plate, spacer and bolts. Coat the bolts with thread compound and torque them to 55 ft. lbs.

10. Install the release plate and retaining ring.

11. Using special tool L-4533, C-4676 or their equivalent, install the clutch disc and flywheel on the pressure plate.

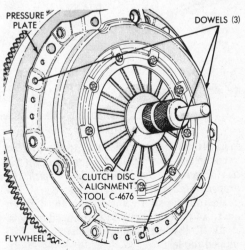

PRESSURE
PLATE

DOWELS (3)

CLUTCH DISC
ALIGNMENT
TOOL C-4676

FLYWHEEL

A-460, 465, and 525 clutch disc alignment

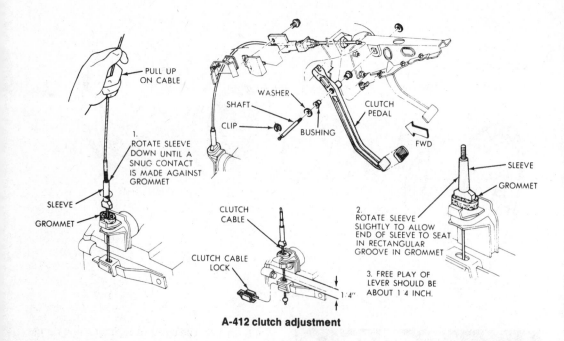

A-412 clutch adjustment

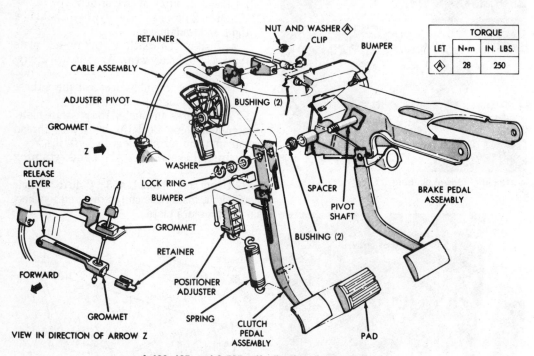

A-460, 465, and A-525 self adjusting clutch mechanism

WARNING: *Make certain that the drilled mark on the flywheel is at the top, so that the two dowels on the flywheel align with the proper holes in the pressure plate.*

12. Install the six flywheel bolts and tighten them to 14.5 ft. lbs. on A-412 equipped models, and 21 ft. lbs. on A-460, A-465, and A-525 equipped models.

13. Remove the aligning tool.

14. Install the transmission.

15. Adjust the freeplay.

CLUTCH FREEPLAY ADJUSTMENT

A-412

1. Pull up on the clutch plate.

2. While holding the cable up, rotate the adjusting sleeve downward until a snug contact is made against the grommet.

3. Rotate the sleeve slightly to allow the end of the sleeve to seat in the rectangular hole in the grommet.

A-460, A-465, and A-525

This unit has a self-adjusting clutch. No manual adjustment is possible.

AUTOMATIC TRANSAXLE

Understanding Automatic Transaxles

The automatic transaxle allows engine torque and power to be transmitted to the front wheels within a narrow range of engine operating speeds. The transaxle will allow the engine to turn fast enough to produce plenty of power and torque at very low speeds, while keeping it at a sensible rpm at high vehicle speeds. The transaxle performs this job entirely without driver assistance. The transaxle uses a light fluid as the medium for the transaxle of power. This fluid also works in the operation of various hydraulic control circuits and as a lubricant. Because the transaxle fluid performs all of these three functions, trouble within the unit can easily travel from one part to another. For this reason, and because of the complexity and unusual operating principles of the transaxle, a very sound understanding of the basic principles of operation will simplify troubleshooting.

THE TORQUE CONVERTER

The torque converter replaces the conventional clutch. It has three functions:

1. It allows the engine to idle with the vehicle at a standstill even with the transaxle in gear.

2. It allows the transaxle to shift from range to range smoothly, without requiring that the driver close the throttle during the shift.

3. It multiplies engine torque to an increasing extent as vehicle speed drops and throttle opening is increased. This has the effect of making the transaxle more responsive and reduces the amount of shifting required.

The torque converter is a metal case which is shaped like a sphere that has been flattened on opposite sides. It is bolted to the rear end of the engine's crankshaft. Generally, the entire metal case rotates at engine speed and serves as the engine's flywheel.

The case contains three sets of blades. One set is attached directly to the case. This set forms the torus or pump. Another set is directly connected to the output shaft, and forms the turbine. The third set is mounted on a hub which, in turn, is mounted on a stationary shaft through a one-way clutch. The third set is known as the stator.

A pump, which is driven by the converter hub at engine speed, keeps the converter full of transaxle fluid at all times. Fluid flows continuously through the unit to provide cooling.

Under low speed acceleration, the torque converter functions as follows: The torus is turning faster than the turbine. It picks up fluid at the center of the converter and, through centrifugal force, slings it outward. Since the outer edge of the converter moves faster than the portions at the center, the fluid picks up speed.

The fluid then enters the outer edge of the turbine blades. It then travels back toward the center of the converter case along the turbine blades. In impinging upon the turbine blades, the fluid loses the energy picked up in the torus.

If the fluid were now to immediately be returned directly into the torus, both halves of the converter would have to turn at approximately the same speed at all times, and torque input and output would both be the same.

In flowing through the torus and turbine, the fluid picks up two types of flow, or flow in two separate directions. It flows through the turbine blades, and it spins with the engine. The stator, whose blades are stationary when the vehicle is being accelerated at low speeds, converts one type of flow into another. Instead of allowing the fluid to flow straight back into the torus, the stator's curved blades turn the fluid almost 90 degrees toward the direction of rotation of the engine. Thus the fluid does not flow as fast toward the torus, but is already spinning when the torus picks it up., This has the effect of allowing the torus to turn much faster than the turbine. This difference is speed may be compared to the difference in speed between the smaller and larger gears in any gear train. The result is that engine power output is higher, and engine torque is multiplied.

As the speed of the turbine increases, the fluid spins faster and faster in the direction of engine rotation. As a result, the ability of the stator to redirect the fluid flow is reduced. Under cruising conditions, the stator is eventually forced to rotate on its one-way clutch in the direction of engine rotation. Under these conditions, the torque converter begins to behave almost like a solid shaft, with the torus and turbine speeds being almost equal.

THE PLANETARY GEARBOX

The ability of the torque converter to multiply engine torque is limited. Also, the unit tends to be more efficient when the turbine is rotating at relatively high speeds. Therefore, a planetary gearbox is used to carry the power output of the turbine to the driveshaft.

Planetary gears function very similarly to

conventional transaxle gears. However, their construction is different in that three elements make up one gear system, and in that all three elements are different from one another,. The three elements are: an outer gear that is shaped like a hoop, with teeth cut into the inner surface. A sun gear, mounted on a shaft and located at the very center of the outer gear, and a set of three planet gears, held by pins in a ring-like planet carrier and meshing with both the sun gear and the outer gear. Either the outer gear or the sun gear may be held stationary, providing more than one possible torque multiplication factor for each set of gears. Also, if all three gears are forced to rotate the same speed, the gearset forms, in effect, a solid shaft.

Most modern automatics use the planetary gears to provide either a single reduction ratio of about 1.8:1, or two reduction gears: a low of about 2.5:1, and an intermediate of about 1.5:1. Bands and clutches are used to hold various portions of the gearsets to the transaxle case or to the shaft on which they are mounted. Shifting is accomplished, then, by changing the portion of each planetary gearset which is held to the transaxle case or to the shaft.

THE SERVOS AND ACCUMULATORS

The servos are hydraulic pistons and cylinders. They resemble the hydraulic actuators used on many familiar machines, such as bulldozers. Hydraulic fluid enters the cylinder, under pressure, and forces the piston to move to engage the band or clutches.

The accumulators are used to cushion the engagement of the servos. The transaxle fluid must pass through the accumulator on the way to the servo. The accumulator housing contains a thin piston which is sprung away from the discharge passage of the accumulator. When fluid passes through the accumulator on the way to the servo, it must move the piston against spring pressure, and this action smooths out the action of the servo.

THE HYDRAULIC CONTROL SYSTEM

The hydraulic pressure used to operate the servos comes from the main transaxle oil pump.

Troubleshooting Basic Automatic Transmission Problems

Problem	Cause	Solution
Fluid leakage	• Defective pan gasket	• Replace gasket or tighten pan bolts
	• Loose filler tube	• Tighten tube nut
	• Loose extension housing to transmission case	• Tighten bolts
	• Converter housing area leakage	• Have transmission checked professionally
Fluid flows out the oil filler tube	• High fluid level	• Check and correct fluid level
	• Breather vent clogged	• Open breather vent
	• Clogged oil filter or screen	• Replace filter or clean screen (change fluid also)
	• Internal fluid leakage	• Have transmission checked professionally
Transmission overheats (this is usually accompanied by a strong burned odor to the fluid)	• Low fluid level	• Check and correct fluid level
	• Fluid cooler lines clogged	• Drain and refill transmission. If this doesn't cure the problem, have cooler lines cleared or replaced.
	• Heavy pulling or hauling with insufficient cooling	• Install a transmission oil cooler
	• Faulty oil pump, internal slippage	• Have transmission checked professionally
Buzzing or whining noise	• Low fluid level	• Check and correct fluid level
	• Defective torque converter, scored gears	• Have transmission checked professionally
No forward or reverse gears or slippage in one or more gears	• Low fluid level	• Check and correct fluid level
	• Defective vacuum or linkage controls, internal clutch or band failure	• Have unit checked professionally
Delayed or erratic shift	• Low fluid level	• Check and correct fluid level
	• Broken vacuum lines	• Repair or replace lines
	• Internal malfunction	• Have transmission checked professionally

Lockup Torque Converter Service Diagnosis

Problem	Cause	Solution

No lockup	• Faulty oil pump
	• Sticking governor valve
	• Valve body malfunction
	    (a) Stuck switch valve
	    (b) Stuck lockup valve
	    (c) Stuck fail-safe valve
	• Failed locking clutch
	• Leaking turbine hub seal
	• Faulty input shaft or seal ring
		• Replace oil pump
		• Repair or replace as necessary
		• Repair or replace valve body or its internal components as necessary
		
		• Replace torque converter
		• Replace torque converter
		• Repair or replace as necessary

Will not unlock	• Sticking governor valve
	• Valve body malfunction
	    (a) Stuck switch valve
	    (b) Stuck lockup valve
	    (c) Stuck fail-safe valve
		• Repair or replace as necessary
		• Repair or replace valve body or its internal components as necessary

Stays locked up at too low a speed in direct	• Sticking governor valve
	• Valve body malfunction
	    (a) Stuck switch valve
	    (b) Stuck lockup valve
	    (c) Stuck fail-safe valve
		• Repair or replace as necessary
		• Repair or replace valve body or its internal components as necessary

Locks up or drags in low or second	• Faulty oil pump
	• Valve body malfunction
	    (a) Stuck switch valve
	    (b) Stuck fail-safe valve
		• Replace oil pump
		• Repair or replace valve body or its internal components as necessary

Sluggish or stalls in reverse	• Faulty oil pump
	• Plugged cooler, cooler lines or fittings
	• Valve body malfunction
	    (a) Stuck switch valve
	    (b) Faulty input shaft or seal ring
		• Replace oil pump as necessary
		• Flush or replace cooler and flush lines and fittings
		• Repair or replace valve body or its internal components as necessary

Loud chatter during lockup engagement (cold)	• Faulty torque converter • Failed locking clutch • Leaking turbine hub seal	• Replace torque converter • Replace torque converter • Replace torque converter
Vibration or shudder during lockup engagement	• Faulty oil pump • Valve body malfunction • Faulty torque converter • Engine needs tune-up	• Repair or replace oil pump as necessary • Repair or replace valve body or its internal components as necessary • Replace torque converter • Tune engine
Vibration after lockup engagement	• Faulty torque converter • Exhaust system strikes underbody • Engine needs tune-up • Throttle linkage misadjusted	• Replace torque converter • Align exhaust system • Tune engine • Adjust throttle linkage
Vibration when revved in neutral Overheating: oil blows out of dip stick tube or pump seal	• Torque converter out of balance • Plugged cooler, cooler lines or fittings • Stuck switch valve	• Replace torque converter • Flush or replace cooler and flush lines and fittings • Repair switch valve in valve body or replace valve body
Shudder after lockup engagement	• Faulty oil pump • Plugged cooler, cooler lines or fittings • Valve body malfunction • Faulty torque converter • Fail locking clutch • Exhaust system strikes underbody • Engine needs tune-up • Throttle linkage misadjusted	• Replace oil pump • Flush or replace cooler and flush lines and fittings • Repair or replace valve body or its internal components as necessary • Replace torque converter • Replace torque converter • Align exhaust system • Tune engine • Adjust throttle linkage

Transmission Fluid Indications

The appearance and odor of the transmission fluid can give valuable clues to the overall condition of the transmission. Always note the appearance of the fluid when you check the fluid level or change the fluid. Rub a small amount of fluid between your fingers to feel for grit and smell the fluid on the dipstick.

If the fluid appears:	It indicates:
Clear and red colored	• Normal operation
Discolored (extremely dark red or brownish) or smells burned	• Band or clutch pack failure, usually caused by an overheated transmission. Hauling very heavy loads with insufficient power or failure to change the fluid, often result in overheating. Do not confuse this appearance with newer fluids that have a darker red color and a strong odor (though not a burned odor).
Foamy or aerated (light in color and full of bubbles)	• The level is too high (gear train is churning oil) • An internal air leak (air is mixing with the fluid). Have the transmission checked professionally.
Solid residue in the fluid	• Defective bands, clutch pack or bearings. Bits of band material or metal abrasives are clinging to the dipstick. Have the transmission checked professionally.
Varnish coating on the dipstick	• The transmission fluid is overheating

This fluid is channeled to the various servos through the shift valves. There is generally a manual shift valve which is operated by the transaxle selector level and an automatic shift valve for each automatic upshift the transaxle provides: i.e., 2-speed automatics have a low/high shift valve, while 3-speeds have a 1-2 valve, and a 2-3 valve.

There are two pressures which effect the operation of these valves. One is the governor pressure which is affected by vehicle sped. The other is the modulator pressure which is affected by intake manifold vacuum or throttle position. Governor pressure rises with an increase in vehicle sped, and modulator pressure rises as the throttle is opened wider. By responding to these two pressures, the shift valves cause the upshift points to be delayed with increased throttle opening to make the best use of the engine's power output.

Most transaxles also make use of an auxiliary circuit for downshifting. This circuit may be actuated by the throttle linkage or the vacuum line which actuates the modulator, or by a cable or solenoid. It applies pressure to a special downshift surface on the shift valve or valves.

The transaxle modulator also governs the line pressure, used to actuate the servos. In this way, the clutches and bands will be actuated with a force matching the torque output of the engine.

Identification

There are three automatic transaxle designations used in the Omni/Horizon model line, the A-404 used with the 1.7L engine 1978-83, the A-413 used with the 2.2L engine 1981-84, and the A-415 which is used with the 1.6L engine in 1984. All of these transaxles are Chrysler built Torqueflite Automatic Transaxles.

SHIFT LINKAGE ADJUSTMENT

NOTE: *When it is necessary to disconnect the linkage cable from the lever, which uses plastic grommets as retainers, the grommets should be replaced.*

1. Make sure that the adjustable swivel block is free to slide on the shift cable.
2. Place the shift lever in Park.
3. With the linkage assembled, and the swivel lock bolt loose, move the shift arm on the transaxle into the Park position.
4. Hold the shift arm in position with a force of about 10 lbs. and tighten the adjuster swivel lock bolt to 8 ft. lbs.
5. Check the linkage action.

NOTE: *The automatic transmission gear selector release button may pop up in the knob when shifting from PARK to DRIVE. This is caused by inadequate retention of the selector release knob retaining tab. The release button will always work but the loose button can be annoying. A sleeve (Chrysler Part No. 5211984) and washers (Chrysler Part No. 6500380) are available to cure this condition. If these are unavailable, do the following:*

1. Remove the release button.
2. Cut and fold a standard paper match stem as shown.

3. Using tweezers, insert the folded match as far as possible into the clearance slot as shown. The match should be below the knob surface.

4. Insert the button, taking care not to break the button stem.

THROTTLE CABLE ADJUSTMENT

1. Adjust the idle speed as previously described.

2. Run the engine to normal operating temperature.

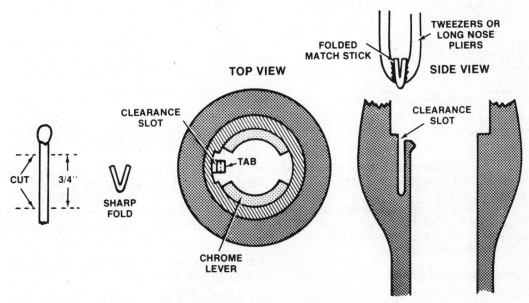

Automatic transmission shifter modification

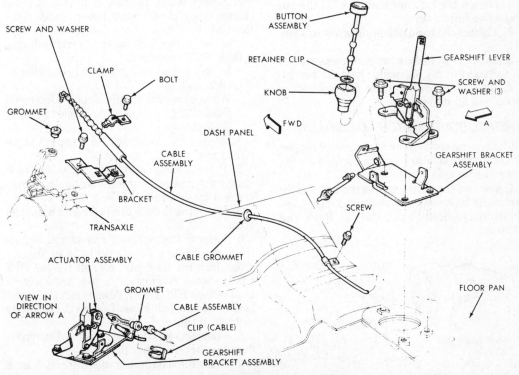

Automatic transmission shift linkage

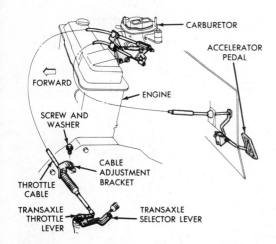

Throttle cable

3. Loosen the adjustment bracket lock screw.
4. Make sure the adjustment bracket is free to slide in its slot.
5. Hold the transmission lever firmly rearward against its internal stop and tighten the adjustment bracket lock screw to 9 ft. lbs.
6. Test the cable operation.

BAND ADJUSTMENTS

Front (Kickdown) Band

Chrysler recommends that the band be adjusted at each fluid change. The adjusting screw is located on the left side of the case.

1. Loosen the lock nut and back off the nut above five full turns.
2. Tighten the band adjusting screw to 72 in. lbs.
3. Back off the adjusting screw exactly 2½ turns except with 1.6L engine, back off 3 turns.
4. Hold the adjusting screw and tighten the locknut to 35 ft. lbs.

NEUTRAL START SWITCH ADJUSTMENT

The neutral start circuit is the center contact of the three-terminal switch located in the transmission case.

1. Remove the wiring connector and test for continuity between the center pin and the case. Continuity should exist only in Park and Neutral.

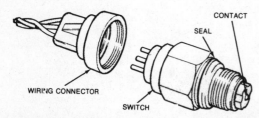

Neutral safety switch

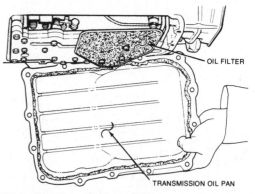

Removing transmission oil pan

2. Remove the switch and check that the operating lever fingers are centered in the switch opening.
3. Install the switch and a new seal and tighten to 24 ft. lbs. Retest with a lamp.
4. Replace the lost transmission fluid.
5. If shift linkage adjustment is correct and the switch still malfunctions, replace the switch.

PAN REMOVAL AND INSTALLATION, FLUID AND FILTER CHANGE

NOTE: *RTV silicone sealer is used in place of a pan gasket.*

Chrysler recommends no fluid or filter changes during the normal service life of the car. Severe usage requires a fluid and filter change every 15,000 miles. Severe usage is defined as:

a. more than 50% heavy city traffic during 90°F (32°C) weather.

b. police, taxi or commercial operation or trailer towing.

When changing the fluid, only Dexron®II fluid change should be performed at every fluid change.

1. Raise the vehicle and support it on jackstands.
2. Place a large container under the pan, loosen the pan bolts and tap at one corner to break it loose. Drain the fluid.
3. When the fluid is drained remove the pan bolts.
4. Remove the retaining screws and replace the filter. Tighten the screws to 35 in. lbs.
5. Clean the fluid pan, peel off the old RTV silicone sealer and install the pan, using a 3mm bead of new RTV sealer. Always run the sealer bead inside the bolt holes. Tighten the pan bolts to 10-12 ft. lbs.
6. Pour the specified amount of Dexron®II fluid through the filler tube.
7. Start the engine and idle it for at least 2 minutes. Set the parking brake and move the

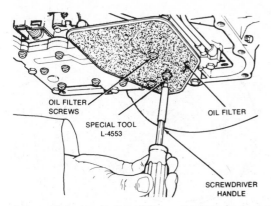

Automatic transmission oil filter attaching screws

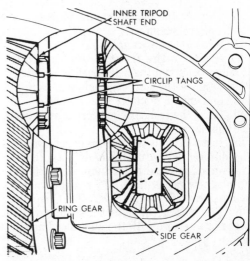

Rotate the driveshafts to expose the circlip ends

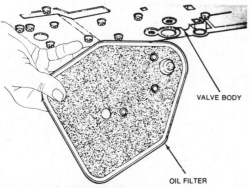

Removing automatic transmission filter

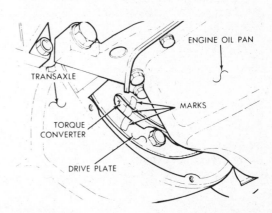

Matchmark the torque converter and drive plate

selector through each position, ending in Park.

8. Add sufficient fluid to bring the level to the FULL mark on the dipstick. The level should be checked in Park, with the engine idling at normal operating temperature.

Transaxle

REMOVAL AND INSTALLATION

The automatic transaxle can be removed with the engine installed in the car, but, the transaxle and torque converter must be removed as an assembly. Otherwise the drive plate, pump bushing or oil seal could be damaged. The drive plate will not support a load; no weight should be allowed to bear on the drive plate.

1. Disconnect the negative battery cable.
2. Disconnect the throttle and shift linkage from the transaxle.
3. Raise and support the car. Remove the front wheels. Refer to "Halfshaft Removal and Installation" to remove or install the halfshafts.
4. Remove the oil cooler hoses.
5. Remove the left splash shield. Drain the differential and remove the cover.

6. Remove the speedometer adaptor, cable and gear.
7. Remove the sway bar.
8. Remove both lower ball joint-to-steering knuckle bolts.
9. Pry the lower ball joint from the steering knuckle.
10. Remove the driveshaft from the hub.
11. Rotate both driveshafts to expose the circlip ends. Note the flat surface on the inner ends of both axle tripod shafts. Pry the circlip out.
12. Remove both driveshafts.
13. Matchmark the torque converter and drive plate. Remove the torque converter mounting bolts. Remove the access plug in the right splash shield to rotate the engine.
14. Remove the lower cooler tube and the wire to the neutral safety switch.
15. Install some means of supporting the engine.
16. Remove the upper bellhousing bolts.

17. Remove the engine mount bracket from the front crossmember.

18. Support the transmission.

19. Remove the front mount insulator through-bolts and the bell housing mount.

20. Remove the long through-bolt from the left hand engine mount.

21. Raise the transaxle and pry it away from the engine.

22. Installation is the reverse of removal. Fill the differential with DEXRON®II automatic transmission fluid before lowering the car. Form a new gasket from RTV sealant when installing the differential cover. See Chapter 1. On 1978 models, be sure the auxiliary horn does not interfere with the oil cooler lines.

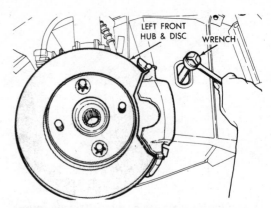

Access plug (in right splash shield) to rotate engine by hand

FRONT SUSPENSION

A MacPherson type front suspension, with vertical shock absorbers attached to the upper fender reinforcement and the steering knuckle, is used. Lower control arms, attached inboard to a cross-member and outboard to the steering knuckle through a ball joint, provide lower steering knuckle position. During steering ma-

neuvers, the upper strut and steering knuckle turn as an assembly.

Strut
REMOVAL AND INSTALLATION

NOTE: *A new bonded mount assembly is now used on late 1978 and later models, replacing the double nut, bearing retainer, isolator and strut retainer previously used. To*

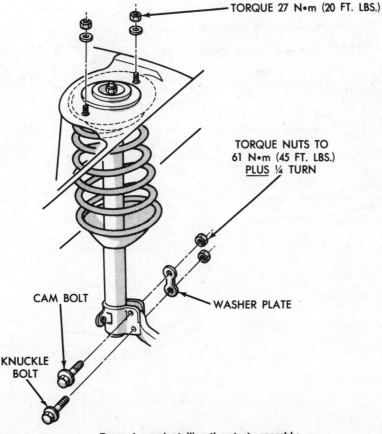

TORQUE 27 N•m (20 FT. LBS.)

TORQUE NUTS TO
61 N•m (45 FT. LBS.)
PLUS ¼ TURN

CAM BOLT

WASHER PLATE

KNUCKLE
BOLT

Removing or installing the strut assembly

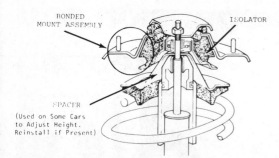

Modified version of strut damper mount

remove the welded nut, grind the hex flats for proper wrench fit.

1. Raise and support the vehicle.
2. Remove the wheel.

NOTE: *If the original strut is to be assembled to the original knuckle, mark the cam adjusting bolt. Remove the cam adjusting bolt, through bolt and brake hose bracket retaining screw.*

4. Remove the strut mounting screws and remove the strut.
5. Installation is the reverse of removal. Position the knuckle leg in the strut and install

the upper (cam) and lower through-bolts. Index the cam bolt with the match marks. Torque the strut mounting screws to 20 ft. lbs.; the brake hose bracket screw to 10 ft. lbs.; the cam bolt to 45 ft. lbs. plus ¼ turn, and the wheel nuts to 80 ft. lbs.

Spring

REMOVAL AND INSTALLATION

NOTE: *A spring compressor is required to remove the spring from the strut. A crow's foot adaptor and torque wrench are also required.*

1. Remove the struts.
2. Compress the spring, using a reliable coil spring compressor.
3. Hold the strut rod and remove the rod nut.
4. Remove the retainers and bushings.
5. Remove the spring.

NOTE: *Springs are not interchangeable from side to side.*

CAUTION: *When removing the spring from the compressor, open the compressor evenly and not more than 9¼" (235mm).*

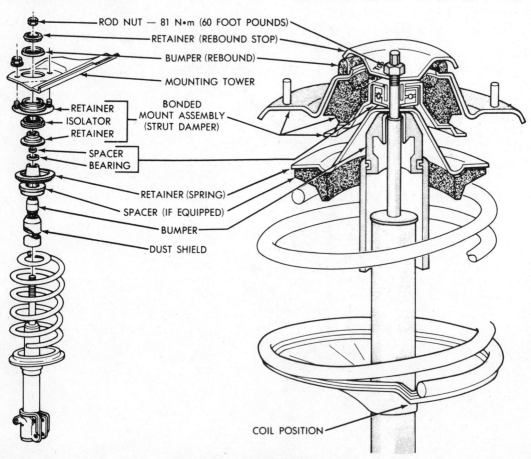

First version of strut damper mount

Troubleshooting Basic Steering and Suspension Problems

Problem	Cause	Solution
Hard steering (steering wheel is hard to turn)	• Low or uneven tire pressure • Loose power steering pump drive belt • Low or incorrect power steering fluid • Incorrect front end alignment • Defective power steering pump • Bent or poorly lubricated front end parts	• Inflate tires to correct pressure • Adjust belt • Add fluid as necessary • Have front end alignment checked/adjusted • Check pump • Lubricate and/or replace defective parts
Loose steering (too much play in the steering wheel)	• Loose wheel bearings • Loose or worn steering linkage • Faulty shocks • Worn ball joints	• Adjust wheel bearings • Replace worn parts • Replace shocks • Replace ball joints
Car veers or wanders (car pulls to one side with hands off the steering wheel)	• Incorrect tire pressure • Improper front end alignment • Loose wheel bearings • Loose or bent front end components • Faulty shocks	• Inflate tires to correct pressure • Have front end alignment checked/adjusted • Adjust wheel bearings • Replace worn components • Replace shocks
Wheel oscillation or vibration transmitted through steering wheel	• Improper tire pressures • Tires out of balance • Loose wheel bearings • Improper front end alignment • Worn or bent front end components	• Inflate tires to correct pressure • Have tires balanced • Adjust wheel bearings • Have front end alignment checked/adjusted • Replace worn parts
Uneven tire wear	• Incorrect tire pressure • Front end out of alignment • Tires out of balance	• Inflate tires to correct pressure • Have front end alignment checked/adjusted • Have tires balanced

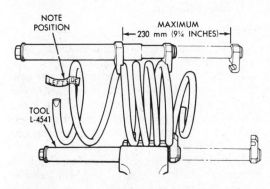

Remove or install the coil spring

6. Assembly is the reverse of disassembly in the following order:
    a. Bumper dust shield
    b. Spring seat
    c. Upper spring retainer
    d. Bearing and spacer
    e. Mount assembly
    f. Rebound bumper
    g. Retainer
    h. Rod nut

NOTE: *Torque rod nut to 55 ft. lbs. before removing the spring compressor. Use a crow's foot adaptor to tighten the nut while holding the rod with an open end wrench.*
Be sure the lower coil end of the spring is seated in the seat recess.

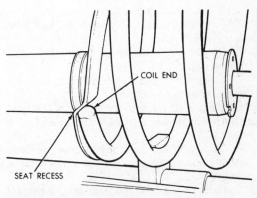

Be sure the lower coil end seats in the recess

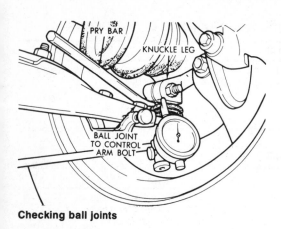

Checking ball joints

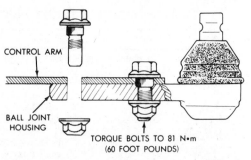

TORQUE BOLTS TO 81 N•m
(60 FOOT POUNDS)

Ball joint bolted to lower control arm—1979–80 models

Ball Joints

INSPECTION

1. Raise and support the vehicle.
2. With the suspension fully extended (at full travel) clamp a dial indicator to the lower control arm with the plunger indexed against the steering knuckle leg.
3. Zero the dial indicator.
4. Use a stout bar to pry on the top of the ball joint housing-to-lower control arm bolt with the bar tip under the steering knuckle leg.
5. Measure the axial travel of the steering knuckle leg in relation to the control arm by raising and lowering the steering knuckle as in Step 4.
6. If the travel is more than 1.25mm, the ball joint should be replaced.

REPLACEMENT

1978 Models

The lower ball joints are permanently lubricated, operate with no free play, and are riveted in place. The rivets must be drilled out and replaced with special bolts.

NOTE: *To avoid damage to the control arm surface adjacent to the ball joint during drilling, the use of a center punch and a drill press are strongly recommended.*

1. Remove the lower control arm.
2. Position the assembly with the ball joint up.
3. Center punch the rivets on the ball joint housing side.
4. Using a drill press with a ¼" bit, drill out the center of the rivet.
5. Using a ½" bit, drill the center of the rivet until the bit makes contact with the ball joint housing.
6. Using a ⅜" bit, drill the center of the rivet. Remove the remainder of the rivet with a punch.
7. Position the new ball joint on the control arm and tighten the bolts to 60 ft. lbs.

8. Install the control arm and tighten the ball joint clamp bolt to 50 ft. lbs.; the pivot bolt to 105 ft. lbs. and the strut stub to 70 ft. lbs.

1979-80

The ball joint housing is bolted to the lower control arm with the joint stud retained in the steering knuckle by a clamp bolt.

1. Raise and support the car.
2. Remove the steering knuckle-to-ball joint stud clamp bolt and separate the stud from the knuckle leg.
3. Remove the 2 bolts holding the ball joint housing to the lower control arm.
4. Remove the ball joint housing.
5. Install a new ball joint housing to the control arm. Torque the retaining bolts to 60 ft. lbs.
6. Install the ball joint stud in the steering knuckle. Tighten the clamp bolt to 50 ft. lbs.
7. Lower the car.

1981-89

NOTE: *This procedure requires special tools and machine shop services.*

The ball joint is pressed into the lower control arm on these models and is retained to the steering knuckle by a clamp bolt. The lower control arm must be removed from the vehicle and placed in a press to perform this operation.

1. Pry off the rubber grease seal.
2. Position the Receiving Cup tool C-4699-2 to support the lower control arm while receiving the ball joint assembly.
3. Install a 1¹⁄₁₆" deep socket over the stud and against the joint upper housing.
4. Apply pressure from the press to remove the joint from the arm.
5. To install, position the ball joint housing into the control arm cavity.
6. Place the assembly in the press with the installer tool C-4699-1 supporting the lower control arm.
7. Align and press the assembly until the ball joint bottoms against the control arm cavity down flange.

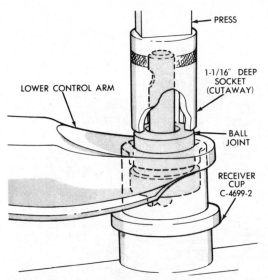

Removing the ball joint—1981 and later

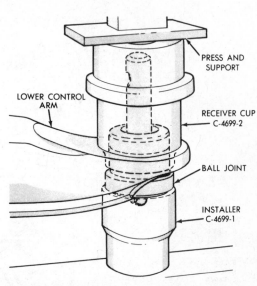

Installing the ball joint—1981 and later

8. With a 1½" socket, press the seal onto the ball joint housing so that it seats against the lower control arm.

Lower Control Arm

REMOVAL AND INSTALLATION

1. Raise and support the vehicle.
2. Remove the front inner pivot through bolt, the rear stub strut nut, retainer and bushing, and the ball joint-to-steering knuckle clamp bolt.
3. Separate the ball joint stud from the steering knuckle by prying between the ball stud retainer on the knuckle and the lower control arm.

WARNING: *Pulling the steering knuckle out*

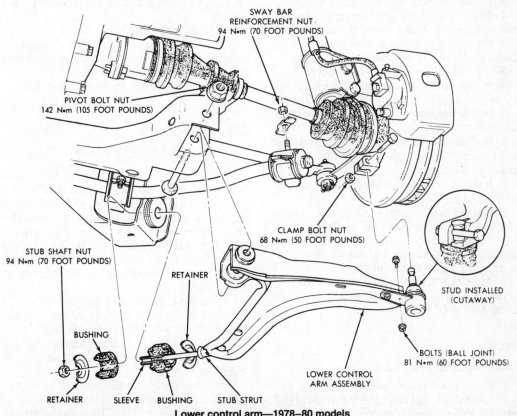

Lower control arm—1978–80 models

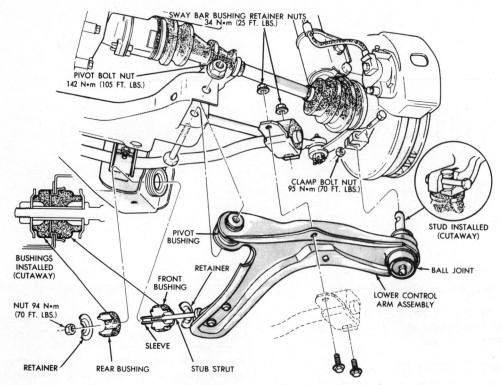

SWAY BAR BUSHING RETAINER NUTS
34 N•m (25 FT. LBS.)

PIVOT BOLT NUT
142 N•m (105 FT. LBS.)

CLAMP BOLT NUT
95 N•m (70 FT. LBS.)

STUD INSTALLED
(CUTAWAY)

BALL JOINT

PIVOT
BUSHING

RETAINER

LOWER CONTROL
ARM ASSEMBLY

FRONT
BUSHING

BUSHINGS
INSTALLED
(CUTAWAY)

NUT 94 N•m
(70 FT. LBS.)

RETAINER   REAR BUSHING   STUB STRUT

SLEEVE

Lower control arm—1981 and later

from the vehicle after releasing it from the ball joint can separate the inner CV-joint.

4. Remove the sway bar-to-control arm nut and reinforcement and rotate the control arm over the sway bar. Remove the rear stub strut bushing, sleeve and retainer.

NOTE: *The substitution of fasteners other than those of the grade originally used is not recommended.*

5. Install the retainer, bushing and sleeve on the stub strut.

6. Position the control arm over the sway bar and install the rear stub strut and front pivot into the crossmember.

7. Install the front pivot bolt and loosely install the nut.

8. Install the stub strut bushing and retainer and loosely assemble the nut.

9. Position the way bar bracket and stud through the control arm and install the retainer and nut. Tighten the nut to 10 ft. lbs.

10. Install the ball joint stud into the steering knuckle and install the clamp bolt. Torque the clamp bolt to 50 ft. lb.

Sway Bar
REMOVAL AND INSTALLATION

1. Raise and support the car.
2. Remove the nut from the control arm end bushing and reinforcement plates.

3. Remove the nut retainers and insulator holding the sway bar to the crossmember linkage.

4. Remove the sway bar.

5. Inspect the sway bar for distortion or fatigue cracks in the metal. Replace any damaged or distorted bushings.

6. Installation is the reverse of removal.

Steering Knuckle
REMOVAL AND INSTALLATION

Service or repair to the bearing, hub, brake dust shield or the steering knuckle itself will require removal of the knuckle. Before attempting this operation, be aware that to reassemble the components it is necessary to torque the front hub nut to at least 180 ft. lbs. You will need a large torque wrench to read that high and a great deal of strength to attain that much torque on the nut.

1. Remove the cotter pin and nut-lock.

2. Loosen the hub nut while the car is resting on the wheels with the brakes applied.

NOTE: *The hub and driveshaft are splined together through the knuckle and retained by the hub nut.*

3. Raise and support the car.

4. Remove the wheel and tire.

5. Remove the hub nut. Be sure the splined

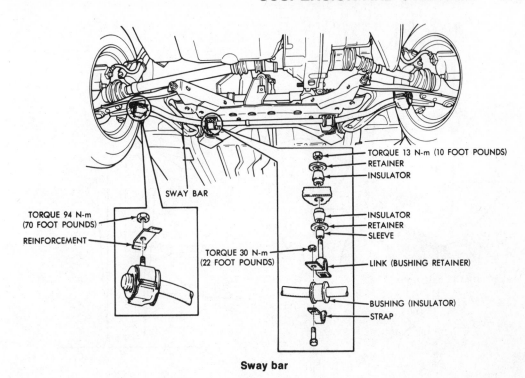

TORQUE 13 N-m (10 FOOT POUNDS)
RETAINER
INSULATOR

INSULATOR
RETAINER
SLEEVE

LINK (BUSHING RETAINER)

BUSHING (INSULATOR)
STRAP

SWAY BAR

TORQUE 94 N-m
(70 FOOT POUNDS)

REINFORCEMENT

TORQUE 30 N-m
(22 FOOT POUNDS)

Sway bar

CAM BOLT
122 N•m (90 FOOT POUNDS)

STRUT DAMPER
(REFERENCE)

ADAPTOR SCREW AND WASHER
115 N•m (85 FOOT POUNDS)

BRAKE CALIPER

DRIVE SHAFT

SCREW
26 N•m
(20 FOOT POUNDS)

BEARING

SHIELD

HUB

RETAINER

WASHER

COTTER
PIN

STEERING LINKAGE
47 N•m (35 FOOT POUNDS)

CLAMP BOLT
67 N•m (50 FOOT POUNDS)

LOWER CONTROL ARM
(REFERENCE)

KNUCKLE

WHEEL BOLT

NUT LOCK

HUB NUT
245 N•m (180 FOOT POUNDS)

Exploded view of front suspension (steering knuckle)—typical

driveshaft is free to separate from the spline in hub when the knuckle is removed.

6. Disconnect the tie rod end from the steering arm.

7. Disconnect the brake hose retainer from the strut.

8. Remove the clamp bolt holding the ball joint stud in the steering knuckle.

9. Remove the brake caliper adaptor screw and washers.

10. Support he caliper on a wire hook.

11. Remove the brake disc.

12. Matchmark the camber adjusting cams and loosen both bolts.

13. Support the steering knuckle and remove the cam adjusting and through-bolts. Remove

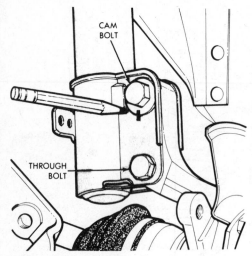

Matchmark the cam bolts

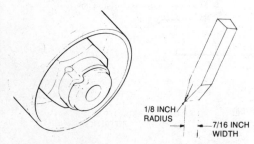

Staking the nut retainer in place in 1978 models

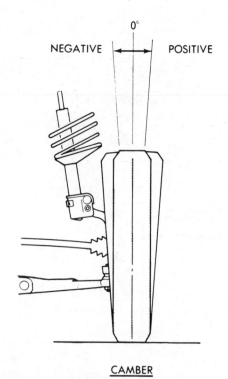

CAMBER

Front suspension camber

the upper knuckle leg out of the strut bracket and lift the knuckle from the ball joint stud.

WARNING: *Do not allow the driveshaft to hang during this procedure.*

14. Service procedures requiring hub removal also require that a new bearing be installed.

15. Installation is the reverse of removal. A new hub nut is required. When the car is resting in the wheels, with the brakes applied, tighten the hub nut to:

- 200 ft. lbs.: 1978 models
- 180 ft. lbs.: 1979 and later models

On 1978 models, stake the hub nut in place. 1979 and later models use a cotter pin and nutlock.

Wheel Alignment

Wheel alignment requires the use of fairly sophisticated equipment to accurately measure the geometry of the front end. The information is given here so that the owner will be aware of what is involved, not so that he can do the work himself.

Before the wheels are aligned, the following checks should be made, since these are factors that will influence the wheel alignment settings.

1. All tires should be of the same size and up to the recommended pressures.

2. Check the lower ball joints and steering linkage.

3. Check the struts for extremely stiff or spongy operation.

4. Check for broken or sagged springs.

5. The wheel alignment should be made with a full tank of gas, and no passenger or luggage compartment load.

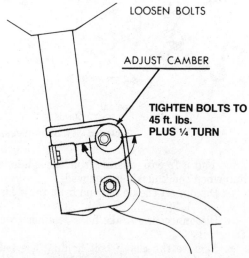

Camber adjusting location

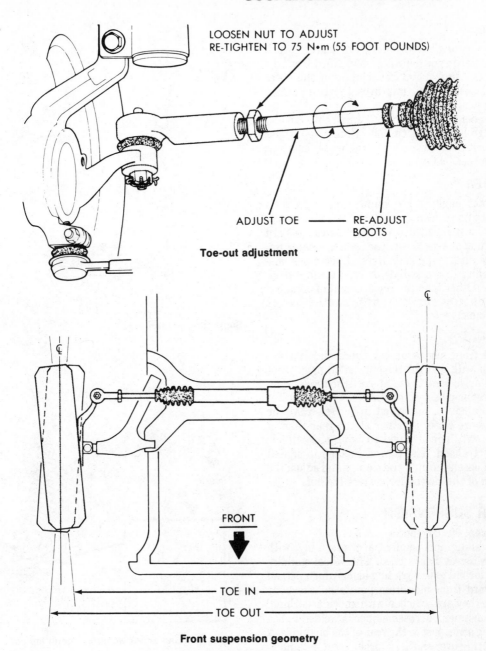

LOOSEN NUT TO ADJUST
RE-TIGHTEN TO 75 N•m (55 FOOT POUNDS)

ADJUST TOE — RE-ADJUST
BOOTS

Toe-out adjustment

FRONT

TOE IN

TOE OUT

Front suspension geometry

Wheel Alignment Specifications

(caster is not adjustable)

Year	Front Camber		Toe-Out (in.)		Rear Camber	
	Range (deg)	Preferred	Front	Rear	Range (deg)	Preferred
'78	¼N to ¾P	5⁄16P	⅛ out to 0	5⁄32 out to 1⁄32 in	1½N to ½N	1N
'79–'81	¼N to ¾P	5⁄16P	5⁄32 out to ⅛ in	5⁄32 out to 11⁄32 in	1½N to ½N	1N
'82–'89	¼N to ¾P	5⁄16P	7⁄32 in to ⅛ out	5⁄32 out to 11⁄32 in	1¼N to ¼N ①	½N

① Rampage/Scamp: 1⅛N to ⅛N

CAMBER

Camber angle is the number of degrees which the centerline of the wheel is inclined from the vertical. Camber reduces loading of the outer wheel bearing and improves the tire contact patch while cornering.

Camber is adjusted by loosening the cam and through-bolts on each side. Rotate the upper cam bolt to move the top of the wheel in or out to the specified camber.

CASTER

Caster angle is the number of degrees in which a line drawn through the steering knuckle pivots is inclined from the vertical, toward the front or rear of the car. Positive cater improves directional stability and decreases susceptibility to crosswinds or road surface deviations. Other than the replacement of damaged suspension components, caster is not adjustable.

TOE-OUT

The front wheels on the Omni and Horizon are set with a slight toe out, as on most front wheel drive cars, to counteract the tendency of the driving wheels to toe-in excessively. Toe out is the amount, measured in inches, that the wheels are closer together at the rear than at the front. Toe is checked with the wheels straight ahead. The tie-rod linkage is adjustable. Loosen the nuts and clamps and adjust the length of the tie-rod for correct toe out.

REAR SUSPENSION

All Except Pickup Models

A trailing, independent arm assembly, with integral sway bar is used. The wheel spindles are attached to two trailing arms which extend rearward from mounting points on the body where they are attached with shock absorbing, oval bushings. A crossmember is welded to the trailing arms, just to the rear of the bushings. A coil spring over shock absorber strut assembly, similar to the front suspension, is used.

Rampage and Scamp Pickup Models

The rear suspension on the Rampage and Scamp pickup models uses leaf springs mounted to a tubular axle. The conventional type rear shock absorbers are mounted on an angle, outboard at the bottom and inboard at the top. This design is used to provide greater side-to-side stability and weight carrying capacity in addition to controlling ride motion. The wheel spindles are attached to the axle assembly and supported by the leaf springs.

NOTE: *It is important that aftermarket load leveling devices are NOT installed on this*

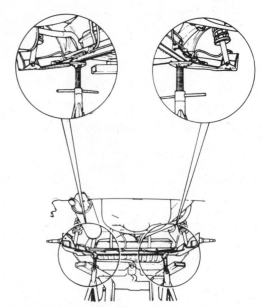

Supporting the rear axle

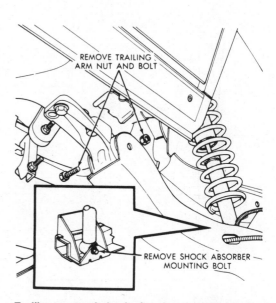

REMOVE TRAILING ARM NUT AND BOLT

REMOVE SHOCK ABSORBER MOUNTING BOLT

Trailing arm and shock absorber mounting bolts

suspension system. The installation of these devices will cause the rear brake height sensing proportioning valve to sense a light load condition that is actually a loaded condition being created by these add-on devices.

Shock Absorber

REMOVAL AND INSTALLATION

All Except Pickup Models

1. Remove the protective cap from the upper mounting nut.

2. Remove the upper mounting nut, isolator retainer and isolator.

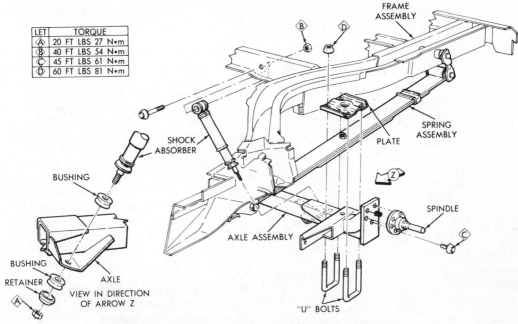

LET	TORQUE	
A	20 FT LBS	27 N•m
B	40 FT LBS	54 N•m
C	45 FT LBS	61 N•m
D	60 FT LBS	81 N•m

Rear shock absorber mounting—Rampage and Scamp models

3. Raise and support the vehicle.

4. Remove the lower strut mounting bolt.

5. Remove the strut and spring assembly.

6. Installation is the reverse of removal. Torque the lower mounting bolt to 40 ft. lbs.; the upper nut to 20 ft. lbs.

Rampage and Scamp Pickup Models

1. Raise and support the truck.

2. Remove the nuts and bolts securing the upper and lower ends of the shock absorber.

3. Remove the shock absorber and inspect the rubber eye and bushings. If these are defective, replace the shock absorber assembly.

4. Installation is the reverse of the removal.

Rear Spring

REMOVAL AND INSTALLATION

All Except Pickup Models

The use of a coil spring compressor, such as Chrysler part #L-4514, is necessary.

1. Remove the strut and spring assembly as described earlier.

2. Install the spring compressor on the spring and place it in a vise.

CAUTION: *Always grip 4 or 5 coils and never extend the retractors beyond 9¼" (235mm).*

3. Tighten the retractors evenly until pressure is removed from the upper spring seat.

4. Loosen the retaining nut.

CAUTION: *Be very careful when loosening the retaining nut. If the spring is not properly compressed, serious injury could result.*

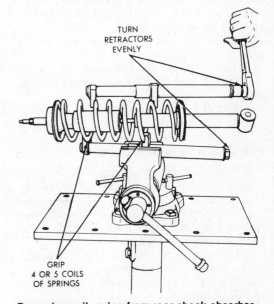

Removing coil spring from rear shock absorber

5. Remove the lower isolator, pushrod sleeve, and upper spring seat.

6. Carefully slip the strut from the spring.

7. Remove the rebound bumper and dust shield from the strut.

8. Remove the lower spring seat.

9. Carefully and evenly, remove the compressor from the spring.

10. Install the compressor on the spring, gripping four or five coils.

11. Compress the spring.

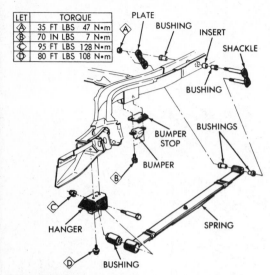

LET	TORQUE	
Ⓐ	35 FT LBS	47 N•m
Ⓑ	70 IN LBS	7 N•m
Ⓒ	95 FT LBS	128 N•m
Ⓓ	80 FT LBS	108 N•m

Rear leaf spring installation—Rampage and Scamp pickup models

12. Install the lower spring seat, dust shield and rebound bumper on the strut.

13. Slip the unit inside the coil spring and install the upper spring seat.

14. Make sure that the level surfaces on the seats are in position with the spring.

15. Install the sleeve on the pushrod and install the retaining nut. Torque the nut to 20 ft. lbs.

16. Install the lower isolator.

17. Install the strut and spring assembly.

Rampage and Scamp Pickup Models

1. Raise the vehicle and support the frame on jackstands while relieving the weight on the rear springs.

2. Disconnect the rear brake proportioning valve spring. Disconnect the lower ends of the shock absorbers at the axle brackets.

3. Loosen and remove the U-bolt nuts and remove the U-bolts and spring plates.

4. Lower the rear axle assembly, allowing the springs to hang free.

5. Loosen and remove the front pivot bolt from the front spring hanger.

6. Loosen and remove the rear spring shackle nuts and remove the shackles from the spring.

7. Installation is the reverse of the removal procedure, taking note of the tightening specifications shown in the illustration.

Rear Wheel Bearings

The rear wheel bearings should be inspected and relubricated whenever the rear brakes are serviced or at least every 30,000 miles. Repack the bearings with high temperature multi-purpose grease.

Check the lubricant to see if it is contaminated. If it contains dirt or has a milky appearance indicating the presence of water, the bearings should be cleaned and repacked.

Clean the bearings in kerosene, mineral spirits or other suitable cleaning fluid. Do not dry them by spinning the bearings. Allow them to air dry.

NOTE: *Sodium-based grease is not compatible with lithium-based grease. Read the package labels and be careful not to mix the two types. If there is any doubt as to the type of grease used, completely clean the old grease from the bearing and hub before replacing.*

Before handling the bearings, there are a few things that you should remember to do and not to do.

Remember to DO the following:
• Remove all outside dirt from the housing before exposing the bearing.

• Treat a used bearing as gently as you would a new one.

• Work with clean tools in clean surroundings.

• Use clean, dry canvas gloves, or at least clean, dry hands.

• Clean solvents and flushing fluids are a must.

• Use clean paper when laying out the bearings to dry.

• Protect disassembled bearings from rust and dirt. Cover them up.

• Use clean rags to wipe bearings.

• Keep the bearings in oil-proof paper when they are to be stored or are not in use.

• Clean the inside of the housing before replacing the bearing.

Do NOT do the following:
• Don't work in dirty surroundings.

• Don't use dirty, chipped or damaged tools.

• Try not to work on wooden work benches or use wooden mallets.

• Don't handle bearings with dirty or moist hands.

• Do not use gasoline for cleaning; use a safe solvent.

• Do not spin-dry bearings with compressed air. They will be damaged.

• Do not spin dirty bearings.

• Avoid using cotton waste or dirty cloths to wipe bearings.

• Try not to scratch or nick bearing surfaces.

• Do not allow the bearing to come in contact with dirt or rust at any time.

1. Raise and support the car with the rear wheels off the floor.

2. Remove the wheel grease cap, cotter pin, nut-lock and bearing adjusting nut.

3. Remove the thrust washer and bearing.

4. Remove the drum from the spindle.

5. Thoroughly clean the old lubricant from the bearings and hub cavity. Inspect the bearing rollers for pitting or other signs of wear. Light discoloration is normal.

6. Repack the bearings with high temperature multi-purpose EP grease and add a small amount of new grease to the hub cavity. Be sure to force the lubricant between all rollers in the bearing.

7. Install the drum on the spindle after coating the polished spindle surfaces with wheel bearing lubricant.

8. Install the outer bearing cone, thrust washer and adjusting nut.

9. Tighten the adjusting nut to 20-25 ft. lbs. while rotating the wheel.

10. Back off the adjusting nut to completely release the preload from the bearing.

11. Tighten the adjusting nut finger-tight.

12. Position the nut-lock with one pair of slots in line with the cotter pin hole. Install the cotter pin.

13. Clean and install the grease cap and wheel.

14. Lower the car.

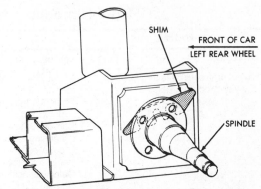

Shim installation for rear wheel positive camber

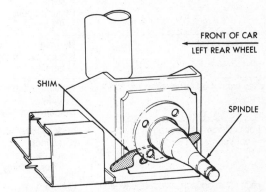

Shim installation for rear wheel negative camber

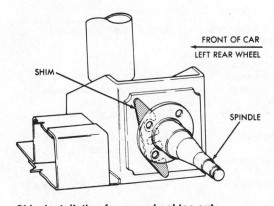

Shim installation for rear wheel toe-out

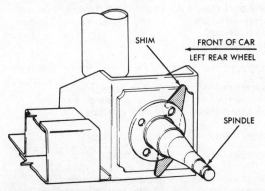

Shim installation for rear wheel toe-in

Rear Wheel Alignment

Due to the design of the rear suspension, it is possible to adjust both the camber and toe-in of the rear wheels. Alignment is controlled by inserting 0.25mm shim stock between the spindle mounting surface and the spindle mounting plate. Each 0.25mm shim stock changes wheel alignment by approximately 0° 18'. Be sure to adjust the rear wheel bearings.

STEERING

The manual steering system consists of a tube which contains the toothed rack, a pinion, the rack slipper, and the rack slipper spring. Steering effort is transmitted to the steering arms by the tie rods which are coupled to the ends of the rack, and the tie rod ends. The connection between the ends of the rack and the tie rod is protected by a bellows type oil seal which retains the gear lubricant.

The power steering system consists of four major parts: the power gear, power steering pump, pressure hose and the return hose. As with the manual system, the turning of the steering wheel is converted into linear travel

Troubleshooting the Steering Column

Problem	Cause	Solution
Will not lock	• Lockbolt spring broken or defective	• Replace lock bolt spring
High effort (required to turn ignition key and lock cylinder)	• Lock cylinder defective • Ignition switch defective • Rack preload spring broken or deformed • Burr on lock sector, lock rack, housing, support or remote rod coupling • Bent sector shaft • Defective lock rack • Remote rod bent, deformed • Ignition switch mounting bracket bent • Distorted coupling slot in lock rack (tilt column)	• Replace lock cylinder • Replace ignition switch • Replace preload spring • Remove burr • Replace shaft • Replace lock rack • Replace rod • Straighten or replace • Replace lock rack
Will stick in "start"	• Remote rod deformed • Ignition switch mounting bracket bent	• Straighten or replace • Straighten or replace
Key cannot be removed in "off-lock"	• Ignition switch is not adjusted correctly • Defective lock cylinder	• Adjust switch • Replace lock cylinder
Lock cylinder can be removed without depressing retainer	• Lock cylinder with defective retainer • Burr over retainer slot in housing cover or on cylinder retainer	• Replace lock cylinder • Remove burr
High effort on lock cylinder between "off" and "off-lock"	• Distorted lock rack • Burr on tang of shift gate (automatic column) • Gearshift linkage not adjusted	• Replace lock rack • Remove burr • Adjust linkage
Noise in column	• One click when in "off-lock" position and the steering wheel is moved (all except automatic column) • Coupling bolts not tightened • Lack of grease on bearings or bearing surfaces • Upper shaft bearing worn or broken • Lower shaft bearing worn or broken • Column not correctly aligned • Coupling pulled apart • Broken coupling lower joint • Steering shaft snap ring not seated • Shroud loose on shift bowl. Housing loose on jacket—will be noticed with ignition in "off-lock" and when torque is applied to steering wheel.	• Normal—lock bolt is seating • Tighten pinch bolts • Lubricate with chassis grease • Replace bearing assembly • Replace bearing. Check shaft and replace if scored. • Align column • Replace coupling • Repair or replace joint and align column • Replace ring. Check for proper seating in groove. • Position shroud over lugs on shift bowl. Tighten mounting screws.
High steering shaft effort	• Column misaligned • Defective upper or lower bearing • Tight steering shaft universal joint • Flash on I.D. of shift tube at plastic joint (tilt column only) • Upper or lower bearing seized	• Align column • Replace as required • Repair or replace • Replace shift tube • Replace bearings
Lash in mounted column assembly	• Column mounting bracket bolts loose • Broken weld nuts on column jacket • Column capsule bracket sheared	• Tighten bolts • Replace column jacket • Replace bracket assembly

Troubleshooting the Steering Column (cont.)

Problem	Cause	Solution
Lash in mounted column assembly (cont.)	• Column bracket to column jacket mounting bolts loose • Loose lock shoes in housing (tilt column only) • Loose pivot pins (tilt column only) • Loose lock shoe pin (tilt column only) • Loose support screws (tilt column only)	• Tighten to specified torque • Replace shoes • Replace pivot pins and support • Replace pin and housing • Tighten screws
Housing loose (tilt column only)	• Excessive clearance between holes in support or housing and pivot pin diameters • Housing support-screws loose	• Replace pivot pins and support • Tighten screws
Steering wheel loose—every other tilt position (tilt column only)	• Loose fit between lock shoe and lock shoe pivot pin	• Replace lock shoes and pivot pin
Steering column not locking in any tilt position (tilt column only)	• Lock shoe seized on pivot pin • Lock shoe grooves have burrs or are filled with foreign material • Lock shoe springs weak or broken	• Replace lock shoes and pin • Clean or replace lock shoes • Replace springs
Noise when tilting column (tilt column only)	• Upper tilt bumpers worn • Tilt spring rubbing in housing	• Replace tilt bumper • Lubricate with chassis grease
One click when in "off-lock" position and the steering wheel is moved	• Seating of lock bolt	• None. Click is normal characteristic sound produced by lock bolt as it seats.
High shift effort (automatic and tilt column only)	• Column not correctly aligned • Lower bearing not aligned correctly • Lack of grease on seal or lower bearing areas	• Align column • Assemble correctly • Lubricate with chassis grease
Improper transmission shifting—automatic and tilt column only	• Sheared shift tube joint • Improper transmission gearshift linkage adjustment • Loose lower shift lever	• Replace shift tube • Adjust linkage • Replace shift tube

Troubleshooting the Ignition Switch

Problem	Cause	Solution
Ignition switch electrically inoperative	• Loose or defective switch connector • Feed wire open (fusible link) • Defective ignition switch	• Tighten or replace connector • Repair or replace • Replace ignition switch
Engine will not crank	• Ignition switch not adjusted properly	• Adjust switch
Ignition switch wil not actuate mechanically	• Defective ignition switch • Defective lock sector • Defective remote rod	• Replace switch • Replace lock sector • Replace remote rod
Ignition switch cannot be adjusted correctly	• Remote rod deformed	• Repair, straighten or replace

Troubleshooting the Turn Signal Switch

Problem	Cause	Solution
Turn signal will not cancel	• Loose switch mounting screws • Switch or anchor bosses broken • Broken, missing or out of position detent, or cancelling spring	• Tighten screws • Replace switch • Reposition springs or replace switch as required
Turn signal difficult to operate	• Turn signal lever loose • Switch yoke broken or distorted • Loose or misplaced springs • Foreign parts and/or materials in switch • Switch mounted loosely	• Tighten mounting screws • Replace switch • Reposition springs or replace switch • Remove foreign parts and/or material • Tighten mounting screws
Turn signal will not indicate lane change	• Broken lane change pressure pad or spring hanger • Broken, missing or misplaced lane change spring • Jammed wires	• Replace switch • Replace or reposition as required • Loosen mounting screws, reposition wires and retighten screws
Turn signal will not stay in turn position	• Foreign material or loose parts impeding movement of switch yoke • Defective switch	• Remove material and/or parts • Replace switch
Hazard switch cannot be pulled out	• Foreign material between hazard support cancelling leg and yoke	• Remove foreign material. No foreign material impeding function of hazard switch—replace turn signal switch.
No turn signal lights	• Inoperative turn signal flasher • Defective or blown fuse • Loose chassis to column harness connector • Disconnect column to chassis connector. Connect new switch to chassis and operate switch by hand. If vehicle lights now operate normally, signal switch is inoperative • If vehicle lights do not operate, check chassis wiring for opens, grounds, etc.	• Replace turn signal flasher • Replace fuse • Connect securely • Replace signal switch • Repair chassis wiring as required
Instrument panel turn indicator lights on but not flashing	• Burned out or damaged front or rear turn signal bulb • If vehicle lights do not operate, check light sockets for high resistance connections, the chassis wiring for opens, grounds, etc. • Inoperative flasher • Loose chassis to column harness connection • Inoperative turn signal switch • To determine if turn signal switch is defective, substitute new switch into circuit and operate switch by hand. If the vehicle's lights operate normally, signal switch is inoperative.	• Replace bulb • Repair chassis wiring as required • Replace flasher • Connect securely • Replace turn signal switch • Replace turn signal switch
Stop light not on when turn indicated	• Loose column to chassis connection • Disconnect column to chassis connector. Connect new switch into system without removing old.	• Connect securely • Replace signal switch

Troubleshooting the Turn Signal Switch (cont.)

Problem	Cause	Solution
Stop light not on when turn indicated (cont.)	Operate switch by hand. If brake lights work with switch in the turn position, signal switch is defective.	
	• If brake lights do not work, check connector to stop light sockets for grounds, opens, etc.	• Repair connector to stop light circuits using service manual as guide
Turn indicator panel lights not flashing	• Burned out bulbs • High resistance to ground at bulb socket • Opens, ground in wiring harness from front turn signal bulb socket to indicator lights	• Replace bulbs • Replace socket • Locate and repair as required
Turn signal lights flash very slowly	• High resistance ground at light sockets • Incorrect capacity turn signal flasher or bulb • If flashing rate is still extremely slow, check chassis wiring harness from the connector to light sockets for high resistance • Loose chassis to column harness connection • Disconnect column to chassis connector. Connect new switch into system without removing old. Operate switch by hand. If flashing occurs at normal rate, the signal switch is defective.	• Repair high resistance grounds at light sockets • Replace turn signal flasher or bulb • Locate and repair as required • Connect securely • Replace turn signal switch
Hazard signal lights will not flash— turn signal functions normally	• Blow fuse • Inoperative hazard warning flasher • Loose chassis-to-column harness connection • Disconnect column to chassis connector. Connect new switch into system without removing old. Depress the hazard warning lights. If they now work normally, turn signal switch is defective. • If lights do not flash, check wiring harness "K" lead for open between hazard flasher and connector. If open, fuse block is defective	• Replace fuse • Replace hazard warning flasher in fuse panel • Conect securely • Replace turn signal switch • Repair or replace brown wire or connector as required

Troubleshooting the Manual Steering Gear

Problem	Cause	Solution
Hard or erratic steering	• Incorrect tire pressure • Insufficient or incorrect lubrication • Suspension, or steering linkage parts damaged or misaligned • Improper front wheel alignment • Incorrect steering gear adjustment • Sagging springs	• Inflate tires to recommended pressures • Lubricate as required (refer to Maintenance Section) • Repair or replace parts as necessary • Adjust incorrect wheel alignment angles • Adjust steering gear • Replace springs

Troubleshooting the Manual Steering Gear (cont.)

Problem	Cause	Solution
Play or looseness in steering	• Steering wheel loose	• Inspect shaft spines and repair as necessary. Tighten attaching nut and stake in place.
	• Steering linkage or attaching parts loose or worn	• Tighten, adjust, or replace faulty components
	• Pitman arm loose	• Inspect shaft splines and repair as necessary. Tighten attaching nut and stake in place
	• Steering gear attaching bolts loose	• Tighten bolts
	• Loose or worn wheel bearings	• Adjust or replace bearings
	• Steering gear adjustment incorrect or parts badly worn	• Adjust gear or replace defective parts
Wheel shimmy or tramp	• Improper tire pressure	• Inflate tires to recommended pressures
	• Wheels, tires, or brake rotors out-of-balance or out-of-round	• Inspect and replace or balance parts
	• Inoperative, worn, or loose shock absorbers or mounting parts	• Repair or replace shocks or mountings
	• Loose or worn steering or suspension parts	• Tighten or replace as necessary
	• Loose or worn wheel bearings	• Adjust or replace bearings
	• Incorrect steering gear adjustments	• Adjust steering gear
	• Incorrect front wheel alignment	• Correct front wheel alignment
Tire wear	• Improper tire pressure	• Inflate tires to recommended pressures
	• Failure to rotate tires	• Rotate tires
	• Brakes grabbing	• Adjust or repair brakes
	• Incorrect front wheel alignment	• Align incorrect angles
	• Broken or damaged steering and suspension parts	• Repair or replace defective parts
	• Wheel runout	• Replace faulty wheel
	• Excessive speed on turns	• Make driver aware of conditions
Vehicle leads to one side	• Improper tire pressures	• Inflate tires to recommended pressures
	• Front tires with uneven tread depth, wear pattern, or different cord design (i.e., one bias ply and one belted or radial tire on front wheels)	• Install tires of same cord construction and reasonably even tread depth, design, and wear pattern
	• Incorrect front wheel alignment	• Align incorrect angles
	• Brakes dragging	• Adjust or repair brakes
	• Pulling due to uneven tire construction	• Replace faulty tire

through the meshing of the helical pinion teeth with the rack teeth. Power assist is provided by an open center, rotary type, three-way control valve which directs fluid to either side of the rack control piston.

Steering Wheel
REMOVAL AND INSTALLATION

1. Remove the horn button and horn switch.
2. Remove the steering wheel nut.
3. Using a steering wheel puller, remove the steering wheel.
4. Align the master serration in the wheel hub with the missing tooth on the shaft. Torque the shaft nut to 60 ft. lbs.

WARNING: *Do not torque the nut against the steering column lock or damage will occur.*

5. Replace the horn switch and button.

Turn Signal Switch
REMOVAL AND INSTALLATION

1. Disconnect the electrical connector at column.
2. Remove the steering wheel as described earlier.

Troubleshooting the Power Steering Gear

Problem	Cause	Solution
Hissing noise in steering gear	• There is some noise in all power steering systems. One of the most common is a hissing sound most evident at standstill parking. There is no relationship between this noise and performance of the steering. Hiss may be expected when steering wheel is at end of travel or when slowly turning at standstill.	• Slight hiss is normal and in no way affects steering. Do not replace valve unless hiss is extremely objectionable. A replacement valve will also exhibit slight noise and is not always a cure. Investigate clearance around flexible coupling rivets. Be sure steering shaft and gear are aligned so flexible coupling rotates in a flat plane and is not distorted as shaft rotates. Any metal-to-metal contacts through flexible coupling will transmit valve hiss into passenger compartment through the steering column.
Rattle or chuckle noise in steering gear	• Gear loose on frame	• Check gear-to-frame mounting screws. Tighten screws to 88 N·m (65 foot pounds) torque.
	• Steering linkage looseness	• Check linkage pivot points for wear. Replace if necessary.
	• Pressure hose touching other parts of car	• Adjust hose position. Do not bend tubing by hand.
	• Loose pitman shaft over center adjustment **NOTE:** A slight rattle may occur on turns because of increased clearance off the "high point." This is normal and clearance must not be reduced below specified limits to eliminate this slight rattle.	• Adjust to specifications
	• Loose pitman arm	• Tighten pitman arm nut to specifications
Squawk noise in steering gear when turning or recovering from a turn	• Damper O-ring on valve spool cut	• Replace damper O-ring
Poor return of steering wheel to center	• Tires not properly inflated	• Inflate to specified pressure
	• Lack of lubrication in linkage and ball joints	• Lube linkage and ball joints
	• Lower coupling flange rubbing against steering gear adjuster plug	• Loosen pinch bolt and assemble properly
	• Steering gear to column misalignment	• Align steering column
	• Improper front wheel alignment	• Check and adjust as necessary
	• Steering linkage binding	• Replace pivots
	• Ball joints binding	• Replace ball joints
	• Steering wheel rubbing against housing	• Align housing
	• Tight or frozen steering shaft bearings	• Replace bearings
	• Sticking or plugged valve spool	• Remove and clean or replace valve
	• Steering gear adjustments over specifications	• Check adjustment with gear out of car. Adjust as required.
	• Kink in return hose	• Replace hose
Car leads to one side or the other (keep in mind road condition and wind. Test car in both directions on flat road)	• Front end misaligned	• Adjust to specifications
	• Unbalanced steering gear valve **NOTE:** If this is cause, steering effort will be very light in direction of lead and normal or heavier in opposite direction	• Replace valve

Troubleshooting the Power Steering Gear (cont.)

Problem	Cause	Solution
Momentary increase in effort when turning wheel fast to right or left	• Low oil level • Pump belt slipping • High internal leakage	• Add power steering fluid as required • Tighten or replace belt • Check pump pressure. (See pressure test)
Steering wheel surges or jerks when turning with engine running especially during parking	• Low oil level • Loose pump belt • Steering linkage hitting engine oil pan at full turn • Insufficient pump pressure • Pump flow control valve sticking	• Fill as required • Adjust tension to specification • Correct clearance • Check pump pressure. (See pressure test). Replace relief valve if defective. • Inspect for varnish or damage, replace if necessary
Excessive wheel kickback or loose steering	• Air in system • Steering gear loose on frame • Steering linkage joints worn enough to be loose • Worn poppet valve • Loose thrust bearing preload adjustment • Excessive overcenter lash	• Add oil to pump reservoir and bleed by operating steering. Check hose connectors for proper torque and adjust as required. • Tighten attaching screws to specified torque • Replace loose pivots • Replace poppet valve • Adjust to specification with gear out of vehicle • Adjust to specification with gear out of car
Hard steering or lack of assist	• Loose pump belt • Low oil level **NOTE:** Low oil level will also result in excessive pump noise • Steering gear to column misalignment • Lower coupling flange rubbing against steering gear adjuster plug • Tires not properly inflated	• Adjust belt tension to specification • Fill to proper level. If excessively low, check all lines and joints for evidence of external leakage. Tighten loose connectors. • Align steering column • Loosen pinch bolt and assemble properly • Inflate to recommended pressure
Foamy milky power steering fluid, low fluid level and possible low pressure	• Air in the fluid, and loss of fluid due to internal pump leakage causing overflow	• Check for leak and correct. Bleed system. Extremely cold temperatures will cause system aeriation should the oil level be low. If oil level is correct and pump still foams, remove pump from vehicle and separate reservoir from housing. Check welsh plug and housing for cracks. If plug is loose or housing is cracked, replace housing.
Low pressure due to steering pump	• Flow control valve stuck or inoperative • Pressure plate not flat against cam ring	• Remove burrs or dirt or replace. Flush system. • Correct
Low pressure due to steering gear	• Pressure loss in cylinder due to worn piston ring or badly worn housing bore • Leakage at valve rings, valve body-to-worm seal	• Remove gear from car for disassembly and inspection of ring and housing bore • Remove gear from car for disassembly and replace seals

Troubleshooting the Power Steering Pump

Problem	Cause	Solution
Chirp noise in steering pump	• Loose belt	• Adjust belt tension to specification
Belt squeal (particularly noticeable at full wheel travel and stand still parking)	• Loose belt	• Adjust belt tension to specification
Growl noise in steering pump	• Excessive back pressure in hoses or steering gear caused by restriction	• Locate restriction and correct. Replace part if necessary.
Growl noise in steering pump (particularly noticeable at stand still parking)	• Scored pressure plates, thrust plate or rotor • Extreme wear of cam ring	• Replace parts and flush system • Replace parts
Groan noise in steering pump	• Low oil level • Air in the oil. Poor pressure hose connection.	• Fill reservoir to proper level • Tighten connector to specified torque. Bleed system by operating steering from right to left—full turn.
Rattle noise in steering pump	• Vanes not installed properly • Vanes sticking in rotor slots	• Install properly • Free up by removing burrs, varnish, or dirt
Swish noise in steering pump	• Defective flow control valve	• Replace part
Whine noise in steering pump	• Pump shaft bearing scored	• Replace housing and shaft. Flush system.
Hard steering or lack of assist	• Loose pump belt • Low oil level in reservoir **NOTE:** Low oil level will also result in excessive pump noise • Steering gear to column misalignment • Lower coupling flange rubbing against steering gear adjuster plug • Tires not properly inflated	• Adjust belt tension to specification • Fill to proper level. If excessively low, check all lines and joints for evidence of external leakage. Tighten loose connectors. • Align steering column • Loosen pinch bolt and assemble properly • Inflate to recommended pressure
Foaming milky power steering fluid, low fluid level and possible low pressure	• Air in the fluid, and loss of fluid due to internal pump leakage causing overflow	• Check for leaks and correct. Bleed system. Extremely cold temperatures will cause system aeriation should the oil level be low. If oil level is correct and pump still foams, remove pump from vehicle and separate reservoir from body. Check welsh plug and body for cracks. If plug is loose or body is cracked, replace body.
Low pump pressure	• Flow control valve stuck or inoperative • Pressure plate not flat against cam ring	• Remove burrs or dirt or replace. Flush system. • Correct
Momentary increase in effort when turning wheel fast to right or left	• Low oil level in pump • Pump belt slipping • High internal leakage	• Add power steering fluid as required • Tighten or replace belt • Check pump pressure. (See pressure test)
Steering wheel surges or jerks when turning with engine running especially during parking	• Low oil level • Loose pump belt • Steering linkage hitting engine oil pan at full turn • Insufficient pump pressure	• Fill as required • Adjust tension to specification • Correct clearance • Check pump pressure. (See pressure test). Replace flow control valve if defective.

Troubleshooting the Power Steering Pump (cont.)

Problem	Cause	Solution
Steering wheel surges or jerks when turning with engine running especially during parking (cont.)	• Sticking flow control valve	• Inspect for varnish or damage, replace if necessary
Excessive wheel kickback or loose steering	• Air in system	• Add oil to pump reservoir and bleed by operating steering. Check hose connectors for proper torque and adjust as required.
Low pump pressure	• Extreme wear of cam ring • Scored pressure plate, thrust plate, or rotor • Vanes not installed properly • Vanes sticking in rotor slots • Cracked or broken thrust or pressure plate	• Replace parts. Flush system. • Replace parts. Flush system. • Install properly • Freeup by removing burrs, varnish, or dirt • Replace part

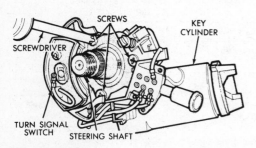

Turn signal switch

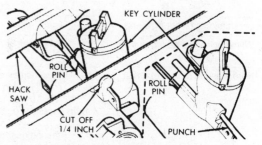

Remove the roll pin in key cylinder

3. Remove the lower column cover.
4. Remove the wash/wipe switch.
5. Remove the wiring clip and the three screws securing the turn signal switch.
6. Installation is the reverse of removal.

Ignition and Steering Lock
REMOVAL AND INSTALLATION

1. Remove the steering wheel.
2. Remove the upper and lower column covers.
3. Using a hacksaw blade, cut the upper ¼" from the key cylinder retainer pin boss.
4. Using a drift, drive the roll pin from the housing and remove the key cylinder.
5. Insert the new cylinder into the housing, making sure that it engages the lug on the ignition switch driver. Install the roll pin.

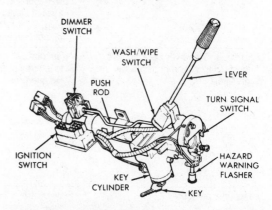

Steering column switch components

Ignition Switch
REMOVAL AND INSTALLATION

1. Remove the connector from the switch.
2. Place the key in the LOCK position.
3. Remove the key.

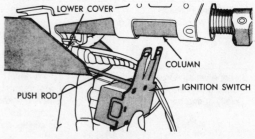

Ignition switch removal

4. Remove the two mounting screws from the switch and pushrod to drop below the jacket.

5. Rotate the switch 90 degrees to permit removal of the switch from the pushrod.

6. To install the switch, position the switch in LOCK (second detent from the top).

7. Place the switch at right angles to the column and insert the pushrod.

8. Align the switch on the bracket and install the screws.

9. With a light rearward load on the switch, tighten the screws. Check for proper operation.

Tie Rod End
REPLACEMENT

1. Loosen the jam nut which connects the tie rod end to the knuckle. mark the tie rod position on the threads.

2. Using a ball joint separator, remove the tie rod end from the knuckle.

3. Install a new tie rod end in reverse of removal. Torque the end nut to 50 ft. lbs.; the locknut to 65 ft. lbs.

4. Check alignment.

Power Steering Pump
REMOVAL AND INSTALLATION

1. Disconnect the power steering hoses from the pump.

2. Remove the adjusting bolt and slip off the belt.

3. Support the pump, remove the mounting bolts and lift out the pump.

4. Installation is the reverse of removal. Adjust the belt to specifications. See Chapter 1.

Manual and Power Steering Gear
REMOVAL AND INSTALLATION

NOTE: *An assistant will be needed to perform this procedure.*

1. Loosen the wheel nuts. Raise the vehicle and support it securely by the body.

2. Detach the tie rod ends at the steering knuckles as described above.

3. Support the lower front suspension cross-

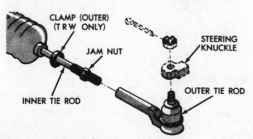

Tie rod end replacement

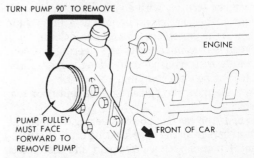

Power steering pump removal and installation—1.7L and 2.2L engines

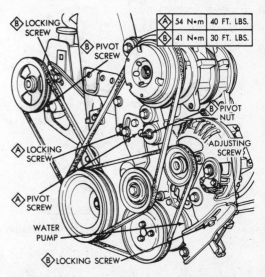

Power steering pump mounting—1.6L engine

Power steering pump mounting—1.7L and 2.2L engines

member securely with a jack. Then, remove all four suspension crossmember attaching bolts. Lower the crossmember with the jack until it is possible to gain access to the steering gear and the lower steering column. Slide the gear off the steering column coupling.

4. Remove the splash shields and boot seal shields.

5. If the car has power steering, remove the fasteners from the hose locating bracket attachment points. Get a drain pan and disconnect both hoses at the opening nearest the steering gear and drain them into the pan. Discard the O-rings.

6. Remove the bolts attaching the power steering unit to the crossmember.

7. Remove the steering gear from the crossmember by pulling it off the steering column coupling and then removing it.

8. To install, first bolt the steering gear to the crossmember, torquing them to 250 in. lbs.

9. Raise the crossmember into position with the jack, lining up the steering column coupling and the corresponding fitting on the end of the steering rack pinion shaft. Have an assistant in-side the car help to position the column. If the car has manual steering, make sure the master serrations are lined up. Then, maneuver the crossmember/rack assembly so as to engage the column coupling and pinion shaft.

10. Position the crossmember so the boltholes will line up. Install the bolts, but do not tighten them—merely start the threads. Tighten the right rear bolt, which serves as a pilot bolt to properly located the crossmember. Then, torque all four bolts to 90 ft. lbs.

11. Reconnect the tie rod ends, as described above.

12. Wipe the ends of the power steering pump hoses and the ports in the steering gear. Install new O-rings on the hose tube ends and coat them with power steering fluid. Then, route the hose carefully in all clips and in such a way as to avoid kinks or close proximity to any exhaust system parts.

13. Make the hose connections and torque them to 25 ft. lbs. Refill the power steering pump with approved fluid.

14. Adjust toe in. Bleed the power steering system. Run the engine and check for leaks.

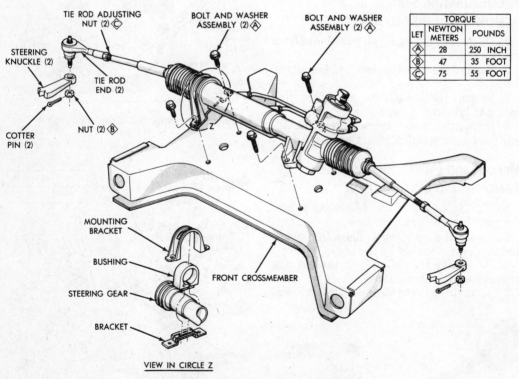

TORQUE		
LET	NEWTON METERS	POUNDS
A	28	250 INCH
B	47	35 FOOT
C	75	55 FOOT

Steering gear assembly—all models similar

BRAKE SYSTEMS

Hydraulic System
BASIC OPERATING PRINCIPLES
Except Anti-Lock Braking System

Hydraulic systems are used to actuate the brakes of all modern automobiles. The system transports the power required to force the frictional surfaces of the braking system together from the pedal to the individual brake units at each wheel. A hydraulic system is used for two reasons. First, fluid under pressure can be carried to all parts of an automobile by small hoses-some of which are flexible-without taking up a significant amount of room or posing routing problems. Second, a great mechanical advantage can be given to the brake pedal end of the system, and the foot pressure required to actuate the brakes can be reduced by making the surface area of the master cylinder pistons smaller than that of any of the pistons in the wheel cylinders or calipers.

The master cylinder consists of a fluid reservoir and either a single or double cylinder and piston assembly. Double type master cylinders are designed to separate the front and rear braking systems hydraulically in case of a leak.

Steel lines carry the brake fluid to a point on the vehicle's frame near each of the vehicle's wheels. The fluid is then carried to the wheel cylinders by flexible tubes in order to allow for suspension and steering movements.

Each wheel cylinder contains two pistons, one at either end, which push outward in opposite directions. In disc brake systems, the cylinders are part of the calipers. One or four cylinders are used to force the brake pads against the disc, but all cylinders contain one piston only. All pistons employ some type of seal, usually made of rubber, to minimize fluid leakage.

A rubber dust boot seals the outer end of the cylinder against dust and dirt. The boot fits around the outer end of the piston on disc brake calipers, and around the brake actuating rod on wheel cylinders.

The hydraulic system operates as follows: When at rest, the entire system, from the piston(s) in the master cylinder to those in the wheel cylinders or calipers, is full of brake fluid. Upon application of the brake pedal, fluid trapped in front of the master cylinder piston(s) is forced through the lines to the wheel cylinders. Here, it forces the pistons outward, in the case of drum brakes, and inward toward the disc, in the case of disc brakes. The motion of the pistons is opposed by return springs mounted outside the cylinders in drum brakes, and by internal springs or spring seals, in disc brakes.

Upon release of the brake pedal, a spring located inside the master cylinder immediately returns the master cylinder pistons to the normal position. The pistons contain check valves and the master cylinder has compensating ports drilled in it. These are uncovered as the pistons reach their normal position. The piston check valves allow fluid to flow toward the wheel cylinders or calipers as the pistons withdraw. Then, as the return springs force the brake pads or shoes into the released position, the excess fluid reservoir through the compensating ports. It is during the time the pedal is in the released position that any fluid that has leaked out of the system will be replaced through the compensating ports.

Dual circuit master cylinders employ two pistons, located one behind the other, in the same cylinder. The primary piston is actuated directly by mechanical linkage from the brake pedal. The secondary piston is actuated by fluid trapped between the two pistons. If a leak develops in front of the secondary piston, it moves forward until it bottoms against the front of the master cylinder, and the fluid trapped between

Troubleshooting the Brake System

Problem	Cause	Solution
Low brake pedal (excessive pedal travel required for braking action.)	• Excessive clearance between rear linings and drums caused by inoperative automatic adjusters	• Make 10 to 15 alternate forward and reverse brake stops to adjust brakes. If brake pedal does not come up, repair or replace adjuster parts as necessary.
	• Worn rear brakelining	• Inspect and replace lining if worn beyond minimum thickness specification
	• Bent, distorted brakeshoes, front or rear	• Replace brakeshoes in axle sets
	• Air in hydraulic system	• Remove air from system. Refer to Brake Bleeding.
Low brake pedal (pedal may go to floor with steady pressure applied.)	• Fluid leak in hydraulic system	• Fill master cylinder to fill line; have helper apply brakes and check calipers, wheel cylinders, differential valve tubes, hoses and fittings for leaks. Repair or replace as necessary.
	• Air in hydraulic system	• Remove air from system. Refer to Brake Bleeding.
	• Incorrect or non-recommended brake fluid (fluid evaporates at below normal temp).	• Flush hydraulic system with clean brake fluid. Refill with correct-type fluid.
	• Master cylinder piston seals worn, or master cylinder bore is scored, worn or corroded	• Repair or replace master cylinder
Low brake pedal (pedal goes to floor on first application—o.k. on subsequent applications.)	• Disc brake pads sticking on abutment surfaces of anchor plate. Caused by a build-up of dirt, rust, or corrosion on abutment surfaces	• Clean abutment surfaces
Fading brake pedal (pedal height decreases with steady pressure applied.)	• Fluid leak in hydraulic system	• Fill master cylinder reservoirs to fill mark, have helper apply brakes, check calipers, wheel cylinders, differential valve, tubes, hoses, and fittings for fluid leaks. Repair or replace parts as necessary.
	• Master cylinder piston seals worn, or master cylinder bore is scored, worn or corroded	• Repair or replace master cylinder
Decreasing brake pedal travel (pedal travel required for braking action decreases and may be accompanied by a hard pedal.)	• Caliper or wheel cylinder pistons sticking or seized	• Repair or replace the calipers, or wheel cylinders
	• Master cylinder compensator ports blocked (preventing fluid return to reservoirs) or pistons sticking or seized in master cylinder bore	• Repair or replace the master cylinder
	• Power brake unit binding internally	• Test unit according to the following procedure: (a) Shift transmission into neutral and start engine (b) Increase engine speed to 1500 rpm, close throttle and fully depress brake pedal (c) Slow release brake pedal and stop engine (d) Have helper remove vacuum check valve and hose from power unit. Observe for backward movement of brake pedal. (e) If the pedal moves backward, the power unit has an internal bind—replace power unit

Troubleshooting the Brake System (cont.)

Problem	Cause	Solution
Spongy brake pedal (pedal has abnormally soft, springy, spongy feel when depressed.)	• Air in hydraulic system	• Remove air from system. Refer to Brake Bleeding.
	• Brakeshoes bent or distorted	• Replace brakeshoes
	• Brakelining not yet seated with drums and rotors	• Burnish brakes
	• Rear drum brakes not properly adjusted	• Adjust brakes
Hard brake pedal (excessive pedal pressure required to stop vehicle. May be accompanied by brake fade.)	• Loose or leaking power brake unit vacuum hose	• Tighten connections or replace leaking hose
	• Incorrect or poor quality brakelining	• Replace with lining in axle sets
	• Bent, broken, distorted brakeshoes	• Replace brakeshoes
	• Calipers binding or dragging on mounting pins. Rear brakeshoes dragging on support plate.	• Replace mounting pins and bushings. Clean rust or burrs from rear brake support plate ledges and lubricate ledges with molydisulfide grease. **NOTE:** If ledges are deeply grooved or scored, do not attempt to sand or grind them smooth—replace support plate.
	• Caliper, wheel cylinder, or master cylinder pistons sticking or seized	• Repair or replace parts as necessary
	• Power brake unit vacuum check valve malfunction	• Test valve according to the following procedure: (a) Start engine, increase engine speed to 1500 rpm, close throttle and immediately stop engine (b) Wait at least 90 seconds then depress brake pedal (c) If brakes are not vacuum assisted for 2 or more applications, check valve is faulty
	• Power brake unit has internal bind	• Test unit according to the following procedure: (a) With engine stopped, apply brakes several times to exhaust all vacuum in system (b) Shift transmission into neutral, depress brake pedal and start engine (c) If pedal height decreases with foot pressure and less pressure is required to hold pedal in applied position, power unit vacuum system is operating normally. Test power unit. If power unit exhibits a bind condition, replace the power unit.
	• Master cylinder compensator ports (at bottom of reservoirs) blocked by dirt, scale, rust, or have small burrs (blocked ports prevent fluid return to reservoirs).	• Repair or replace master cylinder **CAUTION:** Do not attempt to clean blocked ports with wire, pencils, or similar implements. Use compressed air only.
	• Brake hoses, tubes, fittings clogged or restricted	• Use compressed air to check or unclog parts. Replace any damaged parts.
	• Brake fluid contaminated with improper fluids (motor oil, transmission fluid, causing rubber components to swell and stick in bores	• Replace all rubber components, combination valve and hoses. Flush entire brake system with DOT 3 brake fluid or equivalent.
	• Low engine vacuum	• Adjust or repair engine

Troubleshooting the Brake System (cont.)

Problem	Cause	Solution
Grabbing brakes (severe reaction to brake pedal pressure.)	• Brakelining(s) contaminated by grease or brake fluid	• Determine and correct cause of contamination and replace brakeshoes in axle sets
	• Parking brake cables incorrectly adjusted or seized	• Adjust cables. Replace seized cables.
	• Incorrect brakelining or lining loose on brakeshoes	• Replace brakeshoes in axle sets
	• Caliper anchor plate bolts loose	• Tighten bolts
	• Rear brakeshoes binding on support plate ledges	• Clean and lubricate ledges. Replace support plate(s) if ledges are deeply grooved. Do not attempt to smooth ledges by grinding.
	• Incorrect or missing power brake reaction disc	• Install correct disc
	• Rear brake support plates loose	• Tighten mounting bolts
Dragging brakes (slow or incomplete release of brakes)	• Brake pedal binding at pivot	• Loosen and lubricate
	• Power brake unit has internal bind	• Inspect for internal bind. Replace unit if internal bind exists.
	• Parking brake cables incorrrectly adjusted or seized	• Adjust cables. Replace seized cables.
	• Rear brakeshoe return springs weak or broken	• Replace return springs. Replace brakeshoe if necessary in axle sets.
	• Automatic adjusters malfunctioning	• Repair or replace adjuster parts as required
	• Caliper, wheel cylinder or master cylinder pistons sticking or seized	• Repair or replace parts as necessary
	• Master cylinder compensating ports blocked (fluid does not return to reservoirs).	• Use compressed air to clear ports. Do not use wire, pencils, or similar objects to open blocked ports.
Vehicle moves to one side when brakes are applied	• Incorrect front tire pressure	• Inflate to recommended cold (reduced load) inflation pressure
	• Worn or damaged wheel bearings	• Replace worn or damaged bearings
	• Brakelining on one side contaminated	• Determine and correct cause of contamination and replace brakelining in axle sets
	• Brakeshoes on one side bent, distorted, or lining loose on shoe	• Replace brakeshoes in axle sets
	• Support plate bent or loose on one side	• Tighten or replace support plate
	• Brakelining not yet seated with drums or rotors	• Burnish brakelining
	• Caliper anchor plate loose on one side	• Tighten anchor plate bolts
	• Caliper piston sticking or seized	• Repair or replace caliper
	• Brakelinings water soaked	• Drive vehicle with brakes lightly applied to dry linings
	• Loose suspension component attaching or mounting bolts	• Tighten suspension bolts. Replace worn suspension components.
	• Brake combination valve failure	• Replace combination valve
Chatter or shudder when brakes are applied (pedal pulsation and roughness may also occur.)	• Brakeshoes distorted, bent, contaminated, or worn	• Replace brakeshoes in axle sets
	• Caliper anchor plate or support plate loose	• Tighten mounting bolts
	• Excessive thickness variation of rotor(s)	• Refinish or replace rotors in axle sets
Noisy brakes (squealing, clicking, scraping sound when brakes are applied.)	• Bent, broken, distorted brakeshoes	• Replace brakeshoes in axle sets
	• Excessive rust on outer edge of rotor braking surface	• Remove rust

Troubleshooting the Brake System (cont.)

Problem	Cause	Solution
Noisy brakes (squealing, clicking, scraping sound when brakes are applied.) (cont.)	• Brakelining worn out—shoes contacting drum of rotor	• Replace brakeshoes and lining in axle sets. Refinish or replace drums or rotors.
	• Broken or loose holdown or return springs	• Replace parts as necessary
	• Rough or dry drum brake support plate ledges	• Lubricate support plate ledges
	• Cracked, grooved, or scored rotor(s) or drum(s)	• Replace rotor(s) or drum(s). Replace brakeshoes and lining in axle sets if necessary.
	• Incorrect brakelining and/or shoes (front or rear).	• Install specified shoe and lining assemblies
Pulsating brake pedal	• Out of round drums or excessive lateral runout in disc brake rotor(s)	• Refinish or replace drums, re-index rotors or replace

the pistons will operate the rear brakes. If the rear brakes develop a leak, the primary piston will move forward until direct contact with the secondary piston takes place, and it will force the secondary piston to actuate the front brakes. In either case, the brake pedal moves farther when the brakes are applied, and less braking power is available.

All dual-circuit systems use a switch to warn the driver when only half of the brake system is operational. This switch is located in a valve body which is mounted on the firewall or the frame below the master cylinder. A hydraulic piston receives pressure from both circuits, each circuit's pressure being applied to one end of the piston. When the pressures are in balance, the piston remains stationary. When one circuit has a leak, however, the greater pressure in that circuit during application of the brakes will push the piston to one side, closing the switch and activating the brake warning light.

In disc brake systems, this valve body also contains a metering valve and, in some cases, a proportioning valve. The metering valve keeps pressure from traveling to the disc brakes on the front wheels until the brake shoes on the rear wheels have contacted the drums, ensuring that the front brakes will never be used alone. The proportioning valve controls the pressure to the rear brakes to avoid rear wheel lock-up during very hard braking.

Warning lights may be tested by depressing the brake pedal and holding it while opening one of the wheel cylinder bleeder screws. If this does not cause the light to go on, substitute a new lamp, make continuity checks, and, finally, replace the switch as necessary.

The hydraulic system may be checked for leaks by applying pressure to the pedal gradual-

ly and steadily. If the pedal sinks very slowly to the floor, the system has a leak. This is not to be confused with a springy or spongy feel due to the compression of air within the lines. If the system leaks, there will be a gradual change in the position of the pedal with a constant pressure.

Check for leaks along all lines and at wheel cylinders. If no external leaks are apparent, the problem is inside the master cylinder.

Disc Brakes
BASIC OPERATING PRINCIPLES

Instead of the traditional expanding brakes that press outward against a circular drum, disc brake systems utilize a disc (rotor) with brake pads positioned on either side of it. Braking effect is achieved in a manner similar to the way you would squeeze a spinning phonograph record between your fingers. The disc (rotor) is a casting with cooling fins between the two braking surfaces. This enables air to circulate between the braking surfaces making them less sensitive to heat buildup and more resistant to fade. Dirt and water do not affect braking action since contaminants are thrown off by the centrifugal action of the rotor or scraped off the by the pads. Also, the equal clamping action of the two brake pads tends to ensure uniform, straightline stops. Disc brakes are inherently self-adjusting.

There are three general types of disc brake:
1. A fixed caliper.
2. A floating caliper.
3. A sliding caliper.

The fixed caliper design uses two pistons mounted on either side of the rotor (in each side of the caliper). The caliper is mounted rigidly and does not move.

The sliding and floating designs are quite similar. In fact, these two types are often lumped together. In both designs, the pad on the inside of the rotor is moved into contact with the rotor by hydraulic force. The caliper, which is not held in a fixed position, moves slightly, bringing the outside pad into contact with the rotor. There are various methods of attaching floating calipers. Some pivot at the bottom or top, and some slide on mounting bolts. In any event, the end result is the same.

Drum Brakes

BASIC OPERATING PRINCIPLES

Drum brakes employ two brake shoes mounted on a stationary backing plate. These shoes are positioned inside a circular drum which rotates with the wheel assembly. The shoes are held in place by springs; this allows them to slide toward the drums (when they are applied) while keeping the linings and drums in alignment. The shoes are actuated by a wheel cylinder which is mounted at the top of the backing plate. When the brakes are applied, hydraulic pressure forces the wheel cylinder's actuating links outward. Since these links bear directly against the top of the brake shoes, the tops of the shoes are then forced against the inner side of the drum. This action forces the bottoms of the two shoes to contact the brake drum by rotating the entire assembly slightly (known as servo action). When pressure within the wheel cylinder is relaxed, return springs pull the shoes back away from the drum.

Most modern drum brakes are designed to self-adjust themselves during application when the vehicle is moving in reverse. This motion causes both shoes to rotate very slightly with the drum, rocking an adjusting lever, thereby causing rotation of the adjusting screw.

Power Boosters

Power brakes operate just as standard brake systems except in the actuation of the master cylinder pistons. A vacuum diaphragm is located on the front of the master cylinder and assists the driver in applying the brakes, reducing both the effort and travel he must put into moving the brake pedal.

The vacuum diaphragm housing is connected to the intake manifold by a vacuum hose. A check valve is placed at the point where the hose enters the diaphragm housing, so that during periods of low manifold vacuum brake assist vacuum will not be lost.

Depressing the brake pedal closes off the vacuum source and allows atmospheric pressure to enter on one side of the diaphragm. This causes the master cylinder pistons to move and apply the brakes. When the brake pedal is released, vacuum is applied to both sides of the diaphragm, and return springs return the diaphragm and master cylinder pistons to the released position. If the vacuum fails, the brake pedal rod will butt against the end of the master cylinder actuating rod, and direct mechanical application will occur as the pedal is depressed.

The hydraulic and mechanical problems that apply to conventional brake systems also apply to power brakes, and should be checked for if the tests below do not reveal the problem.

Test for a system vacuum leak as described below:

1. Operate the engine at idle without touching the brake pedal for at least one minute.
2. Turn off the engine, and wait one minute.
3. Test for the presence of assist vacuum by depressing the brake pedal and releasing it several times. Light application will produce less and less pedal travel, if vacuum was present. If there is no vacuum, air is leaking into the system somewhere.

Test for system operation as follows:

1. Pump the brake pedal (with engine off) until the supply vacuum is entirely gone.
2. Put a light, steady pressure on the pedal.
3. Start the engine, and operate it at idle. If the system is operating, the brake pedal should fall toward the floor if constant pressure is maintained on the pedal.

Power brake systems may be tested for hydraulic leaks just as ordinary systems are tested.

CAUTION: *Brake linings contain asbestos. Asbestos is a known cancer-causing agent. When working on brakes, remember that the dust which accumulates on the brake parts and/or in the drum contains asbestos. Always wear a protective face covering, such as a painter's mask, when working on the brakes. NEVER blow the dust from the brakes or drum! There are solvents made for the purpose of cleaning brake parts. Use them!*

A conventional front disc/rear drum setup is used. The front discs are single piston caliper types; the rear drums are activated by a conventional top mounted wheel cylinder. Disc brakes require no adjustments, the drum brakes are self adjusting by means of the parking brake cable. The only variances in the system from those found on the majority of vehicles are that the system is diagonally balanced, that is, the front left and right rear are on one system and the front right and left rear on the other. No proportioning valve is used. Power brakes are optional.

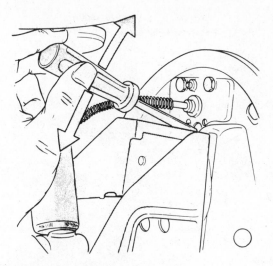

Adjusting rear brakes

Adjustment

All disc brakes are inherently self-adjusting. No adjustment is possible. Even though the drum brakes are self-adjusting in normal use, there are times when a manual adjustment is required, such as after installing new shoes or if it is required to back the shoes off the drum. A star wheel with screw type adjusters is provided for these occasions.

1. Remove the access slot plug from the backing plate.

2. Using a brake adjusting spoon pry downward (left side) or upward (right side) on the end of the tool (starwheel teeth moving up) to tighten the brakes. The opposite applies to loosen the brakes.

NOTE: *It will be necessary to use a small screwdriver to hold the adjusting lever away from the starwheel. Be careful not to bend the adjusting lever.*

3. When the brakes are tight almost to the point of being locked, back off on the starwheel 10 clicks. The starwheel on each set of brakes (front or rear) must be backed off the same number of turns to prevent brake pull from side to side.

4. When all brakes are adjusted, check brake pedal travel and then make several stops, while backing the car up, to equalize all the wheels.

TESTING ADJUSTER

1. Raise the vehicle on a hoist, with a helper in the car, to apply the brakes.

2. Loosen the brakes by holding the adjuster lever away from the starwheel and backing off the starwheel approximately 30 notches.

3. Spin the wheel and brake drum in reverse

and apply the brakes. The movement of the secondary shoe should pull the adjuster lever up, and when the brakes are released the lever should snap down and turn the starwheel.

4. If the automatic adjuster doesn't work, the drum must be removed and the adjuster components inspected carefully for breakage, wear, or improper installation.

Master Cylinder

REMOVAL AND INSTALLATION

With Power Brakes

1. Disconnect the primary and secondary brake lines from the master cylinder. Plug the openings.

2. Remove the nuts attaching the cylinder to the power brake booster.

3. Slide the master cylinder straight out, away from the booster.

4. Position the master cylinder over the studs on the booster, align the pushrod with the master cylinder piston and tighten the nuts to 16 ft. lbs.

5. Connect the brake lines.

6. Bleed the brakes.

With Non-Power Brakes

1. Disconnect the primary and secondary brake lines and install plugs in the master cylinder openings.

2. Disconnect the stoplight switch mounting bracket from under the instrument panel.

3. Pull the brake pedal backward to disengage the pushrod from the master cylinder piston.

NOTE: *This will destroy the grommet.*

4. Remove the master cylinder-to-firewall nuts.

5. Slide the master cylinder out and away from the firewall. Be sure to remove all pieces of the broken grommet.

6. Install the boot on the pushrod.

7. Install a new grommet on the pushrod.

8. Apply a soap and water solution to the grommet and slide it firmly into position in the primary piston socket. Move the pushrod from side to side to make sure it's seated.

9. From the engine side, press the pushrod through the master cylinder mounting plate and align the mounting studs with the holes in the cylinder.

10. Install the nuts and torque them to 16 ft. lbs.

11. From under the instrument panel, place the pushrod on the pin on the pedal and install a new retaining clip.

NOTE: *Be sure to lubricate the pin.*

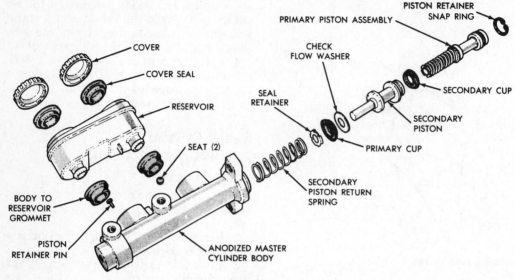

PISTON RETAINER
SNAP RING

PRIMARY PISTON ASSEMBLY

CHECK
FLOW WASHER

SECONDARY CUP

COVER

COVER SEAL

SEAL
RETAINER

SECONDARY
PISTON

RESERVOIR

PRIMARY CUP

SEAT (2)

SECONDARY
PISTON RETURN
SPRING

BODY TO
RESERVOIR
GROMMET

PISTON
RETAINER PIN

ANODIZED MASTER
CYLINDER BODY

Master cylinder exploded view

12. Install the brake lines on the master cylinder.

13. Bleed the system.

OVERHAUL

CAUTION: *Do not hone the master cylinder bore. Honing will remove the anodized finish.*

1. Clean the housing and reservoir.

2. Remove the reservoir caps and empty the fluid.

3. Clamp the master cylinder in a soft-jawed vise.

4. Pull the reservoir from the master cylinder housing.

5. Remove the reservoir grommets.

6. Use needle nosed pliers to remove the secondary piston pin from inside the housing.

7. Remove the snap-ring from the outer end of the housing.

8. Slide the primary piston out of the master cylinder bore.

9. Tap the open end of the cylinder on the bench to remove the secondary piston. If it sticks in the bore, it can be removed with light air pressure.

NOTE: *If air pressure is used to remove the piston, new cups must be installed.*

10. Note the position of the rubber cups and remove all except the primary cup.

CAUTION: *NOTE:*

Do not remove the primary cup from the primary piston. If the cup is worn, the entire primary piston assembly should be replaced.

11. If the brass tube seats are not reusable, replace them using a suitable tool.

12. Wash the entire housing in clean brake fluid and inspect for pitting or scratches. If any are found, replace the housing. If the pistons are corroded, they should be replaced. Discard all used rubber parts and replace piston caps and seals.

13. Before assembly, dip all parts in clean brake fluid.

14. Install the check flow washer.

15. Install the secondary piston into the master cylinder bore. Be sure the cup lips enter the bore evenly. Keep well lubricated with brake fluid.

16. Center the primary piston spring retainer on the secondary piston and push the piston assemblies into the bore up to the primary piston cup.

17. Work the cup into the bore and push the piston in up to the secondary seal. Work the cup into the bore and push on the piston until fully seated.

18. Depress the piston and install the snap-ring.

19. Tap the secondary piston retainer pin into the housing.

20. Install new tube seats.

21. Install the reservoir grommets in the housing. Lubricate the area with clean brake fluid and install the reservoir. All the lettering should be properly read from the left side of the reservoir when it is properly installed. Make sure the bottom of the reservoir touches the top of the grommet.

Pressure Differential Valve and Warning Light Switch

The brake system is split diagonally. That means that the right rear and left front brakes

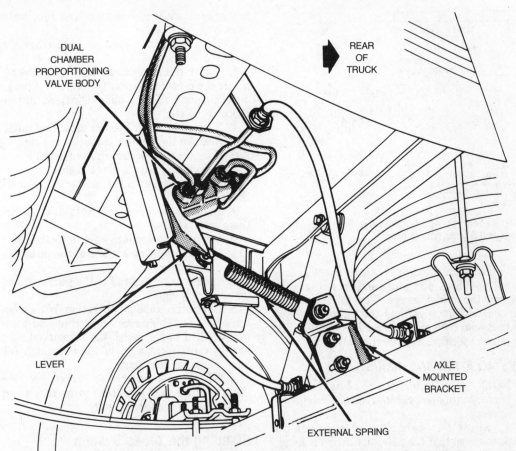

DUAL
CHAMBER
PROPORTIONING
VALVE BODY

REAR
OF
TRUCK

LEVER

AXLE
MOUNTED
BRACKET

EXTERNAL SPRING

Rear brake height sensing proportioning valve—Rampage and Scamp pickup models

are connected to the same reservoir. Both systems are routed through, but separated by, the pressure differential valve, which also contains the warning switch. The function of the valve is to activate the switch in the event of brake system malfunction. The warning light switch is the latching type. It will automatically recenter itself after the repair is made and brake pedal depressed.

The bulb can be checked each time the ignition switch is turned to the ON position or each time the parking brake is set.

Height Sensing Proportioning Valve

The Rampage and Scamp pickup models use a height sensing dual proportioning valve in addition to the regular differential warning switch. This valve is located under the bed just forward of the rear axle. It automatically provides optimum brake balance front-to-rear regardless of the vehicle load condition. The valve modulates the pressure to the rear brakes sensing the vehicle load condition through relative movement between the rear axle and the load floor.

NOTE: *It is important that aftermarket load leveling devices are NOT installed on this brake/suspension system. The installation of these devices will cause the rear brake height sensing proportioning valve to sense a light load condition that is actually a loaded condition being created by these add-on devices.*

TESTING

When a premature rear wheel slide is obtained on brake application, it could be an indication that the fluid pressure to the rear brakes is above the reduction ratio for the rear line pressure and that the proportioning valve is malfunctioning. To test the valve use the following procedures.

NOTE: *During the testing, leave the front brake lines connected to the valve.*

1. Disconnect the external spring at the valve end.

2. Install one gauge and the tee of tool set C-4007-A in the line from either master cylinder port and brake valve assembly.

3. Install the second gauge from tool set C-4007-A to either rear brake line. Bleed the rear brake system.

4. Have a second person exert pressure on

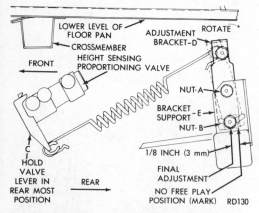

LOWER LEVEL OF FLOOR PAN
CROSSMEMBER
FRONT
HEIGHT SENSING PROPORTIONING VALVE
ADJUSTMENT BRACKET-D
ROTATE
NUT-A
BRACKET SUPPORT-E
NUT-B
C
HOLD VALVE LEVER IN REAR MOST POSITION
REAR
1/8 INCH (3 mm)
FINAL ADJUSTMENT
NO FREE PLAY POSITION (MARK)
RD130

Height sensing proportioning valve adjusting—Rampage and Scamp pickup models

the brake pedal (holding pressure) to get a reading on the valve inlet gauge and check the reading on the outlet gauge. The inlet pressure should read 1000 psi and the outlet pressure should read between 530 and 770 psi. If either is not as specified, replace the valve.

INSTALLATION AND ADJUSTMENT

NOTE: *After installing a new height sensing proportioning valve, both rear brakes should be bled.*

1. Raise the vehicle and support on jackstands so that the rear suspension is hanging free and the shock absorbers are fully extended. Leave the wheels and tires on the truck to help keep the suspension in the full rebound position.
2. Loosen the spring adjusting bracket nuts **A** and **B** as shown in the illustration.
3. Push the valve lever **C** rearward until it bottoms and hold it there.
4. Rotate the spring adjusting bracket **D** rearward until all the free play has been removed from the spring. (Be careful not to stretch the spring). While holding the adjusting bracket in position, release the valve lever. Tighten nut **B** temporarily, to hold the adjusting bracket in this position.
5. Mark the position of the adjusting bracket nut **B** on the bracket support **E**.
6. Loosen nut **B** and rotate the top of the adjusting bracket rearward so that nut **B** is 1/8″ forward of the no free play position. Tighten nut **B** to 21 ft. lbs. while being careful not to move the bracket. Tighten nut **A** to 21 ft. lbs.

Power Booster

REMOVAL AND INSTALLATION

1. Remove the master cylinder; it can be pulled far enough out of the way to allow booster removal without disconnecting the brake lines.
2. Disconnect the vacuum hose from the booster.
3. Under the instrument panel, pry the retainer clip center tang over the end of the brake pedal pin and pull the retainer clip from the pin. Discard the clip.
4. Remove the four booster attaching nuts.
5. Remove the booster from the vehicle.
6. Position the booster on the firewall.
7. Torque the nuts to 20 ft. lbs.
8. Carefully position the master cylinder on the booster.
9. Install the mounting nuts and torque them to 18 ft. lbs.
10. Connect the vacuum hose to the booster.
11. Coat the bearing surface of the pedal pin with chassis lube.
12. Connect the pushrod to the pedal pin and install a new clip.
13. Check the stoplight operation. With vacuum applied to the power brake unit and pressure applied to the pedal, the master cylinder should vent (force a jet of fluid through the front chamber vent port).

NOTE: *Do not attempt to disassemble the power brake unit, since the booster is serviced as a complete assembly only.*

Bleeding the Brake System

Any time a brake line has been disconnected the hydraulic system should be bled. The brakes should also be bled when the pedal travel becomes unusually long (soft pedal) or the car pulls to one side during braking. The proper bleeding sequence is: right rear wheel, left rear wheel, right front caliper, and left front caliper. You'll need a helper to pump the brake pedal while you open the bleeder valves.

NOTE: *If the system has been drained, first refill it with fresh brake fluid. Following the above sequence, open each bleeder valve by 1/2 to 3/4 of a turn and pump the brake pedal until fluid runs out of the valve. Proceed with the bleeding as outlined below.*

1. Remove the bleeder valve dust cover and install a rubber bleeder hose.
2. Insert the other end of the hose into a container about 1/3 full of brake fluid.
3. Have an assistant pump the brake pedal several times until the pedal pressure increases.
4. Hold the pedal under pressure and then start to open the bleeder valve about 1/2 to 3/4 of a turn. At this point, have your assistant depress the pedal all the way and then quickly close the valve. The helper should allow the pedal to return slowly.

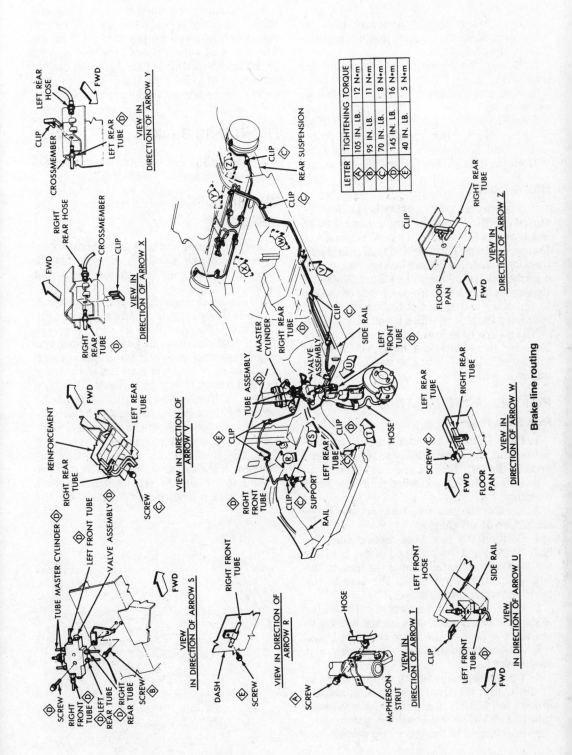

LETTER	TIGHTENING TORQUE	
Ⓐ	105 IN. LB.	12 N·m
Ⓑ	95 IN. LB.	11 N·m
Ⓒ	70 IN. LB.	8 N·m
Ⓓ	145 IN. LB.	16 N·m
Ⓔ	40 IN. LB.	5 N·m

Brake line routing

NOTE: *Keep a close check on the brake fluid in the reservoir and top it up as necessary throughout the bleeding process.*

5. Keep repeating this procedure until no more air bubbles can be seen coming from the hose in the brake fluid.

6. Remove the bleeder hose and install the dust cover.

7. Continue the bleeding at each wheel in sequence.

WARNING: *Don't splash any brake fluid on the paintwork. Brake fluid will soften paint. Any fluid accidentally spilled on the body should be immediately flushed off with water.*

Brake Hoses

It is important to use quality brake hose intended specifically for the application. Hose of less than the best quality, or hose not made to the specified length will tend to fatigue and may therefore create premature leakage and, consequently, a potential for brake failure. Note also that brake hose differs from one side of the car to the other and should therefore be ordered specifying the side on which it will be installed.

Make sure hose end mating surfaces are clean and free of nicks and burrs, which would prevent effective sealing. Use new copper seals on banjo fittings.

REMOVAL AND INSTALLATION

Front Brake Hose

1. Place a drain pan under the hose connections. First, disconnect the hose where it connects to the body bracket and steel tube.

2. Unbolt the hose bracket from the strut assembly.

3. Remove the bolt to disconnect the banjo connection at the caliper.

4. Position the new hose, noting that the body bracket and the body end of the hose are keyed to prevent installation of the hose in the wrong direction. First attach the hose to the banjo connector on the caliper.

5. Bolt the hose bracket located in the center of the hose to the strut, allowing the bracket to position the hose so it will not be twisted.

6. Attach the hose to the body bracket and steel brake tube.

7. Torque the banjo fitting on the caliper to 19-29 ft. lbs.; the front hose to intermediate bracket to 75-115 in. lbs.; and the hose to brake tube to 115-170 in. lbs. Bleed the system thoroughly, referring to the procedure below.

Rear Brake Hose (Trailing Arm-to-Floor Pan)

1. Place a drain pan under the hose connections. Disconnect the double nut (using a primary wrench and a backup wrench) at the tube

mounted on the floor pan. Then, disconnect the hose at the retaining clip.

2. Disconnect the hose at the trailing arm tube. Install the new tube to the trailing arm connection first and torque to 115-170 in. lbs. Then, making sure it is not twisted, connect it to the tube on the floor pan. Again, torque the connection to 115-170 in. lbs. Bleed the system thoroughly, referring to the procedure below.

FRONT DISC BRAKES

Omnis and Horizon models use a floating caliper front disc brake.

Disc Brake Pads

INSPECTION

Disc pads (lining and shoe assemblies) should be replaced in axle sets (both wheels) when the thickness of the shoe and lining is less than $5/16''$.

NOTE: *State inspection specifications take precedence over these general recommendations.*

Note that disc pads in floating caliper type brakes may wear at an angle, and measurement should be made at the narrow end of the taper. Tapered linings should be replaced if the taper exceeds $1/8''$ from end to end (the difference between the thickest and thinnest points).

Always replace both sets on each wheel whenever one pad needs replacing.

NOTE: *Brake squeal is inherent in disc brakes. If the squeal is objectionable and constant it can be reduced by installing new brake pads (Chrysler Part No. 4176767). Af-*

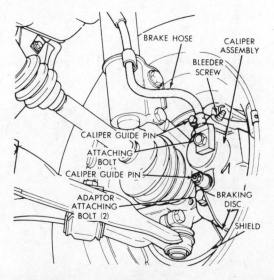

Front caliper attaching points

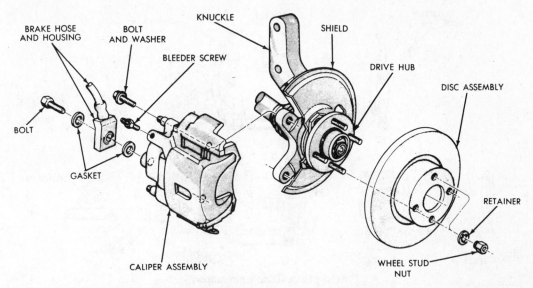

Exploded view of disc brake components

*ter 1000 miles of city driving these new com-
pound pads should reduce noise, although a
very low level of noise may be present under
certain conditions.*

REMOVAL AND INSTALLATION

Kelsey Hayes Type (Double Pin)

1. Raise and support the car.
2. Remove the wheels.
3. Remove the caliper guide pins.
4. Remove the caliper by slowly sliding the caliper off the brake disc. Hang the caliper by a piece of stiff wire. Do not allow it to hang by the brake line.

5. Remove the outboard brake pad from the adaptor.
6. Slide the inboard pad out of the adaptor.
7. To install the pads, place new pads in the adaptor.
8. Loosen the rear cap of the master cylinder reservoir and slowly push the caliper pistons back into the housing.

WARNING: *Be sure the reservoir does not overflow, especially onto painted surfaces.*

9. Hold the outboard lining in position and carefully slide the caliper into position on the adaptor.
10. Install the guide pins (lightly lubricated with silicone grease) and anti-rattle springs.

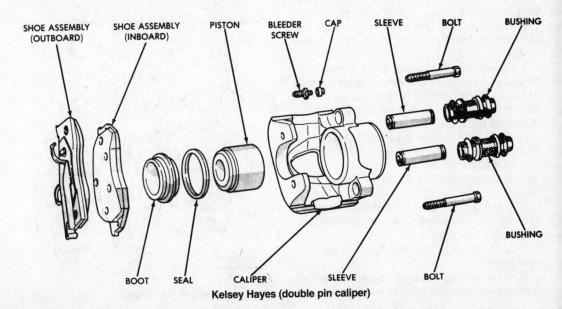

Kelsey Hayes (double pin caliper)

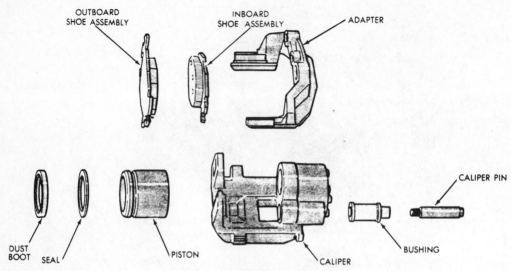

OUTBOARD SHOE ASSEMBLY — INBOARD SHOE ASSEMBLY — ADAPTER — CALIPER PIN — DUST BOOT — SEAL — PISTON — CALIPER — BUSHING

Kelsey Hayes (single pin caliper)

The anti-rattle spring clips are installed with the closed loop toward the center of the car.

11. Bleed the brakes.
12. Install the wheels.

NOTE: *Tighten the wheels in an every-other-nut rotation until all wheels are tightened to ½ specification. Repeat the sequence until all lug nuts are tight to full specification.*

After assembly, pump the pedal several times to remove clearance between pads and rotors.

Kelsey-Hayes System (Single pin)

1. Raise and support the front end on jackstands.
2. Remove the front wheels.
3. Remove the caliper guide pin. To do this, unscrew it until it is free from the threads and then pull it out of the caliper adapter.
4. Using a small prybar, gently wedge the caliper away from the rotor, breaking the adhesive seals.
5. Slowly slide the caliper away from the rotor and off the caliper adapter. Support the caliper securely by hanging it from the body with wire (this is necessary to keep its weight from damaging the brake hose).
6. Slide the outboard pad off the caliper adapter. Then remove the disc by simply sliding it off the wheel studs.
7. Remove the inboard pad by sliding it off the caliper adapter.
8. If the caliper is to be removed, disconnect and cap the brake line. Then, remove it from the hanger and remove it.
9. Lubricate both bushing channels with silicone grease.
10. Remove the protective paper backing from the anti-squeal surfaces on both pads. In-

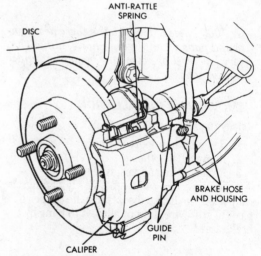

Remove or install the caliper guide pins

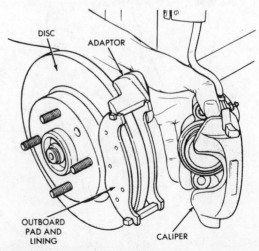

Remove or install the caliper

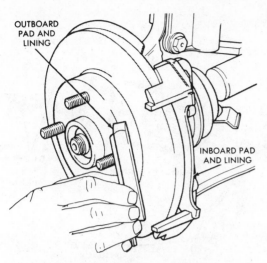

OUTBOARD
PAD AND
LINING

INBOARD PAD
AND LINING

Remove or install the outboard brake pad

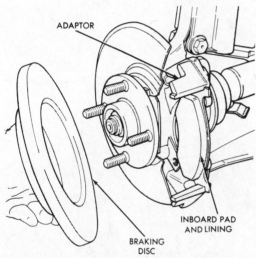

ADAPTOR

INBOARD PAD
AND LINING

BRAKING
DISC

Remove or install the brake disc

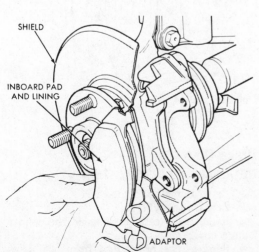

SHIELD

INBOARD PAD
AND LINING

ADAPTOR

Remove or install the inboard brake pad

stall the inboard pad on the adapter. Be careful to keep grease from the bushing channels from getting onto the pad as you do this.

11. Install the rotor onto the wheel studs of the steering knuckle. Install the outboard pad in the caliper and carefully slide it into place over the rotor.

12. If necessary, reconnect the brake line or remove the caliper from the hanger. Lower the caliper into position over the rotor and pads. Install the guide pin and torque it to 35 ft. lbs.

CAUTION: *It is easy to crossthread the guide pin. Start it carefully, turning it gently and allowing it to find its own angle.*

13. Install the wheels and torque the lugs to half the specified torque in a criss-cross pattern. Then, torque the lugs to full torque (95 ft. lbs.). If the brake line was disconnected, bleed the system thoroughly as described above. Pump the brake pedal several times to ensure that the brake pads seat against the rotor. *The pedal must give resistance at the normal position before attempting to drive the car.* Drive the car at moderate speeds in an isolated area in order to apply the brakes several times to test the system and seat the new linings.

ATE Type

1. Raise and safely support front the car.
2. Remove the front wheels.
3. Remove the hold-down spring from the caliper by pushing in at the middle of the spring and pushing it outwards.
4. Loosen, but do not remove the caliper guide pins until the caliper is free from the mount. removal of the guide pins is necessary only if the bushings or sleeves require replacement.

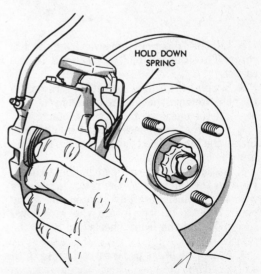

HOLD DOWN
SPRING

Hold-down spring removal—A.T.E.

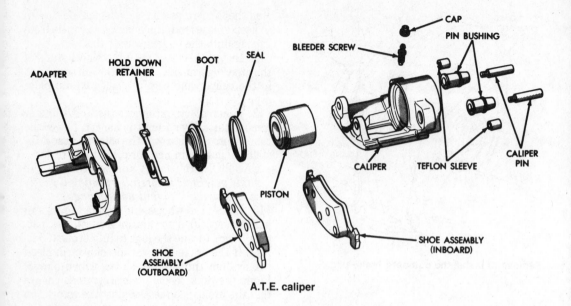

A.T.E. caliper

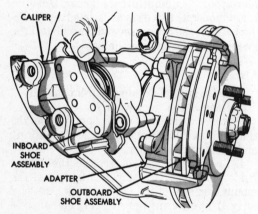

Caliper and inboard pad—A.T.E.

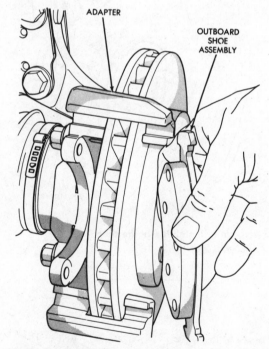

Outboard pad—A.T.E.

5. Lift the caliper out and away from the disc rotor. The inboard pad will remain in the caliper.

6. Support the caliper so that the strain is on the hose. Remove the inboard pad from the caliper. Lift the outboard from the adapter.

7. Push the piston back into the caliper bore. Install the inboard pad with the clamp locating it in the caliper piston.

8. Install the outboard pad in the adapter. Position the caliper over the rotor and secure with guide pins. Carefully tighten the guide pins to 18-22 ft. lbs. Install the hold-down spring. Mount the front wheels and lower the vehicle.

9. Pump the brake pedal several times until a firm pedal is obtained. Check the master cylinder level and road test the vehicle.

Brake Disc

REMOVAL AND INSTALLATION

1. Raise and support the car.
2. Remove the wheels.
3. Remove the caliper. Suspend the caliper from a hook.
4. Remove the brake disc from the drive flange studs.

5. Install the brake disc on the drive flange studs.

6. Install the caliper.

7. Install the wheels. See NOTE at the end of the previous procedure.

INSPECTION

Light scoring is acceptable. Heavy scoring or warping will necessitate refinishing or replacement of the disc. The brake disc must be replaced if cracks or burned marks are evident.

Check the thickness of the disc. Measure the thickness at 12 equally spaced points 25mm from the edge of the disc. If thickness varies more than 0.0125mm the disc should be refinished, provided equal amounts are out from each side and the thickness does not fall below 11mm.

Check the run-out of the disc. Total run-out of the disc installed on the car should not exceed 0.0125mm. The disc can be resurfaced to correct minor variations as long as equal amounts are cut from each side and the thickness is at least 11mm after resurfacing.

Check the run-out of the hub (disc removed). It should not be more than 0.05mm. If so, the hub should be replaced.

Caliper

REMOVAL AND INSTALLATION

1. Raise and support the car.

2. Remove the wheels.

3. Remove the caliper guide pins and anti-rattle springs.

4. Remove the caliper by slowly sliding it off the adaptor.

NOTE: *If the old pads are being reused, mark them so they can be installed in their original position.*

5. If the caliper is being removed for overhaul, disconnect and plug the brake line.

6. To install, attach the brake line if removed.

7. Loosen the rear master cylinder reservoir cap and slowly push the caliper pistons back into the housing.

WARNING: *Be sure the reservoir does not overflow, especially onto painted surfaces.*

8. Hold the outboard pad in position and slide the caliper onto the adaptor.

9. Install the guide pins and anti-rattle springs.

10. Bleed the brakes.

11. Install the wheels.

NOTE: *Tighten the wheels in an every-other-nut rotation until the nuts are tight to ½ specification. Repeat the sequence until all the lug nuts are tight to full specification.*

OVERHAUL

1. Remove the caliper assembly from the car without disconnecting the hydraulic line.

2. Support the caliper assembly on the upper control arm and surround it with shop towels to absorb any brake fluid. Slowly depress the brake pedal until the piston is pushed out of its bore.

CAUTION: *Do not use compressed air to force the piston from its bore; injury could result.*

3. Disconnect the brake line from the caliper and plug it to prevent fluid loss.

4. Mount the caliper in a soft-jawed vise and clamp lightly. Do not tighten the vise too much or the caliper will become distorted.

5. Work the dust boot out with your fingers.

6. Use a small pointed wooden or plastic stick to work the piston seal out of the groove in the bore. Discard the seal.

WARNING: *Using a screwdriver or other metal tool could scratch the piston bore.*

7. Using the same wooden or plastic stick, press the outer bushings out of the housing. Discard the old bushings in the same manner. Discard them as well.

8. Clean all parts in denatured alcohol or brake fluid. Blow out all bores and passages with compressed air.

9. Inspect the piston and bore for scoring or pitting. Replace the piston if necessary. Bores with light scratches or corrosion may be cleaned with crocus cloth. Bores with deep scratches may be honed if you do not increase the bore diameter more than 0.05mm. Replace the housing if the bore must be enlarged beyond this.

NOTE: *Black stains are caused by piston seals and are harmless.*

10. If the bore had to be honed, clean its grooves with a stiff, non-metallic rotary brush. Clean the bore twice by flushing it out with brake fluid and drying it with a soft, lint-free cloth.

Caliper assembly is as follows:

1. Clamp the caliper in a soft-jawed vise; do not overtighten.

2. Dip a new piston seal in brake fluid or the lubricant supplied with the rebuilding kit. Position the new seal in one area of its groove and gently work it into place with clean fingers, so that it is correctly seated. Do not use an old seal.

3. Coat a new boot with brake fluid or lubricant (as above), leaving a generous amount inside.

4. Insert the boot in the caliper and work it into the groove, using your fingers only. The boot will snap into place once it is correctly posi-

tioned. Run your forefinger around the inside of the boot to make sure that it is correctly seated.

5. Install the bleed screw in its hole and plug the fluid inlet on the caliper.

6. Coat the piston with brake fluid or lubricant. Spread the boot with your fingers and work the piston into the boot.

7. Depress the piston; this will force the boot into its groove on the piston. Remove the plug and bottom the piston in the bore.

8. Compress the flanges of new guide pin bushings and work them into place by pressing in on the bushings with your fingertips, until they are seated. Make sure that the flanges cover the housing evenly on all sides.

9. Install the caliper on the car as previously outlined.

REAR DRUM BRAKES

Brake Drums

REMOVAL AND INSTALLATION

1. Raise the car and support it safely.
2. Remove the plug from the brake shoe adjusting hole.
3. Using a brake spoon, release the brake shoes by moving the star wheel adjuster up (left side) or down (right side).
4. Remove the grease cap.
5. Remove the cotter pin, lock nut and washer.
6. Remove the brake drum and bearings.
7. To install, reposition the drum and install the bearings.
8. Adjust the wheel bearings (see Chapter 1).
9. Install the cotter pin, lock nut and washer.
10. Install the gease cap.
11. Adjust the brakes.

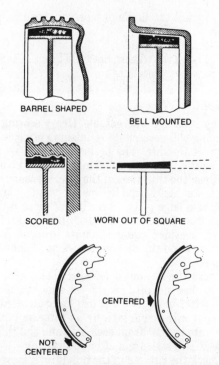

BARREL SHAPED   BELL MOUNTED

SCORED   WORN OUT OF SQUARE

CENTERED

NOT CENTERED

Improperly worn linings are cause for concern only if braking is unstable and noise is objectionable. Compare the lining and drum wear pattern, the drum being more important, since the drum shapes the wear of the shoe

12. Replug the adjusting hole.
13. Lower the car.

INSPECTION

Measure the drum run-out and diameter. If not according to specifications the drum should be replaced. The variation in diameter should not exceed 0.06mm in 30° or 0.09mm in 360°. All drums show markings of maximum diameter.

Once the drum is off, clean the shoes and springs with a stiff brush to remove the accumulated brake dust.

CAUTION: *Avoid prolonged exposure to brake dust.*

Grease on the shoes can be removed with alcohol or fine sandpaper.

After cleaning, examine the brake shoes for glazed, oily, loose, cracked or improperly worn linings. Light glazing is common and can be removed with fine sandpaper. Linings that are worn improperly or below $1/16''$ above rivet heads or brake shoe should be replaced. The NHTSA advises states with inspection programs to fail vehicles with brake linings less than $1/32''$. A good "eyeball" test is to replace the linings when the thickness is the same as or less

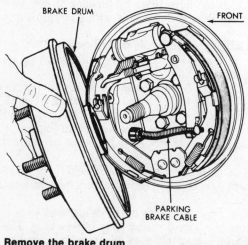

BRAKE DRUM   FRONT

PARKING BRAKE CABLE

Remove the brake drum

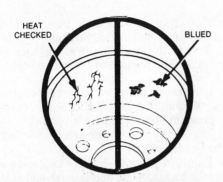

A "blued" or severely heat checked drum and "blued", charred or heavily glazed linings are the result of overheating. The brakes should be checked immediately

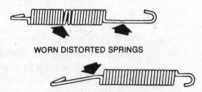

WORN DISTORTED SPRINGS

Check for weak or distorted retracting springs

than the thickness of the metal backing plate (shoe).

Wheel cylinders are a vital part of the brake system and should be inspected carefully. Gently pull back the rubber boots; if any fluid is visible, it's time to replace or rebuild the wheel cylinders. Boots that are distorted, cracked or otherwise damaged, also point to the need for service. Check the flexible brake lines for cracks, chafing or wear.

Check the brake shoe retracting and holddown springs; they should not be worn or distorted. Be sure that the adjuster mechanism moves freely. The points on the backing plate where the shoes slide should be shiny and free of rust. Rust in these areas suggests that the brake shoes are not moving properly.

Brake Shoes

REMOVAL AND INSTALLATION

NOTE: *If you are not thoroughly familiar with the procedures involved in brake replacement, disassemble and assemble one side at a time, leaving the other wheel intact, as a reference.*

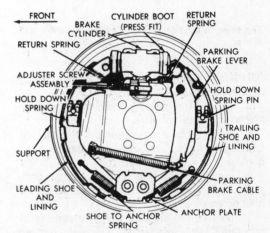

Left rear brake shoes and springs installed

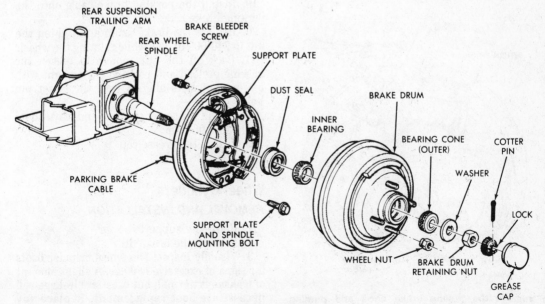

Left rear brake

FRONT →

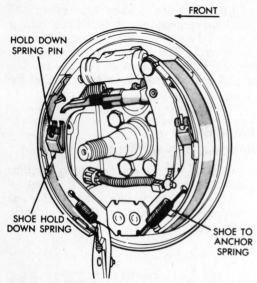

HOLD DOWN
SPRING PIN

SHOE HOLD
DOWN SPRING

SHOE TO
ANCHOR
SPRING

The shoe-to-anchor springs can be removed with pliers

1. Remove the brake drum. See the procedure earlier in this chapter.

2. Unhook the parking brake cable from the secondary (trailing) shoe.

3. Remove the shoe-to-anchor springs (retracting springs). They can be gripped and unhooked with a pair of pliers.

4. Remove the shoe hold down springs; compress them slightly and slide them off of the hold down pins.

5. Remove the adjuster screw assembly by spreading the shoes apart. The adjuster nut must be fully backed off.

6. Raise the parking brake lever. Pull the

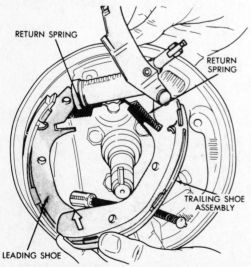

RETURN SPRING

RETURN
SPRING

TRAILING SHOE
ASSEMBLY

LEADING SHOE

Remove the trailing brake shoe and parking brake lever by lifting upward

secondary (trailing) shoe away from the backing plate so pull-back spring tension is released.

7. Remove the secondary (trailing) shoe and disengage the spring end from the backing plate.

8. Raise the primary (leading) shoe to release spring tension. Remove the shoe and disengage the spring end from the backing plate.

9. Inspect the brakes (see procedures under Brake Drum Inspection).

10. Lubricate the six shoe contact areas on the brake backing plate and the web end of the brake shoe which contacts the anchor plate. Use a multi-purpose lubricant or a high temperature brake grease made for the purpose.

11. Chrysler recommends that the rear wheel bearings be cleaned and repacked whenever the brakes are renewed. Be sure to install a new bearing seal.

12. With the leading shoe return spring in position on the shoe, install the shoe at the same time as you engage the return spring in the end support.

13. Position the end of the shoe under the anchor.

14. With the trailing shoe return spring in position, install the shoe at the same time as you engage the spring in the support (backing plate).

15. Position the end of the shoe under the anchor.

16. Spread the shoes and install the adjuster screw assembly making sure that the forked end that enters the shoe is curved down.

17. Insert the shoe hold down spring pins and install the hold down springs.

18. Install the shoe-to-anchor springs.

19. Install the parking brake cable onto the parking brake lever.

20. Replace the brake drum and tighten the nut to 240-300 in. lbs. while rotating the wheel.

21. Back off the nut enough to release the bearing preload and position the locknut with one pair of slots aligned with the cotter pin hole.

22. Install the cotter pin. The end play should be 0.025-0.080mm.

23. Install the grease cap.

Wheel Cylinders

REMOVAL AND INSTALLATION

1. Raise and support the car.

2. Remove the brake drums.

3. Visually inspect the wheel cylinder boots for signs of excessive leakage. A slight amount of leakage is normal, but excessive leakage will necessitate boot replacement. Replace any boots that are torn or broken.

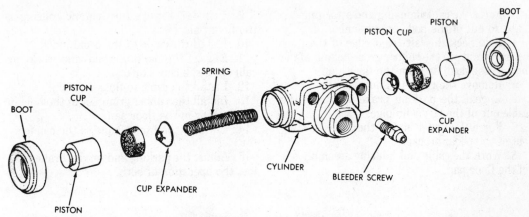

Exploded view of wheel cylinder

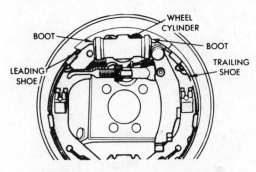

Wheel cylinder installed on backing plate.

4. In case of a leak, also remove the brake shoes and check for contamination.

5. Disconnect and plug the brake line.

6. Unbolt and remove the wheel cylinder.

7. To install, reposition the wheel cylinder and bolt into place.

8. Reconnect the brake line.

9. Install the brake shoes and brake drum.

10. Bleed the brakes.

OVERHAUL

1. Pry the boots away from the cylinder and remove the boots and piston as an assembly.

2. Disengage the boot from the piston.

3. Slide the piston into the cylinder bore and press inward to remove the other boot and piston. Also remove the spring with it the cup expanders.

4. Wash all parts (except rubber parts) in clean brake fluid and dry thoroughly. Do not use a rag; lint will adhere to the bore.

5. Inspect the cylinder bores. Light scoring can usually be cleaned up with crocus cloth. Black stains are caused by the piston cups and are no cause of concern. Bad scoring or pitting means that the wheel cylinder should be replaced.

6. Dip the pistons and new cups in clean brake fluid prior to assembly.

7. Coat the wheel cylinder bore with clean brake fluid.

8. Install the expansion spring with the cup expanders.

9. Install the cups in each end of the cylinder with the open ends facing each other.

10. Assemble new boots on the piston and slide them into the cylinder bore.

11. Press the boot over the wheel cylinder until seated.

12. Install the wheel cylinder.

PARKING BRAKE

ADJUSTMENT

The cable operated parking brake is adjusted at the equalizer (connector) under the car.

1. Adjust the service brakes.

2. Release the parking brake lever and back off the parking brake cable until there is slack in the cable.

3. Clean and lubricate the adjuster threads.

4. Use a brake spoon to turn the starwheel adjuster until there is light shoe-to-drum contact. Back off the starwheel until the wheel rotates freely with no brake drag.

5. Tighten the parking brake adjustment until a slight drag is felt while rotating the wheels.

6. Loosen the cable adjusting nut until both rear wheels can be rotated freely, then back the cable adjuster nut off 2 full turns.

7. Test the parking brake. The rear wheels should rotate freely without dragging.

Front Brake Cable

REMOVAL AND INSTALLATION

1. Raise and support the car.

2. Disconnect the brake cable from the connector.

3. Force the cable housing and attaching clip forward out of the body crossmember.

4. Fold back the left front edge of the floor covering and pry the rubber grommet out of the hole in the dash or from the floor pan.

5. Remove the cable-to-floor pan clip.

6. Engage the parking brake and work the cable out of the clevis linkage.

7. Force the upper end of the cable housing out of the pedal bracket.

8. Work the cable and housing assembly out of the floor pan.

9. To install, rework the cable and housing in the floor pan.

10. Install the cable to the pedal bracket.

11. Engage the parking brake and work the cable into the clevis linkage.

12. Install the cable-to-floor pan clip.

13. Install the rubber grommet in the hole in the dash or in the floor pan.

14. Connect the brake cable to the connector.

15. Adjust the parking and service brakes and test the operation of both.

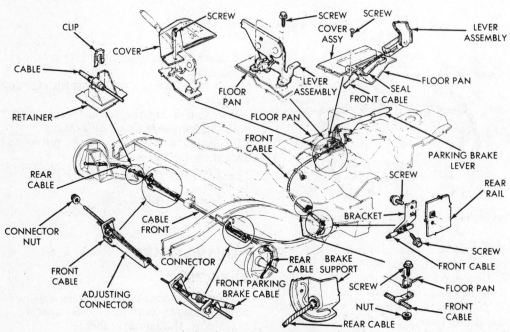

Parking brake cables—all except pickup models

Brake Specifications
All measurements given are (in.) unless noted

Model	Lug Nut Torque (ft./lb.)	Master Cylinder Bore	Brake Disc		Brake Drum			Minimum Lining Thickness	
			Minimum Thickness	Maximum Run-Out	Diameter	Max Machine O/S	Max Wear Limit	Front	Rear
1978–80	80–85	0.625	0.431 ②	①	7.87	7.927	7.927	③	5/16
1981–82	80–85	0.875	0.431 ②	0.004	7.87	7.927	7.927	③	5/16
1983–89	80–85 ④	0.827	0.431 ②	0.004	7.87	7.927	7.927	③	5/16

NOTE: *Minimum lining thickness is as recommended by the manufacturer. Because of variations in state inspection regulations, the minimum allowable thickness may be different than recommended by the manufacturer.*
① Maximum 0.005 in. total combined run-out of disc and hub.
   Run-out of disc (installed on hub)—0.005 in.
   Run-out of hub (disc removed)—0.002 in.
② Thickness of new disc—0.490–0.505 in.
③ 5/16 in.—minimum thickness of lining and backing plate at any point.
④ 1984 and later—95 ft. lbs.

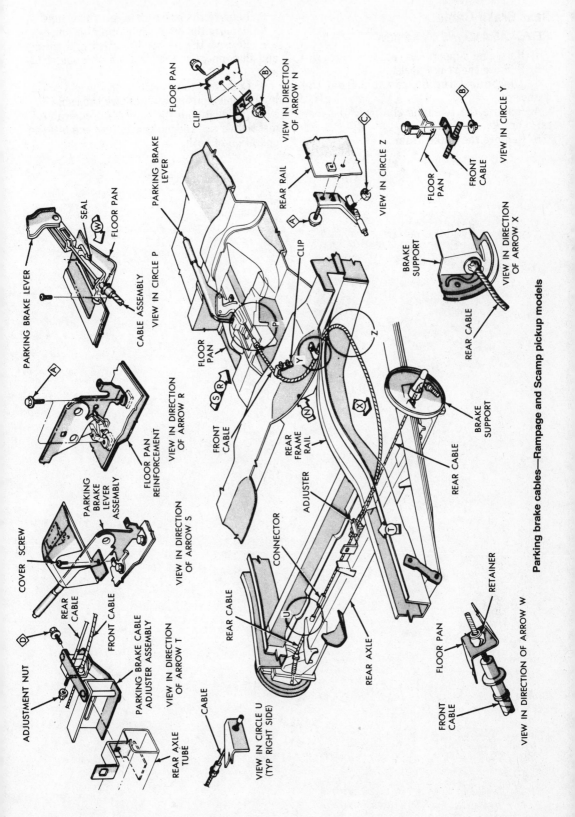

FLOOR PAN

CLIP

VIEW IN DIRECTION OF ARROW N

VIEW IN CIRCLE Z

REAR RAIL

FLOOR PAN

FRONT CABLE

VIEW IN CIRCLE Y

PARKING BRAKE LEVER

SEAL

FLOOR PAN

PARKING BRAKE LEVER

CABLE ASSEMBLY

VIEW IN CIRCLE P

CLIP

BRAKE SUPPORT

VIEW IN DIRECTION OF ARROW X

REAR CABLE

FLOOR PAN REINFORCEMENT

VIEW IN DIRECTION OF ARROW R

FLOOR PAN

FRONT CABLE

BRAKE SUPPORT

REAR CABLE

PARKING BRAKE LEVER ASSEMBLY

VIEW IN DIRECTION OF ARROW S

REAR FRAME RAIL

ADJUSTER

COVER SCREW

REAR CABLE

FRONT CABLE

PARKING BRAKE CABLE ADJUSTER ASSEMBLY

VIEW IN DIRECTION OF ARROW T

CONNECTOR

REAR CABLE

ADJUSTMENT NUT

REAR AXLE TUBE

CABLE

VIEW IN CIRCLE U (TYP RIGHT SIDE)

REAR AXLE

RETAINER

FLOOR PAN

FRONT CABLE

VIEW IN DIRECTION OF ARROW W

Parking brake cables—Rampage and Scamp pickup models

Rear Brake Cable

REMOVAL AND INSTALLATION

1. Raise and support the car.
2. Remove the rear wheels.
3. Disconnect the brake cable from the connector.
4. Remove the retaining clip from the rear cable bracket.
5. Remove the brake drum.
6. Remove the brake shoe return springs.
7. Remove the brake shoe retaining springs.
8. Remove the brake shoe strut and spring and disconnect the cable from the operating arm.
9. Compress the retainers on the end of the brake cable housing and remove the cable.
10. Installation is the reverse of removal. Adjust the service and parking brakes and test the operation of both.

EXTERIOR

Doors

REMOVAL AND INSTALLATION

1. Disconnect the door light wiring harness on models equipped.
2. Remove the door opening check strap.
3. Support the door in the opened position. Use special tool C4614 or C4716 (depending on the size of the hinge pin) and remove the lower hinge pin. Insert special tool C4741 in place of the pin.
4. Remove the upper hinge pin using the suitable special tool. Remove the lower alignment tool and remove the door.
5. Grind a chamfer on the hinge pins to make installation easier.
6. Install the door into the opening using alignment tools C4741 in place of the hinge pins.
7. Use a small hammer and drive in the upper hinge pin from the bottom. Drive in the lower hinge pin from the top.
8. Install the door check strap and reconnect the wiring harness on models so equipped.

ADJUSTMENT

The door hinges are welded to both the door panels and the door pillar. Fore and aft, up and down adjustments may be accomplished by bending the hinges using a special tool C4736. Before bending the hinges, check for correct engagement of the door striker plate. Check hinge pin fit and condition and check for proper weatherstrip installation.

Bend the hinges as follows:
1. Examine the door fit to determine which direction is necessary to bend the hinge for correct alignment.
2. Place the adjusting tool C4736 in position on the hinge to be corrected. The tool must be slipped completely over the hinge to prevent damage to the tool or the hinge.

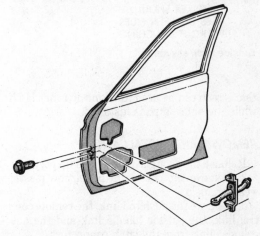

Removing/installing door check

3. Slowly apply pressure to bend the hinge. Check frequently until correct alignment is achieved.

Door Striker

The door latch should engage the striker squarely. The door should not rise up or down on the striker as it is closed. After the striker is adjusted the door should fit flush with the adjoining sheet metal.

ADJUSTMENT

1. Mark the location of the striker for reference.
2. Loosen the striker attaching screws.
3. Move the striker to the desired location and tighten the mounting screws.
4. Check alignment, readjust if necessary.

Door Latch

On late models, the outer latch can be replaced without removing the door trim panel.

The various links will hold the inner latch in position while the outer latch is removed. A

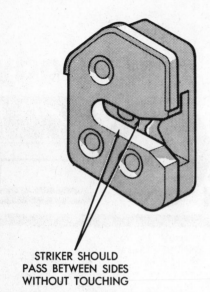

STRIKER SHOULD
PASS BETWEEN SIDES
WITHOUT TOUCHING

Outside latch assembly

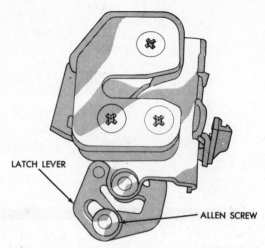

LATCH LEVER

ALLEN SCREW

Door latch adjustment

thin punch can be used to align the inner latch while the outer latch is installed.

REMOVAL AND INSTALLATION

1. Raise the door glass to the full up position.
2. Remove the door trim panel and plastic weathershield.
3. Remove the push rod link, the remote control link, the outside handle link and the key cylinder link from the latch connectors.
4. Remove the latch attaching screws. Remove the outside and inside halves of the latch assembly.
5. Install in the reverse order.

ADJUSTMENT

NOTE: *Door panel removal may be necessary for access to provide full adjustment range.*

1. Insert a $5/32''$ Allen wrench through the access hole provided in the door face and loosen the Allen screw.
2. Move the Allen wrench and screw upwards in the slot to the position required. Tighten the Allen screw to 30 in. lbs.
3. Check the position of the outside door handle for flush appearance to the door panel. Check the operation of the latch. Readjust the latch as required.

Lock Cylinder
REMOVAL AND INSTALLATION

1. Raise the window glass to the full up position.

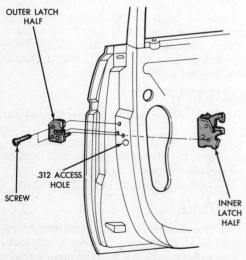

OUTER LATCH
HALF

.312 ACCESS
HOLE

SCREW

INNER
LATCH
HALF

Door latch installation

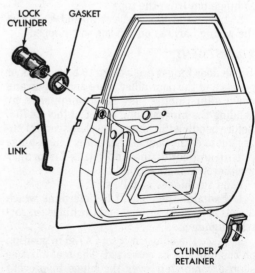

LOCK
CYLINDER

GASKET

LINK

CYLINDER
RETAINER

Door lock cylinder installation

CHILTON'S
AUTO BODY REPAIR TIPS

Tools and Materials • Step-by-Step Illustrated Procedures
How To Repair Dents, Scratches and Rust Holes
Spray Painting and Refinishing Tips

With a little practice, basic body repair procedures can be mastered by any do-it-yourself mechanic. The step-by-step repairs shown here can be applied to almost any type of auto body repair.

TOOLS & MATERIALS

You may already have basic tools, such as hammers and electric drills. Other tools unique to body repair — body hammers, grinding attachments, sanding blocks, dent puller, half-round plastic file and plastic spreaders — are relatively inexpensive and can be obtained wherever auto parts or auto body repair parts are sold. Portable air compressors and paint spray guns can be purchased or rented.

Auto Body Repair Kits

The best and most often used products are available to the do-it-yourselfer in kit form, from major manufacturers of auto body repair products. The same manufacturers also merchandise the individual products for use by pros.

Kits are available to make a wide variety of repairs, including holes, dents and scratches and fiberglass, and offer the advantage of buying the materials you'll need for the job. There is little waste or chance of materials going bad from not being used. Many kits may also contain basic body-working tools such as body files, sanding blocks and spreaders. Check the contents of the kit before buying your tools.

BODY REPAIR TIPS

Safety

Many of the products associated with auto body repair and refinishing contain toxic chemicals. Read all labels before opening containers and store them in a safe place and manner.

• Wear eye protection (safety goggles) when using power tools or when performing any operation that involves the removal of any type of material.

• Wear lung protection (disposable mask or respirator) when grinding, sanding or painting.

Sanding

1 Sand off paint before using a dent puller. When using a non-adhesive sanding disc, cover the back of the disc with an overlapping layer or two of masking tape and trim the edges. The disc will last considerably longer.

2 Use the circular motion of the sanding disc to grind *into* the edge of the repair. Grinding or sanding away from the jagged edge will only tear the sandpaper.

3 Use the palm of your hand flat on the panel to detect high and low spots. Do not use your fingertips. Slide your hand slowly back and forth.

WORKING WITH BODY FILLER

Mixing The Filler

Cleanliness and proper mixing and application are extremely important. Use a clean piece of plastic or glass or a disposable artist's palette to mix body filler.

1 Allow plenty of time and follow directions. No useful purpose will be served by adding more hardener to make it cure (set-up) faster. Less hardener means more curing time, but the mixture dries harder; more hardener means less curing time but a softer mixture.

2 Both the hardener and the filler should be thoroughly kneaded or stirred before mixing. Hardener should be a solid paste and dispense like thin toothpaste. Body filler should be smooth, and free of lumps or thick spots.

Getting the proper amount of hardener in the filler is the trickiest part of preparing the filler. Use the same amount of hardener in cold or warm weather. For contour filler (thick coats), a bead of hardener twice the diameter of the filler is about right. There's about a 15% margin on either side, but, if in doubt use less hardener.

3 Mix the body filler and hardener by wiping across the mixing surface, picking the mixture up and wiping it again. Colder weather requires longer mixing times. Do not mix in a circular motion; this will trap air bubbles which will become holes in the cured filler.

Applying The Filler

1 For best results, filler should not be applied over 1/4" thick.

Apply the filler in several coats. Build it up to above the level of the repair surface so that it can be sanded or grated down.

The first coat of filler must be pressed on with a firm wiping motion.

Apply the filler in one direction only. Working the filler back and forth will either pull it off the metal or trap air bubbles.

REPAIRING DENTS

Before you start, take a few minutes to study the damaged area. Try to visualize the shape of the panel before it was damaged. If the damage is on the left fender, look at the right fender and use it as a guide. If there is access to the panel from behind, you can reshape it with a body hammer. If not, you'll have to use a dent puller. Go slowly and work the metal a little at a time. Get the panel as straight as possible before applying filler.

1 This dent is typical of one that can be pulled out or hammered out from behind. Remove the headlight cover, headlight assembly and turn signal housing.

2 Drill a series of holes ½ the size of the end of the dent puller along the stress line. Make some trial pulls and assess the results. If necessary, drill more holes and try again. Do not hurry.

3 If possible, use a body hammer and block to shape the metal back to its original contours. Get the metal back as close to its original shape as possible. Don't depend on body filler to fill dents.

4 Using an 80-grit grinding disc on an electric drill, grind the paint from the surrounding area down to bare metal. Use a new grinding pad to prevent heat buildup that will warp metal.

5 The area should look like this when you're finished grinding. Knock the drill holes in and tape over small openings to keep plastic filler out.

6 Mix the body filler (see Body Repair Tips). Spread the body filler evenly over the entire area (see Body Repair Tips). Be sure to cover the area completely.

7 Let the body filler dry until the surface can just be scratched with your fingernail. Knock the high spots from the body filler with a body file ("Cheesegrater"). Check frequently with the palm of your hand for high and low spots.

8 Check to be sure that trim pieces that will be installed later will fit exactly. Sand the area with 40-grit paper.

9 If you wind up with low spots, you may have to apply another layer of filler.

10 Knock the high spots off with 40-grit paper. When you are satisfied with the contours of the repair, apply a thin coat of filler to cover pin holes and scratches.

11 Block sand the area with 40-grit paper to a smooth finish. Pay particular attention to body lines and ridges that must be well-defined.

12 Sand the area with 400 paper and then finish with a scuff pad. The finished repair is ready for priming and painting (see Painting Tips).

Materials and photos courtesy of Ritt Jones Auto Body, Prospect Park, PA.

REPAIRING RUST HOLES

There are many ways to repair rust holes. The fiberglass cloth kit shown here is one of the most cost efficient for the owner because it provides a strong repair that resists cracking and moisture and is relatively easy to use. It can be used on large and small holes (with or without backing) and can be applied over contoured areas. Remember, however, that short of replacing an entire panel, no repair is a guarantee that the rust will not return.

1 Remove any trim that will be in the way. Clean away all loose debris. Cut away all the rusted metal. But be sure to leave enough metal to retain the contour or body shape.

2 Grind away all traces of rust with a 24-grit grinding disc. Be sure to grind back 3-4 inches from the edge of the hole down to bare metal and be sure all traces of paint, primer and rust are removed.

3 Block sand the area with 80 or 100 grit sandpaper to get a clear, shiny surface and feathered paint edge. Tap the edges of the hole inward with a ball peen hammer.

4 If you are going to use release film, cut a piece about 2-3″ larger than the area you have sanded. Place the film over the repair and mark the sanded area on the film. Avoid any unnecessary wrinkling of the film.

5 Cut 2 pieces of fiberglass matte to match the shape of the repair. One piece should be about 1″ smaller than the sanded area and the second piece should be 1″ smaller than the first. Mix enough filler and hardener to saturate the fiberglass material (see Body Repair Tips).

6 Lay the release sheet on a flat surface and spread an even layer of filler, large enough to cover the repair. Lay the smaller piece of fiberglass cloth in the center of the sheet and spread another layer of filler over the fiberglass cloth. Repeat the operation for the larger piece of cloth.

7 Place the repair material over the repair area, with the release film facing outward. Use a spreader and work from the center outward to smooth the material, following the body contours. Be sure to remove all air bubbles.

8 Wait until the repair has dried tack-free and peel off the release sheet. The ideal working temperature is 60°-90° F. Cooler or warmer temperatures or high humidity may require additional curing time. Wait longer, if in doubt.

9 Sand and feather-edge the entire area. The initial sanding can be done with a sanding disc on an electric drill if care is used. Finish the sanding with a block sander. Low spots can be filled with body filler; this may require several applications.

10 When the filler can just be scratched with a fingernail, knock the high spots down with a body file and smooth the entire area with 80-grit. Feather the filled areas into the surrounding areas.

11 When the area is sanded smooth, mix some topcoat and hardener and apply it directly with a spreader. This will give a smooth finish and prevent the glass matte from showing through the paint.

12 Block sand the topcoat smooth with finishing sandpaper (200 grit), and 400 grit. The repair is ready for masking, priming and painting (see Painting Tips).

Materials and photos courtesy Marson Corporation, Chelsea, Massachusetts

PAINTING TIPS

Preparation

1 SANDING — Use a 400 or 600 grit wet or dry sandpaper. Wet-sand the area with a 1/4 sheet of sandpaper soaked in clean water. Keep the paper wet while sanding. Sand the area until the repaired area tapers into the original finish.

2 CLEANING — Wash the area to be painted thoroughly with water and a clean rag. Rinse it thoroughly and wipe the surface dry until you're sure it's completely free of dirt, dust, fingerprints, wax, detergent or other foreign matter.

3 MASKING — Protect any areas you don't want to overspray by covering them with masking tape and newspaper. Be careful not get fingerprints on the area to be painted.

4 PRIMING — All exposed metal should be primed before painting. Primer protects the metal and provides an excellent surface for paint adhesion. When the primer is dry, wet-sand the area again with 600 grit wet-sandpaper. Clean the area again after sanding.

Painting Techniques

Paint applied from either a spray gun or a spray can (for small areas) will provide good results. Experiment on an old piece of metal to get the right combination before you begin painting.

SPRAYING VISCOSITY (SPRAY GUN ONLY) — Paint should be thinned to spraying viscosity according to the directions on the can. Use only the recommended thinner or reducer and the same amount of reduction regardless of temperature.

AIR PRESSURE (SPRAY GUN ONLY) — This is extremely important. Be sure you are using the proper recommended pressure.

TEMPERATURE — The surface to be painted should be approximately the same temperature as the surrounding air. Applying warm paint to a cold surface, or vice versa, will completely upset the paint characteristics.

THICKNESS — Spray with smooth strokes. In general, the thicker the coat of paint, the longer the drying time. Apply several thin coats about 30 seconds apart. The paint should remain wet long enough to flow out and no longer; heavier coats will only produce sags or wrinkles. Spray a light (fog) coat, followed by heavier color coats.

DISTANCE — The ideal spraying distance is 8″-12″ from the gun or can to the surface. Shorter distances will produce ripples, while greater distances will result in orange peel, dry film and poor color match and loss of material due to overspray.

OVERLAPPING — The gun or can should be kept at right angles to the surface at all times. Work to a wet edge at an even speed, using a 50% overlap and direct the center of the spray at the lower or nearest edge of the previous stroke.

RUBBING OUT (BLENDING) FRESH PAINT — Let the paint dry thoroughly. Runs or imperfections can be sanded out, primed and repainted.

Don't be in too big a hurry to remove the masking. This only produces paint ridges. When the finish has dried for at least a week, apply a small amount of fine grade rubbing compound with a clean, wet cloth. Use lots of water and blend the new paint with the surrounding area.

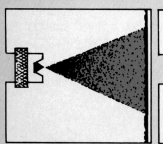

WRONG

Thin coat. Stroke too fast, not enough overlap, gun too far away.

CORRECT

Medium coat. Proper distance, good stroke, proper overlap.

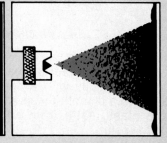

WRONG

Heavy coat. Stroke too slow, too much overlap, gun too close.

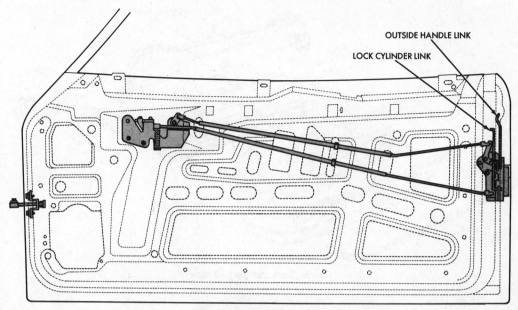

OUTSIDE HANDLE LINK

LOCK CYLINDER LINK

Typical door lock system

2. Remove the door trim panel and plastic air shield.

3. Disconnect the remote link from the lock cylinder lever.

4. Remove the horseshoe retaining clip from the cylinder lock groove. Remove the retainer and the lock cylinder.

5. Install the lock cylinder in the reverse order of removal.

Outside Door Handle
REMOVAL AND INSTALLATION

1. Raise the door glass to the full up position.
2. Remove the door trim panel and plastic air shield.
3. Disconnect the handle link from the latch.

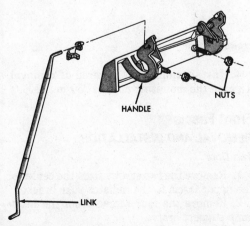

NUTS

HANDLE

LINK

Outside door handle

4. Remove the nuts that attach the handle to the door panel. Lift the handle and link from the door.

5. Install the door handle in the reverse order of removal.

Hood
REMOVAL AND INSTALLATION

1. Mark the hinge outline on the inside of the hood for reinstallation reference.

2. Place a protective padded covering over the windshield and fender ends in case the hood slides out of your grasp when the hinges are disconnected. Place a block of wood below each rear corner of the hood to prevent sudden rear movement when the retaining bolts are loosened.

3. Loosen and remove the retaining bolts and the hood.

4. Install the hood in the reverse order of removal. Align the hood to the scribe marks previously made and tighten the retaining bolts.

ALIGNMENT

Inspect the clearance and alignment of the hood slides in relation to the cowl, fenders and grille panel. Elongated holes in the hood hinges are provided for necessary adjustments. Loosen the hood hinge to hood attaching bolts until the hood can be moved with slight force. Adjust the cowl to hood clearance first. After necessary adjustment has been made and the mounting bolts tightened, check the alignment of the hood latch and safety catch. If adjustment is necessary, loosen the mounting bolts and slide

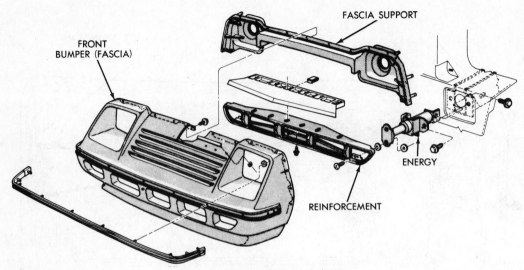

FRONT
BUMPER (FASCIA)

FASCIA SUPPORT

ENERGY

REINFORCEMENT

Fascia (front bumper)—2 door

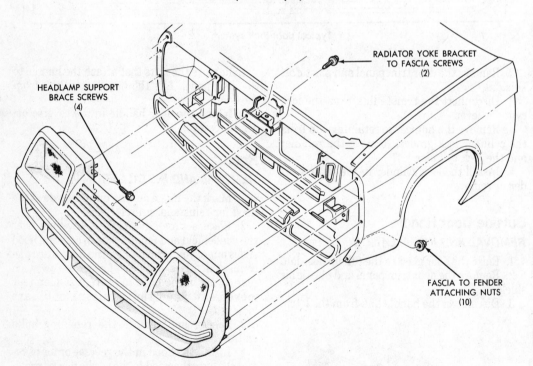

RADIATOR YOKE BRACKET
TO FASCIA SCREWS
(2)

HEADLAMP SUPPORT
BRACE SCREWS
(4)

FASCIA TO FENDER
ATTACHING NUTS
(10)

Fascia attachment screws—2 door

the latch to the required position. Retighten the mounting bolts.

Front and Rear Bumper
REMOVAL AND INSTALLATION
Four Door

1. Remove the push on fasteners securing the boot to the bumper fasteners.
2. Remove the nuts securing the bumper to the energy absorber unit.
3. Lower the bumper to the floor.

4. Installation is the reverse of removal. Tighten the mounting nuts to 250 in. lbs.

Front Fascia
REMOVAL AND INSTALLATION
Two Door

1. Remove the two screws from the center of the upper fascia to the radiator yoke bracket.
2. Remove the four screws from the headlamp support braces.
3. Disconnect the headlamp wire connectors.

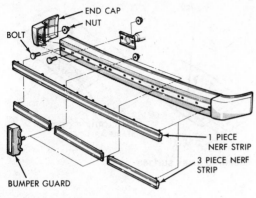

Bumper mounting—4 door

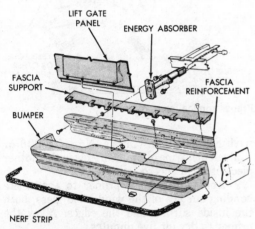

Rear bumper—2 door

4. Raise the vehicle on a hoist and remove the 14 plastic rivets from the splash shields. Remove the shields.

5. Remove the 8 plastic rivets from the underside of the fascia to the fender mounting studs.

6. Grasp the fascia assembly at the upper louver and remove the fascia assembly.

NOTE: *It is recommended that the fascia be stored front side up to prevent permanent distortion.*

Rear Bumper
REMOVAL AND INSTALLATION
Rampage

1. Remove the push on fasteners securing the boot to the bumper fasteners.

2. Remove the nuts securing the bumper to the energy absorber unit.

3. Lower the bumper to the floor.

4. Installation is the reverse of removal. Tighten the mounting nuts to 250 in. lbs.

Two Door

1. Place a support under the bumper.
2. Remove the 10 fascia retainer nuts.
3. Remove the 6 energy absorber to bumper retaining nuts.
4. Lower the bumper to the floor.
5. Installation is the reverse of removal. Tighten the bumper mounting nuts to 250 in. lbs. Tighten the fascia to fender nuts to 60 in. lbs.

Grille
REMOVAL AND INSTALLATION
Two Door

The grille is mounted to the radiator yoke with plastic rivet type fasteners. To remove the grille grasp the center portion of the rivet and pull upward. The rivet may then be removed.

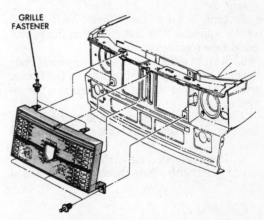

Grille mounting—4 door

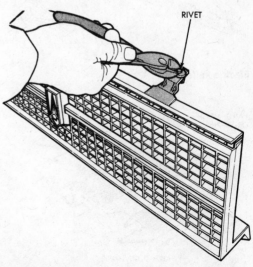

Removing grille rivet—4 door

Windshield

NOTE: *The windshield is mounted with butyl tape, special tools and materials are required for installation.*

REMOVAL AND INSTALLATION

1. Cover all areas around the windshield to prevent damage to the finish.

2. Remove the windshield wiper arm and blade assemblies. Remove the windshield mouldings that interfere with windshield replacement.

3. Use an electric knife (Miller Tool No. 4386 or the equivalent) and cut the existing butyl tape as close as possible to the mounting flange of the windshield frame. Remove the windshield.

4. Remove all remaining adhesive from the mounting flange with naphtha or comparable solvent.

CAUTION: *Follow the warnings on the solvent can.*

5. Apply butyl primer (Chrys. No. 3500883 or the equivalent) on the mounting flange and butyl tape remnants.

6. Start at either side of the windshield body opening and apply the butyl tape to the frame, with the tapered edge of the tape facing the reveal surface.

7. Cut off the excess tape and butt joint the ends. Apply sufficient pressure to ensure a good seal.

8. Clean the bonding surfaces of the windshield glass with clean cheesecloth moistened

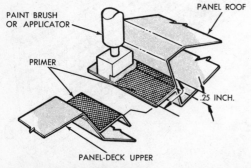

Electric knife

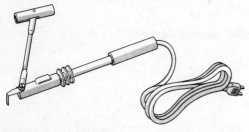

Cleaning metal frame surface

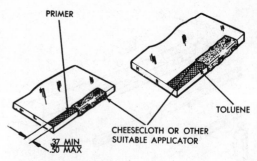

Cleaning glass surface

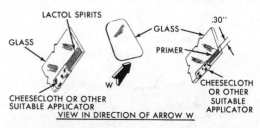

Primer application to glass

with Super-Kleen (Chrys. No. 4026030 or equivalent). Wipe off immediately with another piece of clean cheesecloth.

9. Apply butyl glass primer to the entire bonding surface of the windshield glass, both the inside surface and the edges. Allow the primer to dry for five minutes.

10. Locate the windshield in the center of the opening and made contact with the tape. Place spacers at the bottom of the glass between the glass edge and body opening. Locate one spacer on each side of the glass, over the site of the original spacer. Select spacers, or combination of spacers that will ensure a snug fit between the glass edge and frame while keeping the glass centered.

11. Use maximum hand pressure to push the glass down against the tape.

12. Inspect the bond. If the contact between the glass and tape is poor, repear maximum hand pressure. The bond should be ¼" or greater.

13. Check the spacers to make sure they are in the proper location.

14. Water test the seal. Repair any leaks with secondary sealer application.

15. Install any trim molding and the wiper arm and blade assemblies.

Hatchback Glass

REMOVAL AND INSTALLATION

1. Remove the locking strip center cap and pull the locking strip from the groove.

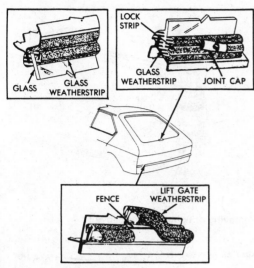

Lift-gate weatherstrips

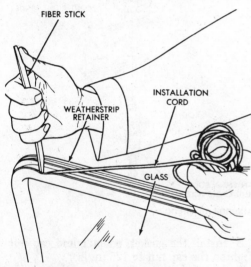

Cord installation

2. Carefully push the glass out of the weatherstrip, starting at one corner and continuing around the glass until it is free from the weatherstrip. Remove the weatherstrip from the hatch frame.

3. Install the glass into the weatherstrip. Install cord between the glass and weatherstrip lip.

4. Place the glass into position in the frame opening. Apply pressure against the glass while an assistant pulls the cord through the window opening which will locate the weatherstripping lip over the frame.

5. Inspect for complete sealing of the weatherstrip around the frame.

6. Install the locking strip starting at the bottom center. Install the center locking cap.

Outside Rear View Mirror
REMOVAL AND INSTALLATION

1. Lower the glass to the full down position.
2. Remove the door trim panel and plastic air shield.
3. Remove the arm rest bracket on models with premium styled arm rest.
4. On remote control mirrors, remove the remote control retaining nut.
5. Remove the remote control cable from the retaining clips.
6. Remove the plastic clip on the cable from the door.

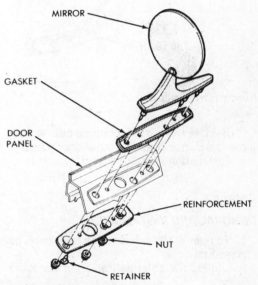

Standard outside mirror—4 door

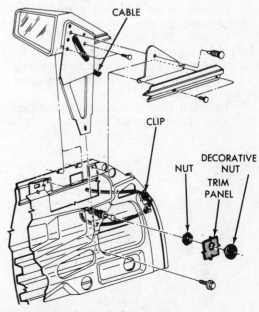

Outside mirror—Tourismo, Charger

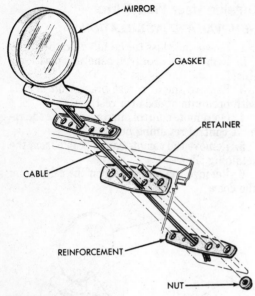

Remote mirror—4 door

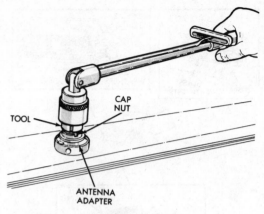

Removing or tightening the cap nut

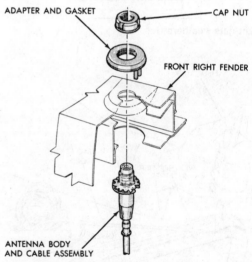

Antenna mounting

7. Remove the mirror retaining nuts and remove the mirror from the outer door panel.

8. Installation is the reverse of removal.

Antenna

REMOVAL AND INSTALLATION

1. To remove the antenna, the radio must be remove first.

2. Unplug the antenna lead from the radio receiver.

3. Remove the antenna mast by unscrewing the mast from the antenna body.

4. Remove the cap nut then remove the antenna adapter and gasket.

5. Unfasten the 3 push pins from the rear of the plastic inner fender shield and bend the shield away to gain access to the antenna body.

6. From under the fender remove the antenna lead and body assembly.

7. To install, position the antenna body and cable from the underneath the fender.

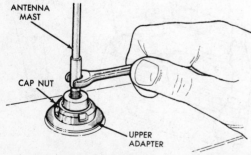

Antenna mast removal

8. Install the gasket, adapter and cap nut. Tighten the cap nut to 125 in. lbs.

9. Install the antenna mast into the antenna body until the sleeve bottoms on the antenna body.

10. Route the cable to the radio.

INTERIOR

Door Panels

REMOVAL AND INSTALLATION

1. Remove the inside door handle and bezel trim.

2. Remove the arm rest and window handle crank.

3. If equipped with a remote door mirror, remove the retaining trim nut.

4. Use a wide prying device and unclip the panel retainers from the door. Remove the panel, and plastic shield.

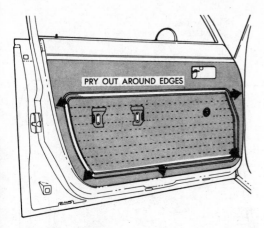

Trim panel removal

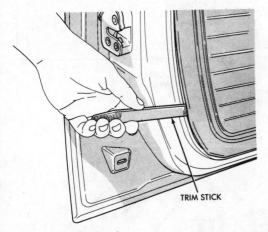

Disengage trim panel

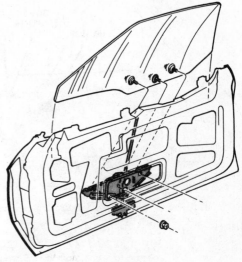

Typical glass fastener locations

5. Install the weather shield and door panel in the reverse order of removal.

Front Door Glass and Regulator
REMOVAL AND INSTALLATION

1. To remove the window glass: Remove the door panel and weathershield.

2. Remove the glass stops and stabilizers.

3. Lower the window until the lift channel fasteners are visible. Remove the fasteners and disengage the glass from the lift channel. Remove the glass through the belt (upper) opening. Install the glass in the reverse order.

4. To remove the window regulator: Remove the door panel and weathershield.

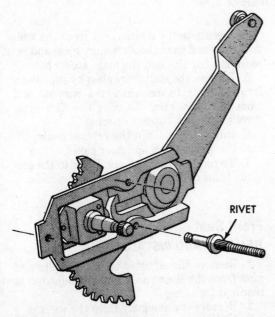

Typical window regulator

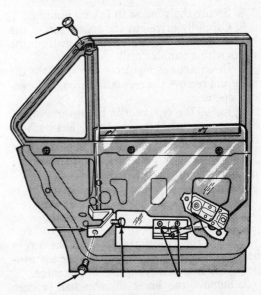

Rear door glass removal points

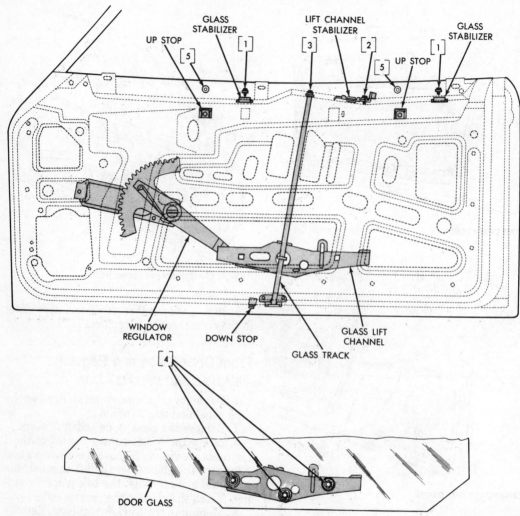

GLASS
STABILIZER

UP STOP
[5]

GLASS
STABILIZER
[1]

LIFT CHANNEL
STABILIZER

[3]

[2]

[5]

UP STOP

GLASS
STABILIZER
[1]

WINDOW
REGULATOR

DOWN STOP

GLASS LIFT
CHANNEL

GLASS TRACK

[4]

DOOR GLASS

Typical glass system on door

5. Secure the window in full up positon.

6. Carefully drive out the center pin of the mounting rivets with a punch, then drill out the rivets with a suitable drill.

7. Disengage the regulator arm from the lift plate and remove the regulator through the access opening.

8. Install the regulator in the reverse order. Secure with suitable size bolts, lockwashers and nuts.

Rear Door Glass and Regulator
REMOVAL AND INSTALLATION

1. To remove the glass: Remove the door panel and weathershield.

2. Align the glass fasteners with the access hole and remove the fasteners. Lower the window glass after removing the lift fasteners.

3. Remove the lower division bar bracket screws and remove the bar bracket.

4. Disengage the division bar from the window glass and from the stationary glass and remove the bar through the main access hole.

5. Remove the stationary glass by applying a forward force to disengage the window seal from the door frame. Remove the door glass through the belt (upper) opening.

6. Install the glass in the reverse order. Install the weatherseal and door panel.

7. To remove the regulator: Refer to the previous front door regulator servicing section.

Front Seat
REMOVAL AND INSTALLATION

1. Remove the adjuster attaching bolts and nuts from the floor pan. Move the adjuster as required for access.

2. Remove the assembly from the vehicle.

3. Install in reverse.

Rear Seat Back

REMOVAL AND INSTALLATION

1. Remove the right side seat belt retractor cover.
2. Remove the retaining clip from the seat back pivot.
3. Push the seat towards the left pivot bracket until the right pivot clears the bracket.
4. Remove the seat back from the vehicle.
5. Installation is the reverse of removal.

Rear Seat Cushion

REMOVAL AND INSTALLATION

1. Remove the rear seat back.
2. Remove the cushion retaining screw.
3. Slide the cushion forward to disengage the front retainers and remove the seat from the vehicle.
4. Installation is the reverse of removal.

Inside Rear View Mirror

REMOVAL AND INSTALLATION

1. Loosen the set screw and slide the mirror up and off of the button.

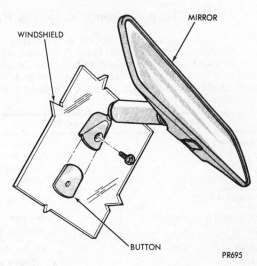

Rear view mirror

2. To install, slide the mirror over the button and tighten the set screw. Care should be exercised not to over tighten the screw.

How to Remove Stains from Fabric Interior

For best results, spots and stains should be removed as soon as possible. Never use gasoline, lacquer thinner, acetone, nail polish remover or bleach. Use a 3' x 3" piece of cheesecloth. Squeeze most of the liquid from the fabric and wipe the stained fabric from the outside of the stain toward the center with a lifting motion. Turn the cheesecloth as soon as one side becomes soiled. When using water to remove a stain, be sure to wash the entire section after the spot has been removed to avoid water stains. Encrusted spots can be broken up with a dull knife and vacuumed before removing the stain.

Type of Stain	How to Remove It
Surface spots	Brush the spots out with a small hand brush or use a commercial preparation such as K2R to lift the stain.
Mildew	Clean around the mildew with warm suds. Rinse in cold water and soak the mildew area in a solution of 1 part table salt and 2 parts water. Wash with upholstery cleaner.
Water stains	Water stains in fabric materials can be removed with a solution made from 1 cup of table salt dissolved in 1 quart of water. Vigorously scrub the solution into the stain and rinse with clear water. Water stains in nylon or other synthetic fabrics should be removed with a commercial type spot remover.
Chewing gum, tar, crayons, shoe polish (greasy stains)	Do not use a cleaner that will soften gum or tar. Harden the deposit with an ice cube and scrape away as much as possible with a dull knife. Moisten the remainder with cleaning fluid and scrub clean.
Ice cream, candy	Most candy has a sugar base and can be removed with a cloth wrung out in warm water. Oily candy, after cleaning with warm water, should be cleaned with upholstery cleaner. Rinse with warm water and clean the remainder with cleaning fluid.
Wine, alcohol, egg, milk, soft drink (non-greasy stains)	Do not use soap. Scrub the stain with a cloth wrung out in warm water. Remove the remainder with cleaning fluid.
Grease, oil, lipstick, butter and related stains	Use a spot remover to avoid leaving a ring. Work from the outisde of the stain to the center and dry with a clean cloth when the spot is gone.

How to Remove Stains from Fabric Interior (cont.)

For best results, spots and stains should be removed as soon as possible. Never use gasoline, lacquer thinner, acetone, nail polish remover or bleach. Use a 3' x 3" piece of cheesecloth. Squeeze most of the liquid from the fabric and wipe the stained fabric from the outside of the stain toward the center with a lifting motion. Turn the cheesecloth as soon as one side becomes soiled. When using water to remove a stain, be sure to wash the entire section after the spot has been removed to avoid water stains. Encrusted spots can be broken up with a dull knife and vacuumed before removing the stain.

Type of Stain	How to Remove It
Headliners (cloth)	Mix a solution of warm water and foam upholstery cleaner to give thick suds. Use only foam—liquid may streak or spot. Clean the entire headliner in one operation using a circular motion with a natural sponge.
Headliner (vinyl)	Use a vinyl cleaner with a sponge and wipe clean with a dry cloth.
Seats and door panels	Mix 1 pint upholstery cleaner in 1 gallon of water. Do not soak the fabric around the buttons.
Leather or vinyl fabric	Use a multi-purpose cleaner full strength and a stiff brush. Let stand 2 minutes and scrub thoroughly. Wipe with a clean, soft rag.
Nylon or synthetic fabrics	For normal stains, use the same procedures you would for washing cloth upholstery. If the fabric is extremely dirty, use a multi-purpose cleaner full strength with a stiff scrub brush. Scrub thoroughly in all directions and wipe with a cotton towel or soft rag.

Mechanic's Data

11

1":254mm
TAX
10.16mm
Liter
Parts
Overhaul

General Conversion Table

Multiply By	To Convert	To	
	LENGTH		
2.54	Inches	Centimeters	.3937
25.4	Inches	Millimeters	.03937
30.48	Feet	Centimeters	.0328
.304	Feet	Meters	3.28
.914	Yards	Meters	1.094
1.609	Miles	Kilometers	.621
	VOLUME		
.473	Pints	Liters	2.11
.946	Quarts	Liters	1.06
3.785	Gallons	Liters	.264
.016	Cubic inches	Liters	61.02
16.39	Cubic inches	Cubic cms.	.061
28.3	Cubic feet	Liters	.0353
	MASS (Weight)		
28.35	Ounces	Grams	.035
.4536	Pounds	Kilograms	2.20
—	To obtain	From	Multiply by

Multiply By	To Convert	To	
	AREA		
.645	Square inches	Square cms.	.155
.836	Square yds.	Square meters	1.196
	FORCE		
4.448	Pounds	Newtons	.225
.138	Ft./lbs.	Kilogram/meters	7.23
1.36	Ft./lbs.	Newton-meters	.737
.112	In./lbs.	Newton-meters	8.844
	PRESSURE		
.068	Psi	Atmospheres	14.7
6.89	Psi	Kilopascals	.145
	OTHER		
1.104	Horsepower (DIN)	Horsepower (SAE)	.9861
.746	Horsepower (SAE)	Kilowatts (KW)	1.34
1.60	Mph	Km/h	.625
.425	Mpg	Km/1	2.35
—	To obtain	From	Multiply by

Tap Drill Sizes

National Coarse or U.S.S.

Screw & Tap Size	Threads Per Inch	Use Drill Number
No. 5	40	39
No. 6	32	36
No. 8	32	29
No. 10	24	25
No. 12	24	17
¼	20	8
5/16	18	F
⅜	16	5/16
7/16	14	U
½	13	27/64
9/16	12	31/64
⅝	11	17/32
¾	10	21/32
⅞	9	49/64

National Coarse or U.S.S.

Screw & Tap Size	Threads Per Inch	Use Drill Number
1	8	⅞
1⅛	7	63/64
1¼	7	1 7/64
1½	6	1 11/32

National Fine or S.A.E.

Screw & Tap Size	Threads Per Inch	Use Drill Number
No. 5	44	37
No. 6	40	33
No. 8	36	29
No. 10	32	21

National Fine or S.A.E.

Screw & Tap Size	Threads Per Inch	Use Drill Number
No. 12	28	15
¼	28	3
6/16	24	1
⅜	24	Q
7/16	20	W
½	20	29/64
9/16	18	33/64
⅝	18	37/64
¾	16	11/16
⅞	14	13/16
1⅛	12	1 3/64
1¼	12	1 11/64
1½	12	1 27/64

Drill Sizes In Decimal Equivalents

Inch	Decimal	Wire	mm
1/64	.0156		.39
	.0157		.4
	.0160	78	
	.0165		.42
	.0173		.44
	.0177		.45
	.0180	77	
	.0181		.46
	.0189		.48
	.0197		.5
	.0200	76	
	.0210	75	
	.0217		.55
	.0225	74	
	.0236		.6
	.0240	73	
	.0250	72	
	.0256		.65
	.0260	71	
	.0276		.7
	.0280	70	
	.0292	69	
	.0295		.75
	.0310	68	
1/32	.0312		.79
	.0315		.8
	.0320	67	
	.0330	66	
	.0335		.85
	.0350	65	
	.0354		.9
	.0360	64	
	.0370	63	
	.0374		.95
	.0380	62	
	.0390	61	
	.0394		1.0
	.0400	60	
	.0410	59	
	.0413		1.05
	.0420	58	
	.0430	57	
	.0433		1.1
	.0453		1.15
3/64	.0465	56	
	.0469		1.19
	.0472		1.2
	.0492		1.25
	.0512		1.3
	.0520	55	
	.0531		1.35
	.0550	54	
	.0551		1.4
	.0571		1.45
	.0591		1.5
	.0595	53	
	.0610		1.55
1/16	.0625		1.59
	.0630		1.6
	.0635	52	
	.0650		1.65
	.0669		1.7
	.0670	51	
	.0689		1.75
	.0700	50	
	.0709		1.8
	.0728		1.85

Inch	Decimal	Wire	mm
	.0730	49	
	.0748		1.9
	.0760	48	
	.0768		1.95
5/64	.0781		1.98
	.0785	47	
	.0787		2.0
	.0807		2.05
	.0810	46	
	.0820	45	
	.0827		2.1
	.0846		2.15
	.0860	44	
	.0866		2.2
	.0886		2.25
	.0890	43	
	.0906		2.3
	.0925		2.35
	.0935	42	
3/32	.0938		2.38
	.0945		2.4
	.0960	41	
	.0965		2.45
	.0980	40	
	.0981		2.5
	.0995	39	
	.1015	38	
	.1024		2.6
	.1040	37	
	.1063		2.7
	.1065	36	
	.1083		2.75
7/64	.1094		2.77
	.1100	35	
	.1102		2.8
	.1110	34	
	.1130	33	
	.1142		2.9
	.1160	32	
	.1181		3.0
	.1200	31	
	.1220		3.1
1/8	.1250		3.17
	.1260		3.2
	.1280		3.25
	.1285	30	
	.1299		3.3
	.1339		3.4
	.1360	29	
	.1378		3.5
	.1405	28	
9/64	.1406		3.57
	.1417		3.6
	.1440	27	
	.1457		3.7
	.1470	26	
	.1476		3.75
	.1495	25	
	.1496		3.8
	.1520	24	
	.1535		3.9
	.1540	23	
5/32	.1562		3.96
	.1570	22	
	.1575		4.0
	.1590	21	
	.1610	20	

Inch	Decimal	Wire & Letter	mm
	.1614		4.1
	.1654		4.2
	.1660	19	
	.1673		4.25
	.1693		4.3
	.1695	18	
11/64	.1719		4.36
	.1730	17	
	.1732		4.4
	.1770	16	
	.1772		4.5
	.1800	15	
	.1811		4.6
	.1820	14	
	.1850	13	
	.1850		4.7
	.1870		4.75
3/16	.1875		4.76
	.1890		4.8
	.1890	12	
	.1910	11	
	.1929		4.9
	.1935	10	
	.1960	9	
	.1969		5.0
	.1990	8	
	.2008		5.1
	.2010	7	
13/64	.2031		5.16
	.2040	6	
	.2047		5.2
	.2055	5	
	.2067		5.25
	.2087		5.3
	.2090	4	
	.2126		5.4
	.2130	3	
	.2165		5.5
7/32	.2188		5.55
	.2205		5.6
	.2210	2	
	.2244		5.7
	.2264		5.75
	.2280	1	
	.2283		5.8
	.2323		5.9
	.2340	A	
15/64	.2344		5.95
	.2362		6.0
	.2380	B	
	.2402		6.1
	.2420	C	
	.2441		6.2
	.2460	D	
	.2461		6.25
	.2480		6.3
1/4	.2500	E	6.35
	.2520		6.
	.2559		6.5
	.2570	F	
	.2598		6.6
	.2610	G	
	.2638		6.7
17/64	.2656		6.74
	.2657		6.75
	.2660	H	
	.2677		6.8

Inch	Decimal	Letter	mm
	.2717		6.9
	.2720	I	
	.2756		7.0
	.2770	J	
	.2795		7.1
	.2810	K	
9/32	.2812		7.14
	.2835		7.2
	.2854		7.25
	.2874		7.3
	.2900	L	
	.2913		7.4
	.2950	M	
	.2953		7.5
19/64	.2969		7.54
	.2992		7.6
	.3020	N	
	.3031		7.7
	.3051		7.75
	.3071		7.8
	.3110		7.9
5/16	.3125		7.93
	.3150		8.0
	.3160	O	
	.3189		8.1
	.3228		8.2
	.3230	P	
	.3248		8.25
	.3268		8.3
21/64	.3281		8.33
	.3307		8.4
	.3320	Q	
	.3346		8.5
	.3386		8.6
	.3390	R	
	.3425		8.7
11/32	.3438		8.73
	.3445		8.75
	.3465		8.8
	.3480	S	
	.3504		8.9
	.3543		9.0
	.3580	T	
	.3583		9.1
23/64	.3594		9.12
	.3622		9.2
	.3642		9.25
	.3661		9.3
	.3680	U	
	.3701		9.4
	.3740		9.5
3/8	.3750		9.52
	.3770	V	
	.3780		9.6
	.3819		9.7
	.3839		9.75
	.3858		9.8
	.3860	W	
	.3898		9.9
25/64	.3906		9.92
	.3937		10.0
	.3970	X	
	.4040	Y	
13/32	.4062		10.31
	.4130	Z	
	.4134		10.5
27/64	.4219		10.71

Inch	Decimal	mm
	.4331	11.0
7/16	.4375	11.11
	.4528	11.5
29/64	.4531	11.51
15/32	.4688	11.90
	.4724	12.0
31/64	.4844	12.30
	.4921	12.5
1/2	.5000	12.70
	.5118	13.0
33/64	.5156	13.09
17/32	.5312	13.49
	.5315	13.5
35/64	.5469	13.89
	.5512	14.0
9/16	.5625	14.28
	.5709	14.5
37/64	.5781	14.68
	.5906	15.0
19/32	.5938	15.08
39/64	.6094	15.47
	.6102	15.5
5/8	.6250	15.87
	.6299	16.0
41/64	.6406	16.27
	.6496	16.5
21/32	.6562	16.66
	.6693	17.0
43/64	.6719	17.06
11/16	.6875	17.46
	.6890	17.5
45/64	.7031	17.85
	.7087	18.0
23/32	.7188	18.25
	.7283	18.5
47/64	.7344	18.65
	.7480	19.0
3/4	.7500	19.05
49/64	.7656	19.44
	.7677	19.5
25/32	.7812	19.84
	.7874	20.0
51/64	.7969	20.24
	.8071	20.5
13/16	.8125	20.63
	.8268	21.0
53/64	.8281	21.03
27/32	.8438	21.43
	.8465	21.5
55/64	.8594	21.82
	.8661	22.0
7/8	.8750	22.22
	.8858	22.5
57/64	.8906	22.62
	.9055	23.0
29/32	.9062	23.01
59/64	.9219	23.41
	.9252	23.5
15/16	.9375	23.81
	.9449	24.0
61/64	.9531	24.2
	.9646	24.5
31/64	.9688	24.6
	.9843	25.0
63/64	.9844	25.0.
1	1.0000	25.4

AIR/FUEL RATIO: The ratio of air to gasoline by weight in the fuel mixture drawn into the engine.

AIR INJECTION: One method of reducing harmful exhaust emissions by injecting air into each of the exhaust ports of an engine. The fresh air entering the hot exhaust manifold causes any remaining fuel to be burned before it can exit the tailpipe.

ALTERNATOR: A device used for converting mechanical energy into electrical energy.

AMMETER: An instrument, calibrated in amperes, used to measure the flow of an electrical current in a circuit. Ammeters are always connected in series with the circuit being tested.

AMPERE: The rate of flow of electrical current present when one volt of electrical pressure is applied against one ohm of electrical resistance.

ANALOG COMPUTER: Any microprocessor that uses similar (analogous) electrical signals to make its calculations.

ARMATURE: A laminated, soft iron core wrapped by a wire that converts electrical energy to mechanical energy as in a motor or relay. When rotated in a magnetic field, it changes mechanical energy into electrical energy as in a generator.

ATMOSPHERIC PRESSURE: The pressure on the Earth's surface caused by the weight of the air in the atmosphere. At sea level, this pressure is 14.7 psi at 32°F (101 kPa at 0°C).

ATOMIZATION: The breaking down of a liquid into a fine mist that can be suspended in air.

AXIAL PLAY: Movement parallel to a shaft or bearing bore.

BACKFIRE: The sudden combustion of gases in the intake or exhaust system that results in a loud explosion.

BACKLASH: The clearance or play between two parts, such as meshed gears.

BACKPRESSURE: Restrictions in the exhaust system that slow the exit of exhaust gases from the combustion chamber.

BAKELITE: A heat resistant, plastic insulator material commonly used in printed circuit boards and transistorized components.

BALL BEARING: A bearing made up of hardened inner and outer races between which hardened steel ball roll.

BALLAST RESISTOR: A resistor in the primary ignition circuit that lowers voltage after the engine is started to reduce wear on ignition components.

BEARING: A friction reducing, supportive device usually located between a stationary part and a moving part.

BIMETAL TEMPERATURE SENSOR: Any sensor or switch made of two dissimilar types of metal that bend when heated or cooled due to the different expansion rates of the alloys. These types of sensors usually function as an on/off switch.

BLOWBY: Combustion gases, composed of water vapor and unburned fuel, that leak past the piston rings into the crankcase during normal engine operation. These gases are removed by the PCV system to prevent the build-up of harmful acids in the crankcase.

BRAKE PAD: A brake shoe and lining assembly used with disc brakes.

BRAKE SHOE: The backing for the brake lining. The term is, however, usually applied to the assembly of the brake backing and lining.

BUSHING: A liner, usually removable, for a bearing; an anti-friction liner used in place of a bearing.

BYPASS: System used to bypass ballast resistor during engine cranking to increase voltage supplied to the coil.

CALIPER: A hydraulically activated device in a disc brake system, which is mounted straddling the brake rotor (disc). The caliper contains at least one piston and two brake pads. Hydraulic pressure on the piston(s) forces the pads against the rotor.

CAMSHAFT: A shaft in the engine on which are the lobes (cams) which operate the valves. The camshaft is driven by the crankshaft, via a belt, chain or gears, at one half the crankshaft speed.

CAPACITOR: A device which stores an electrical charge.

CARBON MONOXIDE (CO): a colorless, odorless gas given off as a normal byproduct of combustion. It is poisonous and extremely dangerous in confined areas, building up slowly to toxic levels without warning if adequate ventilation is not available.

CARBURETOR: A device, usually mounted on the intake manifold of an engine, which mixes the air and fuel in the proper proportion to allow even combustion.

CATALYTIC CONVERTER: A device installed in the exhaust system, like a muffler, that converts harmful byproducts of combustion into carbon dioxide and water vapor by means of a heat-producing chemical reaction.

CENTRIFUGAL ADVANCE: A mechanical method of advancing the spark timing by using flyweights in the distributor that react to centrifugal force generated by the distributor shaft rotation.

CHECK VALVE: Any one-way valve installed to permit the flow of air, fuel or vacuum in one direction only.

CHOKE: A device, usually a moveable valve, placed in the intake path of a carburetor to restrict the flow of air.

CIRCUIT: Any unbroken path through which an electrical current can flow. Also used to describe fuel flow in some instances.

CIRCUIT BREAKER: A switch which protects an electrical circuit from overload by opening the circuit when the current flow exceeds a predetermined level. Some circuit breakers must be reset manually, while other reset automatically

COIL (IGNITION): A transformer in the ignition circuit which steps of the voltage provided to the spark plugs.

COMBINATION MANIFOLD: An assembly which includes both the intake and exhaust manifolds in one casting.

COMBINATION VALVE: A device used in some fuel systems that routes fuel vapors to a charcoal storage canister instead of venting them into the atmosphere. The valve relieves fuel tank pressure and allows fresh air into the tank as fuel level drops to prevent a vapor lock situation.

COMPRESSION RATIO: The comparison of the total volume of the cylinder and combustion chamber with the piston at BDC and the piston at TDC.

CONDENSER: 1. An electrical device which acts to store an electrical charge, preventing voltage surges.
2. A radiator-like device in the air conditioning system in which refrigerant gas condenses into a liquid, giving off heat.

CONDUCTOR: Any material through which an electrical current can be transmitted easily.

CONTINUITY: Continuous or complete circuit. Can be checked with an ohmmeter.

COUNTERSHAFT: An intermediate shaft which is rotated by a mainshaft and transmits, in turn, that rotation to a working part.

CRANKCASE: The lower part of an engine in which the crankshaft and related parts operate.

CRANKSHAFT: The main driving shaft of an engine which receives reciprocating motion from the pistons and converts it to rotary motion.

CYLINDER: In an engine, the round hole in the engine block in which the piston(s) ride.

CYLINDER BLOCK: The main structural member of an engine in which is found the cylinders, crankshaft and other principal parts.

CYLINDER HEAD: The detachable portion of the engine, fastened, usually, to the top of the cylinder block, containing all or most of the combustion chambers. On overhead valve engines, it contains the valves and their operating parts. On overhead cam engines, it contains the camshaft as well.

DEAD CENTER: The extreme top or bottom of the piston stroke.

DETONATION: An unwanted explosion of the air fuel mixture in the combustion chamber caused by excess heat and compression, advanced timing, or an overly lean mixture. Also referred to as "ping".

DIAPHRAGM: A thin, flexible wall separating two cavities, such as in a vacuum advance unit.

DIESELING: A condition in which hot spots in the combustion chamber cause the engine to run on after the key is turned off.

DIFFERENTIAL: A geared assembly which allows the transmission of motion between drive axles, giving one axle the ability to turn faster than the other.

DIODE: An electrical device that will allow current to flow in one direction only.

DISC BRAKE: A hydraulic braking assembly consisting of a brake disc, or rotor, mounted on an axle, and a caliper assembly containing, usually two brake pads which are activated by hydraulic pressure. The pads are forced against the sides of the disc, creating friction which slows the vehicle.

DISTRIBUTOR: A mechanically driven device on an engine which is responsible for electrically firing the spark plug at a predetermined point of the piston stroke.

DOWEL PIN: A pin, inserted in mating holes in two different parts allowing those parts to maintain a fixed relationship.

DRUM BRAKE: A braking system which consists of two brake shoes and one or two wheel cylinders, mounted on a fixed backing plate, and a brake drum, mounted on an axle, which revolves around the assembly. Hydraulic action applied to the wheel cylinders forces the shoes outward against the drum, creating friction and slowing the vehicle.

DWELL: The rate, measured in degrees of shaft rotation, at which an electrical circuit cycles on and off.

ELECTRONIC CONTROL UNIT (ECU): Ignition module, module, amplifier or igniter. See Module for definition.

ELECTRONIC IGNITION: A system in which the timing and firing of the spark plugs is controlled by an electronic control unit, usually called a module. These systems have not points or condenser.

ENDPLAY: The measured amount of axial movement in a shaft.

ENGINE: A device that converts heat into mechanical energy.

EXHAUST MANIFOLD: A set of cast passages or pipes which conduct exhaust gases from the engine.

FEELER GAUGE: A blade, usually metal, of precisely predetermined thickness, used to measure the clearance between two parts. These blades usually are available in sets of assorted thicknesses.

F-Head: An engine configuration in which the intake valves are in the cylinder head, while the camshaft and exhaust valves are located in the cylinder block. The camshaft operates the intake valves via lifters and pushrods, while it operates the exhaust valves directly.

FIRING ORDER: The order in which combustion occurs in the cylinders of an engine. Also the order in which spark is distributed to the plugs by the distributor.

FLATHEAD: An engine configuration in which the camshaft and all the valves are located in the cylinder block.

FLOODING: The presence of too much fuel in the intake manifold and combustion chamber which prevents the air/fuel mixture from firing, thereby causing a no-start situation.

FLYWHEEL: A disc shaped part bolted to the rear end of the crankshaft. Around the outer perimeter is affixed the ring gear. The starter drive engages the ring gear, turning the flywheel, which rotates the crankshaft, imparting the initial starting motion to the engine.

FOOT POUND (ft.lb. or sometimes, ft. lbs.): The amount of energy or work needed to raise an item weighing one pound, a distance of one foot.

FUSE: A protective device in a circuit which prevents circuit overload by breaking the circuit when a specific amperage is present. The device is constructed around a strip or wire of a lower amperage rating than the circuit it is designed to protect. When an amperage higher than that stamped on the fuse is present in the circuit, the strip or wire melts, opening the circuit.

GEAR RATIO: The ratio between the number of teeth on meshing gears.

GENERATOR: A device which converts mechanical energy into electrical energy.

HEAT RANGE: The measure of a spark plug's ability to dissipate heat from its firing end. The higher the heat range, the hotter the plug fires.

HUB: The center part of a wheel or gear.

HYDROCARBON (HC): Any chemical compound made up of hydrogen and carbon. A major pollutant formed by the engine as a byproduct of combustion.

HYDROMETER: An instrument used to measure the specific gravity of a solution.

INCH POUND (in.lb. or sometimes, in. lbs.): One twelfth of a foot pound.

INDUCTION: A means of transferring electrical energy in the form of a magnetic field. Principle used in the ignition coil to increase voltage.

INJECTION PUMP: A device, usually mechanically operated, which meters and delivers fuel under pressure to the fuel injector.

INJECTOR: A device which receives metered fuel under relatively low pressure and is activated to inject the fuel into the engine under relatively high pressure at a predetermined time.

INPUT SHAFT: The shaft to which torque is applied, usually carrying the driving gear or gears.

INTAKE MANIFOLD: A casting of passages or pipes used to conduct air or a fuel/air mixture to the cylinders.

JOURNAL: The bearing surface within which a shaft operates.

KEY: A small block usually fitted in a notch between a shaft and a hub to prevent slippage of the two parts.

MANIFOLD: A casting of passages or set of pipes which connect the cylinders to an inlet or outlet source.

MANIFOLD VACUUM: Low pressure in an engine intake manifold formed just below the throttle plates. Manifold vacuum is highest at idle and drops under acceleration.

MASTER CYLINDER: The primary fluid pressurizing device in a hydraulic system. In automotive use, it is found in brake and hydraulic clutch systems and is pedal activated, either directly or, in a power brake system, through the power booster.

MODULE: Electronic control unit, amplifier or igniter of solid state or integrated design which controls the current flow in the ignition primary circuit based on input from the pickup coil. When the module opens the primary circuit, the high secondary voltage is induced in the coil.

NEEDLE BEARING: A bearing which consists of a number (usually a large number) of long, thin rollers.

OHM: (Ω) The unit used to measure the resistance of conductor to electrical flow. One ohm is the amount of resistance that limits current flow to one ampere in a circuit with one volt of pressure.

OHMMETER: An instrument used for measuring the resistance, in ohms, in an electrical circuit.

OUTPUT SHAFT: The shaft which transmits torque from a device, such as a transmission.

OVERDRIVE: A gear assembly which produces more shaft revolutions than that transmitted to it.

OVERHEAD CAMSHAFT (OHC): An engine configuration in which the camshaft is mounted on top of the cylinder head and operates the valve either directly or by means of rocker arms.

OVERHEAD VALVE (OHV): An engine configuration in which all of the valves are located in the cylinder head and the camshaft is located in the cylinder block. The camshaft operates the valves via lifters and pushrods.

OXIDES OF NITROGEN (NOx): Chemical compounds of nitrogen produced as a byproduct of combustion. They combine with hydrocarbons to produce smog.

OXYGEN SENSOR: Used with the feedback system to sense the presence of oxygen in the exhaust gas and signal the computer which can reference the voltage signal to an air/fuel ratio.

PINION: The smaller of two meshing gears.

PISTON RING: An open ended ring which fits into a groove on the outer diameter of the piston. Its chief function is to form a seal between the piston and cylinder wall. Most automotive pistons have three rings: two for compression sealing; one for oil sealing.

PRELOAD: A predetermined load placed on a bearing during assembly or by adjustment.

PRIMARY CIRCUIT: Is the low voltage side of the ignition system which consists of the ignition switch, ballast resistor or resistance wire, bypass, coil, electronic control unit and pick-up coil as well as the connecting wires and harnesses.

PRESS FIT: The mating of two parts under pressure, due to the inner diameter of one being smaller than the outer diameter of the other, or vice versa; an interference fit.

RACE: The surface on the inner or outer ring of a bearing on which the balls, needles or rollers move.

REGULATOR: A device which maintains the amperage and/or voltage levels of a circuit at predetermined values.

RELAY: A switch which automatically opens and/or closes a circuit.

RESISTANCE: The opposition to the flow of current through a circuit or electrical device, and is measured in ohms. Resistance is equal to the voltage divided by the amperage.

RESISTOR: A device, usually made of wire, which offers a preset amount of resistance in an electrical circuit.

RING GEAR: The name given to a ring-shaped gear attached to a differential case, or affixed to a flywheel or as part a planetary gear set.

ROLLER BEARING: A bearing made up of hardened inner and outer races between which hardened steel rollers move.

ROTOR: 1. The disc-shaped part of a disc brake assembly, upon which the brake pads bear; also called, brake disc.
2. The device mounted atop the distributor shaft, which passes current to the distributor cap tower contacts.

SECONDARY CIRCUIT: The high voltage side of the ignition system, usually above 20,000 volts. The secondary includes the ignition coil, coil wire, distributor cap and rotor, spark plug wires and spark plugs.

SENDING UNIT: A mechanical, electrical, hydraulic or electromagnetic device which transmits information to a gauge.

SENSOR: Any device designed to measure engine operating conditions or ambient pressures and temperatures. Usually electronic in nature and designed to send a voltage signal to an on-board computer, some sensors may operate as a simple on/off switch or they may provide a variable voltage signal (like a potentiometer) as conditions or measured parameters change.

SHIM: Spacers of precise, predetermined thickness used between parts to establish a proper working relationship.

SLAVE CYLINDER: In automotive use, a device in the hydraulic clutch system which is activated by hydraulic force, disengaging the clutch.

SOLENOID: A coil used to produce a magnetic field, the effect of which is produce work.

SPARK PLUG: A device screwed into the combustion chamber of a spark ignition engine. The basic construction is a conductive core inside of a ceramic insulator, mounted in an outer conductive base. An electrical charge from the spark plug wire travels along the conductive core and jumps a preset air gap to a grounding point or points at the end of the conductive base. The resultant spark ignites the fuel/air mixture in the combustion chamber.

SPLINES: Ridges machined or cast onto the outer diameter of a shaft or inner diameter of a bore to enable parts to mate without rotation.

TACHOMETER: A device used to measure the rotary speed of an engine, shaft, gear, etc., usually in rotations per minute.

THERMOSTAT: A valve, located in the cooling system of an engine, which is closed when cold and opens gradually in response to engine heating, controlling the temperature of the coolant and rate of coolant flow.

TOP DEAD CENTER (TDC): The point at which the piston reaches the top of its travel on the compression stroke.

TORQUE: The twisting force applied to an object.

TORQUE CONVERTER: A turbine used to transmit power from a driving member to a driven member via hydraulic action, providing changes in drive ratio and torque. In automotive use, it links the driveplate at the rear of the engine to the automatic transmission.

TRANSDUCER: A device used to change a force into an electrical signal.

TRANSISTOR: A semi-conductor component which can be actuated by a small voltage to perform an electrical switching function.

TUNE-UP: A regular maintenance function, usually associated with the replacement and adjustment of parts and components in the electrical and fuel systems of a vehicle for the purpose of attaining optimum performance.

TURBOCHARGER: An exhaust driven pump which compresses intake air and forces it into the combustion chambers at higher than atmospheric pressures. The increased air pressure allows more fuel to be burned and results in increased horsepower being produced.

VACUUM ADVANCE: A device which advances the ignition timing in response to increased engine vacuum.

VACUUM GAUGE: An instrument used to measure the presence of vacuum in a chamber.

VALVE: A device which control the pressure, direction of flow or rate of flow of a liquid or gas.

VALVE CLEARANCE: The measured gap between the end of the valve stem and the rocker arm, cam lobe or follower that activates the valve.

VISCOSITY: The rating of a liquid's internal resistance to flow.

VOLTMETER: An instrument used for measuring electrical force in units called volts. Voltmeters are always connected parallel with the circuit being tested.

WHEEL CYLINDER: Found in the automotive drum brake assembly, it is a device, actuated by hydraulic pressure, which, through internal pistons, pushes the brake shoes outward against the drums.

ABBREVIATIONS AND SYMBOLS

A: Ampere

AC: Alternating current

A/C: Air conditioning

A-h: Ampere hour

AT: Automatic transmission

ATDC: After top dead center

μA: Microampere

bbl: Barrel

BDC: Bottom dead center

bhp: Brake horsepower

BTDC: Before top dead center

BTU: British thermal unit

C: Celsius (Centigrade)

CCA: Cold cranking amps

cd: Candela

cm^2: Square centimeter

cm^3, cc: Cubic centimeter

CO: Carbon monoxide

CO_2: Carbon dioxide

cu.in., in^3: Cubic inch

CV: Constant velocity

Cyl.: Cylinder

DC: Direct current

ECM: Electronic control module

EFE: Early fuel evaporation

EFI: Electronic fuel injection

EGR: Exhaust gas recirculation

Exh.: Exhaust

F: Fahrenheit

F: Farad

pF: Picofarad

μF: Microfarad

FI: Fuel injection

ft.lb., ft. lb., ft. lbs.: foot pound(s)

gal: Gallon

g: Gram

HC: Hydrocarbon

HEI: High energy ignition

HO: High output

hp: Horsepower

Hyd.: Hydraulic

Hz: Hertz

ID: Inside diameter

in.lb.; in. lb.; in. lbs: inch pound(s)

Int.: Intake

K: Kelvin

kg: Kilogram

kHz: Kilohertz

km: Kilometer

km/h: Kilometers per hour

kΩ: Kilohm

kPa: Kilopascal

kV: Kilovolt

kW: Kilowatt

l: Liter

l/s: Liters per second

m: Meter

mA: Milliampere

mg: Milligram

mHz: Megahertz

mm: Millimeter

mm^2: Square millimeter

m^3: Cubic meter

$M\Omega$: Megohm

m/s: Meters per second

MT: Manual transmission

mV: Millivolt

μm: Micrometer

N: Newton

N-m: Newton meter

NOx: Nitrous oxide

OD: Outside diameter

OHC: Over head camshaft

OHV: Over head valve

Ω: Ohm

PCV: Positive crankcase ventilation

psi: Pounds per square inch

pts: Pints

qts: Quarts

rpm: Rotations per minute

rps: Rotations per second

R-12: A refrigerant gas (Freon)

SAE: Society of Automotive Engineers

SO_2: Sulfur dioxide

T: Ton

t: Megagram

TBI: Throttle Body Injection

TPS: Throttle Position Sensor

V: 1. Volt; 2. Venturi

μV: Microvolt

W: Watt

∞: Infinity

<: Less than

>: Greater than

Index